PENGUIN BOOKS

Think Like a Cat

PAM JOHNSON-BENNETT is one of the most popular and sought-after cat behavior experts in the world. She is the author of seven award-winning books on cat behavior, including *CatWise, Starting from Scratch, Hiss and Tell*, and *Cat vs. Cat*. Pam has a private cat-consulting practice in Nashville, is a popular guest on national TV and radio, has starred on Animal Planet UK's series *Psycho Kitty*, and has spoken on cat behavior at veterinary and animal-welfare conferences around the world. During her more than thirty-year career, she has been profiled widely, has written for many national magazines, and is the former behavior columnist for *Cats* magazine, iVillage, Yahoo!, *Cat Fancy*'s Cat Channel, *Kittens USA, The Daily Cat*, and *Catster*.

A certified cat behavior consultant, she was VP of the International Association of Animal Behavior Consultants and founded the IAABC Cat Division. Pam served on the American Humane Association's Advisory Board on Animal Behavior and Training. She has received many awards, including the Winn Feline Foundation Award, multiple Cat Writers' Association awards, and the IAABC Cat Division Award.

Pam lives in Nashville, Tennessee, with her husband, two children, a rescued Bengal cat, a rescued Sheltie, one well-trained goldfish, and two not-so-well-trained goldfish.

Learn more about Pam's techniques and recommendations at www.catbehaviorassociates.com.

Think
Like a Cat

How to Raise a Well-Adjusted Cat—
Not a Sour Puss

Updated and Expanded Edition

PAM JOHNSON-BENNETT

CERTIFIED
ANIMAL BEHAVIOR CONSULTANT

PENGUIN BOOKS

PENGUIN BOOKS
Published by the Penguin Group
Penguin Group (USA) Inc., 375 Hudson Street,
New York, New York 10014, U.S.A.
Penguin Group (Canada), 90 Eglinton Avenue East, Suite 700, Toronto,
Ontario, Canada M4P 2Y3 (a division of Pearson Penguin Canada Inc.)
Penguin Books Ltd, 80 Strand, London WC2R 0RL, England
Penguin Ireland, 25 St Stephen's Green, Dublin 2, Ireland
(a division of Penguin Books Ltd)
Penguin Group (Australia), 250 Camberwell Road, Camberwell,
Victoria 3124, Australia (a division of Pearson Australia Group Pty Ltd)
Penguin Books India Pvt Ltd, 11 Community Centre,
Panchsheel Park, New Delhi - 110 017, India
Penguin Group (NZ), 67 Apollo Drive, Rosedale, Auckland 0632,
New Zealand (a division of Pearson New Zealand Ltd)
Penguin Books (South Africa) (Pty) Ltd, 24 Sturdee Avenue,
Rosebank, Johannesburg 2196, South Africa

Penguin Books Ltd, Registered Offices:
80 Strand, London WC2R 0RL, England

First published in Penguin Books 2000
This revised edition published 2011

23rd Printing

LIBRARY OF CONGRESS CATALOGING IN PUBLICATION DATA

Johnson-Bennett, Pam, 1954–
Think like a cat : how to raise a well-adjusted cat—not a sour puss /
Pam Johnson-Bennett. —Updated and expanded ed.
p.   cm.
Includes index.
ISBN 978-0-14-311979-1
1. Cats—Training.   2. Cats—Behavior.   3. Cats—Psychology.   I. Title.
SF446.5.J638 2011
636.8'0835—dc23   2011029071

Printed in the United States of America
Set in Adobe Caslon Pro   ·   Designed by Elke Sigal

To my husband Scott, and my two children,
Gracie and Jack. I am so blessed.

In memory of my father, whose love of animals
opened the door to my dreams.

And in memory of one special cat, Ethel,
for a debt I can never repay.

Acknowledgments

After years of working with cats, their owners, veterinarians, and so many people in the animal care field, I've been lucky to learn so much from everyone (two-legged and, most especially, four-legged). Being able to witness, on a daily basis, the love and commitment that owners and cats have for each other has been such a privilege. I'm even grateful to all of the owners who initially viewed me with skepticism (and believe me, there were many) and to the cats who did their very best to run me off. In the beginning, some of them almost did. Challenges became opportunities to grow. Boy, have I had plenty of opportunities. When I started in this business many years ago, it was not the popular field that it is becoming today, and so I was met with many raised eyebrows when I began talking about being able to train a cat. Actually, just a raised eyebrow was one of the more polite responses I received.

When I started out, no one was really focusing on cat behavior, yet alone doing in-home consultations to visit cats and owners on a one-on-one basis to address behavior problems. Dogs were trained—cats were tolerated . . . barely.

Today, though, I am so happy to see that people are receptive to the idea of behavior modification for their cats and how it can truly save a cat's life. Behavior specialists are easier to find these days. I will forever be grateful to the first clients I had because of their trust and willingness to *think like a cat*.

The veterinarians I've had the privilege of working with over the years have been exceptionally generous with their time and knowledge. Veterinarians are truly the unsung heroes for our companion animals. They deal with patients who are less than cooperative and who often prefer to take a bite out of the very doctor saving their lives. I'm impressed at the lightning-fast reflexes some doctors have developed and the patience they show toward even the most fractious cat.

Thanks to my editor, Rebecca Hunt, and my family at Penguin Books.

Thank you to the veterinarians with whom I've had the personal honor of working with. Thank you for your support, guidance, and friendship.

A special thanks to Dr. Mark Waldrop for being an inspiration when it comes to cat care.

Special thanks to my agent and longtime friend, Linda Roghaar, for going above and beyond. Your wisdom has saved me many times.

Thank you Chris Chichuk . . . I'm honored to call you my friend.

Thank you to Marilyn Krieger for a friendship I truly cherish.

Thank you to my incredible family, most especially my husband, Scott.

Thank you to the ever-present spirit of my greatest feline teacher, Ethel. She is the reason I dedicate my life to improving the relationships between humans and cats. Ethel taught me so many of the most valuable lessons in life: love unconditionally, express your true feelings, respect others' territory, protect the family, get enough sleep, and always keep an eye open for mice!

Contents

Introduction

Whew! So much has happened since *Think Like a Cat* first came out over eleven years ago. Over the years I've received so many letters, e-mails, and phone calls from readers who now have a better understanding of why their cats do the things they do. Owners developed better skills for solving behavior problems and were able to prevent future problems. It's amazing how easy it is to solve a behavior problem just by shifting your view and developing a *think like a cat* perspective.

In the last decade, there have been many advancements in veterinary medicine, behavior modification, cat-related products, and nutrition. So it was time to update and expand *Think Like a Cat*. This new version will get you up to speed on the latest information you need to raise a well-adjusted, happy, and healthy cat. Even if you already own the original version, you'll find this new book is packed with many more insights, tips, and techniques.

I've written this book so that a new cat owner can have the tools to provide what a cat needs right away. I don't want you to waste a minute misunderstanding what your cat is trying to communicate, or damaging the relationship by using ineffective training methods. The title of this book truly describes the way I approach training. By understanding your cat's motivations, needs, and communication, you can so easily enjoy a close, wonderful relationship. Even if you're not a cat novice, I'll bet there are many ways you could improve your relationship. Perhaps you've been dealing with a behavior problem and have long since resigned yourself to just accepting it. This book may offer solutions that you didn't think were possible. I want to change the way you look at your cat. I also want to change the way you look at your cat's environment. Instead of seeing it from the vantage point of an adult human, I want you to look through your cat's eyes. What does the world look like when you're ten inches off the ground?

This book will enable you to solve problems by focusing on the good behavior you do want rather than the bad behavior you don't want. Shifting your approach from negative to positive puts you in the mindset of being a successful problem-solver as opposed to a frustrated pet owner. It becomes an easy and logical progression: think about the behavior you want from your cat, and the route necessary to get him there.

My introduction to cats came as it does for many people—accidentally. Growing up in a family of dog lovers, I thought dogs were the greatest pets in the world and cats were, well, *cats*. I believed all the myths I'd heard about them and while I certainly found them to be beautiful, I'd just as soon have a dog.

Then, one Christmas Eve many years ago, my life became forever changed. I was spending the holidays at my parents' home. It was bitter cold and snowy and I was doing some last-minute shopping. I passed a teenage girl standing in front of a church. On the steps beside her was a cardboard box. A handmade sign read FREE KITTENS. Surely this girl wouldn't have kittens outside on a day like this, I thought. I peered over the top of the box, and there inside were indeed two tiny kittens. With just a towel lining the box, the kittens were huddled together, trying to stay warm.

Furious at the lack of compassion and responsibility of this teenager (and the parents who most likely sent her out to do this), I impulsively offered to take the kittens, opened my jacket, and placed them inside my sweater. They felt like two little ice cubes. I doubted they'd even live long enough for me to get them home.

In the car, I turned up the heat full blast and hurried home (quite sure that when I arrived, my parents would probably be less than thrilled at the unexpected addition to their holiday celebration). Luckily, my family's love and compassion for any animals in need outweighed any hint of disapproval concerning what I'd impulsively done.

The quiet Christmas holiday we'd planned became a mad dash of specific responsibilities. My mother began to search for the long-lost heating pad while my father made a makeshift litter pan from a cardboard box and filled it with sand. My sister and I were busy in the kitchen, handling the job of feeding the kittens (we didn't know it at the time, but they were six weeks old).

Once warm and with full tummies, the little kittens curled up in the winter coat I'd tossed on the floor when I'd burst into the house. We all stood around watching as they settled in. Even my parents' two dogs quietly watched the sleeping kittens. As my mother's Christmas cookie dough sat unbaked on the kitchen counter, and the gifts I'd bought that day sat unwrapped in the trunk of the car, two tiny, cold, malnourished, flea-infested, frightened, dirty, unhealthy kittens did something remarkable . . . *they survived*.

Those two kittens survived despite being taken away from their mother much too young, exposed to extremely cold temperatures, and adopted by someone who knew nothing about cats.

Having those two lives totally dependent upon me made me aware of how little I knew about cats, and that what I *did* know wasn't even remotely accurate. Lucy and Ethel (not very original names, I'm embarrassed to admit) endured my well-meaning but often fumbling attempts at care with such grace, tolerance, and love.

Lucy died at the age of three from a congenital heart condition—ironically, on Christmas Day. Ethel, who had the same congenital defect, lived much longer before finally succumbing. Those two cats not only brought such love and happiness into my life, they also inspired me to embark on a career that I (and certainly my family) never could have imagined.

If you're a longtime cat owner, there will certainly be basic information in this book that will seem old hat to you, but I urge you not to rush past subjects you may think don't apply to your situation. While you may not need to learn how to pick out a veterinarian or how to set up a litter box, by looking at your cat's life through his eyes and employing a *think like a cat* approach, you'll solve behavior problems, prevent potential ones, and avoid owner pitfalls. Yes, even experienced owners often can't see the feline forest for the trees.

If you're about to become a cat owner for the first time, congratulations. You are soon to enter into a relationship in which you are unconditionally loved, endlessly forgiven for your mistakes, never judged, and constantly entertained. A cat can make the stresses of your day disappear just by curling up in your lap at night. When you've been working too hard, a cat will walk across your papers to let you know it's time for a break. A cat will show his gratitude for the simplest act, such as scratching him under the chin, by serenading you with his deep, rich purr. A cat will still adore you on those days when you look your worst. A cat is a patient listener, even when you're telling a story for the third time. A cat is the most dependable alarm clock you'll ever have. A cat will show you how to enjoy life.

Get ready, you're about to learn how to *think like a cat*.

Think Like a Cat

1

The Cat of Your Dreams

Will You Be a Match Made in Heaven or the Odd Couple?

Cats aren't shirts that you buy at the store and then return if they don't fit. Nor are they a pair of shoes you can give away or toss out when you've outgrown them. While these comparisons may seem ridiculously obvious to you, the sad fact is that too many cat owners actually do view their cats that way. As a result, countless cats end up relinquished to shelters or just abandoned because they didn't meet their owners' expectations of *the perfect cat*.

Why do you want a cat? Take the time to examine your desires honestly to help ensure a lifetime of love.

Choosing to become a cat owner is, of course, an emotional decision. It's also choosing to take on a serious responsibility because the cat's health and welfare will be completely dependent on you. If your impression of cat ownership involves filling up a food bowl and putting a litter box in the extra bathroom then both you and your cat will soon become very unhappy. Although a cat may *seem* to be a lower maintenance pet than a dog, you must be prepared to meet his emotional, medical, and physical needs.

Being a cat owner also involves a financial commitment which some people aren't prepared for. Cats or kittens acquired for free need the same veterinary and nutritional care as the purebred you paid top dollar for: the initial vaccinations and neuter or spay surgery, then yearly vaccinations for the rest of his life. He'll also undoubtedly need periodic medical care for unexpected ailments or injuries, and veterinary care isn't cheap.

Over the years I've seen many incredibly close cat/owner relationships. I've also seen cats and owners who seem to just co-exist in the same house with no emotional bond. Many times, that's the result of the owner having had the wrong expectations about cats from the start. You have an opportunity now, with this book, to create a close cat/human bond. Even if you already have a cat (maybe you've had him for years), you can create a closer relationship—and that's the key, it *is* a *relationship*.

Rumors, Innuendoes, and Lies

Cats steal the breath from babies.
Cats are aloof.
You must get rid of your cat if you're pregnant.
Litter boxes always stink.
Cats ruin the furniture.
You can't train a cat.

If those were true, why would *anybody* ever want a cat? Unfortunately, people continue to pass along this inaccurate and unfair information. The result? Many people who might have become cat owners get scared off. It's the cats who suffer as they continue to be charged with crimes of which they aren't guilty. Let's take a closer look at some of the common misconceptions so that you can learn fact from fiction and go ahead with plans to share your life with a cat.

Cats are aloof. We've all heard that! In fact, if most people had to describe cats in one word, *aloof* would probably be it. And, if you mention *aloof*, you might as well throw in *independent* as well. I believe these descriptions come from inappropriately trying to compare cats to dogs. We think of dogs as social creatures and cats as unsociable, solitary snobs. In truth, a cat is a sociable animal. His social structure is built upon his sense of territory and the availability of a food source. Cats can and do live happily together. In a free-roaming environment female cats will nurse and care for each other's kittens. One reason why cats may have been inaccurately labeled as solitary is because they are often seen hunting alone. Cats hunt small prey—just enough for one cat. Some cats do however hunt cooperatively as well, so there's always an exception to the rule.

Cats may also appear aloof to some humans because, as hunters, they take in their entire environment. Sometimes the cat may sit on your lap, enjoying your affectionate stroking, but there are other times when he'd prefer just sitting nearby, relaxed yet ready should any prey come on the scene. Cats are stimulated by even the slightest movement which might indicate potential prey.

How kittens were socialized and whether they were handled gently by humans also play a role in how large a personal space they require later. Much of how your individual cat's personality develops, and whether he becomes friendly and sociable versus timid and unfriendly depends on you.

This book will teach you how to understand his language and communicate with him so you two can develop a strong, loving bond. If you expect him to do all of the work then you'll end up with, yes, an aloof, independent, untrusting cat.

The bottom line: stop comparing your cat to a dog, and suddenly you'll start noticing his uniquely wonderful traits. Cats are not small dogs and, surprisingly, that's a hard concept for some people to accept. Cats shouldn't be viewed as acceptable and sociable only when they act "doglike."

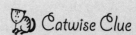 Catwise Clue

The term "domesticated cat" refers to the species being distinct from their species ancestor (the African Wildcat).

Cats can't be trained. False! Once again, you just have to stop thinking DOG and start thinking CAT. My approach to training is based on positive reinforcement, understanding what a cat needs, and what he is communicating by his behavior. If I want my cat to stop doing something, I direct her to something better and then reward her when she gets it right. This *think like a cat* method involves understanding why the cat is behaving a certain way so I can meet those needs in a way that's acceptable to both of us. This training method is easier, more humane, and much more effective than continually reprimanding your cat for doing things that are instinctually natural to him (such as scratching). So throw out all of those old ideas you've had about how cats can't be trained. It's easier than you think.

Cats are dangerous if you're pregnant and *cats steal the breath from babies.* I really hate these. First of all, if you're pregnant, there are precautions you should take concerning the litter box. The box could be a serious health risk to your unborn baby, but it doesn't mean the cat should be tossed out. To get the accurate story, refer to *Toxoplasmosis* in the Medical Appendix in the back of this book. As for that stupid myth about cats stealing the breath from babies, it's not true, yet it continues to resurface again and again. The theory of many cat experts is that long ago, before SIDS (sudden infant death syndrome) was identified, cats were blamed for the unexpected death of sleeping babies.

Litter boxes always stink. Well, actually a litter box will stink IF YOU

DON'T CLEAN IT! As long as you maintain an adequate cleaning schedule, no one will ever have to hold his nose to enter your home.

Cats ruin the furniture. There's some truth to this statement but only if you neglect to provide him with a scratching post. Now I know some of you reading this are thinking, *Well, my neighbor has a scratching post and the cat still ruins the furniture.* My answer to that? Wrong post. Chapter 9 will teach you how to get it right the first time.

So now that we've cleared that up and you're standing on the threshold of cat ownership, let's go get the cat, right? Not quite yet. You have many decisions to make. Do you want a kitten or a cat? Male or female? Will the cat be an indoor or outdoor cat? Where should you get the cat? The shelter? Breeder? The next-door neighbor?

A Kitten or a Cat?

Kittens are cute. I mean really, really cute. Whenever I bring a kitten on television with me, just about everyone on the set has to come by for a closer look. Kittens are definitely smile magnets, but before you fall in love with that adorable little bundle of fur, take the time to understand what'll be required of you as the owner of a kitten.

You need to kitten-proof your home if you decide on a youngster. You have to patrol for dangling electrical cords, dangerous cleansers, poisons, etc. (Even if you decide on an adult cat you'll have to safeguard him from these things as well, but kittens seem bound and determined to get into trouble.) Basically, you have to know where your kitten is at all times to prevent him from hurting himself. Kitten-proofing a home isn't that difficult, but for some people it's not possible. For instance, an artist friend of mine lives in a one-bedroom apartment. She wanted the companionship of a feline but knew that getting a kitten would surely result in spilled paint. Not only would that be messy, but it would cause a serious health risk to a curious little kitty. The artist chose to adopt an adult cat who had a quiet personality. Aside from one incident when the cat accidentally walked across Sonia's palette and left a trail of fuchsia paw prints on the carpet, they have a very compatible relationship.

A family with young children should reconsider the idea of a very young kitten and opt for an older one (at least six months old). Kittens are very fragile and can easily be injured by exuberant young children. An older cat can still be injured, but he is better able to escape from a child's grasp.

If you or anyone in your family is unsure of his footing, a kitten zooming underfoot through the house could create a danger.

Consider how much time you have to devote to a kitten. They require more supervision and can't be left alone as long as an adult cat.

If you adopt a kitten, it affords you the opportunity to have a greater effect on shaping his personality than you might have on an adult cat. By exposing him to a variety of novel stimuli, you stand a good chance of raising a cat who is comfortable around strangers, not afraid of unfamiliar surroundings, adapted to travel, etc.

So why would you want to miss all the fun and get a grown-up? One of the best reasons to choose an adult cat is that you know just what you're getting. You can also get a good sense of his temperament—whether he's active, nervous, docile, sociable, very vocal, quiet, etc. Because all kittens tend to be fuzzy little race cars, you don't know which ones will actually stay that way and which ones will calm down. If you want to be sure of a specific ready-made temperament or personality, go for an adult cat.

Keep in mind, though, that an adult cat who is timid or nervous can be worked with. There's so much you can do to help an adult cat blossom. You also have to take the cat's current surroundings and history into consideration, and how the cat may change in a new environment combined with your *think like a cat* training approach. For example, a shelter cat may initially appear very timid or defensive in that stressful environment. Once he becomes acclimated to your home and family he'll begin to show his true personality and feel comfortable enough to trust. A cat at the shelter may have been relinquished by his previous owner because he had behavior problems. It doesn't mean the problem isn't workable, but you have to be prepared to address whatever situation does arise. Very often, the problem may have been connected with the circumstances of that previous environment and won't continue in the cat's new surroundings. I'll discuss shelter adoptions later in this chapter.

An adult cat doesn't need the seemingly constant supervision that a kitten does.

If you truly have the love and desire to share your life with a cat, adopting an adult could literally save his life. Whether kittens are brought to shelters, found in alleys, or given away outside of grocery stores, they stand a better chance of being adopted than the adult cats. By taking that four-year-old tabby, you might be saving him from a life behind bars or worse, death.

Financially, an adult cat is often less expensive than a kitten. Kittens require a series of vaccinations and the cost of neutering or spaying. Adopting an adult cat from another family or from a shelter often means the cat is up-to-date on vaccinations or at least had the first in the series, and in some cases, already spayed or neutered.

He or She?

This is another area where myths and rumors seem to run wild. If you know someone who has only had male cats, they'll be able to rattle off all of the great qualities of a male and numerous shortcomings of females. They'll tell you how much smarter and outgoing males are. Longtime owners of females will quickly dispute that and add how territorial males are.

Here's the truth. Once a cat is spayed or neutered, it doesn't matter if you choose a male or a female. Hormones are what usually drive undesirable behavior such as a spraying male or a yowling female in heat. Simply by having the cat spayed or neutered, you can control that. Left intact, I don't care whether you choose a male or female, you'll be one unhappy cat owner. Intact males are territorial and they will spray. If allowed outdoors, they'll roam and get into countless fights that could lead to injury or death. Intact females, when in heat call relentlessly in search of a male and will try to sneak outdoors every chance they get. Neutered and spayed cats make much better companions. They won't spend their lives in frustration, their risk of certain types of cancers will be reduced, and you won't spend your days pulling your hair out.

Purebred Cats

Although most cat owners choose non-pedigreed cats, you may have your heart set on a purebred.

Lovers of purebred cats will argue that there are hundreds of reasons to go that route versus mixed-breed, but I'm going to assume you're a novice in the cat world, and focus on what I feel would be of the most importance to a new cat owner.

When considering a purebred, make certain you're aware of any possible genetic health concerns prone to that particular breed. Do your homework before deciding on a purebred. Read breed-specific books and check cat registry Web sites. Talk to your veterinarian, breeders, and owners of the breed you're considering. Visit cat shows in your area to get a closer look. Talk with the breeders who are there to show their cats.

In the dog world you find big dogs, bigger dogs, small dogs, even smaller dogs, hunting dogs, herding dogs, sporting dogs, guard dogs, long-haired, short-haired, floppy eared, perky eared, long-nosed, pug-nosed, vocal dogs, and quiet dogs. Such variety! In the cat world, the greatest variety exists mainly within the purebreds. Let's take size, for example: if you want a very large cat, you'd probably be interested in the Maine Coon Cat. If an athletic cat is more to your liking, there are several breeds to choose from, for example, the Abyssinian. So, if you like specific physical traits or a certain personality type, purebreds can be more predictable. This could be an important factor in your decision-making process. Within the world of purebreds you'll find cats with folded ears, bobbed tails, no tails, kinked fur, no fur, or colors that could only exist in nature; cats who are talkers or known for being couch potatoes.

Some breeds require special attention that you may not have the time, desire, or ability to provide. For example, several of the long-haired breeds—such as Persians and Himalayans—require daily brushing or their hair will mat. Do you have the time required to care properly for this kind of cat?

Use the Internet for researching when considering a purebred because there are many cat-related groups and lists. You can get lots of information from other owners of the type of cat in which you're interested.

Finally, there's money. A purebred will cost you. Some are much more expensive than others but be prepared to pay.

The Long and Short of It: Hair Length

No question about it, a beautifully groomed long-haired cat is a head-turner. Cats such as Persians have the feline world's equivalent of Hollywood glamour. We watch them on TV as they recline on their pillows in their diamond collars, eating out of stemmed crystal glasses. That's probably why Persians are one of the most popular breeds. We see them and fall in love, unaware of the "behind the scenes" work that goes into maintaining that glorious coat.

The coats of many long-haired cats will mat if not brushed daily. That silky coat can get into a knot faster than you can say "detangling spray." Aside from the unsightly look of matted fur, mats can create health risks if left unattended because they can prevent air from reaching the skin. Fleas can also seek refuge under mats. As mats tighten they pull on the skin and make walking painful. The nails of the cat can get stuck in the mats as he attempts to scratch. I've seen neglected Persians who have ripped holes in their skins in an attempt to scratch beneath the mat. If you love the look of a silky long-haired cat, give serious thought to the maintenance.

Not all long-haired cats are prone to matting. Even if you choose a cat whose hair doesn't mat, be aware that all long-haired breeds will still require more frequent brushing. The Maine Coon and Norwegian Forest Cat, for example, have thick, long hair that doesn't mat. Maintenance is still required, though, to keep this coat looking lustrous.

Long-haired cats, whether they mat or not, occasionally need special assistance concerning their personal hygiene. Their long fur can now and then catch and trap pieces of feces. If a long-haired cat develops diarrhea, the cleanup is much more involved than with a short-haired cat.

Hair balls. You've heard of them. You've maybe even seen them. Although any cat, regardless of coat length, can have them, long-haired cats experience more than their share. A good grooming schedule by you, feeding hair-ball-formula food or treats, and a regular dose of hair-ball-prevention gel will help. If you aren't able to maintain the cat's coat, you might be subjecting him to certain hair balls. For more on grooming, refer to Chapter 12.

Some breeds are more fragile than others. The Sphinx, for example—which is a practically hairless cat—requires warmer temperatures and therefore wouldn't be a good choice for someone who prefers keeping the thermostat set low.

Hybrids and Exotic Breeds

Don't choose a cat merely based on its exotic or unique looks. Some people spend lots of money on cats for their physical appeal without researching temperament, personality, and training needs. Bengals are a good example of this. I've met many people who purchased Bengals for their wild look and then became shocked when behavior problems developed because no training was done or the owners had no clue as to the activity and intelligence level of the breed.

If you're interested in one of these cats, carefully research and learn about the breed's personality, care requirements, and potential health risks. Evaluate whether that breed is the right fit for your family and whether you can create the appropriate environment for the cat.

Magnificent Mixed Breeds

Some of the most loved, spoiled, cared for, doted on, cherished cats are the ones who don't come with a pedigree. They're the ones we find lost by the roadside, at our back door, in the neighbor's garage, in the barn, in the local shelter, brought home by our children, or shivering in the parking lot. So many are in need of our rescue. Really, I believe many more actually rescue *us*.

Unless you're already set on a specific breed, are planning to enter your cat in shows (and actually, there are several mixed-breed shows), or embarking on a breeding career (something I strongly advise against), you should consider a mixed breed.

What is a *mixed breed*? It refers to the product of the random matings of different or mixed breeds of cats. Sometimes you see a trace of an identifiable breed but usually, the years of random matings create cats whose histories are mysteries.

Mixed-breed cats come in all shapes, sizes, and colors. From a personality standpoint, you may not get the predictability that you might with purebreds, but in general, what you will get is a hearty, adaptable, trainable cat.

Where to Find Your New Cat

Now that you're sure you want to share your life with a cat, let's examine the many sources out there for acquiring your new companion—whether a kitten, an adult, a purebred, a mixed breed, long-haired, short-haired, male, or female.

As I'm sure you're well aware, cats aren't in short supply. You could probably open up your back door and literally find one hanging out in the yard. I live on three acres and almost every morning I spot a different cat crossing through the field.

While a great many people come across the cat of their dreams through rescue efforts, that method isn't for everyone. The injured or starving cat you pick up from the roadside, or the one you rescue from the shelter's death row, may or may not turn out to be the friendly, trusting, well-socialized animal you'd hoped for. I'm certainly all for anyone who gives a cat a second chance at life, but you should make sure you know what you're getting into. I want you and your cat to spend many, many happy years together. Make sure everyone in your family is on the same page regarding the type of cat you want and the amount of time and patience you have to help that cat get beyond any negative history.

A note of caution: When you begin your search, I recommend that you not bring your children along. Your first visits to shelters, breeders, etc., need to be strictly to evaluate the facilities. I've seen too many owners coming home their first day out with a kitten they weren't prepared for because the children fell in love. Oh, and by the way, children aren't the only ones who suffer from the inability to walk out of a shelter empty-handed—we adults wrote the book on impulsivity.

Shelters—Finding Your Diamond in the Rough

Walking into a shelter is a very emotional experience for an animal lover. Walking out *empty-handed* is very difficult for an animal lover. Be prepared—you can't save all the animals. It's very tough to go from one cage to the next, staring into the eyes of the cats in need of homes. As much as you may want to take the neediest of the cats into your arms forever, be sure you know what it'll require. Making an impulsive decision you aren't ready for could end up being wrong for you and for the cat.

There are many shelters around the country, ranging from public animal control facilities to nonprofit private organizations. In your search, you'll find well-run facilities and you'll come across horrible jailhouses.

Chances are very slim that you'll be able to come across a purebred cat at a shelter but it does happen. If you're looking for a kitten, they go fast—everyone wants kittens, especially around Christmas. But if you're open to the idea of an adult cat, you'll find many ages, colors, and personalities.

Although shelters are staffed by caring people who try their hardest to house the cats in as comforting of an environment as possible, considering how stressful shelter life is, don't expect the cats to be on their best behavior. Very often these cats are in emotional shock. Many have been abandoned by their owners, lost, homeless, injured, or maybe even abused. Suddenly they're put in a cage away from anything even remotely familiar from life as they knew it and they're terrified. Even though your heart's in the right place and you plan on giving a cat the best home in the world, initially he may not act very appreciative. Some cats who've been relinquished to the shelter by a family due to a behavior problem may pose an extra challenge to you. Very often though, a cat adopted from the shelter eventually puts his past behind him and ends up being the love of your life. Some of the smartest, prettiest, most sociable, tolerant cats I've seen came from shelters. I toured nationally with the famous *Friskies Cat Team* and these talented cats who are seen on television and in movies were rescued from shelters. When on tour, that fact always surprised people who assumed that "performing" cats had to be specially raised from kittenhood. Not true! Just ask *Flash, Harley, Squash,* and *Spike*—four feline headliners with shelter beginnings.

Shelter staffs work with cats when they're first brought in to help them become adoptable. Volunteers come in daily to interact with the animals, offer comfort, affection, attention, and playtime. Many shelters now take an active role in providing behavioral information to the volunteers as well so they can interact with the cats in the most productive way. At many shelters, new owners can also find behavior support resources in order to help them through the adjustment period with an adopted cat after the honeymoon period has ended.

Shelters do an amazing job even though they're all overcrowded and underfunded.

Before you decide to go the shelter adoption route, inspect the facility, ask questions, and be completely informed regarding their policies. Some shelters even require an in-home visit first to make sure the environment will be appropriate. Don't be offended at the questions asked of you. The staff is trying to make sure you're matched with the best cat for you.

Cat Rescue Groups

If you'd like to provide a home for a kitty in need through a local rescue agency, keep in mind that as with shelter-adopted cats, you may be dealing with a traumatized animal. These cats need stable, secure, loving homes with owners willing to help them blossom in their own time.

Some of the cats rescued may not have had the advantage of having been socialized to humans during kittenhood. This is an important thing to consider if you absolutely want a cat who will sit in your lap and view life in a carefree way. A cat who has been rescued may need a bit more time before daring to trust. When it happens, though, it's amazing to watch as the cat begins to lower his guard and let you in. The times I've experienced it will stay in my heart forever.

Breeders—The Good, the Bad, and the Bottom of the Barrel

If you truly have your heart set on a purebred, your best source will be a breeder. A *good* breeder isn't so easy to find, though. As with any other business, when money is involved, ethics can get lost on the way to the bank.

A GOOD BREEDER

- is very knowledgeable about the breed
- welcomes any questions you may have
- competes in cat shows
- offers references
- welcomes inspections of his/her cattery
- lets you see the parents of the kittens
- has all registration papers
- requires the buyer to spay or neuter the cat
- has documentation of health exams and vaccinations
- doesn't sell any kitten less than 10–12 weeks old
- prohibits declawing
- specifies in the contract that the cat must be kept indoors
- doesn't pressure you to buy
- displays a genuine love for the breed
- screens you to make sure her/his kitten goes to a good home
- offers a refund and not just a replacement kitten
- requires the kitten be returned if you can't keep him

Good breeders are dedicated to maintaining the integrity of their breed. They lovingly keep a very clean, healthy cattery, and are knowledgeable about cat health, nutrition, and behavior. Good breeders welcome questions and inspections of their catteries. They should also be willing to supply references.

To begin your search for a good breeder, start by attending the cat shows in your area. Even if the nearest one is a bit of a drive, it's worth it. Good breeders *show* their cats. It's a good opportunity for you to talk with several breeders. Unless they're getting their cat ready to be judged, they should be more than happy to answer any questions you have.

Raised underfoot is a phrase you'll hear very often when talking to breeders. That means the kittens have been handled by and socialized to humans as opposed to being locked away in cages. Beware, though, anyone can claim that their kittens were raised underfoot; it's up to you to decide if they're truthful. Make a list of breeders and do research on them. Talk to veterinarians, join online breed groups, check blogs and online review sites. Visit the cattery; ask questions; carefully observe and handle the kittens. Remember, a *registered* kitten means he comes with an official-looking piece of paper. It doesn't guarantee that he's a well-adjusted kitten.

If the breed has congenital defects, a reputable breeder will openly discuss that and what she/he does to reduce that risk.

Look for a breeder who asks *you* lots of questions. If a breeder is quick to sell you a kitten without inquiring about your home and lifestyle, that's not the breeder with whom you should do business.

The breeder shouldn't release kittens until they're ten to twelve weeks old. Don't go with a breeder who is willing to let you have a kitten earlier than that.

Buying by Photograph

Whether you're dealing with a breeder or a private owner, don't agree to purchase a cat you haven't seen. Some breeders who live out of your area will agree to sell cats long-distance. They e-mail a photograph or video and the first time you actually get to meet your cat is when you pick him up at the airport. My word on this practice? DON'T.

If the breeder of the specific breed you want lives far away and you absolutely have to have this kitten, then get on a plane and go see him, evaluate the facilities, and then if all seems right, take the kitten back with you. Don't commit to the sale until you're there in person.

Online and Newspaper Ads

Be cautious. Just because a kitten is advertised for free and the description sounds perfect doesn't necessarily mean things are as advertised.

Treat the owners as you would a breeder by asking questions. How was the kitten or cat raised? In the case of older cats, ask why they need to find another home. The reason may be stated in the ad, but ask for more specific details.

Check out the home carefully. Don't let the owners meet you at the mailbox with the kitten in their arms. You want to see where he was raised and, if possible, see the mother cat.

If the owners are trying to place a cat who has behavior problems and you still want to adopt him, find out *everything* and I mean *everything* you can. Not only what the problem is but where, when, and how it happens. What methods did they use to correct the problem? The behavior problem may be a result of something going on in that household and might be solved just by removing the cat. Just make sure you've received full disclosure and that you're prepared to be patient through the cat's adjustment period.

Sometimes adult cats are put up for adoption because there have been changes in the family. For example, the owner may have passed away and the relatives are trying to place the cat. If you know the reason why the cat is being rehomed, you can be better prepared to help him through the changes.

An adult cat from a previous home often makes a wonderful companion as long as you have the time and patience to help him. Cats who have lost their owners, been abused, or are suddenly shunned (because of something such as rejection by an owner's new spouse), are confused, scared, and in crisis. With your love, though, they stand a chance at a wonderful life.

If it's a kitten advertised and the ad states that initial vaccinations have been given, don't just take a stranger's word for it. Ask to see written proof in the form of a vaccination record and veterinary clinic receipt. Don't be satisfied by one of those little "My Pet's Record" folders where the vaccinations are checked off and the date entered. Anyone with a pen can write in those booklets. Find out who the veterinarian is and call for verification if the owners have no written proof.

If the owner has the mother cat, find out if she is up-to-date on vaccinations and has tested negative for *feline leukemia* and *feline immunodeficiency virus*.

Another big question that should be on your mind is why did this owner allow the cat to become pregnant? Are they backyard breeders who thought they could make a little money by mating their purebred with some friend's male purebred? By purchasing a kitten from such people you only encourage them to continue this practice. If you think you'll be getting a valuable purebred at a bargain, you're sadly mistaken. What you may actually be doing is paying a high price for a low-quality cat with genetic defects.

I'm also upset about the people who don't alter their mixed-breed cats, and then when the cat has a litter, put an ad on *Craigslist* knowing that people are always looking for kittens and they'll be able to get those four or five little *problems* off their hands.

Getting a Kitten or Cat from Your Friend or Neighbor

Refer to the previous section on "Online and Newspaper Ads" because the same dos and don'ts apply. They may be fabulous gardeners or conscientious neighbors but problematic cat owners. Ask the right questions.

Check Out the People, Not Just the Cats

Summon up every intuitive ability you have, and while you're asking questions of the people who have raised the kitten or cat, make sure you're comfortable with their answers. During consultations I've learned that when I ask questions of owners, they'll often give me the answer they think I want to hear rather than the truth. I've had to sharpen my skill at separating fact from fiction. If anything a breeder or private owner says doesn't coincide with what you're seeing, then your antenna should go up. Ask questions and get whatever accurate history is available on the kitten.

When the Cat Chooses You

I'll bet that if you took a poll among cat owners, an overwhelming number of them would tell you that they hadn't been looking for a cat, hadn't planned on one, and maybe didn't even care much for cats—the feline love of their lives just walked in. More often than not, it's the cats who choose us, whether they show up at our doorstep, on the roadside as we take our morning run, or are huddled on the warm hood of our car on a cold winter night. This is the way almost all of my cats have come into my life.

If a cat appears at your door, before deciding to become his owner, make sure he doesn't belong to anyone else. Obviously check for a collar or any other form of identification. Some owners have microchips implanted under the cat's skin. These chips are then read by a special hand-held scanner. Many shelters and veterinarian clinics have these scanners. Check with your local shelter and the veterinarians in your area in case someone has been searching for a lost cat.

Search *Craigslist* and your local newspaper and consider placing an ad yourself. Don't tell everything about the cat, though, so you'll be able to tell who the true owner is. For example, if the cat has a white spot on his back right foot, or is missing a canine tooth, these are the kinds of facts that only the true owners would know. You need to be careful because there are some very cruel people in this world who will take a free cat for inhumane reasons.

Before keeping the cat who seems to have chosen you, he'll need to be tested for diseases such as *feline leukemia* and *feline immunodeficiency virus*. He should also be vaccinated and dewormed, if necessary.

If the cat who chooses you is *feral* (a cat who has reverted back to the wild and has had no human socialization) as opposed to being a *stray* (a cat someone once owned and socialized but has since been on his own for whatever sad reason), then the process of becoming his owner is more complicated. A feral cat hasn't been handled or socialized through contact with humans. These cats can remain mistrustful and distant. They also may not integrate well into households where there are existing cats without a good deal of rehab work and behavior modification.

I don't mean to dissuade you from bringing a feral into your family but I have to caution you because it's not an ideal situation for the average person. Ferals require lengthy trust-building and a solid behavior modification plan. You have to have the skill and patience needed to work at the cat's pace. You also need appropriate living conditions for the cat because he'll initially need to be in a large cage and then eventually housed in one room while you work on trust-building. Ill-equipped owners can be injured by a frightened, defensive feral. The safety of children in the home must also be considered as well as the safety of existing companion animals. If you don't think you have the skills to rehabilitate a feral cat and there is one (or more) in your area, contact the nearest feline rescue group. They will have the information concerning whether there are any skilled foster homes that are feral-specific or whether there is a TNR (trap-neuter-release) program near you. If there are no feline rescue groups in your area then contact your local humane organization.

Pick of the Litter

Rule number one: Don't let anyone sell or give you a kitten taken away from his mother before he's ten to twelve weeks of age. Kittens need to be with their mother and also their littermates until that time. This is the time they're still learning from each other. The playing and posturing kittens do with each other is actually preparing them for adulthood. They're learning valuable social skills. Kittens taken away from their littermates too early may sometimes have difficulty integrating into multicat households later. They may not have appropriate play skills and can have trouble bonding with companion pets. This isn't always the case but you need to be informed so you can make the best choice for your family.

Rule number two: A kitten who wasn't properly socialized may have trouble bonding to humans. The crucial socialization period is between three to seven weeks. It's at this time that frequent gentle handling by humans help kittens learn to trust and become comfortable around us scary-looking giants.

Observe the mother cat if possible, and ask questions concerning the kind of care she gives her kittens. How is the mother cared for? What kind of physical condition is she in? If she looks thin and unhealthy then the quality and quantity of the milk she provided her kittens could be compromised.

With five adorable kittens staring at you, how do you choose just one? It's hard. Your head is calmly saying, "We agreed that we'd get only one kitten," but your heart is saying, "They're so cute, WE WANT THEM ALL!" Stop and think. Your heart may want them all but your resources may be too limited.

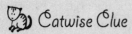 *Catwise Clue*

If you're at a shelter or in a situation where you don't have the opportunity to observe the litter (the kittens may already have been separated), then TAKE YOUR TIME when evaluating whether the kitten you're looking at is right for you. It's a decision you'll both have to live with for a long time.

If you don't have any other cats already at home, though, I would strongly recommend that you do consider taking *two* kittens. Adopting or purchasing two kittens will be a very rewarding experience. They'll continue to learn from each other as they grow, they'll have companionship (because you can't always be around), and from a behavioral standpoint, it's a heck of a lot easier to bring two kittens into a household together than to get just one and decide after he's an adult that he needs a buddy. Adult cats are territorial and introducing a second cat takes finesse. I can't even count how many owners of adult cats have told me how they wished they'd adopted a second kitten when they had the chance.

Finding Your Feline Soul Mate

If there's a litter of kittens, try to see them all. Even if you know in advance that you want a female, and the owners tell you that there's only one in the litter, look at each kitten anyway. Why would I want you to look at the males when you're sure you want a girl? Observing the litter as a whole can help you sort out personality types. You may want a female kitten but maybe you don't want a wild one; by watching the whole group you'll get a sense of where she fits in. You may find a male cat who seems playful and confident but not as revved up. Although you may be tempted to rescue the so-called *runt* of the litter, realize that the kittens who are on the far ends of the scale (i.e., very aggressive or very timid) may develop behavioral problems. I'm not saying that only perfect kittens should be adopted, just that you have to be aware of your expectations and your limiting factors. If your family is expecting that perfect kitten, then bringing them a very frightened kitten who hides at the slightest sound or movement will be difficult for the family and for the kitten.

Many people choose kittens on looks alone. They've always wanted a black cat or maybe it's the orange tabby look that melts their heart. While looks are certainly nice, take a moment to think back over relationships you've had in your life. How successful have your relationships been that were based on looks alone? Would you choose a partner to spend the rest of your life with just because he or she is attractive? If you answered "yes," then I want you to take this book, close it, hold it up to your head, and give yourself a good whack. Shame on you.

Now, let's get back to work. Remember, the cat you choose will, with luck and care, be in your family for twelve or more years. We have a twenty-three-year-old cat at our house. Physical appearance is only a part of what makes up a cat. Now you can get an ice pack for that lump on your head.

Checking Out the Kitten's Temperament

Find out if the kittens have just eaten before attempting to evaluate potential personalities and activity levels, because everyone will most likely be sleepy after a meal.

- Notice who is playful, confident, and friendly.

- Get down on the floor and let the kitten (or kittens) get used to you. How does he react? Does he panic and hide? Does he hiss at you? Basically, he should be comfortable and unafraid.

- Tempt the kitten with anything that will elicit a play response (a feather will do). He should express interest in it, pouncing on it and batting it around, and in general, if he causes you to giggle with his antics, he gets an A+.

- After he's enjoyed a good playtime and has settled down (remember, kittens seem to have bursts of energy), try gently holding him. He shouldn't hiss, spit, or attempt to seriously bite or scratch. He may bite gently in play though, since he is a kitten and hasn't been trained yet. Determine whether the bite is playful, a warning, or a no-nonsense chomp. And, while kittens in general don't tend to want to sit still long enough to be held for any length of time, he should be accepting of handling. Kittens who haven't been well socialized to humans will do everything in their power to get out of your grasp. A little squirming is fine, but biting, fear, and aggression are not.

The Physical Once-Over

While a kitten may not want to stay still long enough for you to do a thorough exam, you should check him out physically before you make your decision. Your veterinarian ought to examine him as well. Once again, I'm not saying you should reject a kitten if he has fleas or ear mites, but be aware of potential health issues. If the kitten is ill, you may be going back and forth to the veterinarian. Can you handle the possible expense? You also don't want to fall in love with a kitten who won't survive. BE INFORMED.

- *Skin and coat.* A healthy kitten has a soft coat with no bald patches or broken hairs (which could indicate ringworm). Sniff the kitten's fur—it should smell clean. If the coat is greasy, rough, dry, or has an odor, it could mean parasites, improper care, or an underlying disease. Keep in mind that most kittens and puppies are born with worms and will get dewormed several times early in life.

The skin should look clean, without any scabs or rashes. Look for signs of fleas or flea dirt (flea excrement—little black specks). Don't reject a kitten just because he has fleas, but be aware that a badly infested kitten may be anemic from the loss of blood caused by the parasites.

- *Body.* When you pick the kitten up, he shouldn't feel fat or skinny. If you can feel his ribs, that's okay. If you can *see* his ribs, then he's too thin. His belly shouldn't feel hard or swollen. If he has a *potbellied* look, then he probably has worms.

- *Eyes.* They should be clear and free of any film or discharge (either watery, milky, or greenish). There should be no sign of squinting and the nictitating membrane (a protective membrane that unfolds to cover the eye) shouldn't be visible. The normal position for the nictitating membrane is to remain folded in the inner corner of the eye.

- *Ears.* They should look clean inside. Head shaking or the appearance of gritty brownish/black exudate indicates a strong probability of ear mites. While not a reason to reject a kitten, be aware that he'll require medication for about three weeks (the life cycle of the ear mite).

- *Mouth.* The gums should be pink, not red, and not pale. Teeth should be white. Look for signs of periodontal disease (red, inflamed gums, tartar buildup, loose teeth, foul breath) in adult cats. Ask about the kitten or cat's diet and appetite. Make sure a kitten is able to eat solid food.

- *Tail.* To be more precise, it's what is *under* the tail area. It should be clean, with no signs of discharge or diarrhea.

Be realistic when evaluating the kitten or cat. Don't reject him just because he may have something such as tapeworms, fleas, or ear mites, but be cautious of potentially serious problems.

Documentation, Guarantees, and Paperwork

If you're purchasing from a breeder, read every word of the contract and guarantee. Question anything you don't understand. It should be written in the guarantee that when you take the cat to be examined by the veterinarian, if he is determined to be unhealthy, you can return him. I know it sounds cold, almost as if you're buying a washing machine and not a living creature, but keep in mind that some people spend thousands of dollars for certain breeds of cats and there are some breeders who will knowingly sell you an unhealthy pet then refuse to refund your money.

If it's written in the guarantee that should the kitten be deemed unhealthy by the veterinarian, you can choose another cat but not a refund, insist on having that changed. None of the remaining kittens may be what you want. The option should be yours to decide if you want to take your business elsewhere, rather than being locked into taking the "best of the worst."

The "Special Needs" Kitty

Not everyone looks for the perfect kitty. Some are drawn to the kitten or cat no one else wants. Cats with physical disabilities very often turn out to be the most amazing companions—some should even be applauded for being kitty role models, so to speak. But sadly, some don't do well. If you have it in you to give a kitten or cat a second chance at life, consult your veterinarian to discuss what you can expect in terms of care required and long-term prognosis.

If you decide that you do want to adopt and nurse an ill kitten or cat back to health, make sure you're prepared for the time, expense, and possible heartbreak should your best efforts fail. Bringing a sick cat home to a household where there are existing cats will also mean isolating him to keep everyone safe. Think everything through carefully before committing to the welfare of a cat with special needs.

2

Head to Toe

A Guided Tour of Your Cat and the Ways He Communicates

Take the time to go on a little tour of your cat's body. He's not just a cute little ball of fur who chases mice and sleeps in the sun. A cat's body is perfectly built for hunting and every piece of feline equipment performs intricate, well-timed functions. And what about those meows? Do they really mean anything? Cats are masters of communication and use multiple forms: olfactory, visual, and auditory. Become familiar with your cat's language and it will unlock the mysteries of behavior problems and cat/owner misunderstandings.

Let's start with some basic information on the internal/external workings of this marvelous creature:

Temperature

Temperature can range from 101.5–102.5 degrees Fahrenheit. Under stress, the cat's temperature can rise (for example, while being examined by the veterinarian), so depending on the circumstances, a temperature of 102.5 degrees Fahrenheit would be considered normal.

Heart

The cat's heart averages around 120 to 240 beats per minute. The number of beats will increase in times of stress, fear, excitement, or physical activity. A fever can also cause an increase in the number of beats.

Respiratory Rate

About twenty to thirty breaths per minute is the average for a resting cat. Humans average about half of that.

Blood

There are three blood types: *A*, *B*, and the extremely rare *AB*. Most domestic short-haired cats are type A. Before a transfusion both the donor cat and patient must be typed.

The Eyes

Cats have binocular vision, this means an image is seen by both eyes at the same time. This provides the cat with excellent depth perception.

Cats, being hunters, are very stimulated by movement going across their visual field. The prey-drive is strongly triggered by movements going away from the cat.

Cats have a layer of cells beneath the retina called the *tapetum lucidum*. These act as a mirror and reflect light back into the retina, which allows the cat to use all available light. This makes the eye about 40 percent more efficient. You've seen this glowlike effect as your car's headlights are reflected in the eyes of animals at night.

People mistakenly assume that cats can see when it's totally dark, which isn't the case. They can, however, see in conditions we consider total darkness.

The light path from the cat's pupil to the retina is shorter than that of humans. This enables the pupil to open wider and constrict smaller.

Cats have a third eyelid known as the *nictitating membrane*. This pale pink membrane normally rests at the inner corner of the eye. If protection of the eye is needed, it will unfold and cover the surface. Since cats generally hunt in tall grass and brush, the nictitating membrane protects the eye from injury. When a cat is ill, more of the nictitating membrane may also be exposed.

Kittens are blind at birth and then as their poorly focusing eyes develop, they are very sensitive to light. Kittens also are born with blue eyes. Their true eye color will develop several weeks later.

Cats' eyes come in several colors, the most common being green or gold. White cats with blue eyes suffer from congenital deafness. Frequently, odd-eyed cats have deafness on the side with the blue eye.

Cats have limited color vision. They can see blues, grays, yellows, and greens. They don't see reds. Limited color vision isn't as important as being able to detect sound, scent, and movement.

Your cat's eyes can help indicate what he's feeling. The pupils dilate when a cat is stimulated, surprised, or fearful. Constricted pupils may indicate tension or potential aggression. Of course, available light must be taken into consideration.

Avoiding direct eye contact is one method a cat uses to try to prevent a violent confrontation with another cat. An offensively aggressive cat will make direct eye contact.

The Ears

Because cats are hunters, their sense of hearing is as important as their sight or smell. A good predator has to be able to detect the faintest rustling in the grass. A cat's hearing range is better than that of a human and at the higher end is better than even that of a dog. Their hearing is so sensitive that cats can distinguish between two similar sounds from dozens of feet away. They can hear about two octaves higher than us.

The *pinna* is the flap of the ear that is shaped like a cone. It collects sound waves, funneling them to the inner ear. The many muscles in the pinnae are what allow the cat to rotate his ears in a wide arc, enabling him to locate the source of sounds accurately. Your cat's ears can rotate 180 degrees and one ear can rotate independently of the other.

Your cat's ears are also mood indicators. Ears flattened sideways and down reflect irritation or possible submission. An anxious cat may twitch his ears. When the ears face forward, it often indicates alertness. During a fight (or in anticipation of one), the ears are rotated back and flattened to prevent them from being damaged by an opponent's claws or teeth.

The Nose

A well-developed sense of smell is vital for survival in the cat world. It enables the cat to identify territories, relays specific information about the opposite sex, informs him of the presence of potential enemies, alerts him to the presence of potential prey, and detects the temperature and safety of food. A cat isn't a scavenger and the cat's sense of smell directly affects his appetite. A cat who can't smell can become anorexic.

The cat's sense of smell is better than a human's but inferior to a dog's.

The cat's nose has approximately two hundred million scent cells. To give you an idea of how your cat's nose compares to yours, humans only have about five million.

The inside of the cat's nose is lined with a mucous membrane that traps foreign particles and bacteria in an effort to prevent them from entering the body.

The mucous membrane also warms and moisturizes inhaled air before it continues on through the respiratory tract.

Some cats have to work harder than others when it comes to breathing due to the differences in muzzle shapes. Flat-nosed breeds, such as Persians, have a compromised breathing ability due to the distorted shape of their compact nose. Their sense of smell may be compromised as well.

Cats also have an extra scent "analyzer" that plays a specific role in identifying sex-related odors in urine (see *The Mouth*).

The Mouth

Kittens get their temporary teeth at four weeks of age. The permanent teeth are usually in by six months. There are thirty teeth in total. The two canine teeth are used for severing the spinal cord of prey and delivering the killing bite. The six incisors located in the front of the mouth in both the upper and lower jaws are for tearing off small bits of meat and plucking feathers. The premolars and molars cut off larger pieces of flesh from the prey. Cats don't chew or grind these pieces, but rather, they're swallowed whole.

The cat's tongue is covered with tiny backward-facing barbs (papillae) that are used for grooming, and also for removing meat from the bones of prey.

When it comes to drinking water, cats use their tongue to lap water at an incredibly fast speed. New research has been done on this by Pedro M. Reis and Roman Stocker of the Massachusetts Institute of Technology, along with Sunghwan Jung of Virginia Polytechnic Institute and Jeffrey M. Aristoff of Princeton University. The *New York Times* published the results in an article in the November 11, 2010, science section (based on the researchers' writings in *Science* magazine). The cat curves the upper side of his tongue downward and darts his tongue lightly onto the surface of the water. The speed at which he does this is so fast that as a column of water is drawn up by his tongue, the cat will close his mouth to collect the water just at the moment gravity begins to pull the water column back down. The researchers are engineers and they created a machine to mimic the cat's tongue. They determined that the cat laps four times per second.

The cat's tongue has fewer taste buds than that of a human. The cat generally has no desire for sweet tastes although some develop a taste for sweet goodies if repeatedly offered by owners.

Cats use their tongue very efficiently to keep their coats well groomed. Grooming is vital to survival. After eating, the cat uses his tongue to remove all traces of prey from his fur so it won't alert other prey to his presence. It also decreases the cat's risk of becoming prey to a larger predator.

Grooming serves a behavioral function as well. In a stressful situation a cat may groom himself to displace the tension he feels. You may notice this if your cat is sitting at the window watching a bird outside. If the bird flies off, the cat may begin a round of self-grooming to defuse the energy he was storing and the frustration he feels.

Located in the roof of the mouth is a scent organ known as the *vomeronasal organ*, with ducts leading into both the mouth and the nose. The cat inhales, opening his mouth and curling his upper lip. The odor is then picked up on his tongue. It's almost a cross between smelling and tasting. He then moves the tongue toward the roof of the mouth with the collected odor, passing it to the vomeronasal organ. While performing this scent analysis, the cat's lips are pulled back into a sort of grimace (called a *flehmen reaction*). This behavior is most commonly performed by males reacting to the urine or pheromones of females in heat.

The Whiskers

Whiskers (*vibrissae*) are used as a sensory device, relaying messages to the brain. Whiskers are located on the upper lip, cheeks, above the eyes, and on the forelegs. The whiskers on the muzzle are in four rows. The upper two rows can move independently of the bottom two rows. The upper whiskers, which extend beyond the head, also help guide a cat through darkness by gauging air currents. Whiskers on the forelegs are used to sense any movement of prey trapped under the cat's front paws.

The muzzle whiskers also help a cat to determine if he can fit through a tight spot. In theory, the width of the whiskers should match the width of the body. In reality, though, many cats are overweight so their body width far exceeds the whisker tips.

Whiskers play an important role in feline body language as well. Whiskers that are forward-facing and spread out usually indicate that the cat is alert and ready for action. The whiskers of a relaxed cat are positioned sideways and not as fanned out. Fear or potential aggression is communicated by the whiskers being tightly spaced and flattened back against the face.

The Nails

Cats have five toes on each forefoot and four on each hind foot. The fifth toe on the inside of the forefoot is known as the dewclaw and doesn't come in contact with the ground. Some cats, referred to as *polydactyls*, have extra toes.

When a cat scratches on a tree or scratching post, the outer sheath of the nail is removed. This allows the new growth to come through. If you look at the base of where your cat normally scratches, you'll probably find little discarded crescent-shaped sheaths.

Unlike dogs, the nails on the cat's forefeet don't wear down because they remain sheathed until needed.

The Tail

The tail is one-third of the spine, is used for balance, and also serves an important role in communication. The tail helps the cat balance on high, narrow places and assists in high speed directional changes. An upright tail when the cat is standing or walking lets you know he's alert. It's also the position used in greeting. A relaxed cat's tail is horizontal or somewhat down. When your cat flicks his upright tail at you, it's usually meant as a greeting. In most cases, the message he's sending is "Hi, I've missed you. When's dinner?" A lashing or thumping tail reflects arousal or irritation. If you're petting your cat when this happens, it's a very good idea to back off. When a cat is resting, an occasional twitching or sweeping motion of the tail is his way of saying he's relaxed but still alert. A frightened cat will puff out the hairs on his tail (*piloerection*) so it looks more than twice its size. A tail in an inverted "U" shape indicates that the cat is fearful and potentially defensively aggressive. A subordinate cat will tuck his tail between his legs or around his body, trying to be as small and invisible as possible.

Injury to your cat's tail can result in a permanent loss of balance and create severe or fatal bladder problems.

OTHER INTERESTING BODY FACTS

- Cats have a floating clavicle that is not attached to bone. This gives them the ability to squeeze into tighter spaces.
- Cats have a sprinting speed of about 30 miles per hour.
- Cats can jump about five times their height.
- Only cats have the ability to retract their claws.
- Cats are *digitigrade* walkers, which means they walk on their toes. This increases their stealth, speed, and ability to make quick directional turns.

Relating the Feline Aging Process to Ours

Just about everyone is familiar with that age-old saying about how a dog ages seven years for every one of our human years. Applying that principle to cats is inaccurate. It isn't even entirely accurate for dogs.

The first two years of cat life are the approximate equivalent of twenty-four human years. That's a lot of growing and maturing that a cat goes through in a short amount of time. Each year after the age of two equals approximately four human years.

With dogs, life expectancy can vary based on breed. Large dogs tend to have shorter life spans than the small breeds. With cats, breed doesn't affect life expectancy as much as lifestyle does. An indoor cat who is well cared for stands a much better chance of living to a ripe old age than an outdoor cat who only sees the veterinarian for emergencies, if at all.

Cat's Age	Equivalent Human Years
1 year	15–18 years
2 years	21–24 years
3 years	28 years
4 years	32 years
5 years	36 years
6 years	40 years
7 years	44 years
8 years	48 years
9 years	52 years
10 years	56 years
11 years	60 years
12 years	64 years
13 years	68 years
14 years	72 years
15 years	76 years
16 years	80 years
17 years	84 years
18 years	88 years
19 years	92 years
20 years	96 years

Vocal Communication

Cats use vocal communication along with marking and body language to effectively convey messages.

Cat owners become very familiar with the subtle, and some not so subtle, nuances of their cat's vocabulary. Almost every owner can identify the differences between the vocalization that says "play with me" and "you're late with my dinner."

A cat's vocal repertoire is quite extensive. It ranges from soft contented murmurs and vowel patterned sounds to strained intensity sounds. There's no such thing as a simple "meow." Here are some general examples of the cat's vocabulary.

Purr

It's the most charismatic and endearing sound that a cat makes. How the purr is actually produced remained a mystery for a long time. Experts had various theories but the most current information is that the purr is created by contractions of the laryngeal muscles and diaphragm, which create pressure in the glottis.

Cats purr during both inhalation and exhalation and it is done with a closed mouth. Studies have shown that vibrations of 25 hertz applied to extremities promote wound healing, and increase bone density and muscle mass. They also help with pain relief. The cat's purr is 25 hertz (25 cycles per second).

Initially, the purr is produced by the mother as a way to communicate with her kittens. They feel the vibrations of the purr, which helps them to locate her. The purr may also help the queen with pain relief after birth and during nursing.

Although we as owners are most familiar with the purring our cats do during times of contentment or nursing, they also purr in a variety of other, less expected situations. Cats often purr to self-soothe during times of illness or fear. When a cat is close to death is also a time that purring can occur. Euphoria has been reported by some terminally ill human patients, so perhaps cats may experience this as well.

Purring may also be how a cat attempts to soothe an opponent in an effort to thwart an attack.

Meow

A meow is a greeting that is usually directed toward humans and is generally not a cat-to-cat form of communication. Variations on "meow" are used to communicate to their owners. Body postures and environmental specifics must be taken into consideration to determine what the cat is asking for (food, attention, greeting, request to be left alone, etc.).

Mew

A cat-to-cat communication that may be used for location or identification purposes.

Chirp

A soft sound that a cat makes in anticipation of something desired that he is about to receive (usually a meal or treat).

Trill

A more musical version of a chirp that is often used as a happy greeting.

Chattering

The sound an excited cat makes when spotting prey. Owners may be familiar with this sound if they've ever watched their indoor cat sit at the window watching a bird or squirrel.

Murmur

A closed-mouth soft sound that is often issued as a greeting.

Grunt

Sound produced by newborn kittens.

Hiss

The hiss is used as a defensive warning, and is created when a burst of air is forced out through an arched tongue and an open mouth with the lips pulled back. The creator of the sound is most likely hoping the vocalization and accompanying body posture will deter potential violence. Aggression will likely follow should the danger persist.

Spit

A quick popping sound, spitting often accompanies the hiss. It's produced in reaction to being threatened or taken by surprise. A menacingly quick slap to the ground with a paw often adds to the drama of spitting.

Growl

This is one of the cat's strained intensity sounds. A steady, low-pitched warning sound produced with an open mouth. Just as a cat tries to appear larger by piloerection of fur, the deep growl may also be an attempt to seem threatening to the enemy. Growling can be either offensive or defensive.

Snarl

An intimidating expression of upper lip curling. I include it in this section on vocal communication because it is often accompanied by a growl.

Shriek

Most commonly associated with the female as she cries out after copulation. The male's penis has tiny barbs on it that most likely hurt her as he withdraws. The shriek can be heard when there is sudden pain or in very intense aggressive encounters.

Moan/Yowl

A loud call expressing confusion or discomfort. Older cats may issue a bewilderment yowl when disoriented. This often happens at night when everyone has gone to bed and he's walking around a dark and quiet house. Some cats may moan just prior to vomiting.

Mating Call

The estrous female gives out a two-syllable call. The male's call resembles "mowl." These nightly sounds are what elicit slipper throwing, water squirting, and various four-letter words from sleep-deprived humans.

Body Language and Communication Basics

In general, body language can be broken down into two general categories: *distance-increasing* and *distance-reducing*. The posture can indicate an indifference, acceptance, or even desire for interaction, or else the posture can say "don't come any closer" or even "go away." For example, a play solicitation posture is a distance-reducing display while a cat standing stiff-legged and displaying piloerection (hair standing on end) is clearly requesting an increase in distance.

Self-Grooming

Cats are famously fastidious and can be seen grooming themselves on a regular basis. The cat's saliva contains a natural odor neutralizer and that's why the kitty's fur smells so fresh after a tongue bath.

Grooming removes dirt, loose hairs, parasites, and other debris.

In an outdoor environment, grooming is more than just a cleanliness issue—it's a survival instinct, as discussed earlier, for the cat to rid himself of all scent traces.

Cats will also self-groom as a displacement behavior when they're anxious or unsure of a situation. Taken to the extreme, some cats can groom themselves so much they create bald patches. There are several underlying medical causes for extreme self-grooming. For example, a cat may overgroom an area that is painful, and certain diseases such as hyperthyroidism can cause overgrooming.

Allogrooming

Mutual grooming between cats serves many functions. It's most often a bonding and social behavior between familiar cats. It can also be used to reinforce status as well as relieve stress. Cats may also groom each other to create one familiar, communal scent.

Your cat may also enjoy grooming you and this usually is a very special bonding moment.

Bunting and Rubbing

Using the scent glands on the forehead and face, the cat rubs or nudges his face against you or a companion pet. This behavior is called *bunting*. As he rubs, he deposits a scent onto the person or animal. This is typically an affectionate behavior and probably has more to do with bonding than marking.

Allorubbing

This refers to one cat rubbing against another, and is a component of social communication among familiar cats. Allorubbing is usually done by one cat rubbing his flank along the side of another cat. Cats who are friendly to each other may also engage in bunting behavior before or during allorubbing. This behavior is also displayed by cats toward humans.

Piloerection (aka Halloween Cat)

Just about everyone is familiar with this famous defensive posture. The cat arches his back with piloerection of hair. He will also turn sideways and this is all done to appear larger and more threatening to an approaching opponent.

Offensive Aggressive Posture

The cat will be standing stiff-legged to appear as tall and imposing as possible. Piloerection of hair adds to that imposing appearance. The cat will give a direct stare at the opponent. The pupils are constricted. Ears are flattened back and slightly down. Tail position is down but not tucked under the body.

Defensive Aggressive Posture

The cat stands sideways and although his head is facing his opponent, he avoids a direct stare. The tail is usually tucked and he holds his body lower to the ground or raises up and assumes a puffed up stance with piloerection. Pupils are dilated and ears are flattened.

Side Step

In a playful, friendly environment, a cat may solicit a companion to participate in play by standing sideways with a slightly arched back and arched tail. Although the posture is similar to the defensive Halloween cat image, there's no piloerection, no facial tension, and no desire to fight.

Stomach Exposure

Often misinterpreted to be a request for a tummy rub, stomach exposure is NOT an invitation for you to scratch or pet this most vulnerable area. The exact meaning of a stomach display depends on the specific circumstances. When confronted with an opponent, a cat may roll onto his back as a defensive display. The message he's conveying is that he doesn't want to engage in battle but if the opponent persists, the cat will use all weapons (i.e. teeth and claws). This posture is used in the hope that the opponent will move on.

In a relaxed setting, a cat may expose his tummy as he naps or rests and this is truly a sign of ultimate trust and security. Don't ruin the moment by attempting to pet him there because it'll trigger an automatic defensive response.

Often a cat may roll onto his back when requesting to play with a companion cat.

Kneading

This is the milk tread that kittens initially do to stimulate milk flow from the mother's teats. It's a behavior that many adult cats retain and display when on an owner's lap or on a soft material such as a blanket. It's a sign of contentment and relaxation.

Slow Blinks

It's believed by many to be a sign of trust and affection when a cat gives a slow eye blink to an owner or companion cat. Affectionately referred to as *cat kisses*, you can try giving a slow blink back to your cat.

Ears Flattened Against Head

Depending upon the exact position, and other accompanying body signs, it indicates offensive or defensive aggression. Either way, it's a sign that your cat shouldn't be touched.

Airplane Ears

No, this doesn't mean kitty is getting ready to take off and fly. It refers to the ears being held in a horizontal position that resembles airplane wings. A cat may do this to show agitation and increasing aggression. A cat may also display this with one or both ears if he has an ear infection, ear mites, or other ear discomfort.

Tail Lashing

When the cat starts whipping his tail back and forth it's an indication of increasing agitation or tension. If you're petting your cat at that moment, it means it's time to stop—right now. An indoor cat sitting at the window watching an outdoor bird may start swishing his tail back and forth as a way of displacing all that built-up tension and impatience.

Scent-Marking Communication

Cats have scent glands that produce chemicals called *pheromones*. These scent glands are found on the forehead, around the mouth and chin, on the paw pads, and around the anal region. The cat's use of scent marking is elaborate and highly developed. For example, secretions from a female's scent glands provide the tomcat with information concerning her hormonal condition.

To help you get an idea of a cat's emotional state during specific marking behaviors, picture your cat in profile. The pheromones produced on the front end (facial rubbing) have a calming effect on the cat. They're usually reserved for marking in the cat's familiar environment. The pheromones that come from the back end (urine spraying) are high intensity and are produced as a result of anxiety, fear, aggression, and uncertainty.

The glands located between the cat's toes secrete a scent whenever he scratches on objects such as a tree or a scratching post. This activity provides an olfactory territory mark in addition to the visual.

Another gland involved in feline communication is located at the tip of the tail. This rather mysterious sebaceous gland is more active in intact males. Occasionally, the gland can become overactive and the tail gets a greasy look. This condition is referred to as *stud tail*.

Cats also use scent as a way of recognizing and communicating with each other. Two familiar cats will recognize each other and exchange greetings by engaging in nose-to-nose sniffing and then possibly anal sniffing.

Urine Marking

The pheromones in urine are the least subtle way for a cat to communicate or mark territory. Unneutered males are very territorial and tend to establish their ownership by spraying this strong-smelling urine. Having your cat neutered before he gets into this habit is very wise. The perimeters of the turf may be sprayed along with pathways and crossings. Let there be no doubt whose territory you are about to enter.

The cat who is about to spray turns his back to the object, and you very often will notice his tail twitching. When a cat sprays (as opposed to engaging in normal urination), the urine is sent out at a high level to make it convenient for another cat's nose to catch the scent. Spraying, as opposed to urinating a small puddle on the ground, also allows the cat to cover a wider area.

Outdoors, urine spraying by an intact male is also used to entice females.

3

Watch Out for
That Hot Tin Roof

Creating a Safe Home for Your Unstoppable Kitten

Tragically, many times we learn lessons too late. It isn't until the kitten gets burned at the stove or swallows some thread that we rearrange things in our home. Don't think that just because you put the crystal vase up on a shelf, that a curious, adventurous kitten won't find a way to get up there and knock it over.

Before you bring the kitten home and everyone gets caught up in the excitement is the time to go through your home and create a safe environment.

Especially if it is a kitten you are bringing home, you'll need to go room by room through the house, because her energy, curiosity, and lack of experience will cause her to try some potentially dangerous stunts. If it's an adult cat you're bringing in, you'll still need to "cat proof," but it's the relentlessly curious kitten who will have to depend on you to keep her out of trouble.

Later in this chapter, I'll discuss how to bring your kitten or cat into the house and create a room for her so she can begin to adjust to her new life. For now, though, you have some preventative kitten-proofing to do.

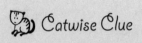 Catwise Clue

From your kitten's point of view, if it's not nailed down, bolted to the ceiling, or glued to the wall, it's a potential toy.

A House Is a Dangerous Thing

When you bring a new pet home you have two immediate safety concerns: protecting your *pet* and protecting your *house*.

Even though the kitten may be a tiny little thing, there's very little out of her reach. To get a proper perspective on how a kitten views our world, get on your hands and knees and crawl around a little. Come on, don't be embarrassed—no one's looking. Do you notice how your perspective changes? Look at how those dangling electrical cords, that you as a human never notice, are now in plain view? And look at that sewing basket by the chair—from here it's a basket of yarn, thread, and other things that a kitten could hardly resist viewing as toys. Now, bear with me a little longer, and go from being on your hands and knees to lying flat on your stomach. Now look around. The perspective changes again (and now you're truly kitten height). What do you see? Perhaps you notice the aspirin tablet that you lost last night when it rolled under a chair. Oh, and there's a needle on the carpet next to the sewing basket. And there's that jelly bean that your daughter dropped yesterday. Perhaps you even notice how there's enough space behind the refrigerator for a kitten to get stuck. And look at those dust-balls rolling around—uh-oh, better get the vacuum cleaner out.

The next exercise I want you to do is look up, way up, from your current position on the floor. (If someone walks in on you, just tell them you're doing your yoga exercises.) From this position, you'll be able to see how a little kitten could find many ways to climb to where all the interesting stuff is. After she scales the back of the couch, what's waiting for her on the end table? Is an ashtray full of cigarette butts sitting there? A candy wrapper with half of a chocolate bar left inside? Once she climbs the curtain, will she reach an open window without a screen?

We have a lot of work to do!

Electrical Cords and Phone Cords

Three main dangers exist here: 1) the risk of electrical burns should your kitten chew through the cords, 2) the chance of her pulling something such as a lamp or an iron over on top of herself; and 3) the possibility that she could get tangled up in a cord.

Try to avoid having dangling cords, especially the mass of cords that are often around electronic equipment and computers. Hide cords as well as you can by tucking them out of sight and out of reach. You can find cord containment devices at your local office supply store. They come in several configurations. You can even make them yourself if you prefer with tubing or PVC pipe from your local home improvement center. Make a lengthwise slit along one side and push the cords through. Some home improvement stores sell cord containment systems that run along the baseboard and get secured to the wall with metal clips. Any exposed part of the cords should be coated with a bitter tasting anti-chew substance. On a regular basis, go around and check any exposed cords for signs of teeth marks or damage.

The danger of a kitten tugging on a cord and having whatever is on the other end topple over on her is a real one. If you're using a small appliance such as an iron, hair dryer, curling iron, and so on, be sure to secure the cord out of kitty's reach when you're done.

To prevent your kitten from sticking her paw in an electrical outlet, use outlet covers that can be purchased in the baby safety section.

If you're a dinosaur like me and still have one corded phone, you need to ensure your kitten doesn't view it as another toy or chew object. Believe it or not, I actually know a few dinosaurs older than myself who have phones with very long cords. If mobility is really important while you're on the phone, switch to a cordless unit in areas where the cat will have access, or use a retractable cord.

Even though it was a fair amount of work when I first started cat-proofing my home, there were two extra benefits that I hadn't anticipated. The first was that my home and especially my office looked so much neater without tangles of cords in sight. The second benefit was that by the time my first child came along, our home was mostly baby-proofed already. I just needed to do a little tweaking, but life with our cats had already made us conscientious parents.

Strings and Things

A cat has backward-facing barbs on her tongue so if she eats certain objects she has to swallow them because they can't be dislodged. String objects in particular pose a danger. You may see lots of cute pictures of kittens playing with balls of yarn, spools of thread, or Christmas tinsel, but in real life these things can cause very serious injury. The same holds true for string, ribbon, and rubber bands.

It's ironic that it can be nearly impossible to give your cat a pill should medicating be necessary, yet that same cat happily swallows the most unlikely objects such as earrings, pills not intended for her, or pieces of toys, among many other seemingly unappetizing objects. As you go around your house, if an object looks small enough to swallow or like something a kitten might bat around with her paw, put it away.

Prevent Disappearing Acts

As part of her ongoing investigation, a kitten will inevitably find, and try to get into, the smallest, narrowest spot in the house—the space behind the refrigerator or the inside of a shoe in the closet, for instance. Block access to dangerous areas and use child-proof locks on cabinets that don't have secure latches.

Always check on the whereabouts of your kitten when opening and closing drawers and doors. Closets are a popular hangout for kittens and cats. If you plan on allowing your kitten to sleep or play in a closet, fix the door so it won't close all the way and shut her in. Foam finger-pinch door guards work great in this situation. They slip on and off the door easily and are readily available in the child

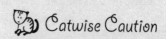

Catwise Caution

Should you find thread or string hanging out of either the kitten's mouth or rectum, DON'T pull it. A needle could be attached to the other end. The string may also have gotten tangled enough that pulling would cause internal damage. Get your cat to the veterinarian or emergency clinic right away.

safety section of many stores. Whenever you go into any closet, always check before closing the door. Kittens have often been accidentally locked in closets for an entire day because their owners didn't notice them before closing the closet door and leaving for work.

Boxes, bags, and even piles of laundry can also be great hiding places, so check to be sure your kitten isn't in one before throwing a box away or putting a pile of laundry in the washer.

Kittens can climb inside of an open drawer before you're even aware of it so close any drawer as soon as you're through, but check inside it first. Kittens can easily be trapped behind the drawer as well, and you could injure her when you close the drawer.

Another thing to remember is that you'll have to change some of your pre-cat habits. If you used to stand at the front door, holding it open as you waved good-bye to your school-bound children, you'll now have to stand on the porch or wave from behind the safety of the closed door.

Later in this chapter, we'll go room by room and work on specific kitten-proofing methods.

Innocent-Looking Poisons

A surprising number of household items are poisonous to cats—from the detergents and cleansers you store under your sink to the mothballs in your closet. It's not enough just to be careful that lids are tight, you also must be sure the cabinet doors are securely latched so there's no chance of your kitten finding her way to the danger. Even if the cap is tightly on the bottle, any drips that have run down the outside can be harmful should the kitten lick them or rub up against the bottle.

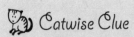 *Catwise Clue*

When you spray a bitter anti-chew spray on your plants, take the plants outdoors or cover the floor with newspaper or a towel to avoid getting the spray all over everything. Be sure to wash your hands as soon as you've finished because you definitely don't want to taste this stuff or get it in your eyes.

Most plants are poisonous to cats, causing reactions that range from irritating to outright deadly. Keep poisonous plants out of kitty's reach. Trim hanging plants so they aren't a temptation and spray the leaves with an anti-chew spray made especially for plants. It doesn't harm the plants and its bitter taste will discourage your kitten from munching on the leaves.

Your medications and vitamins pose a serious danger to your kitten. Acetaminophen (such as *Tylenol*) is so toxic that just one pill can be fatal. Don't leave any medications around because your kitten could be tempted to play with it and wind up ingesting something deadly.

Antifreeze is toxic to animals and just a small amount can be deadly. The added danger of this chemical is that it has a sweet taste, which can attract pets. A few companies manufacture less toxic products now. Check with your local auto supply store or online.

Windows

Many people are under the assumption that cats have perfect balance and, even if they fall, always land on their feet. While they do have the ability to right their body while falling, if the distance is too short they won't have time, and if they fall from a higher distance, the impact can cause serious injury to their legs and chest. A fall from a high window can kill a cat no matter how she lands. Do you think the ability to land on your feet would make much difference in a ten-story fall?

All windows should have sturdy well-fitting screens that can't be pushed out.

An unscreened window opened just a crack can still be wiggled through by a determined cat chasing a fly or curious to get at the sights and smells of the outside.

Don't make the very tragic mistake of assuming your placid cat understands how high up she is and will just sit on the window sill sunning herself. It only takes being distracted by a passing bird or insect for her to lean too far out and lose her balance.

Cords from window blinds and drapes can also be very dangerous. A cat can get tangled in them and possibly end up hanging herself. Secure all cords by rolling them up and tucking them out of reach or use a cord containment device.

Room-by-Room

The Kitchen

This is a dangerous room that looks so deceptively innocent. Everywhere you turn, there's something that could potentially cause harm to your pet. Let's start with the appliances.

A kitten who is able to get up onto the counter (and it doesn't take long before she'll be big enough to make it in one easy leap) could walk across a hot stove. Enticing food aromas make that danger even greater.

When cooking at the stove, keep a squirt bottle handy in case your cat shows any sign of attempting to jump. This is the one place where using an immediate deterrent is necessary because there is never a reason for your cat to come anywhere near the danger of the stove.

Because of the immediate danger that hot burners pose, be on your guard if she's in the kitchen with you. From her point of view, all she knows is that there are tempting smells coming from the area. She won't realize until it's too late that the surface is hot. Use burner covers if needed after removing the food from the stove.

I've seen curious kittens crawl up into the refrigerator without the owners even being aware of it. Before closing the door, always check for the possibility that your kitten is hiding behind the mayonnaise jar.

To keep your kitten from getting behind the refrigerator, tape a piece of cardboard across the space, blocking the way.

Oh, the delicious smells coming up from the garbage disposal—from a cat's point of view, of course. Keep it clean and empty; never allow food to sit in the disposal, which creates a dangerous temptation. Routinely running fresh lemon slices through the disposal will help keep it clean and provide a citrus scent which isn't appealing to cats. As an added safety feature, keep a drain-stopper over the opening.

Check before you close the dishwasher door to be sure a sneaky kitten hasn't crawled in while you were loading it and not looking.

Kittens very often don't know what food is good for them. As far as they're concerned, the world is just one big buffet. Some foods can be deadly (these include chocolate as well as chicken bones) and some spicy or rich foods can cause illness. Keep food in containers and never leave tempting food unsupervised. Use covered garbage cans in your kitchen or secure the can in a cabinet with a child-proof latch.

Glasses and other breakable items can be knocked to the floor and shattered when a cat jumps on the counter. I think it's a must that from the beginning you establish boundaries for where your kitten may and may not venture. The kitchen counter should always be off limits. For training tips, refer to Chapter 7.

Rodent or insect poisons, traps, and baits you may have placed in certain areas of the kitchen might not be as out of kitty's reach as you think. Be very careful about which products you use and where you place them. If you're having a pest problem, consult a professional exterminator and your veterinarian for information on the best products to use.

Sharp utensils that contain food residue may cause injury if left out. A dirty steak knife or the big one used to carve the Thanksgiving turkey can injure a cat's tongue should she attempt to lick the tasty juices clinging to the sharp edge. The same holds true for the sharp-pronged corn-on-the-cob holders, toothpicks, skewers, etc.

Speaking of toothpicks, don't ever leave them on the counter because of the danger of your cat chewing on them. Store them in a closed container in the cabinet. If you're testing a cake for doneness by using a toothpick, don't leave it out before or after you use it.

The Bathroom

Get in the habit of keeping the toilet lid closed. A kitten attempting to jump onto the seat and not expecting an opening there can easily slip and fall right in. An adult cat may be able to jump out but a kitten is unable to and will most likely drown. Keep the lid down to also prevent pets from drinking the water. If you use an automatic toilet disinfectant, its chemicals will harm an adult cat or a kitten if ingested. I strongly advise against using the automatic bowl disinfectants just because of the risk to pets. Even if you leave a note over the toilet to remind all family members and guests, someone might still neglect to close the lid. Keeping a closed toilet lid will also prevent the things your kitten knocks off the tank from falling into the bowl.

Hair dryers, curling irons, and electric rollers shouldn't be left on the bathroom counters. Should the kitten pull the dangling cords, there's a risk that the appliance would come down on her.

Not only medications but also makeup, nail polish, polish remover, and perfume are all toxic so keep those tightly capped if you leave them on counters.

The wastebasket in the bathroom should have a snap-on lid or should be kept in a cabinet. Dangerous things such as dental floss, discarded razor blades, and disposable razors can lurk in there.

Keep all bathroom cleansers put away in cabinets and make sure that your clever cat can't open the doors.

The toilet paper roll is something that many cats think is a special toy installed just for their playtime pleasure. Many owners have come home to find shreds of toilet paper from one end of the house to the other with not one single piece left hanging on the roll itself.

There are a couple of ways to cat-proof the toilet paper. You can start with the easiest way, which may deter your cat if she tends to give up easily, though not many of us are lucky enough to have such a cat. Before you put the toilet paper on the roller, push in on it so the cardboard center isn't perfectly round anymore. It won't unroll as easily once it's installed. Then, install it so the paper unrolls from underneath and not up over the top. This will also make it less likely that the cat will successfully be able to unroll it when she braces her paws up on the roll and starts scratching.

For cats who are not easily deterred, there are baby-proofing products that work very well for cats as well. There are toilet paper devices with hinged covers that easily snap onto the roller. Safety 1st makes one called Toilet Roll Saver, but there are others available online.

The Living Room

Take a cat's eye view of your furniture. Is there anything that could potentially be a danger to your kitten? Rocking chairs are notorious for landing on cat tails and paws. If you have a recliner, it poses a very serious risk to your cat should you forget to be sure she isn't underneath before attempting to raise or lower the footrest.

If you have a fireplace, you'll need a very sturdy screen to keep your kitten out of danger. Don't ever leave the kitten unsupervised in the room when you have a fire going.

Cats love warm places, so check before closing any doors to an entertainment cabinet to be sure your kitty isn't curled up on top of the TV or DVR.

The Bedroom

As I've said, be careful not to lock the cat in the closet and check before closing any drawers. An added danger in some closets and drawers are mothballs. Just the fumes from mothballs can cause serious liver damage to a cat, so don't put them in any closet or drawer that your kitty might have access to.

Be careful about small jewelry items. Make sure they are put away in a box or drawer so your kitten won't swallow them or bat them to the floor.

Many cats, especially frightened ones, will claw at the material underneath the box-spring part of a mattress. Once they make a hole they often crawl up inside because it feels safe. To prevent this, slide a fitted sheet over the bottom of the box-spring.

The Laundry Room

When I worked at an animal hospital, we had several clients who tragically failed to check the clothes dryer before closing the door. They were unaware that their kittens had crawled inside. The thought of how horribly those kittens died continues to haunt me. I check my washer and dryer without fail before I close the door and turn the machine on. I don't just look, I also feel around. When I'm unloading the laundry, I check again before closing the door to make sure none of my cats are trapped in the empty machine. Detergents and bleaches should be safely put away out of the kitten's reach.

If your laundry room has a door, close it when you're doing laundry to keep your kitten out of there. This is one very important reason why I don't really like having the litter box located in the laundry room.

When you do your ironing, don't leave the iron and ironing board unsupervised. Should your kitten try to jump up on it, the board and the iron could topple over onto her. As soon as you've finished, unplug the iron, wrap the cord around the base, and put it in a safe place to cool.

If your family normally leaves dirty clothes in a pile or even in a laundry basket, there's a good chance the kitten will discover it to be a great place for a nap. Don't just toss the pile into the washer or even the hamper without first checking. Having the kitten around could be a good excuse to ask your family to be a little neater. Ask them to toss their dirty duds in the hamper and always make sure to close the lid immediately.

The Home Office

As I write this, there is one cat on my lap and another on the chair next to me. I couldn't imagine not having at least one cat near me whenever I'm in my office, but cats aren't always compatible with computers so you have to take precautions to protect not only your pet but your equipment as well.

What with the computer, printer, fax, phone, copier, lamps, and whatever else you have that requires an outlet you usually wind up with a big mess of cords behind your desk. Refer to the section on *electrical cords* earlier in this chapter to learn how to keep them safely away from kitty.

Don't leave your computer keyboard exposed and unattended if you have a kitten who feels compelled to type a million Zs or Qs with her dancing paws. A keyboard drawer is a great idea when you have a keyboard-loving kitten.

If you use a paper shredder, take precautions to make sure your kitten isn't in the vicinity. The moving parts of any of your office machines can be dangerous, so watch your kitten carefully.

To reduce the amount of cat hair that will inevitably find its way into your equipment, you may want to invest in plastic covers to put over them when they're not in use if they aren't secured in cabinets. You'll probably want to invest in a supply of compressed air and other computer cleaning equipment to reduce the build-up of cat hair.

All small items, such as thumbtacks, push pins, rubber bands, paper clips, etc., should be kept in covered containers or in drawers.

If your cat consistently attempts to chew on rubber bands that are wrapped around piles of papers or even loves to nibble on the paper itself, set up a few dummy papers coated with an anti-chew product. Lay out a few treated papers and coat any rubber bands that are wrapped around the papers. Set these out every time you're at the desk working so your kitty gets the consistent message that this stuff tastes awful. Don't leave the rubber bands out if you're not there to supervise, though. Of course, if you do have a paper chewer, the best solution would be to keep paper put away or out of your cat's reach. You could also try to keep her totally out of the office, but that's not always possible. If you feel as if you're battling with your kitty over shreds of paper but you don't want to lock her out of your home office then set up some constructive distraction for her. Keep a supply of safe toys for her to enjoy when you're working in your office. Food-dispensing puzzle toys are a great distraction.

When I first set up my home office, one lesson I learned the hard way was to put my answering machine where my cats were least likely to step on it. One cat stepped on the outgoing announcement button once and erased my businesslike recording and replaced it with a well-timed "meow." While I thought that was so cute and clever of him, I was less pleased a few days later when he stepped on the *erase* button and wiped out all of my incoming messages.

Children's Play Room

Modeling clay, tiny toys, or any game pieces that could be swallowed should be put away when your children are finished playing with them. I'm a mother and I know it's often a losing battle to get kids to pick up their toys but the consequences of not doing it can be worse—such as having to take your kitten in for emergency surgery to remove a blockage.

Look around—balloons, ribbons, strings, etc.; anything that looks tempting or dangerous needs to be secured.

The Basement, Attic, and Garage

These are three areas where your kittens shouldn't ever be allowed to go.

When you need to go into the attic, I urge you first to close the kitten in another room. A dark, interesting attic can be irresistible to a kitten. Contact with insulation can cause breathing difficulty and skin irritation. And should you shut the door without realizing that your kitten has hidden in the attic, exposure to the extreme temperatures could result in her death.

Basements and garages also hold lots of danger in the form of stored paints, cleaning agents, pesticides, antifreeze, etc. There are also sharp-edge tools and other equipment that can cause injury to the curious kitten.

If you park your car in the garage, on cold days a cat might crawl up into the engine, seeking warmth and end up getting killed when you start the engine. Antifreeze that leaks from your car and sits on the garage floor is also a deadly danger for your cat.

An automatic garage door can kill a cat should she be attempting to get in or out while the door is closing. Garage doors typically come with sensors that prevent them from closing if something is in the path, but older models may not have that safety feature.

Because of all the potentially deadly hazards in basements and garages, I don't feel that your kitten should ever be near them. You have a big enough job making sure you create a safe *indoor* environment—why take unnecessary risks by exposing her to these additional hazards?

Balconies

A cat shouldn't ever be allowed on a balcony. Railings don't offer much protection for a cat who can slip underneath or through the bars. All it takes is for your cat to get distracted by one bird or flying insect, and a tragedy could result. Don't mistakenly believe that *supervision* will keep her safe. Should a passing bird entice your cat, her instinct to leap after her prey will cause her to go over the railing long before you can grab her.

If you're still under the assumption that cats always land on their feet, refer back to the section on *windows*.

It's a Jungle Out There—Outdoor Life

Whether a cat should be allowed outdoors is a hot topic among cat owners. Hopefully, after reading this book you'll have a good understanding of outdoor dangers and with your *think like a cat* training knowledge you'll be able to set up a stimulating and fun indoor environment.

I don't think the outdoors is any place for a cat. There are too many dangers and a little eight-pound cat is no match for cars, trucks, large dogs, mean people, disease, and other very real hazards. Your cat stands a much greater chance of living a longer life if you confine her indoors. Everything she needs is inside your home. As you read through this book, you'll learn how to create all the best that the outdoors has to offer without exposing her to any of the dangers.

Even though my indoor cats may still get sick or injured, I take great comfort in knowing that they won't get hit by cars, attacked by dogs, poisoned, abused by cruel people, or get into fights with other cats. Every night when I go to sleep I know my cats are safe.

If you're going to allow your cat access to the outdoors, you'll have to be very careful about the fertilizers, weed killers, and pesticides you use on your lawn. Secure all outdoor trash-can lids with bungee cords to prevent a cat from rummaging through the garbage.

Leaks from the bottom of cars, such as antifreeze, are deadly.

In the winter, the salt used to melt ice can burn the pads of a cat's paws and burn her mouth when she grooms her paws. You will have to use a pet-safe ice-melting product. Check with your local pet supply store or online.

Finally, although you may take great pains to assure your cat's safety when she's in your yard, should she wander onto a neighbor's property, you have no idea what hazards she may face.

Collars and Identification

Even if you never plan on allowing your cat outdoors, she should wear identification. Indoor cats can accidentally get outside and from your neighbors' point of view, one gray-striped tabby running through a yard looks like any other. Identification can mean the difference between getting her back or losing her forever.

Identification tags are available at your local pet supply store or through mail order. You can choose metal or plastic. Many companies offer plastic in neon colors, which make them extremely visible. Reflective tags are also available. Most people engrave the cat's name, owner's name, and phone number on the tag and—if there's room—an address. For an outdoor cat that's fine, but for an indoor cat I recommend a few changes. My indoor cats' tags read as follows:

> **INDOOR CAT**
> **I'M LOST**
> **IF FOUND, CALL**
> **(NAME)**
> **(PHONE NUMBER)**

In my yard I come across many cats wearing tags with their names and their owners' name and number. So many times I've called the owner only to be told that the cat is allowed to roam and isn't lost. So how do you tell the lost cats? From the vital information on the tag. My cats' names on the tags aren't as important as the information that they're indoor cats.

When you shop for a collar, choose a *breakaway*. This type of collar has an elastic insert so there is no chance that your cat will strangle herself should she get caught on a tree branch.

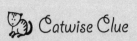 Catwise Clue

Don't weigh your cat's neck down with all kinds of bells, thinking that it will warn away any birds. I'm convinced that a cat with the disadvantage of bells is forced to become even stealthier and faster at the hunt.

When you fit the collar around your cat's neck, be careful that it's not too tight. You should be able to get two fingers underneath. If you are fitting a kitten, keep in mind that she's constantly growing and you must frequently check her collar. Don't let a day go by without testing the fit.

To get your cat used to the idea of wearing a collar, put it on her, then distract her with playtime or feed her dinner. While she may scratch and paw at it initially, if you focus her attention elsewhere, she'll become comfortable soon enough. If she continues to struggle, take it off and try again at the next mealtime. Until you're sure she's used to the collar, don't leave it on her when you're not around to supervise.

Other forms of identification are available to pet owners. You can have a microchip that can be read by a hand-held scanner implanted just under the cat's skin. Veterinarians and humane shelters are equipped with scanners that read the information on the chip. I personally think the combination of the microchip and visible ID tag is best. The visible tag allows your neighbor or someone driving along a road to immediately contact you. The microchip is a great backup in case the collar gets hung up on a branch or removed by someone. If you really want your kitty protected, use both methods.

Always Keep a Current "Lost Cat" Picture

In addition to identification on your kitty, always have at least one clear picture to use in case the unthinkable happens and she gets lost. As she grows and changes, take a few good shots in which her face and markings are clearly visible. As a pet owner, I certainly have loads and loads of pictures but in a crisis, I don't want to have to go searching through a stack for the right one. I have my "lost cat" pictures in an envelope clearly marked so no time will be wasted should that disaster ever occur. For tips on how to find your lost cat, see Chapter 14.

Your Cat Isn't the Only One Who Needs Protection

Perhaps your son has a pet lizard or your daughter has a gerbil. Maybe you have a bird or keep fish. How do you train the cat to leave these creatures alone? You don't. Cats are natural predators. While your kitten may seem to get along well with your parakeet, don't take chances. Keep these pets in separate locations in the house—*always*.

Fish tanks must have super secure cat-proof lids. I've had clients whose cats have managed to figure out even the most complicated, weighted-down tank covers and luckily, the owners were home and able to save both the cats and the fish.

Some kittens who are raised around birds or mice may not view them as prey but I think it's too big a risk. If you're thinking that a cat-proof bird or mouse cage will allow everyone to coexist, keep in mind the anxiety that the mouse or bird will experience by having a predator so close by.

Bringing Kitty Home

Whether you're bringing home a tiny little kitten weighing in at less than one pound or a full-grown Maine Coon at a whopping eighteen pounds, you'll need a *carrier*. If you already have a cat at home, don't use the same carrier for the new kitty. Refer to Chapter 14 for the types of carriers and how to transport a cat safely.

Why should you bring her home in a carrier? Because this is a *really big* step in her life. She's leaving what she knows for something totally unfamiliar. Even if her previous life was bad, she has no idea what's in store for her and this can be very frightening. The carrier will keep her safe during the trip to your house and provide her with a little hiding place.

Place a towel in the bottom of the carrier for comfort and also to absorb any messes. I also always bring an extra towel so I can replace the other one should it get soiled.

Because this is such a big step for a little cat (and for you), if you can arrange it, the best time to bring her home is at the start of a weekend or when you have a day or two off.

If you haven't taken your kitten to the veterinarian yet, make sure it's done in the next few days. If you already have cats at home, the kitten MUST be taken to the veterinarian to be tested for feline leukemia virus and feline immunodeficiency virus, given a physical, and vaccinated before she is exposed to your current cats or vice versa. The last thing you want to do is bring an unhealthy kitten home. Even if your cats are up-to-date on their vaccinations, no vaccine is 100 percent foolproof. You also don't want your new kitty bringing any unwanted visitors along with her, such as fleas or ticks, because parasites would certainly enjoy the opportunity for an all-you-can-eat buffet in the form of your current resident pets.

Prepare the Sanctuary Room

The whole family is excited; even the dog is eagerly wagging his tail in anticipation of the new cat's arrival. In your sweetest voice, explain to them that for the time being, the cat will need a small space of her own and some time to adjust to her new surroundings. As you watch your family's smiles fade and the dog's tail droop, remember—you're doing the right thing.

So why am I being such a meanie and not allowing you to let the cat run free about the house, especially since you've already taken the time to kitten-proof it? Because I don't want to overwhelm her. She's a small cat and it's a big house. Imagine if I whisked you off and dropped you in the middle of a large, unfamiliar city. I then tell you that you have to find your way around the entire city right away. You'd probably get lost, overwhelmed, frustrated, scared, and your initial impression of this strange place might be negative. Basically, that's what you'd be doing to your cat if you gave her the run of the place—you'd be dropping her in a strange city (a foreign one, no less).

Much of a cat's sense of security centers around her territory, so allow your cat to begin acquainting herself with her new home a little at a time. This is crucial for a kitten because she won't know where any of her necessities are.

If you're bringing an adult cat into the house, this is a big change in her life and you must make her feel safe. Safety for her comes in the form of a little sanctuary place. When you set up the sanctuary room, place the litter box on one side of the room and the food/water bowls on the other. It's important to keep a good distance between them because cats don't eat in the same area they use for elimination.

Place her in the room but leave her in the carrier. Open the door to the carrier and let her come out in her own time. A kitten will most likely eagerly charge right out, but an adult may not be sure of herself. Even after she has stepped out of the carrier, leave it in the corner of the room as an extra hiding place.

She may hide under the bed for two days, but that's okay. The fact that she *can* hide will make her feel better. After you've closed the door and left her alone is when she can begin to investigate the room around her. Inch by inch is how she may expand her comfort zone, in quiet, in private, and without a bunch of eyes watching her every move.

No matter what kind of room you've chosen to be your kitty's sanctuary, make sure that there are plenty of hiding places. Don't put her in an empty room where she'll feel totally exposed and threatened. If it's not a room with furniture, place boxes lined with towels around. One trick is to cut a doorway into the side of a box with a lid or a box placed upside down to make a little cardboard cave. Another option is to purchase a couple of soft-sided, flexible kitty tunnels from your local pet supply store.

Create a comfortable and cozy bed area for your new kitty. You can either purchase a pet bed at the store or line a box with some old clothes. I prefer to line a box with a couple of sweatshirts that I've worn so the cat can get used to my scent.

If you're bringing in a kitten at a cold time of year, her room should be warm enough and draft-free.

If you're bringing your new cat into a household of existing cats, a sanctuary room set up for her is absolutely necessary or the fur will fly! How to introduce a new cat to your other pets is covered in Chapter 11.

How much interaction should you initially have with your new cat? Each case is different. If you brought home a kitten, you'll need to give her plenty of time and attention because she'll be anxious to bond with you. If the new arrival is an adult cat, you'll have to use your judgment and base it on her emotional state. If she acts threatened, back off and give her some time by herself. Introduce yourself slowly as you begin the trust-building process.

How will you know when it's time to spring your new cat from kitty jail? If she's a kitten, you can do it as soon as you're sure she has the routine down: eating, drinking, and using the litter box. Keep in mind, though, that the litter box needs to be convenient for her since her litter box habits are still in the learning stage. Don't be too anxious to give her the run of a two-thousand-square-foot house. An adult cat may take longer to feel comfortable about venturing outside of the sanctuary room. You should wait for her to resume normal activities and behavior: i.e., eating, drinking, using the litter box, and demonstrating an increased sense of securtiy. If she's still hiding in the back of the closet, buried beneath a pile of shoes, she's not ready. If you already have cats in the house, the new cat will need to stay in the room for a while so you can do a gradual introduction (see Chapter 11).

Your main concern for a kitten is to make sure she stays safe and has enough time and privacy to eat, sleep, and use the litter box. Everyone is going to want to hold her and play with her, but she's still a fragile baby and needs your watchful eye.

When you do decide to open the door, let her investigate the house a little at a time.

How do you introduce a new adult cat to your family? *Slowly*. She could easily become overwhelmed. I come from a very small family and when I think back to the first time I met my husband's large family I remember feeling overwhelmed. Do your cat a big favor and let her have all the personal space she needs. Don't rush anything. After all, you're going to have many years together, so start things off right.

Your children may have a difficult time understanding the importance of the kitty's need for a sanctuary room. They may be anxious to have the kitty sleep in bed with them. Use your judgment based on the kitty's age, level of comfort, and any other specifics of your situation. Make sure the cat absolutely knows where her litter box is and routinely uses it before trusting her in other rooms. A kitten doesn't have training perfected yet and could have an accident on your child's bed because she may not remember the location of her box.

Taking in a Timid or Fearful Cat

Be prepared—this is a slow process. Taking in a cat whose history is unknown means you have to give her a wide comfort zone and work slowly on building trust.

Just because you've rescued this skinny, hungry, cold, and lonely cat, don't expect her to instantly recognize her sudden good fortune. Depending upon how much contact she has had with humans (if any at all), it may take a long time before she becomes the loving, sociable, happy cat you want, and in some cases, she may remain somewhat timid or hesitant.

The first thing on your list with a stray should be a trip to the veterinarian. The cat must be tested and vaccinated. If she's healthy enough at the time, make plans to have her spayed as well. She should be checked for parasites and if there's so much as one flea on her, take care of that right away so you won't be bringing the little pests home to your other pets.

Once home, she should be kept in one room just as you would with any new kitty. Make certain there are plenty of hiding places in the room because she'll need the security as she gets her bearings. If the room doesn't have enough hiding places, bring in a bunch of boxes and scatter them around the room. Place them on their sides so she'll have a cover over her head. Another great way to create a hiding place yet allow her to move around is to buy a few soft-sided cat tunnels. You can also make a tunnel by connecting several cardboard boxes together. Cut out the bottoms and then tape the boxes together to create a snake-like path. This may help the cat feel more secure as she tries to go from the closet to the litter box or from under the bed to the food bowl. If you create several hiding place options throughout the room, it can encourage her to start investigating. If you just put the cat in a bedroom without multiple hiding places and security options, she might just stay curled up under the bed, only venturing out for a quick trip to the litter box or the food bowl. And in some cases, a very frightened cat may be too afraid to come out for any reason at all.

One of the best ways to start building a relationship with a stray cat is through food. Even if she doesn't yet feel secure enough to eat in your presence (which she probably won't), *you* will be the source of the food supply and she'll eventually make that connection.

At night, leave just a small night-light on for the cat. Don't leave a regular light on because she'll feel more comfortable moving around in darkness. By having a night-light on, you'll be able to enter the room and be aware of where she is (in case she tries to bolt out the door), without having to switch on a bright light, which could be unsettling to her.

Start spending time in the room by just sitting on the floor. Don't try to approach the cat. Let her have total control of the pace of the interaction. While you sit on the floor, quietly talk to her so she gets used to the sound of your voice. Your body language and voice should be casual and nonthreatening and convey a sense of calm.

After a few times of just going in to visit, bring in some special food that the cat will hopefully find irresistible. If she's starving and goes for anything, try handfeeding her, otherwise, in the beginning, just place the food a safe enough distance away from you. If she responds, you can move it a little closer. Each time you feed her, place the food a fraction of an inch closer to you. If using wet food, handfeeding can be done with a soft baby spoon or a wooden tongue depressor. Watch her comfort level, though. If she gets nervous, you need to back up a few steps. Remember: go slowly. Don't rush the trust-building process. Let her dictate the pace. Don't make any sudden moves and don't try to reach out and pet her.

In between mealtimes, bring in an interactive toy (one with a fishing pole design works best) and casually move it around. Don't go in her direction because she could get frightened. Just nonchalantly move it to catch her interest. She may or may not feel bold enough to go after it, but at least you'll be getting her interest. If she does go after the toy, be careful not to bring it too close to you. Work up to that point slowly. After a few play sessions you can let the toy get close to you.

After mealtime or playtime, lay down on the carpet and remain motionless for a while. This may be the time the cat feels brave enough to begin checking you out. When I did this with one of my rescue kitties, I would usually end up falling asleep, then would wake to find her curled up on my legs. The bonding process was taking place. One day I awoke and found that sweet little ball of fur nuzzled up next to my head. It had been a slow trust-building process but that day I saw the light at the end of the tunnel. After quite a while of hiding, fear, and mistrust, she was beginning to let me in. Your patience will pay off, so hang in there.

Have a Safe Holiday

Holidays can be stressful for everyone. For cats, though, it's an especially confusing time because their whole world can be turned upside down. There are often many strangers coming into the house, and the cat may be overlooked by the busy owner. Using your *think like a cat* skills, try to look at the events from your kitty's point of view. An owner's guests may be viewed as intruders by the cat as they attempt to pick her up and hold her. Usual playtime rituals may get forgotten even as the cat follows the owner around waiting for the appearance of a favorite toy. Unfamiliar kids may be running around the house. It may be too loud, and if kitty can't find a safe place to sleep she'll end up hiding under the bed. Doesn't sound much like a happy holiday to me. Then there's the food. Why eat that boring old cat food when there's a feast spread out on the kitchen counter?

Aside from the general holiday dangers, each special day can hold specific dangers, as outlined here.

Christmas

For some cats, Christmas, with all its decorations, must seem like the feline version of *Disneyworld*. For others, Christmas holds no particular interest. To be safe, even if your cat doesn't seem to express any interest in the goings-on of the holiday, don't take chances. Use safe decorations and avoid hazardous temptation.

First, there's the tree. I know many people who spend lots of time and money decorating their beautiful trees, only to find them later that evening lying across the carpet. Don't be fooled—your six-pound cat can knock a six-foot tree right over. Use a heavy, sturdy base so the tree won't be top heavy. Choose a tree that's wide at the bottom, rather than tall and narrow. You can even install a hook in the wall and attach a strong line from it to the tree. Choose a location where there's a picture on the wall behind the tree. Remove the picture and place the hook there, where it will be hidden once the picture is replaced after the holiday.

Get your cat used to the tree before you put decorations on it. Leave the bare tree up for at least a day, so you can see how your cat is reacting. If she starts chewing the needles, use a bitter anti-chew spray for plants. If she attempts to climb the tree, blow a quick spritz of compressed air (the kind used to clean electronic equipment) onto an area of the tree near her. *Don't spritz the cat directly.*

If you have a live tree, be careful to keep your cat away from the water in the reservoir. The pine sap that comes off the tree and ends up in the water is toxic to cats. So are any life-extender chemicals you might add. Cover the exposed part of the reservoir with netting so you can water easily but your cat can't get to it to drink.

Now let's decorate the tree. Start with the lights. Coat each strand with a bitter anti-chew cream to discourage your kitty from munching on the cords. Wear disposable gloves when you do this to limit your exposure to the unpleasant substance and be sure and wash your hands afterward before touching your face. Put the lights deeply into the tree branches. Wrap the light cords around the branches to minimize dangling. To keep the cord that goes from the tree to the outlet safe, slide it through a small piece of PVC pipe. After you purchase the plastic pipe, you can spray-paint it green so it doesn't look so obvious sitting behind the tree. You can also cut a lengthwise slit in the pipe and then push the cords into it. There are also cord containment devices available to minimize the amount of visible loose cords coming from the bottom of the tree to the wall outlet.

The ornaments you choose should be cat-proof. If you have breakable ones, the best place for them is back in their boxes. That said, if you really want the fragile ones on the tree, place them higher up, out of cat's reach. The ornaments on the lower third of the tree shouldn't have any sharp or breakable pieces, string, or anything that could be dangerous.

Ornament hooks can be hazardous too, not just for the cat but for children as well. Instead of hooks, find safer ways to attach your ornaments, such as green twist ties. They're invisible and securely keep the ornaments on the branch. Ribbon-type ornament hangers can also be used. Coat them first with a bitter anti-chew product to discourage your kitten from attempting to munch.

The gifts you so lovingly wrap and place under the tree need to be cat-safe too. Ribbons are not only a big hazard but unfortunately, the most tempting accessories. Keep your gift wrapping simple. Use a plain bow on top rather than the thin curling ribbon with long tendrils of easily chewable strands. If there are gifts you want to wrap elaborately with lots of flowing ribbon, put them away until it's time for them to be opened. And, speaking of opening gifts, that's the time when an unnoticed little kitten can get into trouble. Your family is busy tearing open packages and no one notices that the kitten grabbed the ribbon that was tossed on the floor. Another major potentially dangerous time is when you gather up the discarded wrapping paper and boxes to toss in the outside trash. A kitten could easily be buried in there. If your kitty isn't in sight, go through every piece of paper and every box before tossing it away.

Be careful about seasonal plants such as poinsettias, holly, and mistletoe. Some are toxic and all cause intestinal problems. Keep them out of your cat's reach. Another very serious threat to your cat's safety is the many holiday candles. Don't leave any candles unattended. A cat's tail can easily come in contact with the flame or knock the whole candle over. There are many companies that make realistic-looking flameless candles these days. They're safer for families with pets and small children.

Now we come to my favorite part of Christmas—the food. The rule here for your cat should be simple. Keep her away from it. The rich foods we eat during the holidays will cause your cat digestive upset. Also be very careful of things such as turkey bones, which, if your cat gets hold of, can cause her to choke or suffer serious intestinal injury. Don't leave the turkey or roast sitting out on the counter if no one's in the room.

Don't leave chocolate anything—candies, cookies, alcohol—out unattended when there's a kitten wandering around. Chocolate is deadly to cats.

Another problem cats and other pets face at Christmas is the sudden invasion of strangers. From the cat's point of view, strangers suddenly burst through the door. The cat is often pursued by unfamiliar children, denied access to certain favorite spots (such as the guest room), and is all but forgotten by her usually attentive owner. House guests can let your cat outside, step on her, or just downright frighten her. If you're having a house full of guests for the day, provide your cat with a temporary sanctuary—perhaps in your bedroom or some other area where guest traffic won't be allowed. Put her litter box in there, along with some water (and food if you free-feed). When I do this for my cats, I first engage them in an interactive play session and then put on some soft classical music. That way, they're hopefully ready for a nap while I go and attend to my guests. The music acts as a bit of a buffer from the noises coming from the other side of the door. Before leaving the room, I also set up a few solo activities for my cats. This could be in the form of a few puzzle feeders, some tunnels, or other toys my cats enjoy. I also place a sign on the bedroom door requesting that visitors not enter there because my cats are inside.

A word of caution: with all the partying, shopping, visiting, and other hectic activity at holiday time, don't neglect kitty. Cats are creatures of habit and rely on the comforting familiarity of their normal activities. Don't neglect regular playtime schedules, grooming, feeding, litter box cleaning, and other routines.

Thanksgiving

Food, food, and more food. Everywhere you look there's food. The turkey, stuffing, creamed onions, candied yams, wine, pumpkin pie—all of it needs to be kept away from your kitten. Read the previous section on *Christmas* for why it's important to keep kitty away from this stuff.

If your adult cat is on a diet or seems to become possessed in the presence of food, for her sake, don't give in and let her have snacks. Sometimes people feel their pets deserve extra special food at the holidays. You won't be doing her any favor and you risk endangering her health.

Halloween

This is the most frightening day of the year if you own a cat. There are people in this world who seek out cats on this day to hurt, torture, and even kill. Protect your cat by not allowing her outdoors at all, starting at least a day or two before Halloween. Even cats who are exclusively outdoor cats should be kept inside during this period to be safe. All cats are at risk but black cats are at the most risk. Most humane shelters won't adopt black cats out to anyone during the entire month of October. If you're trying to find a home for your cat or a litter of kittens, don't do it close to Halloween and don't give away or sell any black cats during the entire month.

Your front door will be opened repeatedly so keep your cat in another room, away from the hectic activity. With her litter box, food, and water, she can spend quiet time away from all the chaos. If she's frightened of the doorbell or if she gets upset because the family dog barks at the doorbell, keep her at the far end of the house to help keep her more relaxed.

Although cats don't generally have a sweet tooth, some cats will try to get into the candy. Chocolate, as you know by now, is lethal to cats. You also have the wrapping around the candy to be aware of.

One more thing to watch out for is costumed children frightening the cat. Sometimes children dressed as monsters or ghosts get so excited that they go around attempting to scare other family members or pets, so keep an eye on your cat.

Fourth of July

Even I find it hard when the neighborhood kids shoot off firecrackers all night long. I must be getting old because I find myself preferring the quieter holidays.

This is not a good day or night for a cat to be outdoors. The noise of the firecrackers can be very frightening. And, as with Halloween, there are some people who take sick pleasure in frightening or hurting animals and might throw firecrackers at your cat. Even if a firecracker isn't thrown directly at the animal, the noise can cause her to bolt in panic and she could run right into the road—and an oncoming car.

Keep your cat indoors and play music or turn on the TV. Engage in a play session, and everyone will get through this safely.

Birthdays

Balloons, ribbons, and lighted candles are the three major safety hazards. If you're having a birthday party, kitty will also have to contend with noise-makers, lots of activity, and the possibility of getting stepped on, grabbed, or petted without her consent. Find a safe room for your cat to wait out the party.

Birthday cake, candy, and any other goodies should also be kept out of the cat's reach. If you're hosting a children's party, there's a very good chance that some cake or candy will end up on the floor, so it's best to do your cleanup before allowing the cat back into the general part of the house.

"Save Our Pet"

Despite all your precautions, emergencies and unexpected situations do arise—and you may not even be home to help your cat. Have a visible sign to alert authorities that there's a pet (or pets) inside your house should an emergency, such as a house fire, occur while you're away. Many companies make window or door sticks for this very purpose. Or you can get a sign on a post to stick in the ground. Put the sign near the front of the yard and away from the house to make it easily visible for authorities, rescue workers, or neighbors.

Make sure there's a place on the sign for you to indicate what kind of pet you have and how many.

What If Something Happens to *You*?

I know it's weird; it's not something any of us like to think about. Unfortunately, though, it may happen. What if you have to be hospitalized? What if you're no longer able to care for your cat? If you live alone, this is a very important consideration and one worth being well prepared for. In Chapter 17, which is primarily about coping with the loss of a cat, there's a section on how to make sure your cat is provided for in your will.

4

The Doctor Is In

The Other Most Important Person in Your Cat's Life and How to Tell If Your Cat Is Sick

No matter where you got your cat, he's going to need veterinary care. Whether purchased or rescued, he'll need to be monitored throughout his life.

Your relationship with your veterinarian is more than just a yearly visit for vaccinations. Together, you and the veterinarian are responsible for keeping your cat healthy. The veterinarian will depend on you to notice changes in your cat and bring them to his/her attention immediately. Your observations of your cat will be valuable information that aids your veterinarian in making a diagnosis.

Beginning the Search

Step One

Take some time to think about what qualities you're looking for in a veterinarian and what services matter most to you. Would you prefer a large, multidoctor practice or a small, one-doctor clinic? Do you want a veterinarian whose practice is limited to cats? There are numerous veterinarians around the country who are board-certified feline practitioners.

You'll want to know if the veterinarian provides after-hours care or if there is an animal emergency clinic in your area. Animals have a knack for getting sick on holidays or after everyone has closed up for the night, so having emergency care available is a must.

WHAT YOUR VETERINARIAN CAN PROVIDE

- preventative medical care throughout the life of your cat
- nutritional guidance
- answers to care, behavior, and training questions
- emergency medical care (maybe through an emergency clinic)
- access to information on groundbreaking medical care
- information regarding other pet-related services (such as pet sitters)

- lost and found resources
- bathing/grooming services (optional)
- boarding services (optional)
- emotional support during a feline health crisis
- long-term care of ongoing medical conditions
- referrals to veterinary specialists such as veterinary ophthalmologists, dermatologists, and behaviorists

You may prefer a veterinarian who personally owns cats. Although that shouldn't keep you away from one who doesn't, you may feel you can relate better to a cat owner.

Do you want a young doctor recently out of veterinary school or an older one?

Finally, although it won't have any effect on ability, you may have a preference concerning gender.

Step Two

Ask friends and neighbors you think take particularly good care of their pets for their recommendations. Don't just ask for names, ask your friends what specifically they like or don't like about their veterinarian.

Check out Web sites that offer reviews as well.

Step Three

Once you've accumulated some names, narrow down the list to the two or three who seem to be the most likely candidates. If a friend gave you a name of a great veterinarian who's on the other side of town, that may rule him/her out.

Next, you'll need to visit the clinic to view the facilities and meet the veterinarian. I suggest that you call ahead to let them know you're coming, so someone will be available to give you a tour. When you get to the clinic, begin your assessment from the moment you walk in the door. How does the clinic smell?

Does it look clean? The receptionist who greets you should be friendly and knowledgeable. As you take your tour of the hospital, pay attention to how the staff interacts with each other. I've toured hospitals in which I've heard bickering between technicians and even foul language being used toward the animals. Keep your eyes and ears open. As you walk past the cages, notice how they're kept. Are they clean and are messes taken care of as soon as possible? One thing I always check for is if the surgery patients are given towels or blankets to keep them warm or if they're just left to shiver on the few sheets of newspaper that line the bottom of the cage.

When you meet the veterinarian, keep in mind that he or she may be very busy with patients (another reason why it's always a good idea to call ahead) and won't have time for a long chat. Within a few minutes you should, however, get an idea of how well he or she communicates and if you feel comfortable.

Your relationship with your veterinarian is very important, as you're both responsible for the health of your cat. If after the first few times you visit the veterinarian with your kitten you don't feel comfortable, change veterinarians. Just ask for a copy of your cat's records and go somewhere else. Don't stick with a veterinarian you're not happy with, but before making the decision to switch, think about whether or not your expectations are unrealistic. For example, some clients call the veterinarian several times a day and expect to be put through immediately, not taking into consideration that the doctor may be in surgery or with another patient. Additionally, give the veterinarian the opportunity to correct whatever is bothering you. If you then decide that your expectations are realistic, and you've either talked with the veterinarian or given the staff an opportunity to correct the situation to no avail, then just move on.

Transporting Your Kitten to the Veterinarian

Even though he may be just a tiny little thing right now and easy to hold in your arms, he'll feel more secure in a carrier. Transport him in a carrier to eliminate the chance that he could suddenly become frightened and leap right out of your arms. Begin getting him acquainted with the carrier at an early age. It'll be much easier now than later. It will also protect him in the waiting room, where other patients may not necessarily be as polite as he is. For all of the specifics on carriers, see Chapter 14.

What to Expect at Your Kitten's First Veterinary Visit

No matter where you got your kitten or what you were told about how healthy he is, he must be taken to the veterinarian. If you already have other cats at home it is especially important that the kitten be taken to the veterinarian before you expose your cats to him.

When you bring your kitten in, you should also bring along a sample of his feces, so the doctor can test it for internal parasites. Almost all kittens who haven't already been dewormed have internal parasites, so your veterinarian will begin a series of dewormings. The fecal check will help the veterinarian detect other internal parasites that aren't part of the normal deworming schedule.

If you're going to bring a fecal sample in, try to collect the freshest one. If your kitten defecates in the morning but your appointment isn't until later in the day, wrap the sample in a plastic bag or container and put it in the refrigerator. Write yourself a note and leave it on the front door so you won't leave for the clinic without taking the sample. If the kitten doesn't cooperate by providing you with a sample or you object to keeping the sample in the refrigerator, don't panic—the veterinarian can get a sample from him in the office. It's much less traumatic for the kitty, though, if he volunteers one peacefully at home in his litter box.

If the kitten hasn't been tested for feline leukemia (FeLV) and feline immunodeficiency virus (FIV), or if there's any question regarding the reliability of any previous tests, he should be tested. This involves taking a very small blood sample (for more information on FeLV and FIV, refer to the Medical Appendix). This is usually done by a technician before the veterinarian examines the kitten.

While the blood and stool tests are being completed in the lab, the veterinarian begins the kitten's physical exam. The kitten will have already been weighed and had his temperature taken by a technician. The veterinarian begins at the kitty's head and works his or her way to the tip of the tail. The veterinarian will check inside the ears with an otoscope (a conical light). If ear mites are suspected, the veterinarian will swab a sample of exudate from the ears for microscopic examination. Next, the kitten's eyes and nose will be checked for any signs of discharge. The veterinarian will open the mouth and make sure all looks normal in there as well.

The doctor will run his or her hands along the kitten's body, feeling for anything out of the ordinary, then he or she will use a stethoscope to listen to the kitten's heart and lungs.

Your veterinarian will also go over the vaccination schedule needed and will cover the basics of kitten nutrition, flea control, grooming, and training.

Your kitten will then begin to receive his vaccinations. You will have to bring him back for a return visit in three to four weeks, so he can get the next series. Your veterinarian will instruct you on how many visits will be needed and which vaccines should be administered, based upon your cat's age and risk factors.

Some vaccines, depending on the type and the manufacturer, are combined. Some are even administered intranasally rather than via injection. Your veterinarian will explain specifically about each vaccination as it is being drawn up for administration. The veterinarian should also explain any potential side effects, what to watch for (such as breathing difficulty), and how your kitten may react over the next twenty-four hours.

If internal parasites were detected from the stool sample, your kitten will be given a dewormer. Depending on the type of dewormer, a second dose may be needed on the kitten's return visit. If ear mites were found, you'll be given medication to administer. Refer to the Medical Appendix for more information on ear mites.

Your first visit with the veterinarian is the time to get a demonstration on how to trim your kitten's nails. If there's anything else you feel unsure about, such as how to give any prescribed medication, how much to feed, how to groom your kitten, ask it now. Have your veterinarian explain anything you're not sure about. Your veterinarian's main concern is starting you and your kitten off right.

Less Stressful Veterinary Visits

Every time your kitten visits the veterinarian is an opportunity to form positive associations with the experience. If you want a cat who doesn't turn into a claw-baring, whirling dervish then start from the very beginning training him to accept and, dare I say it, actually not mind being at the clinic.

Your kitten is learning with each experience. Training is occurring all the time. Whether that training is beneficial or counterproductive is up to you.

Behavior modification associated with the veterinary clinic is easy to implement. By the way, this technique isn't just reserved for kittens. You can retrain your veterinarian-hating adult cat as well.

Start by bringing treats with you or a small supply of the kitten's food. When you arrive at the clinic, ask the receptionist to offer your kitten a treat or two (of course, offering food will be dependent on the specific reason for the clinic visit). If your kitten is comfortable, remove him from the carrier so the receptionist or other staff member can pet and/or hold him.

While sitting in the waiting room, offer your kitten a treat. If he's nervous you can cover the carrier with a towel or even a sheet of newspaper.

Once inside the exam room, ask the technician to take a little time before checking vitals such as weight and temperature. The technician can offer the kitten a treat, pet him, or even hold him (if the kitten enjoys being held). If the kitten doesn't accept the treat from the technician's hand it can be tossed on the exam table for him to retrieve. If using wet food, place a small amount on a tongue depressor.

One way to make the exam room less scary is to limit the cat's exposure to the cold, hard exam table. If the carrier you use is the plastic kennel type, unfasten the top so kitty can remain in the bottom part. If you've placed a towel in the bottom of the carrier it will provide even more security. One of the worst things you or the technician can do is to reach into the carrier and yank the cat out. It's far less stressful for the kitten if he feels some sense of familiarity.

When it comes time for the technician to begin taking vitals you can continue to offer treats. For a very nervous kitty try offering a small amount of canned food or favorite treat. Pack some canned food in a small container and bring a small, soft-tipped baby spoon, or use a tongue depressor. This way, you can distract the kitten during uncomfortable procedures such as temperature-taking.

Once the veterinarian comes in, he or she should greet the cat before beginning an exam or procedure. If vaccinations or any other uncomfortable procedure is going to be performed, use the distraction technique here as well. With many cats, less restraint will keep the cat calmer. It makes me sad when I see technicians, veterinarians, or cat owners automatically assume that a cat has to be scruffed and restrained for a procedure.

You may find that placing a dab of canned food on the exam table is enough to distract the kitten while vaccinations are being administered. Many times the kitty isn't even aware that a needle is being inserted.

Since the veterinary clinic is a place your kitten will have to go many times throughout his life, invest the time now in creating positive associations. The more often he goes and receives petting, treats, and minimal restraint, the less stressful future visits will be. Even go so far as to take your kitten there just to be petted by the staff and offered treats. The more he is exposed to the sights, sounds, and scents of the clinic at an early age, the less stressful it will be for everyone.

General Kitten Vaccination Schedule

Your veterinarian will customize specific vaccine protocols according to your cat's risk factors, including age, health status, potential for exposure to a particular disease, and geographical location. There are core vaccines recommended for all cats and there are noncore vaccines recommended for higher-risk cats. There are also noncore vaccines that may not be recommended due to questions of efficacy.

Your kitten will also get a series of dewormings which are given orally.

Some Common Diagnostic Procedures

X-Ray

X-rays taken of your cat are the same kind taken of humans and used for the same diagnoses of fractures, obstructions, tumors, malformations, etc. Cats are usually tolerant of the procedure, but if yours is in pain because of a fracture or other injury, he'll be sedated beforehand.

Blood Tests

There are numerous tests performed on the blood to help diagnose a vast array of disorders. Blood tests can help determine how well a particular organ is functioning, if there's a disease present, the number of red and white cells, etc. Some tests can be performed at the veterinarian's office but many are sent to an outside diagnostic lab for processing.

If only a small amount of blood is needed, it can be drawn from the vein in the cat's foreleg. Larger amounts of blood are drawn from the jugular vein in the neck.

Ultrasound

Ultrasound uses high-frequency soundwaves to create a picture of the cat's internal organs. It's a painless and noninvasive procedure and can provide the veterinarian with valuable information concerning the shape, size, and condition of particular organs.

Electrocardiogram

Contact leads are attached to the cat's skin so the ECG machine can record the heart's electrical functions to determine any abnormalities. It's not painful and cats are usually very tolerant of the procedure.

Urinalysis

Urine samples are used to help diagnose urinary tract disorders, diabetes, and kidney disease, and to determine the function of other organs.

A urine sample can be obtained by your veterinarian using a needle and syringe (cystocentesis). The needle is injected into the bladder and the urine is drawn up into the syringe. This is the method used when a sterile sample is needed so no outside bacteria contaminate the urine. Urine can also be collected through catheterization, manual expression of the bladder (done under sedation), catching the urine in a container as the cat voids, or through the use of nonabsorbent litter.

Biopsy

A sample of tissue is taken and sent to a diagnostic lab for analysis. Biopsies are used to identify growths, determine if a growth is benign (noncancerous) or malignant (cancerous), and also to confirm that all of the cancer has been removed (this is done by examination of the edges of the tumor).

Fecal Examination

The color, consistency, and odor of the cat's feces provide the veterinarian with valuable clues regarding the cat's health. The veterinarian or technician will check a fecal sample to make sure it looks normal and check for signs of blood or mucous.

As a routine part of the examination, a small sample is also mixed with a special solution and examined under the microscope in order to check for signs of parasites.

Some parasites such as giardia are very difficult to detect and your veterinarian may request stool samples from your cat over a period of several days if infection is suspected.

Which Way to the Emergency Clinic?

If there's an animal emergency clinic in your town, it's wise to be familiar with its location before an emergency hits. That way you won't be driving through unfamiliar streets in the middle of the night with a sick or injured cat. GPS is wonderful but don't depend on it. Know where your nearest emergency clinic is located.

When Should Your Kitten Be Spayed or Neutered?

These two terms refer to the sterilization procedure—*spaying* for females and *neutering* for males.

Some shelters perform the procedure on kittens as young as eight weeks.

The most common time to spay a female is before she goes into her first heat—at about six months of age. Males are usually neutered somewhere between six to eight months old.

If you're unsure about whether to have your kitty spayed or neutered, let me assure you the benefits of doing so go beyond helping to cut down on pet overpopulation. There are far more behavioral problems with intact pets. Intact cats are more territorial, tend to roam and fight, the females will go into heat, and if you haven't already experienced the scent of tomcat urine, be prepared, because intact males spray. From a medical standpoint, intact cats are at a higher risk of certain cancers than spayed and neutered pets. If you have any questions, discuss it with your veterinarian.

Health Insurance for Your Cat

Money. It can be the deciding factor for whether a pet lives or dies. When you first get a kitten, the last thing you want to think about is what horrendous diseases, injuries, or disorders this very healthy animal could be subject to down the road.

Huge strides are continually being made in veterinary medicine. Unfortunately, though, the breakthrough procedure that could now save your cat's life may be unaffordable for you.

Check with your veterinarian concerning the plans available in your state. When considering insurance plans, do your homework because some are better than others. Keep in mind as well that insurance won't cover routine visits and vaccinations.

How Do You Know If Your Cat Is Sick?

Your cat depends on you for his health and comfort. Cats don't really have nine lives, so it's up to you and your veterinarian to be responsible for his health and welfare.

Become familiar with your cat's normal routine. Notice how much water he usually drinks. This will be important information because an increase or decrease in water consumption can be a symptom of certain diseases. Are you familiar with your cat's litter box habits? If so, you may be able to detect diarrhea, constipation, and potential urinary tract problems early. Become familiar with his usual volume of urine or feces, as well as its color.

A regular grooming schedule gives you the opportunity to examine your cat's body so you'll be alerted to changes in the norm such as lumps, sores, external parasites, bald patches, rashes, etc. Check your cat's ears, eyes, teeth, genitals, stomach, under his tail, and even the pads of his paws on a regular basis.

SIGNS TO WATCH FOR

- change in appearance of coat: dull, dry, sparse, bald patches, greasy-looking
- change in normal grooming behavior
- inflamed or irritated skin: any change in normal color or texture
- change in usual behavior: cat who doesn't play anymore, is lethargic, hides, is nervous, aggressive, irritable
- change in eating habits: increased/decreased appetite, weight change, difficulty eating
- increased or decreased water consumption
- vomiting: frequency, food vs. liquids, color, volume
- change in urination: urinating outside of litter box, more frequent urination, straining, blood-tinged urine, inability to urinate (this is an absolute emergency), crying during urination, change in urine odor
- change in bowels: eliminating outside of litter box, diarrhea, constipation, mucous-coated stool, unusual color, blood in stool, unusually foul-smelling stool, volume of stool produced
- limping or pain
- weakness
- excessive vocalization, crying, howling
- fever or low body temperature
- sneezing
- coughing
- change in eyes: discharge, film, appearance of nictitating membrane, squinting, enlargement or reduction of pupil size in one or both eyes, pawing at eyes
- discharge from nose (note color and consistency)
- discharge from ears, appearance of exudates, pawing at ears, head shaking
- swelling on any part of the body
- shivering
- lumps on or below the skin surface
- lesions or bruises
- change in breathing: rapid, shallow, labored
- change in appearance of gums: swelling, paleness, blue or gray color, bright red color
- bad breath
- excessive drooling
- strange odor
- neurological changes: seizures, tremors, palsy, etc.

Cats are experts at hiding the fact that they don't feel well. Sometimes you'll have to rely on the slightest change in his behavior. When you talk to your veterinarian, provide the following information:

- A description of the problem

- How long the cat has had the problem

- The frequency of the problem

For example, don't just say, "My cat is vomiting." The veterinarian needs to know what the vomitus consists of: Food? Liquid? What color is it? Did the vomiting start today? Last night? How often is it happening? Does the cat vomit immediately after meals? Has he thrown up five times today in the space of an hour? An accurate description by the owner provides valuable diagnostic clues to the veterinarian.

How to Take Your Cat's Temperature

Taking your cat's temperature may seem close to impossible, but if you do it gently and calmly, both you and your cat will survive the procedure unscathed. You may never need to take your cat's temperature, but the situation could arise so it's helpful to know the easiest procedure. If your cat gets very agitated during a veterinary visit, the veterinarian may suggest that you take the temperature at home when the cat is calm.

A cat's temperature is taken rectally using a *rectal* thermometer or in the ear with a digital thermometer. Never try to take a cat's temperature *orally*. The cat's natural reflex is to bite down, which will break the thermometer and could cause injury.

If you're going to take the temperature rectally, it will probably be much easier if you have an assistant. Even the most good-natured cat may react quite uncooperatively to a thermometer, so if help is offered, take it!

Before inserting the thermometer into the rectum, lubricate the tip with a little petroleum jelly or K-Y jelly.

Give the cat time to get used to the procedure by placing him on the table, touching him gently on the back, or holding his tail while offering a treat. Place the treat on the table in front of him. Just a bit of canned food might help the cat stay distracted during the procedure.

Raise the cat's tail with one hand and gently insert the thermometer one inch into the anal canal. Hold it in place for the time indicated on the instructions that came with the thermometer. If you have trouble inserting the thermometer, lightly scratch or pet your cat at the base of the tail as this sometimes causes a relaxation of the rectal muscles. The thermometer may also slide in more easily if you gently twist it. Be patient and use gentle pressure. Try to keep the cat as calm as possible because if he gets too anxious, it may give you an inaccurate reading.

When you remove the thermometer, wipe it clean with a tissue, read the temperature, then clean the thermometer with alcohol before placing it back in its case, or follow any specific cleaning protocols indicated on the instructions that came with the thermometer.

For a less stressful way to take your cat's temperature, use an instant-read digital ear thermometer. This thermometer gets inserted just inside the ear.

Which thermometer to use will be based on how your cat reacts.

How to Take a Cat's Pulse

Feel the inside of the hind leg where it meets the groin for the *femoral artery*. You can do this with your cat in a standing position. Press your fingers on the artery until you feel the pulse. Count the number of pulsations you feel within a fifteen-second period. Multiply that by four to get the pulse count per minute. The normal rate for an adult cat is 160–180 beats per minute. A kitten's pulse is much higher (usually around 200).

Respiratory Rate

Observe the movement of the cat's chest or abdomen. Counting the number of movements that take place in sixty seconds will give you the respiratory rate.

Don't attempt this if the cat is excited or hot, because the rate will be abnormally high. The average respiratory rate for a cat at rest is about twenty to thirty breaths per minute.

Rapid breathing can indicate pain, shock, dehydration, or disease. Panting is normal if your cat has engaged in strenuous physical activity.

Panting that appears labored or is accompanied by restlessness can indicate a serious medical condition such as heatstroke.

Medicating Your Cat
Pills

Not an easy task to be sure. Some owners would prefer having their teeth drilled by the dentist to giving a pill to their cat. You and your cat can quickly become wrestling opponents as he squirms and wiggles and you turn into a contortionist, trying to unclamp his steel-trap jaws. I've witnessed some of the most horrified expressions I've ever seen on a person's face when I worked in an animal hospital, and they were in response to the veterinarian telling the owners, "Give your cat one of these pills every day."

You may think that the easiest way to pill a cat is to hide it in food but there are several reasons not to do that. First, some pills are coated to protect the contents from being destroyed by stomach acid before they can be absorbed in the intestines. Also, some pills have a strange smell or a bitter taste and your cat may refuse to eat the foods they are in. Cats are *very* adept at detecting altered food due to their extremely acute sense of smell.

If you really believe your cat will fall for a pill hidden in your special concoction of cream cheese and sardines, check with your veterinarian first to be sure it won't destroy the pill's effectiveness. Some pills shouldn't be given with meals.

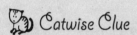

Catwise Clue

Many tablets can be made into a liquid by a compounding pharmacist. If your cat handles liquids better than pills, your veterinarian should be able to recommend a compounding pharmacist.

Many liquids can also be flavored to increase appeal. Some medications can also be compounded for transdermal application.

Some cats will take pills more easily if they have been disguised in a tasty gel such as Nutri-Cal by Tomlyn.

One of my favorite ways to administer a pill is in a Greenies Pill Pocket. This is a soft, pliable treat with a slit in it for hiding the dreaded pill. Not every cat will fall for it but many do. Pill Pockets are available at your local pet supply store and online.

If pilling is the only method for you, the best approach is subtlety and speed—with a lot of emphasis on the latter. Don't make a big production out of it because the more fuss you create, the more worried your cat will be. Just be organized and choose your *timing* carefully. For instance, if your cat is more receptive to handling when he's sleepy, then that's the time to pop the pill.

The procedure: You may prefer to place the cat on a counter so you don't have to crouch down. Put the palm of your hand over the top of the cat's head. Tilt the head up *slightly*. Open his mouth by applying gentle pressure with your thumb on one side and middle finger on the other against the area behind the canine teeth (they're the ones that look like daggers but don't let that thought intimidate you). Hold the pill between the thumb and index finger of your free hand, and with the middle finger, press the lower jaw open. Drop the pill on the back of the tongue. Coating the pill with butter will make it easier to swallow (but sometimes harder to release from your fingers). Let go of the cat's mouth so he can swallow but keep hold of him so he doesn't escape and spit the pill out. Don't clamp his mouth shut or he won't be able to swallow. You can gently massage the throat in a downward motion to help ease the pill down.

After you have administered the pill, observe your cat to make sure it went down and that he doesn't spit it out. If his tongue comes out to lick his nose or mouth, that's a sure sign that the pill has been swallowed. If the cat begins coughing, it means the pill may be lodged in the windpipe. Release your hold on him so he can cough it up. If it doesn't come up, grasp your cat by his hips and turn him upside down to dislodge the pill.

An alternate pilling position is to first kneel on the floor, and then sit back on your heels with your legs open in a V position. Place the cat between your legs, facing away from you. This way, if he tries to back away, he has nowhere to go.

If you find you can't pill with your fingers or if your cat bites, you can buy a plastic pill gun from your veterinarian or local pet supply store. The pill is grasped on the end of the syringe by plastic fingers. When you push the plunger, the pill gets deposited onto the tongue. I find pill guns more difficult than just using my fingers, but what's important is getting the pill into the cat without being bitten, so use whatever method works for you.

To acclimate your cat to the process of being pilled with the pill gun, do some sessions where you put moist cat food on the end of the pill gun and let your cat lick it off.

If your cat squirms and scratches, try wrapping him in a towel. If he's very difficult to handle, enlist the aid of an assistant, although it's often hard to find a volunteer willing to help pill the family cat.

Once you've pilled the cat, it's important to make sure the pill doesn't remain lodged in the esophagus in order to avoid potential irritation. Since humans swallow pills with a liquid in order to ensure smooth transit to the stomach, it's helpful to offer your cat some water, chicken broth, or at the very least, a few laps of moist cat food. If using cat food, make sure the instructions state that it's safe to give the pill with food.

Liquid Medication

You'll need a plastic dropper or syringe. Don't use a glass dropper because it could break if your cat bites down. Don't use a spoon because it always spills and you won't get the accurate amount into your cat. Also, using a spoon for liquids that are thick and sticky presents a greater risk of you getting it all over your cat's fur.

The easiest way to administer liquids is into the cheek pouch (the space between the cheek and the molars). Put the cat on a table or counter, measure the correct amount of liquid into the dropper and place it in the cat's cheek pouch. Administer in small amounts, allowing the cat to swallow each time. If you try to dispense too much liquid at once, you risk having him inhale the medicine. He may also just let most of it dribble out of his mouth. Keep the cat calm so he doesn't panic and aspirate the liquid. If someone can assist, he or she can gently hold and stroke the cat while you administer the medication.

If you find it impossible to get liquid medication into your cat, ask your veterinarian whether the liquid can be mixed with food. If it can, use a stronger-tasting food to disguise the taste. Don't use a large amount of food because your cat may not eat it all, and as a result won't get an adequate dose of medicine.

Many liquids can be flavored. Ask your veterinarian about the options.

Powders

Powders can usually be mixed with moist food. If the powder has an unpleasant taste, mix with a strong-tasting food. Ask your veterinarian about the preferred method of administration.

Compounding Medication

Some medications can be formulated into liquids, gels, or chewables and flavored in order to make administering it less stressful to you and tastier for your cat. Popular flavors for compounded medications include chicken, tuna, beef, and malt. The medicine is compounded by a compounding pharmacist. This type of medication is becoming more and more popular and the number of pharmacies offering this option is increasing. Ask your veterinarian if the prescription for your cat can be compounded. If there isn't a compounding pharmacy in your area and your veterinarian is unsure whether a specific prescription can be compounded (not all can be), an online pharmacy may be able to help you.

Transdermal Medications and Patches

Some oral medications can be reformulated into a transdermal delivery system. This way you're able to medicate the cat by rubbing a paste or cream on the inner ear tip for absorption into the skin. For cats who are impossible to medicate orally, this method may allow you to administer medication and have the cat think he's actually just getting a little ear massage.

For transdermal medication you'll need to wear a finger cot to ensure the entire prescribed dose is delivered to the cat and none is absorbed into your skin. Wash your hands after administering a transdermal medication.

Some pain medications often work well in skin patch form. The pain medication is delivered slowly over time. Patches must be carefully applied to shaved skin in an area where the cat can't lick or chew it off. Your veterinarian will apply the initial patch.

Injections

There are some medical conditions (such as diabetes) that require the cat to receive injections. If the condition is ongoing, you'll most likely have to learn to administer these injections yourself. Should this need arise, your veterinarian will give you instructions as well as demonstrations for the correct procedure.

Depending on the medicine, injections are given either subcutaneously (under the skin) or in the muscle. The injections you would most likely have to administer would be subcutaneous.

Ointments/Creams

The easiest way to apply these may be to sit in a chair with the cat in your lap. Begin by first stroking to relax him and then stroke on the ointment. Continue to stroke the cat and try to keep him on your lap (but don't force him) so the ointment has time to be absorbed and the amount of medicine he'll lick off once he gets down is decreased. You may find that the cat will fall asleep on your lap and then the medicine gets to do its work without any feline interference. If your cat doesn't enjoy sitting on your lap, distract him with interactive playtime or a meal to give the medicine more time to absorb.

If licking is sabotaging the healing process, ask your veterinarian about using a special collar that prevents the cat from being able to chew or lick his body. This type of collar goes around the neck and prevents the cat from reaching around. There are several types of collars and some are more comfortable than others.

Eye Medicine

Place the cat on the counter or you can sit with him in your lap or in the V position previously described above.

Administering ointment: make sure your hands are clean and thoroughly rinsed of soap. Tilt your cat's head slightly upward with one hand. Rest the hand holding the tube against your cat's cheek so you won't poke him in the eye if he should make a sudden move. Gently pull the lower lid down and apply the amount in a strip along the lid. Be careful not to touch the eye with the applicator. There's no need to rub the eyelid; this could cause further irritation. The ointment will automatically spread as the cat blinks.

Administering drops: tilt the cat's head upward. The hand holding the dropper should rest against the cat's cheek to prevent injury in the case of sudden movement. Drop the prescribed amount into the eye, being careful not to touch the eye with the applicator. Let go of the cat to allow him to close his eyes.

Never put any drops in your cat's eyes unless they have been prescribed by your veterinarian.

Ear Medication
Ear medications work best in clean ears so gently swab the ears with a cotton pad or tissue unless it's sensitive. Your veterinarian will instruct you on whether to use an ear cleansing solution.

Place the cat on the counter, your lap, or in the V position on the floor. Be sure your hands are clean, then hold the ear and steady the cat's head. Don't hold the tip of the ear, hold it at the base, or fold the tip back. Be gentle, because if the ear needs medication, it may also be irritated and sensitive. Put the prescribed amount of medication into the ear. Hold onto the cat's head gently to keep him from shaking his head immediately. This gives the medication time to travel down the ear canal. If the ear isn't irritated, you can gently massage the base to distribute the medication. If the medication is for ear mites, don't massage because the ear is already very irritated.

One tip: don't wear your best clothes when administering ear medication because your cat won't realize that shaking his head (which all cats do after you put medicine in their ears) will splatter the antibiotic ointment all over your favorite shirt.

Nursing an Ill Cat
Taking care of an ill cat at home is a big responsibility. Although your cat may prefer the comfort of his own familiar surroundings over the unfamiliarity of being in a hospital, make sure you're confident about your abilities and comfortable with all of the instructions given to you by the veterinarian. If you have

questions or are unsure about a particular procedure, ask for a demonstration before attempting to do something on your own.

The Room

The cat should be placed in a peaceful, quiet room. This is especially important in busy households where there are children or other pets.

The room should be warm enough and free of drafts, so the cat doesn't get chilled. If you have an air purifier, this is a perfect time to use it.

Set up a low-sided litter box near the cat so he won't have far to walk. If he's unable to get up, you may have to assist him by placing him in the box and providing support.

The Bed

Provide a comfortable bed, covered in towels, so you can keep it clean in case he has accidents. Keep the bed clean and dry and change the towels as soon as needed. Orthopedic beds are available at pet supply stores and online. These beds allow for air circulation and can make a cat much more comfortable. If you can't find one, buy an egg crate foam bed covering, cut a good-sized piece, and cover it with towels.

If your cat seems chilled, there are heated pet beds available in all shapes and configurations. Some automatically go back to normal room temperature when the cat's body weight isn't on it. If using a heated bed, keep another unheated bed nearby as well, so the cat has the choice of which to use.

Food

Your cat may not have much of an appetite. He may prefer several smaller meals. Just make sure he's getting enough nutrition. If he's not on a special diet you might have success using a strong-smelling food, or warming it slightly. Your veterinarian may also prescribe a highly palatable convalescence formula food. If he's unable to keep food down the cat may also be prescribed an antinausea medication.

If using baby food, make sure it's a brand that doesn't contain onion powder.

If your cat won't eat any food, no matter what you've tried, your veterinarian may instruct you to syringe-feed. Don't do this unless advised by your veterinarian. If you're instructed to syringe-feed, your veterinarian will prescribe a very smooth, liquid-type food. You'll be instructed on how much to feed and how often, based on your cat's specific needs.

If your cat isn't drinking enough water, your veterinarian may instruct you to administer it orally with a syringe. Since a cat can easily aspirate water into his lungs, mix the water with a little cat food or chicken broth so he'll be able to taste something. Giving water by syringe can be very dangerous, so do it in small amounts, giving him adequate time to swallow and rest. Don't give water by syringe unless specifically instructed to do so by your veterinarian. Often, as long as the cat will eat moist food, the high water content of that diet will be adequate.

Grooming

An ill cat often isn't up to maintaining his normally high standards of hygiene. If he vomits or is being syringe-fed, has diarrhea, or urinates in his bed, his coat and skin will need extra attention.

If you're syringe-feeding him, there's a good chance that a significant amount of food will spill onto his chin and down his neck. To reduce the mess, put a small towel over his check to create a bib to keep his coat clean. Use a warm, moist washcloth to clean his face immediately after you've finished feeding. Don't allow food or medicine to dry on his fur.

If your cat has urinated on himself or has diarrhea, clean him up immediately to prevent the skin from being scaled by urine or irritated by diarrhea. If the cat has chronic urinary or bowel problems, the hair around the anus and genitals may need to be clipped short to help make cleaning easier.

Gently brush your ailing cat regularly to keep his skin and coat healthy. If you have a long-haired cat, you'll have to brush a little every day to prevent mats. If your cat can't move, be sure and turn him occasionally to allow circulation to the skin and prevent sores from developing.

Loneliness and Depression

Keep your little patient's spirits up by spending time with him. If he doesn't enjoy being petted or touched, you can sit with him, providing comfort just by your presence. Spend some time reading a book or working on your laptop in the same room as your cat.

When I worked in an animal hospital, one of the most important recovery aids for the animals was being comforted and touched as they lay scared, confused, and hurting in their cages. I petted heads, scratched under chins, and kissed noses. I held the ones who wanted it and for those who viewed me with suspicion, I tried to comfort with a soothing tone of voice.

If other pets or family members provide a sense of comfort for the patient, then allow them to have access to him. But keep everyone calm and quiet. If there's any tension in your multipet household or if your other pets become nervous or aggressive around the sick cat, keep him separated from the family while he recovers. The patient doesn't need any additional stress.

Hospitalization and Surgery (What to Expect)

The following descriptions of anesthesia and surgical procedures are very general outlines. Every veterinarian has different protocols based on patient age, surgery to be performed, length of procedure, even personal preference.

In most cases a presurgery evaluation will be conducted. This evaluation involves diagnostic tests to make sure there are no underlying conditions that could pose an added risk to your anesthetized cat. Generally the tests may include a physical exam, ECG, complete blood workup, and X-rays. Preanesthetic lab work helps to evaluate such things as kidney and liver function. This doesn't guarantee anesthesia will be safe, but it can help screen for underlying problems that could interfere with the anesthesia or surgical recovery.

The Night Before

The cat will need to have an empty stomach on the morning of the surgery, so you'll be instructed to withhold food after midnight. Your veterinarian will also instruct you as to whether water must be withheld as well.

If your cat is on medication, in most cases you'll continue to give him his usual p.m. dosage but always check with your veterinarian to be sure and to find out if you should administer his a.m. dose the morning of the surgery.

Hospital Admission

You'll bring your cat to the hospital first thing in the morning. At that time you'll be given consent forms to read and sign. The consent forms confirm that you give permission for the doctor to administer an anesthetic to your cat and perform the scheduled procedure.

Most hospitals have a section on the consent form regarding additional pain medication. Because it could be an added expense, they may require your permission to administer any additional medication. Be sure you give your permission for this because many cats (like many people) have varying thresholds of pain. You want your cat to be as comfortable as possible.

Premed

Once your cat has been admitted, he'll be examined by the veterinarian and may be given a "premed." This is an injection which will contain one or more mild sedatives to help him relax. These sedatives not only relieve some of your cat's anxiety but serve to reduce the amount of general anesthetic needed.

Anesthesia

After the premed has taken effect, your cat will be brought to the surgical prep area. A small strip of hair on the foreleg will be shaved and the leg will be cleaned. An anesthetic will be injected into the vein of the leg. Immediately, the cat will become unconscious.

An endotracheal tube is then placed in the cat's windpipe. Once it's in place, it's connected by another tube to the anesthesia machine. The anesthetic, along with oxygen, keeps your cat at the correct degree of unconsciousness. The level of anesthetic is monitored, as well as your cat's vital signs during the entire procedure.

Surgical Prep

The area of the cat's body to be operated on will be prepared for surgery. The surgical nurse will clip the hair and clean the skin with a surgical antibacterial scrub.

In the meantime, the veterinarian prepares him/herself by scrubbing with a surgical antibacterial soap. He/she will wear a sterile surgical gown, cap, eye protection, and of course, gloves. Surgical nurses will prepare themselves in the same way.

Surgery

A sterile surgical pack containing the instruments needed for the procedure is opened. Additional equipment, if and as needed, will also be opened from sterile packs.

Before beginning the procedure, the veterinarians or surgical nurse will cover the cat with a sterile surgical drape. This drape has an opening positioned over the site where the incision will be made.

Post-Op Recovery

After the cat is disconnected from the anesthesia machine, he is taken to the recovery area. Here he's monitored by the staff until he wakes. Because the body temperature lowers under an anesthetic, the cat is usually placed on a heated pad.

Additional pain medication is administered if needed.

Hospital Discharge

Depending upon the surgery, you may be able to pick up your cat later the same day or the following morning. Don't be in too much of a rush to bring your cat home, though, if the veterinarian recommends that he remain hospitalized overnight. The first twenty-four hours after surgery are usually when any potential complications arise. Follow your veterinarian's suggestions. If you want to visit your cat, ask your veterinarian if he or she feels that would be all right.

You'll be given instructions for any at-home care. You'll also be told when to return for a follow-up examination or to have sutures removed.

Follow all instructions to the letter and remember, even though your cat may want to go back to his normal routine, you have to make sure he has adequate rest and recovery time. If he has sutures, check them regularly to be sure that he hasn't chewed on them. Watch for signs of drainage, swelling, or infection. Call your veterinarian right away if something doesn't look right.

A cat recovering from surgery needs plenty of rest and shouldn't go outdoors. If he's on medication (especially pain medication), his reflexes may be sluggish and his sense of balance may be compromised, so be careful that he doesn't attempt to do something such as jump to a place from which he might fall. Keep him in a safe area and be sure he gets all the prescribed medication as directed by your veterinarian.

Before you leave the veterinarian's office, be certain that you're comfortable with whatever medication procedures you'll need to perform. If you're unsure of things, you may tend to be nervous during administration and your cat will pick up on this. If you're calm and confident it will help your kitty stay calm. If there is any administration of medication or at-home nursing care that you feel unable to take care of, inquire about at-home visits by one of the veterinary staff. Very often a veterinary technician will make a house call for an additional fee. The most important thing is your cat's recovery, so don't be shy about asking for help if you don't feel you can handle it by yourself.

If your cat will be on pain medication, your veterinarian may prescribe a skin patch for a gradual transdermal delivery through the skin.

5

House Rules

Basic Training

Training. What a misunderstood word. For many owners, the very word conjures up an image of a behavioral tug-of-war between owner and pet. I want you to rethink your definition of the word *training* to include your responsibility to understand what your cat is actually telling you by her behavior. Also, training means communicating with your cat in a language she understands. Stop looking at her as a pet in need of training and get inside her head. How can you combine your training expectations as an owner with her daily needs as a cat? Get on her level physically, emotionally, and mentally in order to map out an effective training plan.

Training a cat correctly not only makes her a pleasure to be around, but you'll also realize that you *can* have nice furniture without worrying about it being damaged. You won't have to battle constantly to make her stay off the counter and you'll know that she'll come whenever you call her, won't attack the guests, and will be a wonderful companion.

There are some people who think cats come pretrained, meaning they will already know how to use the litter box, will know not to scratch the furniture, and will know not to wander off if they're let outside. I feel sorry for those owners, but I especially feel sorry for those cats because they are the ones that end up abandoned, at the shelter, or dead.

In order to successfully train a cat, you have to understand how a cat communicates and what constitutes normal cat behavior. This is where getting on her level and seeing things as she does will offer valuable insight. For instance, if your cat is scratching the furniture, although it may make you angry, for her it's a very normal behavior. Because scratching is a natural feline behavior, you can spend your days yelling at your cat and chasing her around the house, but she'll never understand why she's being punished. All you'll have accomplished is that you've made your cat afraid of you. The better way to train her is to first understand that scratching is natural, and then provide her with an acceptable scratching surface (i.e., a good scratching post or pad).

Too many times we confuse training with discipline or dominance. So, after attempting to set our cats straight about who's boss, we come to the conclusion that they're just untrainable. The cat is a social creature (this comment still surprises many people) but she's also a hunter. She's territorial and often hunts alone because she hunts small prey. As a hunter, she's always tuned in to her environment. While your dog is sitting at your feet, anxiously watching you for signals, your cat is sitting next to you, keeping an eye on her territory and watching for potential prey. If you want to succeed in training your cat, learn her language and what makes her tick instead of insisting that she bend to your demands.

Your *think like a cat* training method is really a simple concept. Your cat has a valid reason for engaging in specific behaviors. Animals are very smart. They don't repeat behaviors unless they serve a purpose. Even though you may not understand or like the behavior doesn't mean it isn't serving a necessary purpose for the animal. So the key to your *think like a cat* approach is to:

1. Figure out what purpose the behavior serves. What's the "payoff" for the cat?
2. Offer an alternative behavior that is of equal or increased value.
3. Reward the cat for choosing the alternative.

Where owners get tripped up is in assuming the cat's behavior is motivated by anger, spite, or stupidity.

The Litter Box

The use or nonuse of the litter box can be a deal-breaker in a cat/owner relationship. Too many owners are under the assumption that the cat will automatically use the box no matter what—even if we never clean it, put it in the wrong place, or buy a brand of litter that the cat finds objectionable.

In order to avoid litter box problems you have to understand what's important to a cat when it comes to this part of her life. Your "Litter Box Survival Guide" can be found in Chapter 8.

The Dreaded Scratching Dilemma

No, you don't have to declaw your cat. No, your furniture doesn't have to end up shredded—but yes, you *do* have to have a scratching post. Not all posts are created equal, though. Once again, it comes down to what *we think* our cats need versus what *they know* they need. In Chapter 9, I'll show you how to save your furniture and create a scratching post that'll actually get used! What a concept.

Clicker Training

This is surprisingly easy and can serve a dual purpose. It is not only used to train your cat to do tricks, it's also a tool for behavior modification.

With clicker training you use a small device that makes a cricket-type sound when depressed by your finger or thumb. Clicker training works well because it "tells" the cat the precise behavior that is being rewarded. Since most cats are pretty food-motivated, you immediately follow a click with a food reward. The clicker is a sound not normally heard in the cat's environment and so works well as an audible marker. Clickers are available at pet supply stores and online.

Why do we use a clicker instead of just tossing a treat? Because the clicker is more immediate. You want the cat to know that the very behavior performed at that second was exactly what you wanted. You can click faster than you can toss the treat. By the time you toss a treat to the cat she won't know what behavior is being rewarded.

How to Start Clicker Training

The first step is to teach the cat to associate the clicker with a *payoff.* She needs to learn that the sound of the clicker means a treat is coming. Break up the treats into small pieces so you won't overfeed. Click the clicker and then toss a treat. Before doing it again, wait for the cat to look at you before repeating the sequence. This helps the cat associate YOU with the reward. Do it about ten times or however long the cat remains interested and engaged. If your cat is on a restricted or prescription diet, take a small portion of her regular amount and use that as her food reward. If you use wet food, put a tiny amount on the edge of a soft baby spoon or on a tongue depressor.

The first few sessions should be brief. If your cat appears disinterested it may be because she isn't hungry or the treat isn't motivating enough. If you free-feed you may need to switch to scheduled meals so you can use the food for training purposes.

Rewarding a Behavior

Believe it or not, within a couple of minutes you can probably teach your cat her first trick. "Sit" is an easy one to start with. Get down on the floor in front of your cat. Hold a treat or a small amount of wet food on a spoon just slightly up and over her head. As her eyes follow the treat her back end will naturally go down into a sit. Don't hold the treat too high or she'll reach up. As soon as her hindquarters touch the floor, click and give her the treat. Repeat this exercise multiple times. Once she consistently has the behavior down you can then add the verbal cue of "sit." Soon you'll be able to phase out the food lure when she responds to the verbal request instead of just watching the hand with the food.

There are many behaviors you can teach your cat: *down, roll over, high five, circle, come*, and so many more. The key is to be consistent and make the training sessions fun. If you get frustrated or the cat is not in the mood for training then it won't be successful.

Once a behavior is learned and performed consistently, you can begin giving intermittent food rewards. You won't have to keep a supply of cat treats in your pocket at all times. You can alternate food rewards with praise, petting, or a toy.

Timing

It can be easy to get carried away when you see your cat doing something positive and start clicking excessively. You can also easily miss the behavior and click too late. Timing is important because the cat is associating the sound of the clicker with what she is doing at that exact moment. If you click too late she may have already moved on to another behavior. If you click too many times she won't know what the heck she's being rewarded for. Click only once and be precise.

The Benefits of Clicker Training

You may be wondering why you'd need to teach your cat to roll over or give you a high five. Your cat doesn't actually need to know those specific behaviors but by working on at least a couple with your cat you both develop the skill of clicker training. Your cat starts learning in a positive, rewarding way. Good behavior has good consequences. Unwanted behavior doesn't have good consequences. Your cat is smart—she'll start focusing on the behaviors that have the good consequences.

Clicker training also helps the cat feel as if she has more control over her environment, which can help relax her so she'll be less inclined to exhibit negative behaviors. Clicker training is also a wonderful way to strengthen the bond between cat and owner.

You can use the clicker to train your cat to perform specific "cued" behaviors such as *sit* or *down*, but you can also use it to reinforce un-cued behaviors such as when kitty stops giving a direct stare or walks by a spot where, in the past, she has always inappropriately urinated, or when she walks into the room when company is present instead of hiding under the bed. Clicker training gives you a whole new way to communicate with your cat. You can click and reward for subtle behaviors that let the cat know time and time again that good behavior results in good consequences.

As you go through this book you'll see I mention opportunities to use clicker training, but the decision to use it is up to you. You can do behavior modification without the clicker or you can opt to incorporate it.

Teaching Your Cat to Respond to His Name

This is actually a very important behavior to teach. When you need to locate your cat before you leave the house or you need to get your cat away from something dangerous, being able to depend on her to come when called can be a lifesaver.

I have three rules about teaching a cat her name. They are:

Rule #1: Pick an easy name for your kitten to recognize. Long names such as "Cinderella's Prince Charming, Frederick the Fabulous" aren't a good idea. I didn't make that name up. I know a cat with that name and he wouldn't answer when called. It wasn't until his owner started referring to him as "Fred" that he began to respond to her when she called.

Rule #2: Don't use ten different nicknames for your kitten and expect her to respond to them. Stick to one name so she learns to make the association.

Rule #3: Never call your kitty's name in anger. If you call her by her name and then proceed to punish her when she comes, she'll never want to come to you again.

Begin teaching your cat to associate positive things with her name. While you're petting her, repeat her name over and over in a soothing, quiet, friendly voice. As you're preparing dinner, call her name. Hand-feed her a little before you fill her bowl. Say her name repeatedly as you give her a kibble. After a few repetitions of this exercise, put her food in the bowl and let her eat. Don't overdo the sessions. Keep them short and positive.

In between meals, take a few pieces of broken up treats and practice calling her name multiple times a day. When she comes, give her a treat. If you are clicker training, you can add the verbal cue of "come" after saying her name. Click as soon as she comes to you and then immediately offer the treat.

Work up to calling her from another room. Once she has learned her name you can offer treats intermittently, but always offer praise when she has responded. Even when you are no longer giving food rewards for coming when called, she should always know that something good awaits her.

Once kitty has learned to respond to her name, don't forget Rule #3. Never call her in anger. It can be easy to abuse that rule if you come across something she has damaged or a urine spot on the carpet. Resist the urge to call her to you for punishment. The price you'll pay for potentially damaging the trust bond between the two of you won't be worth it. Punishment is counterproductive and inhumane anyway.

How to Pick Up and Handle Your Cat

When your cat becomes an adult, it will prove to be very valuable if you have spent the time when she was a kitten getting her used to being picked up and handled. Everyone wants a cat whom they can pick up, hold, pet, medicate, and groom without ending up looking like a victim from one of the *Friday the 13th* movies. The key is to start early. Hold your kitten with two hands, no matter how small she is, to give her a feeling of security. No kitten wants to be carried around with her middle squeezed and her legs dangling in the air.

Get your kitten comfortable with being handled by incorporating gentle touch manipulations into your petting sessions. Place the kitten on your lap and gently handle each paw. Run your fingers down her leg, hold her paw briefly, and then very gently expose her little claws, touching the top of each one. This helps her to become comfortable with having her paws handled so you'll be able to trim her nails later. Gently touch her ears and look inside. Pet her as you do this and talk soothingly. This prepares her for future ear cleaning and necessary medicating. Offer treats or small food rewards as you touch different parts of her body.

Stroke your kitty along the sides of the mouth (she'll actually enjoy that) and under her chin (she'll really enjoy that). Then gently slide your finger inside her lips and massage her gums. This prepares her for having her teeth brushed. Offer a treat. Go back to rubbing her under the chin and down her back, then return to her mouth. Carefully open it by placing one hand over the top of her head and gently supporting her upper jaw while you pull down on the lower jaw with the finger of your other hand. That's all, make it quick, and then let her close her mouth. Offer a treat. Go back to petting, and then engage in a play session. If you do these exercises on a regular basis, your kitten will grow up to be a cat who is more comfortable with touch.

If you have an adult cat who isn't used to being held, you'll have to go very slowly so that she'll never feel confined or trapped. You may first need to get her comfortable with being petted with one or two strokes, then gradually work up to using slower strokes so your hand stays in contact with her body for longer periods. Clicker training during each step will help your cat make positive associations with your touch. If you are not clicker training offer treats or food rewards.

When you pick up your cat, always use two hands. Don't grab her by the scruff of the neck and carry her with her hind legs dangling, and never scoop her up with one hand around her middle or she'll feel as if her chest is being crushed.

The proper way to pick up a cat is by putting one hand on her chest, just behind her front legs, and use the other hand to cradle her hindquarters and hind legs. Bring her in close to you so that she can lean against your chest. Her front paws can rest on your forearm. This method allows her to feel supported, yet not trapped. This method of holding is for when you have her in a safe location such as inside your home.

When you put your cat down, do so gently. Don't let her leap out of your arms. You don't want to train her that the only way she can get out of your grasp is to struggle and jump for her life. Let her down before she struggles and she won't associate being held with confinement. Your responsibility as an owner is to stay very aware, sense the moment she's getting restless, then immediately place her back down. Initially, you may only be able to hold your cat for a few seconds, but as she gradually realizes that being held is not such a terrible thing, she'll relax in your arms.

Don't try to hold your cat in your arms like a baby. She'll feel trapped because it's not a natural position for her.

Make sure your cat sees you before you attempt to pick her up. If you startle her by coming up from behind, not only will that make her grow more nervous about being touched but it could also cause you to get scratched.

The other way to hold a cat is the method most often used in veterinary clinics. The following technique is a good way to ensure that the cat doesn't leap out of your arms. This method is best used for unpredictable cats or if you're transporting a cat in an unfamiliar environment—such as a veterinary clinic setting.

The method involves bracing the cat's hind end against your side with one arm, so her rear legs are left free below your forearm and against your hip. The hand of the same arm that's bracing the cat comes up under the chest to gently grasp the forelegs. Place one finger between the forelegs. Your other hand comes over the top of the cat's head to either gently pet it or offer gentle restraint. This method prevents the cat from wriggling away or leaping out of your arms.

Determining Boundaries

You'll never have a well-trained cat if you aren't consistent about what she's allowed to do and where she's allowed to do it. You'll just create confusion and frustration if one family member lets her on the bed but another one doesn't. Is she going to be allowed on kitchen counters? The dining room table? Only when there's no food on it? Well, how is she supposed to know the difference?

Sit down with everyone in the family and go over what the boundaries are. It's not fair to your cat if you're inconsistent, because she'll end up in trouble for things that are truly *your* fault.

Who's Been Sleeping in My Bed?

Are you someone who would enjoy curling up in bed with a cat at your feet? Do you look forward to sharing your pillow with your cat and haven't the least concern for shedding hairs? Or do you want your bedroom to be strictly off limits at night? Be consistent right from the beginning about where your cat will sleep, because it'll be harder to change the rule later.

If you want a kitten to share your bed, no problem. She'd probably like nothing better than to snuggle up with you and enjoy the warmth and companionship. It's one of the tenderest ways for kittens and their owners to bond. If you've adopted an adult cat, she may or may not choose to sleep on your bed. Depending upon her personality and comfort level, she may prefer to stay in the main part of the house or find her own private place to sleep. Some owners, in an attempt to entice a cat to sleep on the bed, will bring her in and close the bedroom door (allowing for litter box access in there) in the hope that she'll learn to like it. If you bring her into the bedroom and she doesn't want to sleep on the bed, there may not be another place in the room where she feels comfortable. If you do decide to go this route, at least place a cat tree or window perch in the bedroom as well.

When you buy a cat bed, keep in mind that cats generally prefer elevated places for sleeping and lounging. If you put a cat bed on the floor in the corner, it may be doomed to being forever unused, or used only by your dog. Observe the places, fabrics, and elevations your cat goes to and that will help you create the most comfortable spot for her. Does she like to be hidden? Does she like to be up high? Does she like to sleep on something that has your scent? Pay attention to her preferences to create the ideal sleeping area.

Cats aren't dogs so don't try to create matching sleeping arrangements. Your dog may happily sleep on the little bed you fixed up for him in the corner. That same arrangement for your cat will most likely fail because it doesn't meet her safety requirements.

If you close your cat up in a separate room during the night make sure it's one she likes being in. It should have more than one sleeping option. If there's room, put a cat tree in with her. Install one of the window perches made especially for cats so she'll have something to keep her occupied during the long night. Carefully scrutinize the room to be sure it doesn't seem like a kitty prison. Create a cozy bed with one of your worn sweatshirts. If the room is chilly, provide the option of a heated pet bed. This is a situation where adopting two kittens works well. If you don't want the kitten in bed with you, they'll have each other to cuddle and play with instead of being lonely.

Since some cats are active during the night, you can also set up some fun activities for her to keep her occupied, so she doesn't sit by your door and meow. Have an arrangement of puzzle feeders, toys, and seek-and-find activities that are reserved just for her nighttime enjoyment.

If your kitty isn't enjoying the sleeping arrangement you've chosen for her, do a little training to help her make a positive association with the spot. You can do some clicker training to reward her whenever she goes up on her cat tree or on her window perch. Eventually you can give the behavior a cue such as "go to bed."

If your cat scratches on the carpet under the door in an attempt to dig her way out, play with her right before you both go to bed, offer her some food (divide her daily portion so you aren't overfeeding), and be sure you've left her with an interesting array of puzzle feeders and toys. To protect your carpet, place a plastic carpet protector under the door.

Ho Hum, Just Another Boring Day

Misbehavior is often just the result of a cat needing something to do. Cats are hunters and benefit greatly from environmental enrichment.

Start your kitty off right by making sure she has enough in her environment to keep her interested. A kitten can be fascinated by the piece of lint that falls from your clothing, but as she grows it may take more thought on your part to provide sufficient stimulation. A window that overlooks outdoor bird activity may be to your cat's liking. Maintain a regular schedule of interactive playtime (see Chapter 6) and rotate your cat's solo toys to keep them from becoming boring. Set up solo activities such as food-dispensing toys, cat tunnels, and other puzzles for kitty to enjoy during the long hours alone. Consider getting a second cat if your work or social schedule leaves your cat home alone all day and then much of the evening.

When you walk in the door at the end of the day, remember that your cat has been alone for hours and will be looking forward to interacting with you. A good balance of stimulation and affection from you will help her become a happy, sociable, and well-behaved cat.

A Place of Her Own

Throughout this book, you'll notice that I refer to cat trees. A cat tree consists of two or three (sometimes more) perches that sit on top of posts of varying lengths. The posts can be bare wood or covered with bark or rope. They serve many purposes. Cat trees provide comfortable window viewing, serve as sturdy scratching posts, and their elevation allows the cat to feel more secure. Multi-tiered trees enable two or more cats to enjoy bird watching without having to crowd each other. One of the most important functions of a cat tree, though, is that it's truly the cat's furniture and will only have her scent as opposed to other pieces of furniture such as chairs and sofas that will contain unfamiliar scents of guests.

My cats use their cat trees during the day for playing, scratching, bird watching and sleeping. Because they're on my furniture less, it cuts down on the amount of cat hair on the sofa. A cat tree in the corner of the living room can be enough of a security blanket for a shy or tentative cat to stay in the room with the family instead of going off somewhere.

Think Vertically

Humans live in a horizontal world but cats live in a vertical one. The more you make use of vertical space in your home, the more territory you'll create for your cat. Even the smallest apartment can be made bigger from a cat's point of view by making use of wall space. Think along the lines of cat walks, perches, and cozy hideaways and you can turn that wall space into valuable feline real estate. Environmental modifications can be as basic as a few secure perches on the wall to an elaborate elevated cat walk encircling the room. For access to a cat walk you can create a mini stairway or stagger a few perches for easy jumping. For safety, cover the perches and cat walks with a nonslip surface. Also, if you have a multicat household, you should provide access to a cat walk on two ends so one cat will never be trapped up there should another cat approach. Even installing a couple of shelves with cat beds on them can add some vertical security for your cat.

When you look around your environment, don't limit yourself to elevated areas but also consider lower territory as well. Place a tunnel behind your sofa for fun, playtime, or as a way for a timid cat to navigate around the room. You can make a homemade tunnel by cutting the bottoms out of paper bags and then taping them together. Environmental enrichment doesn't have to break the budget.

If you have more than one cat, it's important to think vertically because it can help your cats establish a peaceful coexistence. An assertive cat who might normally want to engage in a confrontation may be content to claim the highest perch in the room as a show of his position. This may greatly reduce the amount of actual physical altercations.

Even if you have only one cat, provide some variation in vertical territory (high, middle, and low areas) for her to create a more stimulating environment.

At the very least, invest in a multiperched cat tree and you'll be off to a good start.

Don't Raise a Scaredy-Cat

Kittenhood is the time to start desensitizing your cat by gently exposing her to a variety of novel situations in everyday life. This will help her as she grows up to be unafraid of ordinary things such as the vacuum cleaner or unfamiliar people.

Get your kitten used to potentially scary sounds such as the vacuum or the hair dryer by first running one in another room while you play with her or offer treats. If she isn't bothered by the faraway sound, you can bring it a little closer. You can then try setting a hair dryer on *low* and running it in the same room. Have some treats or a toy in the bathroom with you whenever you dry your hair, so that if the kitten is nearby you can offer a reward for being in the vicinity of the scary noise. The reason you want her to become comfortable with the hair dryer is that you may at some point need to bathe and dry her, and for many cats, the noise is the most frightening part.

The sound of the vacuum cleaner was what sent my cats under the beds, into the closets, and up to the ceiling fixture. So I began their desensitization by running the vacuum in a distant closed room. The sound was far enough away that it wasn't too unsettling. I then began playing with the cats or feeding them while my husband would run the vacuum in another room (by telling my husband this exercise was for behavior modification purposes I was able to get out of vacuum duties for a week). Every day I moved the vacuum cleaner a little closer, but still in a closed room, and had my husband run it while I engaged my cats in something positive. When I finally brought the vacuum cleaner out into the largest open area of the house, I didn't turn it on. I got my cats comfortable with it just being in the same room with them. While my cats were initially startled when I first turned it on, they soon got used to it. The key was that I took the process very slowly and never advanced to the next step until I was sure my cats were totally comfortable with the current noise level.

You can turn many of the scary aspects of life into things your kitten may barely notice with gradual desensitization and counterconditioning. Counterconditioning involves having the cat engage in an activity that would normally be counterintuitive to her in that surrounding. By running the vacuum far enough away from my cats I was desensitizing them to the sound through gradual exposure. The counterconditioning was having them engage in playtime, eating treats or meals while the vacuum was running. I was having them do something they wouldn't normally do with a scary noise in the background.

Introduce your cat to grooming when she's a kitten. Although as a kitten she may not have any mats to worry about, or even very much hair, getting her used to the feel of the brush, the nail trimmers, and being handled will make both of your lives much easier as she grows.

A common behavior problem that develops in single-owner homes is that the cat becomes so used to the sound, touch, and movements of one person, that when just one guest comes over, the cat panics. Imagine the cat's terror should the owner get married (especially if children and other pets are part of the package). Early, gentle exposure to a variety of situations will help your kitten grow up well-adjusted rather than a cat nobody ever sees or worse, the kind your friends label as "the attack cat."

An important reminder, though: the object of these exercises is to desensitize your kitten gradually. If she shows fear, you've gone too far too fast. Always proceed at a slower pace than you think is required. Two important tools for raising a well-adjusted cat are *love* and *patience*. We usually get the *love* part down right away; it's the *patience* aspect of being a pet owner that we often have to work harder on.

Kitten Kindergarten

If the new cat is a kitten, find out if there are any kitten kindergarten classes in your area. These classes are usually conducted at veterinary clinics. I know you're probably shaking your head at the thought of kitten classes but why should puppies have all the fun?

The classes help kittens become familiar with being handled in the veterinary clinic as well as become more comfortable with other kittens and people. Owners learn litter box basics as well as cat care information.

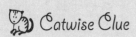 Catwise Clue

Kitten kindergarten classes offer a safe environment for socializing kittens.

There are vaccination and age requirements for the kittens attending in order to prevent the spread of disease. Disposable litter boxes are provided as well.

Kitten kindergarten classes are fun and informative. Contact the veterinary clinic in your area to find out if there are any scheduled in your community.

Leash Training

I don't think the outdoors is a safe place for a little cat to roam freely. If you absolutely insist on letting your cat experience the outdoor world then do it in a safe way by leash training. Even if you never plan on taking your kitty outdoors, leash training is valuable. If you travel with her, it will give you added control when you take her out of her carrier.

Not every cat is a good candidate for leash training. A timid, nervous cat may find more security in the unchanging world of her indoor environment. All the unpredictable noises, scents, and sights of the outdoors could fuel her anxiety. A cat who gets very upset while looking out the window at the mere sight of another cat in her territory might become even more agitated if she's outside and confronted with the scents of unfamiliar cats.

You may also be setting yourself up for a cat who starts demanding to be let outdoors or who decides she doesn't need to wait for permission and attempts to escape. Another negative is that your cat will be at increased risk for getting fleas, ticks, and contagious diseases.

Leash training a cat doesn't mean going for a brisk walk. The way you walk with your dog will in no way resemble the way you'll walk with your cat. First of all, you'll need to confine your walking to your own yard. It'll be much safer because there's less of a chance of running into other animals. Should your cat become upset or if you drop the leash, she'll be in more familiar territory in your own yard and you won't have far to go if you have to pick her up and carry her inside. She may also be less inclined to panic because she'll be in familiar surroundings. Another reason to stay within your own yard is that you don't want to teach her that it's okay to roam beyond her own territory. That way, should she ever get out of the house, she may be inclined to stay closer to home.

How to Leash Train

The right equipment comes first. You'll need to purchase a lightweight leash. Don't get a chain or a heavy leather leash—you're not walking a rottweiler. The lighter the leash the better, because it'll be more comfortable for both of you and it'll take less time for your cat to get used to it. You'll also need a cat harness rather than a regular collar. Your leashed cat will pull out of a collar. There are several types of harnesses on the market. I use the Come with Me Kitty harness by Premier with my cats and clients' cats due to its safety and comfort for the cats.

Make sure your cat's vaccinations are up-to-date before exposing her to the outdoors. She'll also need an identification tag just in case she escapes from you. If it's flea season, be sure she's protected (see Chapter 13).

Start leash and harness training indoors for the first couple of weeks. The first time you put the harness on your cat just be casual about it, then give her a treat, feed her, or distract her with playtime. Mealtime usually works best. Leave the harness on for about five to fifteen minutes. Repeat the procedure before the next meal. If your cat is normally fed free-choice, use treats or playtime to divert her attention away from the harness. If your cat struggles too much as you try to put the harness on, don't attempt to buckle it; just get the harness on her and then immediately distract her.

As your cat gets more comfortable, put the harness on her for longer periods during the day and always provide a positive diversion should she begin to resist it. Don't leave it on her when you're not there to supervise because she could get herself all worked up.

In week two, introduce the leash. Attach it to the harness but don't tug on it. She has to get used to the idea of being connected to something. If the leash is light enough, let your kitty drag it behind her while you provide a distraction. Be careful that she doesn't get the leash caught on anything. It's best to do this step in one room where she won't be able to run off and possibly get tangled in something. Once she's comfortable with this new attachment, you'll begin the next phase of training.

Very important warning: don't tug on the leash at this point or your mild mannered cat will turn into a thrashing, growling, fur-covered chain saw. The way to introduce her to walking on a leash is through positive reinforcement. Here's where clicker training can work as well. Have a supply of treats in your pocket. If your cat responds better to wet food, hold a small container of canned food and feed the cat a tiny amount from a soft-tipped baby spoon. If you feel as if you need an extra arm in order to handle the leash, clicker, food, and spoon, tape an extension onto the spoon and then tape the clicker to the end. That way you can click and reward with one hand. You can also attach a trainer's pack to your belt and put a small opened container of wet food in there.

With the leash loosely in your hand, take a step out in front of your cat. Hold a treat out at her eye level. When she starts walking toward the treat, click the clicker and give her the treat. Take another step forward, holding another treat and repeat the process. You can also use a target stick: hold it out in front of her and then click-and-treat when she takes a step forward. Continue this until she becomes used to walking with you. Gradually introduce a slight tug as you step forward. Don't pull or yank the leash. It should be a gentle tug that's barely detectable. Remember to give her time to eat her treat; don't expect her to stay in motion all the time.

When your cat is comfortable with this exercise, you can pair the behavior with a cue such as "let's walk." Do your walking sessions around the interior of the house. Don't attempt to go outdoors with your cat until she's totally comfortable walking on a leash. She shouldn't struggle when you slightly increase tension on it. Be prepared for this to take anywhere from one to three weeks.

> ### 🐱 Catwise Caution
>
> **Think long and hard about whether leash-walking outdoors is really a good idea for your cat. Carefully examine whether your outdoor environment will create a positive or negative experience. There is much risk with being in an environment you and your cat can't control.**

When you go outdoors, stick close to the house and don't stay out too long. This is a new experience for your cat, so it'll be overwhelming. Your initial sessions should ideally be limited to the back deck or just around the backyard. Carry a towel with you so that if she becomes upset you can pick her up by wrapping the towel around her. This way you won't get injured. You may also want to wear your trainer's pack with some wet food inside and carry your spoon so you can divert your cat's attention to the food reward should it be needed.

6

Fast Forward . . . Stop . . . Rewind . . . Play

Playtime Techniques Used for Behavior Modification

I know, I know, you're scratching your head while looking at this chapter title and thinking, *Why would cats need instructions on how to play?* Well, actually they don't—*you* need them. Do you make any of the following common mistakes in playing with your cat?

- Do you play with her using your hands as toys or use your hands to "wrestle" with her?

- Do you assume that if you just supply the toys, the cat will play by herself, whenever she wants to?

- Do you play with your cat now and then or whenever you have time? Once a week? Once a month?

By *thinking like a cat*, you'll view playtime as more than just fun and games—it's a powerful behavior modification tool, and it can help raise a confident, sociable, well-behaved kitten. If your cat is an adult, playing with her can help correct behavior problems, ease stress or depression, help her lose weight, and improve her overall health. In general, cats sleep about sixteen hours a day. If your cat has extended that to twenty-four hours, a regular play schedule will help her reestablish a more normal sleep pattern. Play can also accelerate acceptance of a new cat into a multicat household. If you want to strengthen the bond you share with your cat, playtime can be almost magical.

Defining Play

Cats engage in two forms of play: *social* play and *object* (or solo) play. Social play involves another cat, pet, or human. With a young kitten, social play begins with her littermates. This type of play behavior helps the kitten develop motor coordination and gives her the opportunity to bond with her companions. Kittens take turns playing the aggressor as they learn about their own and each other's abilities. Their playful interactions are a controlled and inhibited version of their natural predatory behavior. The kittens' inhibited bites, nonaggressive body posture and facial expressions demonstrate that this is for fun and learning rather than for real.

Object play also builds and strengthens a kitten's motor coordination as well as teaches her about her environment. What might appear to you to be just an amusing game of a kitten chasing a toy around the house is actually a vital educational process. She's learning about different surfaces and textures, how each feels and how they affect her movements. She's also learning about her emerging ability to climb, and what objects are safe to land on. Much to everyone's dismay, she'll also discover what objects aren't for kitten landings.

Littermates will play socially mostly before twelve weeks of age. After that, social play sessions become shorter and sometimes end with a little genuine aggression. Object play becomes the main focus as kittens mature. This is an important time for you to teach your kitten how to play appropriately with objects and to accept being handled and petted, so they don't direct their playfulness toward your fingers.

Successful, frequent playtime helps build confidence. I know you may be thinking that this sounds silly—*confidence* for a cat? But it makes a lot of sense when you really think about a cat's nature. Cats being predators are attracted by movement, especially if that movement resembles the behavior of prey. If an outdoor cat had to depend on hunting for food but was afraid of and distracted by every leaf that fell from a tree, or every sound of a distant car horn, she'd soon starve. The cat who spies her prey makes a quick assessment to make sure *she's* not in danger, focuses in on her hunt, and then eats. She begins to strengthen both her *air hunting* skills for flying prey and *ground hunting* skills for rodents, insects, and other creepy crawlies. Each success also builds her confidence and she learns how to modify her technique, depending on whether she's hunting a bird, mouse, snake, or butterfly. The more she hunts, the more athletic she becomes.

When I go on consultations, one of the first things I ask about is the cat's playtime routine. Many owners will show me the cat's basket of toys but often can't recall actually seeing the cat play with any of them recently. When owners say they do play with their cats, I always ask for a demonstration. After years of doing consultations and working with cats and owners, I realized that many people don't know *how* to play with their cats. The worst is, too many cats—troubled by anxiety, boredom, obesity, or other problems—eventually give up on playing.

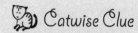 Catwise Clue

Many people assume the outdoor cat who "plays" with his prey after injuring or killing it, is being cruel. In reality, though, the behavior is most likely a displacement due to the excitement and anxiety of the hunt. During the hunt the cat must deal with the fear of getting injured himself in the process.

Interactive Play

While your new kitten may seem to have the whole play routine down to a fine art: zooming ninety miles an hour around the house in pursuit of a dust ball, *your* participation is still greatly needed. That's where *interactive* play comes in.

Interactive play is so powerful throughout a cat's entire life—from the day you bring her home as a kitten to her golden years as the geriatric queen of the house. If you're just starting out with a kitten, establishing an interactive playtime schedule may help develop the bond you share, will teach her what is and isn't acceptable to bite, and will help avoid many potential behavior problems. If you have an adult cat, especially a troubled one, interactive playtime can redirect her negative behavior toward something positive and help correct many problems.

Interactive play involves *you* participating in the game with your kitten or cat, using a fishing-pole type toy. Now, you may already feel that you engage in lots of playtime with your kitty, but what toys do you use? Your hands? Little furry mice? Unfortunately, many owners use the most readily available toys—their *fingers*—to play with their kitten. While it may not be bad now, as your kitten grows, a bite from her adult teeth *will* hurt. You're also sending a very bad message to the kitten when you use your fingers as toys—you're telling her it's okay to bite skin. Never encourage biting, not even in play. If you start a kitten off correctly, you'll avoid having to retrain her once she has grown.

Okay, so maybe you've never allowed your cat to bite your fingers but you use those furry little mice or a light spongy ball for playtime. What's wrong with that? First, it puts your fingers and the toy in close proximity so you stand a greater chance of being accidentally scratched or bitten by an excited kitty. Also, you can't control the movements of the toy very well. Fishing-pole type toys give you greater control and you can create a more preylike movement.

The concept of an interactive toy is simple: pole, string, and a toy target dangling on the end. What I love about these toys is that you can make the toy move as prey naturally would. If you're going to *think like a cat*, you have to understand how they react to prey. The problem with all of the cute little toys that are strewn about the house is that they're essentially dead prey. In order to play with them, the cat must work as both prey and predator. She has to bat at the toy to make it move. Once it slides a little on the floor it dies again and remains lifeless unless the cat pushes it back into motion. An interactive toy lets you create the movement so the cat can just enjoy being a predator.

There are many interactive toys on the market. Some are pretty basic and others are very elaborate. When shopping for one, again, use your *think like a cat* approach. Look at the toy and imagine what kind of prey it resembles and how your cat, based on her personality, would react to it. Because cats are opportunistic hunters, which means they hunt whatever is available, look for several different types of interactive toys. Try to cover the various types of prey such as: birds, mice, insects, and snakes. Your cat will be more interested if you vary the toys, because she'll never know just which prey to expect.

Several interactive toys have feathers on the end to make them resemble birds. My all-time favorite is called Da Bird by Go Cat, available in most pet supply stores and online. This fishing-pole type toy has a swivel device at the end of the string where the feathers are connected. As you wave the toy through the air, the feathers spin around, so it looks and sounds like a bird in flight. Cats go crazy for it. This toy will make even the most sedentary cat dust off her hunting skills.

For simulating the movements of a cricket or a fly, nothing beats the Cat Dancer by Cat Dancer Products. It has been around a long time and for good reason. The toy consists of a wire with a small, tightly rolled-up cardboard target on the end. If you just move it subtly, the Cat Dancer darts and moves as unpredictably as a fly does. This toy makes your cat use her concentration skills and best reflexes.

WHY YOUR KITTEN NEEDS INTERACTIVE PLAY

- helps her bond with her new family
- helps coordination and muscle tone
- helps her become comfortable with her environment
- reduces fear
- helps teach her what is and isn't acceptable to bite or scratch
- prevents damage to items in your home
- reduces tension in multicat households due to addition of the new kitten
- eases discomfort after a traumatic episode
- it's a natural part of a kitten's daily life

There are many interactive toys out there on the market. You may find one that fits your cat's personality or play skill even better. Before buying it, though, make sure it is a good match for your cat. Sometimes it takes a couple of toy purchases to find the one your cat prefers. A shy, timid cat might be overwhelmed by a large toy that makes lots of noise, and a cat who lives to air hunt may not find the slithery movements of a snakelike toy very appealing.

Bubbles and Lasers

A popular game is to blow bubbles and let your cat run around after them. Some bubbles are even catnip scented. Some cats love this. My problem is that she doesn't actually get to capture anything. The bubbles always pop and she's left with nothing. A cat is a very tactile creature and she wants to feel the "captured prey" underneath her paw. If your cat enjoys the bubble game then move into an interactive play session right afterward, so she gets to achieve an actual capture. If you have children who enjoy blowing bubbles for the cat, instruct them not to blow the bubbles at her, especially at her face.

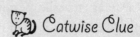 Catwise Clue

If you bought an interactive toy and your cat isn't interested, don't give up. It may take a few attempts to get her interested or it may not be the right toy for her. Luckily, there are many terrific options to choose from.

Laser toys for cats are extremely popular. I think their success is based on the fact that they require minimal movement from the owners. You can sit in your chair, watch TV, and point the laser all over the room. For some owners the pleasure comes from the comical scene of watching their cats almost body-slam the wall in an attempt to reach the little red light pointed half way up the ceiling. As with the bubbles, the cat never actually "gets" anything. A major component of interactive playtime is capturing the prey under her paw and letting her carpal whiskers detect movement.

Using laser lights regularly may also lead to potential compulsive behaviors in some animals. Some become reactive to other forms of flashing light. There are also differing opinions on whether the lasers are actually even safe or not. To be sure, NEVER point the laser in your cat's face and don't allow children to play with laser toys. If you really want to use the laser light with your cat, start with it, then continue the game with an actual interactive toy. Point the laser at the target on the end of the interactive toy and then let the tactile part of the game begin. Since the purpose of interactive playtime is to create stimulation and leave the cat happy and confident, it's important to provide your cat with opportunities to succeed.

How to Use Interactive Toys

First, imagine your living room or den is about to be transformed into a hunting ground. The sofa, chairs, and tables will now become trees, bushes, rocks, and other things that the cat can hide behind. If you have a big, open space, scatter some pillows, cushions, or even an open paper bag to provide additional cover for your little predator.

A common mistake made by well-meaning owners is to play with their cat by dangling the toy in front of her. The cat bats at the toy repeatedly. She sits up and appears to almost box the toy. Although this play method may look amusing and seem as if she's having fun, it isn't a natural form of cat playing/hunting. Remember that playtime is supposed to be a make-believe hunt. What self-respecting prey would hover in front of the cat and hang around to be repeatedly batted? The cat ends up just using reflexes instead of using her best tool—her brain. This method of playing will only serve one purpose—it'll annoy your cat.

Another playtime mistake I often see is that the owner keeps the toy out of the cat's reach during the entire game. It becomes a marathon race throughout the house with the cat never able to grasp even one paw on the prey. Cats don't chase to exhaustion, they silently stalk and ambush when they've gotten close enough. In the wild, a cat uses every rock, tree, and bush for cover as she inches closer to her prey (that's where your sofa, chairs, table, and cushions come in). Therefore, much of her efficient hunting technique involves her *patience, plan-*

ning, and *precision*. Your cat has incredible stealth and she wants to make good use of that during playtime. Play with your cat in a way that's natural and satisfying to her. Use your toy to simulate the way prey would truly move in a real hunt: it would get the heck out of there and run for cover. Move *away* from the cat, not *toward* her. Movements going across your cat's visual field are easier for her to see and movements going away from her strongly trigger her prey-drive. Movements coming toward her are confusing, more difficult to see, and potentially viewed as threatening. Guide the toy over to a hiding place and then entice your cat by letting it just peek out. Think prey!

Because the purpose of the game is for the cat to have fun, not become frustrated, don't frantically wave the toy around at the speed of light, out of reach. Let her have many successes. If she grasps it in her paws, let her savor the victory and then gently try to get it away.

Try to emmulate the natural intensity curve of a real hunt. For example, when you work out you have a *warm-up*, the *actual exercise*, and the *cool-down*. Your playtime should provide this as well. Don't play like crazy with your cat, ripping around having a grand time, and then, discovering it's time to leave for work, suddenly ending the game. If she hasn't had enough opportunities to capture and kill her prey, she'll be left frustrated. A cool-down will leave her satisfied and content. To cool kitty down, begin to move the prey as if it's becoming injured and allow the cat to capture it. I know that in the real world the bird very often gets away, but with you as the producer/director of this hunt, you can let your cat win every time. That's how you inspire confidence in your cat, by allowing her to be the Mighty Hunter. So, when you feel it's time to end the game, begin to let your prey slow down.

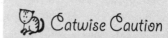 **Catwise Caution**

Always put all interactive toys away in a closet, out of kitty's reach, when the game is over so she won't chew on the stringed parts.

When your cat has achieved her great capture, reward her by either serving her dinner or giving her a treat—the *hunt* and then the *feast*. You're going to have one happy kitty.

When to Play

For play sessions to be most effective and have long-term positive effects, they should be a part of your daily schedule. Ideally it would be great if you could fit in two sessions a day (ten to fifteen minutes each, or whatever your schedule will

INTERACTIVE PLAYTIME TIPS

- If you're using a birdlike interactive toy, remember to incorporate frequent landings into the game. Birds don't fly all the time, they also walk. This gives your cat time to plan.

- Frequent freezes in action, with the prey staying absolutely still, can be very exciting. This is the time the cat thinks and plans her next move.

- Don't forget sound effects. I'm not talking about bird chirps or rodent squeaks, but the little sounds of the toy slightly tapping on the floor or the subtle sound of it inside a paper bag.

- Vary the speed of your movements—not everything should be fast. Just

barely quivering the toy will drive your kitty wild!

- You're not conducting a kitty marathon here, so don't exhaust your cat. Her sides shouldn't be heaving and she shouldn't be gasping for breath. If you get her too worked up, she won't have the opportunity to plan and stalk. Remember, this exercise should be *mentally*, as well as *physically*, rewarding.

- Whenever she gets the toy in her mouth or paws, allow her to savor each victory for a few seconds.

- Reward her with a treat or serve dinner after the game. She caught her prey: well done!

allow). I can hear you now: "Where am I going to find this extra time each day?" If you can't fit in a half hour a day for your cat, maybe you shouldn't be a cat owner. This little creature's whole world revolves around you. Surely you can squeeze in fifteen to thirty minutes a day to bond with her. It's amazing how, if you really try, you can become very adept at doing two things at once. Combine watching television in the evening with a playtime. Talk on the phone and play with your cat. Read three or four fewer e-mails at night and spend that time playing with your cat. The key is to play every day with your cat. Whether it's five minutes, ten minutes, or forty-five minutes, your cat needs that stimulation and activity every day.

Unless you're using specific play sessions to work out behavior problems (see section later in this chapter), I'd recommend that the first session be in the morning before you leave for work, because after you go, your kitty will be sleeping on and off for the entire day. The second session should then be in the evening. A third session right before bedtime will help a cat who tends to keep you up at night with her after-dark activities.

A kitten may require more play sessions during the day but of shorter duration. She may play like a little maniac for five minutes and then go off to sleep. A kitten needs playtime, but she also needs frequent little naps. Don't exhaust her.

Schedule your play sessions to coincide with your particular kitten or cat's active times. Don't wake her up to play (especially a kitten), unless you're dealing with a depressed or sedentary cat who sleeps twenty-four hours a day.

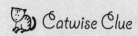

Catwise Clue

Remember to include environmental enrichment for your cat's enjoyment while you're gone during the day by setting out puzzle feeders and other adventure toys.

Interactive Playtime in Multicat Households

A cat has to focus completely on her prey and plan her attack. Two or more cats stalking the same toy will be distracted by each other. Also, the more assertive cat will take charge, leaving the other cat to sit on the sidelines. That certainly isn't much fun for her.

Interactive playtime should provide pleasure and confidence, so make sure each cat has her own toy. Your goal isn't achieved if they simultaneously pounce on a toy and one cat crashes into the other. That will result in hisses, swats, and somebody running away in fear. But you can avoid that problem. Either take one cat at a time into another area of the house and conduct an individual play session, or hold a fishing pole toy in each hand. It's tricky at first but you'll get used to it. The secret to working two toys at once is to keep the cats far enough apart so they avoid crashing into each other. With two toys you're obviously not going to be as adept at imitating precise preylike movements, but it's better than nothing. You could also enlist another family member to help. Unlike when it's time to medicate the cat, you can usually find a willing assistant for play sessions.

If you have *more* than two cats, you'll have to arrange individual play sessions to be sure that everyone gets his or her turn. You can still do group sessions using two toys (obviously the cats will have to take turns) but you have to be very aware of who might be backing away from the game. Make sure everyone gets a shot and don't allow two cats who maybe aren't on the best of terms to find themselves eye to eye. If you are going to do individual sessions, leave the radio or TV on to create background noise for your other cats. The sound will hopefully cover the familiar sound of the interactive toy off in the distance.

After a group play session, provide everyone with a treat for a job well done. Then go lie down and put a cold cloth over your eyes.

Interactive Play for Behavior Modification

Because a cat is first and foremost a hunter, you can use an interactive toy to switch her focus from something negative to positive. Here's a common example: your cat hides whenever she hears a strange noise. You look under the bed and find two eyes staring at you in terror. Get out one of your interactive toys and *casually* move it around the room. There's a good chance you'll get your cat to focus on it. She may not come out from under the bed right away, but she'll at least give the toy some attention. Your casual attitude sends a signal to her that all is okay in the house. The wrong thing to do after she dives under the bed in terror is to reach down and pull her out so you can hold her. The last thing she wants is to be clutched in your arms. First of all, she'd feel confined (cats don't tend to like that) and second, she'd pick up the message from you that whatever the noise was, it must've been something as bad as she thought. Clutching her would be reinforcing her view that the event was the end of the world. Casual playtime, on the other hand, allows her to keep the comforting option of remaining under the bed, but helps her to realize she doesn't need to.

Cats, like children, require two very specific emotional things from us to feel secure. Affection is one. Humans and animals both benefit from being touched and provided with a reassuring physical connection. What parent doesn't enjoy holding her child, and what cat owner doesn't cherish any opportunity to hold or pet her cat? The other thing you must provide is reassurance. For example, parents (much like cat owners) must allow their children to gain confidence by letting them accomplish things on their own. If you are a parent, I'm sure you've watched your child try to do something new or maybe even a little scary, such as going down a slide for the first time. Instead of confirming her fears by clutching her in your arms and agreeing that the slide is a big, scary thing, you explain to her how much fun it is. You reassure her that you'll be at the bottom to catch her but that she's going to love it. Your reassurance, calm voice, and light manner (maybe you even go down the slide yourself), calm her fears. When she does finally go down the slide, you're waiting at the bottom, and she immediately forgets the fears she had and wants to do it again! Casual interactive playtime with your troubled cat works the same way. Your impulse may be to hold your cat when she reacts to something scary, but in many cases that may only convince her that her fear is valid. Refocus her attention on something positive by triggering her prey-drive. This doesn't mean you have to engage her in a rip-roaring, high-intensity play session, but rather, just shift her focus. Maybe she'll play—maybe she won't. What matters is that your casual and calm body language reassures her that she is safe and secure and offers her a little anxiety-relieving distraction.

You can use toys to counteract many negative situations. Play sessions can help two cats who don't get along by distracting them from focusing so intensely on each other. As soon as you see the tension building, pull out a couple of toys. The cats become distracted by the toys. As they play (remember, use *two* toys so they don't have to compete), they begin to associate fun playtime with being together. They get used to being in the same room without having tension.

Interactive toys can also be used to help combat emotional problems; they could possibly reignite a depressed cat's spark for life. Interactive sessions can also help a cat become more comfortable in a new home. And cats who tend to be aggressive benefit from this sort of play because they can take their aggression out on the toy instead of their owners or other pets.

If your cat hates your new spouse or significant other, have that person engage in most of the interactive play sessions. This will help build trust at a safe distance from the cat's point of view. Through play, the cat will begin to associate the spouse with positive experiences.

If your cat is spraying in a certain area, conduct an interactive play session in that spot to help change his association with that section of the room. By playing there, it becomes a positive, fun area. For more on spraying behavior, refer to Chapter 8.

If you're expecting a new baby, interactive playtime will help the cat adjust to the frightening changes. Play a tape of baby sounds at a low volume while conducting interactive play sessions.

When you're dealing with a timid cat, provide many opportunities for *cover* during playtime. For example, if you're playing in a wide open room with all the furniture close to the walls, the timid cat might be too nervous to step out into the open and expose herself. Cats in an outdoor setting prefer not to hunt in wide open fields. They depend on tall grasses, trees, bushes, stumps, and other objects to allow them to make full use of their stealth. When you're playing with your timid indoor cat, place boxes, bags, cushions, pillows, or whatever objects are handy in the middle of the room to create hiding places and thus more security for her. Once she ventures out and eventually starts playing, she'll become more at ease. If you'd prefer, you can purchase several soft-side cat tunnels that can be connected to one another. Several of these placed around a room can be sufficient to help make a timid cat feel invisible enough to attempt to hunt. You can also make tunnels by cutting the bottoms out of several paper bags.

Interactive play sessions appeal to a cat's natural instincts and that can help

WHY YOUR ADULT CAT NEEDS INTERACTIVE PLAY

- strengthens the bond you share
- provides exercise for overweight or sedentary cats
- eases tension in multicat households
- helps diffuse aggression
- provides beneficial stimulation for depressed cats
- builds confidence in shy or nervous cats
- encourages a normal, healthy appetite
- reduces fear
- corrects inappropriate biting and scratching
- accelerates acceptance of new family members
- eases reactions to traumatic events
- eases discomfort of a new environment
- builds trust
- builds confidence
- allows you to interact with an unpredictable cat without risk of injury

change her focus and behavior. As you go through this book, you'll find I've indicated many situations in which play sessions would be beneficial. That's how important playtime is to your cat.

Catnip

Not enough owners understand the value of catnip or how to use it correctly. Catnip is a minty herb that contains a substance known as *nepetalactone*. It is a substance that causes a pleasure-release in the brain, and cats react to it with ecstasy. They rub, roll, play, lick, jump, munch, and basically act as if they're going through second kittenhood. Very often cats will eat catnip (it's safe), but the pleasure-inducing effect is actually only achieved by smelling the herb. The effects, which last about fifteen minutes, are completely harmless and nonaddictive, and after those fifteen minutes of ecstasy and zany fun, cats are relaxed and ready for a nap.

Catnip can be used to help everyone get past a stressful situation, it can jump-start a play session, or just light a fire (figuratively speaking) underneath a sedentary kitty. It's one of the perks of being a cat—that is, being able to experience such a joy-inducing substance without any side effects, repercussions, or danger.

Here's what many owners don't know about catnip: if you leave catnip or catnip-filled toys out for your cat all of the time, she can become immune to its effects. I explain that to my clients whenever I enter their homes and see dozens of catnip-filled toys. How sad for the kitties that their owners may be ruining this feline pleasure without knowing it. Limit catnip to once or twice a week. You can always add an extra session now and then if needed, for instance, after a visit to the veterinarian or other stressful event.

Buy good quality catnip. I prefer to buy loose, dried catnip instead of all the catnip-filled toys because unless I'm familiar with the toy manufacturer, I don't know whether the catnip is of good quality. Some manufacturers don't even use real catnip. Check the label on loose catnip to make sure only *leaves* and *blossoms* are used. Lower quality catnip contains *stems*, which do nothing but fill up the package. Dried stems are also very hard and sharp. If your cat enjoys eating catnip (which most do), stems are uncomfortable. Stay away from supermarket brands. Better quality catnip can be found in pet supply stores, cat specialty shops, and online, or you can grow your own!

You can fill toys with catnip as well. Check your local pet supply store and you'll find many soft cat toys that have open pouches in them for packing with catnip. You can also put some catnip in a small sock, knot the top, and you've created your own inexpensive catnip toy. Cats will also enjoy loose catnip. To release the aromatic oil, rub the catnip between your hands before you sprinkle loose catnip on the floor or carpet. If filling a sock with it, rub the sock between your hands to release the full potency.

Keep unused catnip tightly sealed in an airtight container, out of kitty's reach. I'd also recommend that instead of buying all those catnip-filled toys, buy a few furry mice toys and drop them in the catnip container. When you pull one out after it has been "marinating," it will have acquired the real scent of top quality, potent catnip.

🐾 Catwise Clue

If you have a large quantity of catnip, store it in the freezer in several small airtight containers to prolong its freshness. All you have to do is take out one little packet and allow it to come to room temperature before giving it to your cat.

Growing Your Own

You can grow your own catnip plant. If you plant it outdoors, though, I warn you, word will spread within the feline community and you'll soon have every cat in the neighborhood visiting your garden. Catnip spreads so you'll have to keep it pruned to prevent it from taking over your garden. Find a safe place to grow it outdoors (good luck), or grow the plant indoors in a sunny window. Packets of catnip seeds are available at garden centers and online. Planting and growing instructions will be on the packet. To ensure peak potency, don't allow the plant to flower or you'll

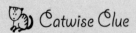 Catwise Clue

Some cats enjoy nibbling on the fresh leaves of the catnip plant. This is totally safe.

end up with skinny branches. Keep nipping those flower buds. To harvest and dry catnip, cut the branches, tie them in bunches, and hang them upside down in a dry, dark place. Once the herb has dried (the leaves will look shriveled), carefully sort the leaves into an airtight container and discard all stems. You don't want to release the potent oil until it's time to use the herb so don't crumble or crush the catnip.

Unexpected Reactions

Not every cat reacts to catnip. There is actually an inherited catnip-response gene that some cats don't possess. It has been estimated that approximately one-third of the cat population lacks this special gene. So if your kitty seems unimpressed, don't worry, there's nothing wrong with her. Kittens don't respond to catnip either, so don't attempt to entice yours until she's at least a year old. Kittens have enough natural energy anyway!

If you have a male cat in a multicat household, the first time you give him catnip, do so away from the other cats. There are some males who actually display aggressive behavior while under the influence of catnip. You also never want to give it to any cat (male or female) who is showing aggression because catnip can cause them to lose inhibition, which may escalate the undesirable behavior.

Environmental Enrichment Through Solo Activity Toys

One of the reasons cats become overweight is because they have no activity but eating. They sleep, waddle a few steps to their food bowl, eat, and then waddle back to the sofa to sleep until it's time to eat again. They don't have to hunt for their food—heck, they don't have to do *anything* for their food except show up.

Lack of activity because of insufficient stimulation also contributes to boredom and depression. A cat whose owner works long hours or has little time for interaction can lose her spark. An interactive toy is the best way to guarantee that your cat gets enough stimulation, but what if you're never home to do it? Or, what if you'd like a way to supplement your interactive sessions? Puzzle feeders and activity toys may work for you.

Puzzle Feeders

If you're away from home a lot or are looking for a way to supplement current playtime, activity toys and puzzle feeders can help. The concept behind a puzzle feeder is that it encourages the cat to work for food—the way nature intended. Whether she works for her actual meals or just extra treats will be up to you depending upon her weight, health, and what behavior issues there are. For the most part, activity toys and puzzle feeders will greatly enrich your cat's life and can be a valuable tool in preventing or resolving behavior problems. Activity toys and puzzle feeders are very popular behavior modification tools in the field of dog behavior due to their success in reducing the high degree of separation anxiety felt by many dogs. Owners place several toys around the house, each with a biscuit or some food in them, and the dog discovers and works on them over the course of the day. These types of toys work beautifully with cats as well. The way a puzzle feeder works is that you place several treats or pieces of her regular dry food inside the toy, and the cat works on removing the food reward. Puzzle feeders come in various configurations. The most basic is the food-dispensing ball. It's a hollow plastic ball with a hole on one side. Snap the ball open, fill halfway with dry food, close the ball and leave it in your cat's play area. As she rolls the ball around, pieces of kibble randomly fall out.

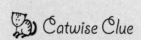 Catwise Clue

If you have a dog who shares space with your cat, don't use small puzzle feeders where the dog has access.

Puzzle feeders can keep an overweight cat busy and allow her to eat slowly as she paws at the ball. Puzzle feeders can create activity for a bored or depressed cat and can help ease anxiety for the nervous kitty. I love toys that require a cat to *think*. Keep your cat occupied with a "thinking" activity and you can probably avoid many potential behavior problems in addition to providing valuable enrichment.

Puzzle feeders are an outstanding way for your cat to engage in normal hunting behavior and be rewarded for her efforts. If your cat doesn't seem to be grasping the concept of the food-dispensing ball you can use the following method to train her. Start by first placing the empty ball in her bowl of dry food. In order to get at the food she'll have to roll the ball around. This gets her familiar with the basic concept. Next, snap the ball apart and place dry food in the bottom half of the ball. Set the bottom ball-half in the food dish so kitty will now start eating the food out of the ball. The next step is to place dry food in the ball, snap it closed, and place it in an empty food bowl. You may have to use a large dish instead of kitty's usual food bowl in order for there to be adequate space for the ball to roll around. Finally, the last step is to place the food-filled ball on the floor.

There are several food-dispensing toys on the market. Play-N-Treat Ball by OurPets is a very popular one. There's also the Egg-Cersizer by Premier, which is my cats' favorite. You can adjust the openings on the Egg-Cersizer to set the degree of difficulty. Premier, the company that manufacturers the Egg-Cersizer also makes a food-dispensing toy that can be hung from the doorway. The Aïkiou Stimulo, an interactive cat feeder, is another terrific food puzzle that has little plastic cups imbedded in a base. Your cat has to use his paw to reach the kibble. Some cups are deeper than others and you can change the level of difficulty.

Another option for a puzzle feeder is to use the Kong. This is a toy meant for dogs but the petite puppy-sized ones will work great for cats. Put a drop of cream cheese or some canned food just inside the edge.

You don't even have to spend money to create puzzle feeders. Homemade ones work well too. Cut a few holes in the center of a cardboard toilet-paper roll. Cut the holes larger than the size of the dry food. Close up the ends and you now have a fun puzzle feeder. For a longer version use a paper towel roll.

A small cardboard box makes a great puzzle toy as well. Cut a few paw-sized holes in the box, close the flaps securely, and put kibble in there.

More complex puzzle feeders include the plastic version of the Nina Ottosson Dog Brick Game. This is actually a dog toy but the plastic version is very adaptable for cats. It's a plastic box with multiple compartments with sliding covers. The cat must slide one of the little covers (shaped like a bone) over to reveal the food inside.

Even if you just take some small dishes and hide tiny amounts of food around your cat's play area, you'll be creating environmental enrichment.

Nonfood Activity Toys

Boxes and paper bags can be used in so many ways to hide toys, create tunnels, and up the enjoyment factor in your cat's daily life. An empty tissue box with a ping pong ball inside can be a fun challenge for a kitty. You can also put a toy inside an open paper bag.

Peek-a-Prize by SmartCat is a wooden activity toy that has many holes in it for your cat to paw at the balls inside. It is available at pet supply stores and online. You can also make your own inexpensive version of this with a small, flat box. Cut paw-sized holes in it, tape the flaps closed, and drop several Mylar balls, spongy balls, or ping pong balls inside.

Dangerous Toys

Ribbons, strings, yarn, rubber bands, and dental floss may seem like fun things for cats to play with, but they're extremely dangerous if swallowed. With all of the safe toys available, don't take a chance with any of these.

Any stringed toy, even an interactive one, should be used only when you are present. Put it away, out of the cat's reach, when the game is over.

Plastic bags should be kept away from your kitty because of the risk of suffocation. Plastic bags with handles pose an added risk of strangulation.

Aluminum foil is dangerous if swallowed. Don't start the practice of wadding up aluminum foil into a ball for your cat to play with. Some owners create aluminum foil balls from foil that had been wrapped around food, so there is an irresistible smell on the ball. That's just asking for trouble because it'll be hard for the cat to resist chewing off pieces of the foil.

How to Tell If Your Cats Are Playing or Fighting

Sometimes it's hard to tell the difference, but here are a few general guidelines:

- When cats are *playing*, one or both may hiss once or twice, but if they hiss several times, they're more likely engaged in a *fight*.

- Cats who *play* together usually take turns in the offensive and defensive postures. When they're *fighting*, there's usually no role reversal—one cat remains offensively aggressive and the other becomes defensive.

- There should be no yowling or screaming in *play*.

- No cat gets hurt during *play* (unless it's accidental). *Fighting* cats may give or receive a scratch or bite wound.

- When *play* is over, the cats should act normal and not avoid each other. After a *fight*, one or both of the cats often stay out of the other's way or appear afraid of each other.

- If two cats who aren't normally friendly to each other appear to be engaged in *play*, be careful. There's a good chance that it's actually a *fight*. If you're in doubt, distract them with a noise such as the opening of a can of cat food, the shaking of a box of treats, etc. Keep it positive, though. If they were really *playing*, you don't want to discourage their blossoming friendship.

Misunderstood Intentions

In multicat households, one cat may misread another's playful intentions. Cats don't have a typical play request such as the play bow displayed by dogs. A kitten who was taken away from her littermates too early and didn't engage in social play behavior may be more comfortable with object play. When your other cat, who may be very social and playful, comes over to her and communicates an invitation to play, the kitten may interpret it as a threatening gesture.

If you're raising a litter of kittens, be aware if any of the males play too aggressively. That could cause the females to react by not responding favorably to any play invitations.

Keep Your Camera Ready

I always keep a camera within easy reach because even my geriatric cats will strike poses I want captured forever.

You don't have to have expensive equipment or be a professional photographer to take great pictures of your cat. Almost everything a cat does is photogenic. A few basics and patience will allow you to capture both posed and action shots. Digital cameras and phones have really made life easier for those of us who want to get creative with our pictures or include them in e-mails. They also allow us the freedom to take many pictures at a time and easily discard unwanted ones. If you don't have a digital or cell phone camera, you can still take wonderful pictures with an inexpensive point-and-shoot camera. Cats are great subjects!

Action Shots

Your kitten will be more than happy to provide you with many of these. What you have to be careful about, though, is a poorly timed shot, which can result in a blurry photo of a ball of fur. This usually occurs when you grab the camera and try to center it on your moving cat too quickly. To avoid this, watch your kitten playing through the camera's viewfinder until you have a steady hand.

Try to be aware of the background so the picture doesn't look too busy or the kitten doesn't blend in so much she disappears—for instance, if you're photographing your calico kitten playing with a toy on a patterned, multicolored rug. The pattern of the carpet will compete with the cat's coat and the toy will also disappear against the busy background.

Posed Shots

It's best to start with a relaxed kitten, so don't decide that you want a still shot when your kitty's revved up to play.

If you want to try for a more formal shot with a solid background, you can use a sheet or buy rolled paper at an art supply store. Choose a color that will highlight your cat's coat color. If you want to highlight the cat's eyes, choose that same color for your background.

Your cat probably won't want to just sit in front of the background. Place a basket, a pillow, or some other object for her to sit near if she needs a little security initially. If you're photographing a kitten, set your props up in front of the background. If you're using a basket with a toy in it, when she starts playing in the basket, make an enticing sound. That millisecond when she pops her head out of the basket and looks in your direction is the moment to snap the picture. Don't overdo the sound—you're not trying for a look of terror.

To photograph an adult cat more formally, avoid a straight-on pose. Stand a little to the side so your cat's body will show, that way she won't look like just a head with legs. Entice her with a toy or a sound and you'll get her ears to prick forward and eyes to look alert. If you want her focus off to the side, dangle a peacock feather to your right or left. Don't make the feather movements too exciting or your cat will run right toward you in anticipation of playtime. You might want to use a tripod to keep the camera steady, so you'll have one hand free. If you use an assistant, make sure it's someone your cat is comfortable with.

To avoid red-eye in pictures, don't shoot directly at the cat's eye level—shoot from a little above. If all else fails, there's always Photoshop.

Don't try too hard for avant-garde camera angles or you may wind up with a photo of a cat who looks very out of proportion.

Be Patient

Don't ever force your cat to sit still while you try to pose her. Your best photos will most likely be the candid shots anyway. If you want to attempt a posed shot, do it when your cat isn't in play mode. After she has eaten and is relaxed is the best time. If things aren't working, let her go. Leave the background set up, your camera nearby, and before you know it, you'll find your kitty stretched out right where you want her.

My digital camera is handy and I frequently snap pictures of my cats to keep them used to the experience. This way, they remain less concerned about the flash and what I'm doing so I stand a better chance of getting the shot I want.

7

Sour Puss

Solving Common Behavior Problems,
Serious Problems, and the Ones You're Too
Embarrassed to Tell Anyone About

How Do Behavior Problems Begin?

We ask so much of our cats. We leave them alone all day with nothing to do, thrust unwanted companions on them, lay down ever-changing rules and force them to adjust their natural schedules to coincide with our more convenient ones. We don't walk them and then insist they use a litter box that often falls way below their standard of cleanliness. We're positive that the motivation behind their furniture scratching is willful destruction, because there's a scratching post somewhere in the house—oh yeah, it's in the laundry room (so what if that's also where the dog sleeps). We spank our cats and then don't understand why they're defensive. We yell at them and then act surprised when they no longer want to be around us. We rub their noses in their messes because somebody somewhere told us that's the way to train a pet. We punish our cats when we come home from work at night for something they did earlier in the day—it doesn't matter that the cat is now peacefully sleeping in his bed—he'll *know* why he's being yelled at. We play with our cats when it's convenient but push them away if they playfully bat at the newspaper we're try to read. We treat our cats as children, adults, friends, enemies, confidants, even dogs—but not often enough as *cats*. Finally, we think our cats should *know better*, when in reality, *we're* the ones who should.

We create most of the behavior problems in our cats. There are certainly other contributing factors toward behavior problems and disorders, such as medical conditions, lack of socialization, history of abuse or neglect, but for the most part, we're the ones who mess things up.

Your relationship with your cat is just that—a *relationship*. As with any relationship, you have to communicate with each other and understand one another's needs. People too often take on the responsibility of becoming cat owners, then expect the cat to do all of the work: suppress his natural behaviors and then magically understand the wishes of a giant who is speaking a language he can't possibly make out.

You know by now that it's your responsibility as a cat owner to educate yourself about this beautiful creature you've chosen to spend your life with. Learn to interpret what your cat is communicating, what his needs are, and finally, if you hope to solve a behavior problem, learn to understand his behavior. Many of the behaviors we label as "bad" are actually normal in the cat's world. Animals aren't stupid. They don't repeat behaviors unless they're serving a function. A behavior that's normal for a cat may be unacceptable to us, but to view it as bad or abnormal will prevent you from finding a solution and could actually damage the relationship between you and your cat. You need to understand the motivation behind the behavior—the "payoff," so to speak. It's only when you look at the behavior from the cat's point of view that you'll be able to see what function it serves and find a solution that works for both of you. The owner's misreading the cat's motivation, and misunderstanding what he's communicating, is most often why he'll grant the cat a one-way ride to the local animal shelter. Behavior problems kill more cats than any disease ever will.

So what triggers behavior problems? For cats, the cause can be as seemingly minor as a change in routine. A cat is a creature of habit, so when his daily rituals are disturbed, it can cause anxiety. We humans are quick to make changes without realizing how a sudden shift in the comfort of familiarity might affect our cats. Boredom can also cause problems as the cat searches for something, anything, to do. Cats are predators, so it's natural for them to seek stimulation throughout the day, and all too often, we don't provide that. If a cat feels his territory is being threatened, that can spark a behavioral change. So even though you may bring home a companion animal for your cat with the best intentions, the method of introduction, if done incorrectly, may trigger major stress and territorial issues. There are also numerous medical conditions that can lead to behavior problems and, all-too-often, these go undetected because some owners are so convinced a problem is strictly behavioral that they don't get the cat to the veterinarian for a proper diagnosis. Improper early socialization, abuse, and inappropriate punishment are also on the list of potential causes of behavior problems. The point is, it's up to you to identify the motivation or cause of the behavior you don't want.

A wonderful thing happens when you stop looking at your world through your eyes and start seeing it from your cat's view—not only do you stand an excellent chance of solving the current behavior problem, but you'll probably be able to head off future ones as well.

Here are some common training mistakes made by owners:

- misreading motivation

- inconsistency

- unfair changes (for example, now that you've bought a new couch, the cat is punished when he attempts to get into his usual spot there)

- punishment

- reinforcing unwanted behavior (for example, your cat meows at five a.m. so to quiet him you go to the kitchen and put food in his bowl)

- no training whatsoever

Changing Undesirable Behavior

If you're attempting to change a long-standing problem, stop whatever it is you've been doing in the past, because it obviously hasn't worked so far. Don't force your cat to do or *not* do something. Don't go head-to-head with your cat in a battle of wills. Step back, take a deep breath, make yourself a cup of tea, and I'll help you plan out a new strategy.

As you go through this chapter, remember the *think like a cat* perspective:

- determine the motivation or cause

- create an alternative that is of equal or increased value to the cat

- reward the cat for choosing the alternative

Litter Box Problems

This is such a complex subject that it needs a chapter all its own. Refer to Chapter 8.

Destructive Scratching

Another big one. See Chapter 9.

Destructive Chewing

Pica

This is defined as the eating of nonfood items. With dogs, the targets chosen for ingesting are typically feces, rocks, grass, dirt, small toys, or other small objects. Cats, though, usually stick to clothing, blankets, plants, and plastic bags. Although you can't imagine why a sweater or blanket would seem appetizing, wool-chewing cats can turn a pair of socks into swiss cheese in a matter of minutes.

The theory about fabric-related pica is that some cats crave fiber and some breeds appear to have a higher need than others. Siamese cats, for example, are often wool chewers. It may also be an anxiety-relieving behavior.

To solve this problem, first remove all temptation. That means no more tossing your socks on the floor, leaving the bed unmade, or the plastic grocery bags on the floor. Keep sweater drawers closed and don't store any sweaters on open closet shelves within reach of a wool-chewing kitty.

If you're feeding your cat wet food, consult with your veterinarian about increasing the fiber by adding about a half-teaspoon of canned pumpkin (the exact amount will depend on your cat's weight, age, and other specific factors). The pumpkin seems to work well and cats generally don't mind the taste at all. Be sure and start slowly, though, and add just a little at a time when you're increasing fiber in the diet. Before making any dietary changes be sure to check with your veterinarian.

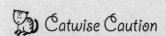 Catwise Caution

The desire to ingest nonfood items can have an underlying medical condition. Have your cat examined by the veterinarian.

Grow some kitty greens for your cat (see section on Plant Attack). Make sure there's always a supply of kitty greens, so your cat won't go looking for an afternoon snack in the form of your daughter's brand new wool sweater or your favorite floor plant.

Use environmental enrichment to provide alternate means of anxiety relief. Food dispensing toys will help redirect the cat's energy while providing an appropriate reward (food) for his hard work. If the pica is due to separation anxiety, the environmental enrichment can help divert your cat's focus.

Interactive playtime and a predictable daily routine helps as well. Be consistent and reliable with meal schedules as well. Consistency provides comfort.

If there is hostility in a multicat home, that situation must be addressed to control the anxiety level in the cat.

Wool Sucking

Wool sucking may be the result of abrupt or early weaning but it can also be an attention-seeking behavior, a play behavior, anxiety relief, or the result of boredom. The kitten continues the nursing-like behavior on clothing, shoelaces, blankets, etc. Some cats have specifically targeted types of fabric.

Have your cat checked by the veterinarian to rule out underlying medical causes such as dental problems, gastrointestinal issues, etc. The best way to stop the cat's behavior is by creating a more enriched environment with lots of opportunities for appropriate playtime and foraging. Address causes of anxiety (such as intercat issues), remove access to targeted items, and possibly increase dietary fiber (talk with your veterinarian). You can provide access to safe chewable items such as rawhide and dental chews.

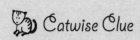

Catwise Clue

Siamese and Burmese cats top the list when it comes to wool sucking behavior.

Plant Attack

As you know, most plants are deadly or at least highly toxic to cats. For a list of dangerous plants refer to the ASPCA Web site (see Resource Guide).

Many cats enjoy munching on greenery and you can provide a safe alternative by purchasing one of the many kitty grass kits available in pet supply stores and online. Keep it in a convenient location. Your cat will prefer this grass over your nasty-tasting ferns. Follow the setup directions, water as indicated and in no time you'll have lush greenery that's safe for your cat's afternoon snack. The only thing I don't like about many of the kits is that they come in lightweight containers. If your cat pulls on the grass with his teeth instead of just munching, the container moves around. I usually transfer the contents to a heavier pot such as a terra cotta or ceramic one. You can even make your own kitty greens by sprinkling rye or oat seeds in a pot of soil. Be sure and use sterilized potting soil. Cover lightly with a ¼" layer of soil, water well, and allow to drain. Mist daily with a plant sprayer so you don't disrupt the tiny seeds. Keep the pot in a dark, warm place until you see the little green heads peek out of the soil, then place it in a sunny location. As soon as the grass is tall enough, place it in a location convenient for your cat.

You can also buy patches of wheat grass at your local organic food store.

Self-Chewing and Overgrooming

Some cats groom excessively to the point of creating thinning hair or actual bald spots. A few cats not only groom but begin chewing on themselves to the point of creating sores. Some cats don't chew, but lick repeatedly until they create bald areas. Sometimes the cat even pulls the hair out.

If your cat is engaging in this behavior, he needs to be examined by your veterinarian to make sure there isn't an underlying medical condition causing the problem. Even a flea infestation can cause some cats to chew themselves raw. Hyperthyroidism is another common reason for overgrooming. A cat in pain may repeatedly lick or chew at that area on his body in an attempt to relieve the discomfort. There are many medical reasons for self-chewing and over-grooming and before you assume it's behavioral, your cat needs to get checked out medically.

If it turns out that the problem is behavioral, the trigger must be identified. The chewing or overgrooming is an anxiety-relieving mechanism. Whatever is causing the cat to feel so anxious is the real problem. It could be anything from a change in your work schedule to the addition of a companion animal, living in an ongoing stressful environment, the death of a companion, or moving to an unfamiliar environment—*anything* can cause this behavior. The stress builds up to such a point that the cat must do *something* to relieve his anxiety. The medical term for this is *psychogenic alopecia*.

Provide as much stability, consistency, and positive activity for your cat as possible. Make sure his environment is as stress-free as you can. If the dog barks at him or relentlessly pursues him, make sure he has access to safe areas where he can get away from other household pets. The area in which he eats should be stress-free. When you place his food bowl on the floor, if you notice that he's constantly looking around, frequently stopping to check out his surroundings, then you should move his feeding station to an area that is more secure for him. Try feeding him on top of a cat tree or in a quieter room.

As much as you want to hold and cuddle him, he needs to feel in control of his environment, so interactive playtime should be a regular part of his daily schedule. Two or three sessions a day will not only help dispel his anxiety, they'll build up his positive associations with his environment. Leave activity toys and puzzle feeders out when you're not at home so he has opportunities to find rewards and engage in anxiety-relieving behavior that's healthy. Make sure he has enough distractions when you're not around. A cat tree in a window, so he can watch the birds, will help him pass the time as well.

Pheromone therapy may help in the environment. Use the Comfort Zone with Feliway diffuser in the area where the cat spends the most time.

Psychogenic alopecia usually requires the use of medication in conjunction with behavior modification. Your veterinarian will advise you on whether anti-anxiety medication is required. He/she may also refer you to a veterinary behaviorist, certified applied behaviorist, or certified animal behavior consultant in order to establish the most effective behavior modification plan for your cat's specific set of circumstances.

Trash Can Invaders

There are a few cats who, no matter what you feed them, insist on using the self-serve buffet found in the kitchen trash can. Your cat may dine on the most expensive cat food money can buy and then later that evening rummage through discarded vegetable peelings and used napkins to lick the aluminum foil you used to cover the roast.

There may be a medical reason behind your cat's behavior that needs to be addressed. If your cat is dumpster diving, consult your veterinarian. There may be a dietary adjustment that needs to be made or there may be an underlying medical problem.

You could try booby traps and elaborate deterrents, but the first line of defense when it comes to feline dumpster diving is to have a trash can with a lid or keep the can in a closed cabinet. The more you booby-trap the can, the more trouble it becomes for you to throw something in it. If you have a cabinet that doesn't latch, attach a magnetic closure to it or install a baby-proof latch. I've come across many Houdini kitties who have learned to paw open the cabinet door, and the baby-proof latches are the only things that stop them. Hopefully, you won't have to go to that extreme to protect your cat, but keeping kitty safe is what's most important.

Excessive Vocalization

If the excessive vocalization is a change from your cat's normal behavior, be sure and consult your veterinarian.

If you have a Siamese, then you might as well skip over this section because he's not going to change. Siamese cats love to provide running narratives on their daily activities and aren't shy about voicing opinions. Know this and accept it.

Other cats may become vocal for many reasons. Mostly, it's a surefire way of getting your attention. When the less subtle method of staring you down, walking back and forth in front of your computer monitor, or sitting on your chest doesn't do the trick, nonstop meows usually work. The odds are that because he's born with patience, determination, and unrelenting persistence, you'll eventually cave in and give him what he wants. It may take five minutes of meowing, but he now knows that as long as he doesn't give up, you'll give in. Whether it's to be let outside, fed, or petted, he knows that you know the only way to quiet him is to surrender. Of course, once you give in, you've just shown him that his meowing has successfully trained you. How do you change this behavior? Ignore his vocal demands. Don't reward negative behavior. Even if you hold out for twenty minutes and then in desperation finally get up and put some food in his bowl he'll remember that persistent meowing works. It took an inordinate amount of time, but it worked.

Instead of rewarding his negative behavior, when you notice your cat may be about to enter into his meowing phase, click and reward him with a treat when he's silent. Keep some treats in your pocket or get a trainer's treat bag that attaches to your belt. This way you'll be prepared to train at any time. When kitty meows, turn away. When he's silent, click and treat.

One reason your cat may be meowing is because he isn't sufficiently stimulated. Make sure you are engaging in daily interactive play sessions and have incorporated environmental enrichment techniques.

An older cat may yowl or meow at night after everyone has gone to bed or when the house is very quiet and there's no activity. As he walks through the darkened house, his declining senses may cause him to become disoriented. Have him checked by the veterinarian to make sure he's not in pain or experiencing age-related cognitive dysfunction. When you hear your older cat yowling or meowing at night, call out to him so he can find you. If it begins to happen on a regular basis or if he seems to be disoriented, confine him to your room at night. For more on helping older cats, refer to Chapter 16.

The Fearful Cat

Fear can be the result of inadequate socialization, a traumatic past experience, pain, illness, improper handling, and exposure to unfamiliar people or things. Fearful behavior may also be inherited.

Cats hate sudden change and prefer the security of their familiar territory. It's only natural then that new people, places, or things may cause certain cats to be fearful. One common situation a cat may fear is having strangers come into the house. As soon as the doorbell rings, he may take off for the farthest closet. Here's an exercise you can do: Ask a friend to come over (make sure it's not someone your cat already hates). Have him or her sit in the living room while you go into the room where your cat is hiding. With total nonchalance, sit down on the floor and casually conduct an interactive playtime (key word: *casually*). Don't try to force your hiding cat out, just lightly play with a toy, gently moving it around a small area of the room. Use your voice in a calm, comforting way. The effect is for your cat to start picking up the signal from you that this is no big deal. So what if there's a guest in the house—who cares? You want to play with your cat. If you're relaxed and make no attempts to force your cat out of his comfort zone, he'll start to relax too. He may not actually play or even venture out of the closet the first few times, but he will begin to relax.

If you've been clicker training you can use a target stick (it can be a chop stick, the eraser on a pencil, a true target stick, or even a thin wooden dowel), and if kitty comes out from under the bed to sniff the stick, click and reward.

After several minutes with your cat, leave him alone. But instead of going back to your guest, sit on the floor in the hallway. Engage in a quiet conversation with the guest but dangle the toy gently to get your cat's attention. Although your cat may not come out of the room, he may risk leaving the closet or coming out from under the bed. He may even come as far as the hallway. If clicker training, click and reward for any positive behavior,

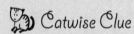 Catwise Clue

A fearful cat often tries to make himself look as small as possible. He may crouch down, lower his head, tuck his feet underneath, and wrap his tail closely around. Ears will be flattened back in preparation for a defensively aggressive move. The cat may pant or drool. You also may notice that he is shedding more hair than normal. If there's an opportunity for escape, the cat will take it.

HELPING THE FEARFUL CAT

- Don't force him to be in the room with you
- Make sure he has access to a hiding place
- Let him determine how close he wants to get
- Use gentle interactive playtime or treats for distraction
- Keep your tone of voice soothing
- Reward any signs of relaxed body posture or interaction

- Do daily training where you gradually expose your cat to a particular stimulus at a level significantly lower than what would cause a reaction
- Gradually increase the level of the stimulus
- Take several deep breaths to relax yourself
- Introduce changes in a cat's life gradually

however small. If he'll play, engage in a session but don't try to take it any farther into the living room. Have your guest leave, and then reward your cat again. Ask your friend to return again the next day and repeat the same exercise. Keep up these visits and move, inch by inch, closer to the living room. You can also alternate the friends who come over, just be sure that each person chosen is someone your cat doesn't already have a negative association with and that the person is on the calm, quiet side. Eventually your cat should be calm enough that he'll make an appearance as you sit in the living room—however brief. If he can be distracted with playtime, let your guest conduct a game with him. The guest must remain in his or her seat, though, so as not to frighten the cat. Remember to give your friend a treat too (like lunch) for being such a good sport.

This slow and steady method helps a cat get over whatever frightens him. Conduct light play sessions. Let your cat dictate the pace, though. If he only wants to come as far as the hallway, then be content with that for now. Eventually, as he sees there's no threat, he'll inch closer. Your behavior throughout should be casual and relaxed. Very often, in an attempt to comfort a cat, the owner tries to hold the struggling animal. The owner's voice often sounds worried, and the cat interprets this as confirmation that there really is something to fear. He needs to know there's a secure place for him besides the back of the closet.

Is Your Cat Stressing Out?

Any cat in a stressful situation long enough can change from being healthy and sociable to nervous and fearful.

What would a cat possibly have to stress about? Don't they just sleep, eat, and play the day away? I wish life for cats did just involve sleeping, eating, receiving affection, and playing, but unfortunately they encounter many negative things that can have an impact. We often forget how much security a cat finds in familiarity. Therefore, change—however minor we consider it—can be very upsetting for some cats.

First, let's think about the things that would stress *us*. A death in the family, a divorce, a move to a new home, a move to a new city, illness, a natural disaster, even getting married can certainly be stressful (after all, a wedding wouldn't be a wedding without a truckload of stress). These affect your cat as well. Plus, he gets a double whammy because for him it comes out of the blue. One day he's sleeping in his favorite spot and the next thing he knows, everything's being boxed up around him. A few days later he's whisked off to an unfamiliar place.

BIG-TIME CAUSES OF STRESS

- death in the family
- marriage
- new baby
- divorce
- a move to a new home
- renovations
- natural disasters
- house fires
- abuse
- neglect
- loneliness
- illness or injury

Okay, so you're not surprised that those things could stress your cat. What you may not realize, though, is that seemingly little and insignificant things can cause stress as well. Some cats negatively react to *any* change. The box on page 125 lists situations we might overlook in terms of how they affect a cat.

In order to help a stressed-out cat, you must identify the cause of the stress and if possible, eliminate or modify it. The best method, if you know something potentially stressful is coming up, is to prepare your cat gradually for it. Whether

CAUSES OF STRESS OWNERS
OFTEN OVERLOOK

- dirty litter box
- change in litter type
- change in food
- food and litter in close proximity
- litter box in a noisy location
- children
- holidays
- travel
- change in your work schedule
- boarding

- buying new furniture or rearranging
- new carpet
- addition of another pet
- ongoing appearance of another cat in yard
- not having access to hiding places
- ongoing loud noises
- rough or improper handling
- punishment

it's a small thing such as a change in food or a big, big one such as a move to a new house, *prepare* him ahead of time. Introduce changes gradually. For example, when you want to change the cat's food, mix a little of the new food into the current diet and increase the amount of the new food over the course of a week. If the change is a move to a new house, you should pack in stages, keep calm, and when you get to the new home, put your cat in one room. Let him get his bearings gradually (see Chapter 14). The bigger the change, the more prep time needed. When there is an unexpected crisis, such as a death in the family (human, feline, or canine), realize that your cat is experiencing the same emotions as you. Provide lots of playtime, keep his schedule as normal as possible, and monitor his eating and litter box habits. At these times he needs as much consistency and normalcy from you as possible.

Because playtime puts cats in a more confident frame of mind and creates positive associations with their surroundings, I use interactive toys to keep them distracted from the negative situation and focused on something rewarding.

Make sure the cat has access to a security zone (preferably several)—meaning safe hiding places away from noise, other pets, or people.

Incorporate environmental enrichment to keep your cat occupied when you can't be around.

There are bound to be situations that arise that will be stressful and some will be unexpected so you won't have the luxury of being able to prepare your cat in advance. There will also be many situations where you'll have enough advanced warning, so use these opportunities to ease your kitty through the adjustment. Happy kitty = happy owner. Stressed kitty = stressed owner. Keep the odds in your favor.

The Depressed Kitty

Sophia was a big (but not fat), beautiful mixed-breed cat. Her gray and white coat was lush, shiny, and kept meticulously clean by this very fastidious feline. She was a cat who loved to be in the center of things and was always in the lap of one of her owners, Patricia or Marc. Sophia was doted on, played with, and truly loved. Because she had been adopted as a kitten, this was the only life Sophia knew and there was no reason for anyone to think it would change anytime soon, but it did. When Sophia was seven, Marc had a heart attack at work. He was rushed to the hospital and died a few hours later.

Patricia and Marc had been married for twenty years. Patricia came home from the hospital that night, obviously still in shock. Over the next few days she began the long and painful process of grieving for her beloved husband. Friends and family remained by her side offering help. She was watched over and cared for.

Sophia, who didn't understand any part of what was happening, began a slow descent into depression. From her point of view, one of her owners had suddenly vanished and her other owner was acting totally out of character. Sophia would attempt to climb into Patricia's lap, but one of the visiting family members would shoo her off. There were lots of strangers in the house, but no one paid any attention to Sophia. In an effort to help Patricia, a neighbor was coming over to feed the cat twice a day and take care of the litter box. Sophia's attempt at contact, though, was ignored. Everything in her world had been turned upside down. Eventually she began to withdraw. She kept to herself, coming out from under the bed only to eat and use the litter box. She became neglectful of her personal hygiene. Her coat started looking messy and dirty. She began using the litter box sporadically, choosing instead to eliminate in the corners of the closets. Food lost its appeal. Sleep became the focus of Sophia's life. As months went by, Sophia's deteriorating appearance and behavior concerned a guilt-ridden Patricia, so she called the veterinarian. A consultation with me was recommended after the initial physical examination and diagnostic tests.

When I arrived at the house, the cat I saw was a depressed, thin, dirty cat who in no way resembled the robust, social beauty she had been based on pictures and a behavioral history received from the client. Cats get depressed over many of the same things we do: death, divorce, illness, loneliness, you name it. How do you recognize depression? Look for changes in your cat's normal routine, especially if there has been a crisis in the household. Keep in mind that the crisis may have happened some time ago. By the time some owners recognize the outward signs of depression, the internal deterioration is already taking place. Note any changes in personality, activity level, appetite, grooming habits, litter box habits, sleep patterns, or overall appearance. You know your cat—if something seems amiss, it probably is.

After you've consulted with your veterinarian, begin to bring the spark back in your cat's life. Use lots of interactive playtime. Incorporate environmental enrichment. If there was ever a time when the fun factor has to be improved, it's now. Add cat tunnels, set out puzzle feeders, and put a cat tree by the window. Play a cat-entertainment DVD on the TV, hide some toys in fun places, install a couple cat shelves on the wall, set up some cozy hideaways, and so on. Use your imagination to improve your cat's environment. If the cat is home alone for long periods, have a friend or pet sitter come over for daily play sessions if needed. If you haven't been clicker training, this would be a good time to start working with your cat. Also, if kitty has been neglecting grooming duties, help him out with daily brushing. The massage of the brush will feel great. Don't forget to break out the catnip occasionally too.

If your cat's depression is because you have changed your lifestyle and you're gone for long periods and the environmental enrichment alone isn't enough, consider getting him a companion cat.

Bottom line—make life fun again!

> ### 🐾 Catwise Caution
>
> **Depression is a serious issue and can impact your cat's health. Pay close attention to your cat's eating and litter box habits. If kitty stops eating, contact your veterinarian immediately. It's dangerous for a cat to go without eating for more than twenty-four hours. In some cases, the veterinarian may prescribe psychotropic medication for the cat. Stay in close contact with your veterinarian.**

Attention-Seeking Behavior

A cat may exhibit attention-seeking behavior when he doesn't receive a consistent level of stimulation. In a home with inadequate environmental enrichment, the owner often becomes the only source of activity. Even in a home where the owner engages in lots of playtime with the cat, if he hasn't been taught how to occupy himself with solo activity toys, he may rely strictly on the owner for playtime opportunities.

A cat may also exhibit attention-seeking behavior if he's unsure of what the owner is expecting of him in terms of acceptable behavior.

Typical attention-seeking behavior may include: following the owner around, pawing at the owner, jumping up onto a surface to be closer to the owner, weaving in and out of the owner's legs, vocalizing, biting, and inappropriate play behavior toward the owner.

Treatment involves not giving any attention to the cat when he's displaying this behavior. Even saying "no" or pushing the cat away may be interpreted as receiving the much-wanted attention. *Extinction* is the method that works and that involves the cat realizing that his behavior gets him nothing—no attention, no fun, no interaction, no payoff.

Do not engage in any physical punishment for attention-seeking behavior because in addition to being inhumane, it also provides attention—however painful, it's still attention.

Reward the cat when he isn't engaging in attention-seeking behavior. So if kitty paws at you or vocalizes when he wants attention, ignore that behavior but then pet him or interact with him when he's being quiet.

Maintain a routine of playtime, interaction, petting, etc., so the cat knows when to expect acknowledgment and playtime. The more consistent with every aspect of life as possible, from playtime to mealtime, the less anxious he'll be. Less anxiety leads to less of a need to solicit your attention at the wrong times.

Noisy Nightly Adventures

You're in bed and just about to drift off to sleep when suddenly there's a *crash* in the other room. You sit bolt upright in bed, convinced you also heard the sound of a horse galloping down the hall. What in the world is going on? You get out of bed, switch on the light, and walk out into the hallway. Standing there, looking as innocent as can be, is your cat. On the floor next to him are the dozen roses you received from your husband that day. Also on the floor is the crystal vase that once held the roses. Of course, now it's in several pieces in a puddle of water. Your cat blinks his eyes, flicks the tip of his tail, and goes off down the hall. What sounded like a horse to you was merely your eight-pound cat revving up for a night of fun.

While some of us are lucky enough to have cats who graciously agree to adjust to our schedules, others of us aren't so fortunate. In order to ensure sleep for yourself, you'll need to add a few things to your prebedtime preparations.

If you feed your cat on a schedule, divide his meals up so you can save a final portion for this prebedtime behavior modification session. Before you go to bed, and I mean *just* before, conduct a ten- to fifteen-minute interactive play session with him and then feed him his last meal portion for the day. The exercise will release his built-up energy and then the meal will most likely lead him to sleep afterward. Wind the action down at the end of the game so your cat is left relaxed. Don't make the mistake of abruptly ending the game and then having to deal with a cat who feels he still has lots of extra energy to burn. Even with the wind-down and the meal, if he still insists on using your stomach for a trampoline as you try to sleep, put out some puzzle feeders or activity toys for him to discover in the evening. Put noisy toys in a more distant area of the house so the noise doesn't wake you up.

If you can, leave curtains open in a window. Put a cat tree there so your cat can look out at the nightly activity. I keep the shutters open in the sitting room off my bedroom because my backyard is private. My cats love to sit on the cat tree and keep track of the insects and frogs conducting their nightly business.

You can also have a special set of toys and puzzle feeders that are only brought out at night. That will make them seem extra special to your cat.

Be consistent in your nightly prebedtime routine. It should be stimulating and satisfying so your cat gets to release his energy and then feel relaxed when it's done.

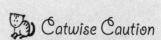 Catwise Caution

Don't conduct your nighttime interactive play session on your bed. You don't want your cat to get the idea that the bed is a landing strip for his pounces, leaps, and sneak attacks.

Paw Prints on the Counter

The house is quiet. No one seems to be doing anything interesting so the cat walks into the kitchen and looks around. Nothing much happening on ground level, so in one graceful leap, he lands on the counter. Suddenly, out of nowhere comes his owner, yelling, charging the cat, aiming a squirt bottle in his direction, and then blasting water in his face. Panic stricken, the soaking wet cat scrambles off the counter, runs through the house, and dives under the bed. There, the terrified cat stays for the next hour. His owner replaces the squirt bottle on the shelf and goes back to watching TV in the den. What the owner is thinking: *I'll train that cat yet!* What the cat is thinking: *My owner is a lunatic!* The bottom line: this training method stinks.

The best way to keep your cat off the counter, table, or whatever furniture you decide should be forbidden is to remember your *think like a cat* technique. Figure out what he likes about the counter, supply an alternative, and reward him for choosing the better option. We're also going to add a little incentive here by making the counter unappealing. Remember to be consistent about which areas are to be off limits to kitty. Don't confuse him by allowing him to be on the table or counter as long as you're not eating, but forbid him when there's food. He won't understand the difference, and it's not fair to expect him to.

Why your cat likes the counter is important information you need in order to create an appropriate and appealing alternative.

- Does he want food up there? If so, then set up puzzle feeders to provide a more acceptable alternative. Additionally, keep all food put away and not left out on the counter after meals.

- Are there plants up there to chew on or other interesting potential play objects? Remove plants from counters and keep small objects put away in drawers and cabinets.

- Does he want to look out the window? Place a window perch or cat tree near another window that offers an interesting view of outdoor activities. When I'm on consultations I often see cats on the kitchen counters in homes where there are no other elevated options. I've seen houses where tables were cluttered with so many items that there isn't one free inch of space for a cat to sit on in order to look out the window. In many of these houses there isn't a cat tree or window perch to be found.

- Is the counter a preferred napping area? Perhaps he loves being able to stretch out on the counter. Time to create an alternate elevated resting area that's large enough for him—a cat tree with large perches, perhaps, or even a large pet bed or towel spread out on a table near a window.

- Does kitty feel safer on the counter? Create alternative elevated places. Additionally, if there's hostility between other pets, work on repairing those relationships. Your cats need to feel they have safe places within your house. If kitty feels he needs to be on the counter to be safe, it probably is because he wants the maximum visual warning time to see if an opponent is approaching along with the reassurance that no one can sneak up behind him. Some cats seek the safety of the counter to get away from children or other family members as well. If so, it's time to work on improving the relationship to allow kitty to feel calm in addition to creating alternate elevated areas.

- Does kitty want your attention? Incorporate regularly scheduled interactive play sessions and set up solo activities for environmental enrichment. If he's jumping on the counter to engage with you, even the very act of you picking him up to remove him can be the interaction he wants. I've even seen owners who shoo their cats off the counters by picking them up, talking to them, and petting them as they place them back down on the floor. What kind of message do you think that sends to the cat? Jumping on the counter = loving attention from my owner.

My method is to use sheets of plastic carpet protectors. You can buy a small roll of this from your local home improvement store. Get the kind with little pointy feet on the underside. Cut the plastic into pieces so they'll fit on and cover the counter, yet be easy to stack and store when not needed. Place the plastic with the feet side up, all along the counter. This makes the counter surface unappealing and the first time your cat jumps up there he'll immediately want to jump back down. Keep the plastic pieces on the counter, or on any surface where you don't want the cat to lounge. Remove them only when you need access to the surface, then immediately replace them when you're through. Eventually your cat will decide that the counter isn't such a great place after all. Don't be too quick to remove the plastic permanently. A few more days of inconvenience are worth it to end up with a well-trained and happy cat. When you do begin removing the plastic pieces, do it one at a time over the course of several days. Keep the pieces closest to the front edge of the counter in place the longest so your cat will think all of them are still in place.

If you find your cat on a surface that doesn't have the plastic pieces on it, and it's an area where you don't want your cat lounging, just pick him up, say "no" (don't yell or scream, just say "no"), and place him on the floor. Don't knock him off the furniture or drop him on the floor. On the other hand, don't pick him up and kiss or cuddle him before placing him on the floor. If your cat jumps on the surface as an attention-seeking behavior, don't make eye contact with him as you put him back down on the floor. Just place him down and walk away. He'll eventually see that being on the counter leads to you walking away from him.

Biting and Scratching During Play

I can usually identify the owner of a new kitten just by looking at his or her scratched-up hands. Those ten fingers make such convenient and enticing toys when you're trying to get a kitten's attention. However, the message the kitten receives is that biting skin is acceptable. You won't like that very much as your cute little kitten grows. From the very beginning, use the interactive toys for playtime so there's never any confusion. As with all the other aspects of training, consistency is important. If one family member lets the kitten bite, then he'll never be trained.

What to do if your kitten accidentally bites you during play: Say a high-pitched "ouch" or other sound to startle him to let him know he has hurt you and to inform him that this isn't part of the game. If his teeth are still in contact with your hand, don't pull away. This is important because if you do pull away from him, he'll instinctively bite down harder. He's responding to the movement of prey. Just freeze. If he doesn't let go of your fingers, *gently* push *toward* him which will automatically release you from his grasp. It will also confuse him momentarily. Prey never willingly heads toward the predator, so he'll relax his mouth, loosening his grip. After you've gotten out of his grasp, ignore the kitten for a few seconds. Then, get an interactive toy so you can teach him the appropriate object for biting.

The same approach should be used if the kitten accidentally scratches you in play, because if you pull away, the curve of the nails will cause them to dig in deeper.

Never punish, hit, or scold your kitten for play-biting. The best way for him to learn is to show him that the game stops when he bites an inappropriate object, then redirect him toward an acceptable toy. Don't ever break the "no biting" rule no matter what. If you're in bed wiggling your fingers under the sheet to entice your kitten and he bites you, you'll have set the training process back several steps. Don't send mixed messages.

Charging the Door

Whether or not your cat is allowed outdoors, you certainly don't want him charging past you as you're opening the door.

You should never greet or pet your cat right at the front door (or whatever door you use to enter and exit). If you call to your kitty the moment you walk in the door, he may begin to wait there as the time of your arrival grows closer. The sound of your key in the lock could be his cue to slip through as you open the door. Instead of greeting your cat right at the door, walk over to a spot a few feet inside the entrance and make that the official greeting area. Ignore him until you get to that spot. If you do this repeatedly, he may begin to wait for you closer to that inside spot rather than at the door.

To prevent your cat from running out the door when you're trying to *leave* the house, say your good-bye to him in a specific spot (such as at his cat tree). You could place a treat-filled activity toy there as you are going so he'll have something with which to occupy himself. If your cat isn't food-motivated at the moment you're going out, toss a toy away from the door.

If all redirection methods fail and your cat keeps charging the door, there is a last resort method to use. Be sure to try the other methods first, though, before using this deterrent technique. Have someone stand outside the door and open it just a little (not enough for your cat to squeeze through). If the cat goes to the door, the person is to squirt him with water or a quick spritz from a can of compressed air to startle him. Remember to NEVER aim for the cat's face. Since the cat will be facing forward, aim for the chest or front legs. It's important that the cat not see the person. You want him to think the door itself is responsible for this experience.

Begging Is Not an Attractive Quality in a Feline

I'm a pretty easygoing person, but I do have a few absolutely unbreakable rules in our house. No animals are to be fed from the table—ever. When I'm invited to a friend's home for dinner, I find it extremely distracting to eat while their dog stares at me, forming little puddles of drool on the floor in front of him. I also don't appreciate it when the cat jumps on the table or claws at my leg.

Feeding your cat from the table often upsets his nutritional balance, creates a finicky eater, contributes to obesity, and poses a health risk because many of the foods we eat are too rich and spicy for cats.

If your cat begins the behavior of begging, give him an activity toy, puzzle feeder, or schedule his meal for when you eat yours.

Aggression

It's a scary subject. You don't want to think about the possibility that your sweet little kitty could turn into a growling, biting, scratching attack cat, but to ignore warning signs could be disastrous for both you and your cat.

A cat who acts aggressively isn't being mean or defiant or taking pleasure in watching you recoil in fear. A cat acts aggressively because he feels he has no other choice. A cat displaying aggressive behavior feels cornered and trapped. It isn't fair to merely categorize a cat as being "aggressive." That blanket label doesn't do anyone any good (cat or human who interacts with him) because *any* animal is potentially capable of aggression under the right circumstances. What would be more productive is to identify what triggers the aggressive behavior so appropriate behavior modification can be done. By understanding more about what triggers aggression and what the different kinds of aggression are, you can, in many cases, avoid it from ever surfacing.

In the wild, aggression is a crucial part of a cat's survival. It enables him to catch prey, defend territory, mate, and keep himself alive. For female cats, maternal aggression helps keep her kittens safe.

Very often there will be warning signs leading up to aggression—such as low volume growling, skin twitching, tail lashing, and paw smacks with sheathed claws. Some cats give several signs, some give only a brief one, and there are some cats who give no warning whatsoever that an attack is about to occur. If you find yourself in a situation where your cat is suddenly and unexpectedly being aggressive, the best thing to do is leave him alone. Any attempt to touch, pet, comfort, or restrain him will only heighten his panic and possibly get you injured. And since aggression is a behavior that can actually be caused by numerous potential medical conditions, consult your veterinarian to make sure the problem doesn't have an underlying medical cause. Even if the problem is medical, your veterinarian may recommend that your cat be seen by a behavior specialist.

The following are some forms of aggression seen in cats:

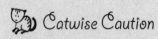 Catwise Caution

Don't overlook the importance of having your cat examined by the veterinarian so an accurate diagnosis can be made. Don't assume a problem is behavioral until your veterinarian has given your cat a clean bill of health.

Intercat Aggression

This may be part of the normal ongoing dynamic between two cats. You may have two cats who have barely tolerated each other for years. Intercat aggression can also occur when one cat comes home from a veterinarian visit and smells different.

The more cat-dense the population in your home, the greater the chances of intercat aggression.

If you add a new cat to the environment, you may find the original cats, who were normally friendly, now display aggressive behavior toward each other.

Intercat aggression can be the result of a territorial threat or can be a case of redirected aggression from a different episode.

Aggression can be subtle and show up as guarding, stalking, and spray-marking, or it can be as overt as hissing, growling, swatting, and outright ambush.

Treating intercat aggression involves finding the underlying cause, making any necessary environmental changes, and incorporating appropriate behavior modification. Look at feeding station placement, number and location of litter boxes, location and number of scratching posts, and sleeping areas. It's important for each cat to have his own safe areas and nonstressful access to resources.

In some cases the cats need to be separated and then reintroduced as if they've never met before. Have them together but at a distance during treat-giving or mealtimes. If one cat ambushes another on sight, use baby gates or a screen door to provide a little bit of a buffer during this exposure, or put one cat on a harness and leash. You can also place them each in carriers (separate carriers, obviously) during the mealtime or treat-giving. In subsequent sessions, move the food bowls closer together as the cats show increased relaxation.

Clicker training will help as well. Click and reward any sign of relaxation or nonaggressive behavior.

If the aggression is severe, contact your veterinarian for a referral to a certified behavior expert.

If there is one cat who is initiating the aggression, place a collar with a bell on him to give the other cat some advance warning of his whereabouts.

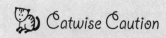 Catwise Caution

If there's any tension in your multicat home, don't add another cat.

Play-Related Aggression

This behavior directed toward a human is not acceptable. Your unsuspecting ankles are usually the victims of this. You walk by the bed and suddenly your feet are ambushed by a set of teeth and razor-sharp claws. It's a hit-and-run at-tack, though, because he's gone in a flash, racing out of the room and down the hall. In most cases, the cat offers an inhibited bite that doesn't break the skin, but sometimes a cat is so aroused that he may draw blood.

It's not unusual for the cat to hide in anticipation of someone (human family member, cat companion, or the family dog) to ambush. The cat may hide behind a door, under the bed, or behind furniture.

An orphaned cat or one who was taken away from his littermates too early may display this type of aggression because he didn't experience the social play period that occurs in kittenhood. This type of aggression can also be the result of a cat who isn't getting enough playtime or stimulation, so he has to go for whatever moving targets he can find. Your feet are usually the most tempting. The cat may not have learned to keep claws retracted during play.

To correct this behavior, use interactive toys and play with your kitty at least two or three times a day. You'll help him get all that energy out while also teaching him what objects are acceptable to bite (the toys) and what aren't (your feet). Rotate his regular toys as well to prevent boredom. Set up activity toys and puzzle feeders for solo playtime to increase environmental stimulation. Make sure there's at least one cat tree or climbing structure for the cat to use.

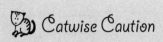 **Catwise Caution**

If your cat tends to attack your feet when you walk, stop all action and merely stand still. It is the movement that attracts him. Additionally, redirect your kitten to an appropriate toy so he learns more acceptable behavior.

Be aware of certain trigger areas where your cat may hide. Keep some solo toys handy so you can toss them away from you in advance of an attack.

Remember to never let your cat bite your fingers in play. If you allow your fingers to be toys, then he'll assume that toes and other body parts are toys as well.

To reduce injury done by claws (should the cat wrap his paws around your ankles), keep his nails trimmed. Never physically punish your cat for this behavior because it could trigger a fear of you as well as encourage more serious aggression.

Fear Aggression

This is displayed by a cat who needs to be left alone if at all possible. A cat who is terrified isn't thinking clearly and will view most attempts at comfort as a threat.

A cat displaying fear aggression will often be crouched low to the ground with pupils dilated and ears flattened. He'll very likely be hissing and growling. His body is usually facing sideways, but his head and front paws often face his "attacker." This position says that his body is ready to get the heck out of Dodge, but his head and front paws are ready to defend himself. Fear aggression is a conflicting emotion for a cat, because he doesn't want to be in that position, but he will fight if necessary. He'll hiss and swat if you approach and if you don't retreat, he'll attack with claws and teeth.

Fear aggression is a behavior many veterinarians see when cats are brought into their clinics. This may be the only time owners ever see such menacing behavior from their cats. If frightened enough, the cat may even urinate and/or defecate. Sometimes anal glands are expressed as well.

If your cat is showing this behavior, leave him alone. If you're at home, leave the room and let him calm down. If you know the source of his fear and can remove it, do so quickly and calmly. Leave your cat alone and don't attempt to interact with him until he resumes normal activity such as eating, using the litter box, or soliciting attention from you. If your cat is injured and showing fear aggression, transport him safety to the veterinarian (see Chapter 18).

If your cat has a tendency to show fear aggression at the veterinary clinic, be sure to transport him in a carrier. He may be calm on the way there but impossible to hold once you walk through the door. If your cat is too aggressive for you to handle while at the veterinarian, let the doctor and staff handle him.

For a cat who tends to display fear aggression at the veterinary clinic, I've found that using the kennel-type carrier works best. You can unscrew the top and allow the cat to stay in the familiar bottom half rather than placing him onto the exam table.

Bring treats with you to help him make positive emotional associations with the clinic staff.

If the fear aggression is due to another animal in the home, you may need to separate them and do a gradual reintroduction. This is basically the same as introducing two new animals to each other. Rather than continuing the ongoing negative cycle, you just stop right where you are and start at the beginning. For the introduction technique, refer to Chapter 11.

Fear aggression related to another human family member should be handled very gradually. A common example is when the cat displays fear aggression toward a new spouse. The behavior modification technique consists of having the family member in question become the *good guy*. The best way to do this?

Positive association, of course. This family member should be the one who offers the meals and treats. He/she should also be the one who conducts the interactive play sessions. One note of caution, though—it's crucial that you go through this at the cat's pace. Allow the cat to remain in his comfort zone. Don't let the family member rush the trust-building process. The cat will be learning from a safe distance that this family member is someone who is not a threat and then, in time, the relationship will begin to grow more comfortable. If the cat is actively displaying aggression, don't try to interact with him. Let him calm down by himself in another room where he feels safe. When he is no longer reactive, open the door and let him out again.

For a cat who shows fear aggression on a regular basis, consult your veterinarian. You may need a referral to a certified behavior specialist if the source of fear can't be identified.

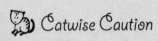

Catwise Caution

Pay attention to the cat's posture and warning signals. Don't attempt to handle a cat displaying aggression.

Petting-Induced Aggression

It seems to come out of the blue. Your cat is lounging on your lap, enjoying your loving strokes his back, when suddenly, seemingly without warning, he turns his head and either sinks his teeth into you or wraps his paws around your hand with claws unsheathed. Let's look back at what happened. Your cat was relaxing on your lap and you were petting him. It seems innocent enough. Then, from your point of view, he suddenly attacked without warning. That's where the communication breakdown occurred, because he more than likely gave you advance warning that he had had enough. The signs that an owner often misses include tail lashing or thumping, skin twitching, or a shifting of body position. Sometimes the cat looks back at you several times, trying to figure out why you're not getting the message. By the time he whips around and scratches or bites, his overstimulation has reached a breaking point. Some cats have low thresholds for how much touch they can tolerate before pleasure turns to discomfort. For some cats the pleasure of being stroked soon becomes overstimulating. Other causes may include sensitivity, pain, or static electricity. The episode can also be triggered by petting a certain area on your cat. It's not unusual for a cat to be relaxed and happy as you stroke behind his head or under his chin, but then become agitated if you stroke too far down his back or tail. Many cats have specific preferences so if your cat is prone to petting-induced aggression, pay attention to how he reacts as your hand moves along different areas of his body.

Become more aware of your cat's body language so you can tell if he's approaching overstimulation. If he starts exhibiting the warning signs, stop petting immediately. Let him just stay where he is so he can calm back down. The best thing is to try not to even reach the warning phase again. If you know your cat starts getting uncomfortable after five minutes of petting, stop after three minutes. Stop before he begins to feel uncomfortable, that way you'll both enjoy this interaction more and he won't associate your hands with something unpleasant. You certainly don't want your cat believing that the only way to stop you from petting him is by inflicting injury on you.

If your cat has no tolerance for so much as one little stroke down the back, be content to just let him sit on your lap or on the sofa next to you. Build trust by not attempting to pet him. Provide a high-value treat reward when the cat sits in your lap. After several sessions, hold your hand out and scratch him once under the chin or on the back of the head. These two spots tend to have the highest tolerance to touch. Some cats don't like having their backs stroked at all, but each cat has their own individual preferences. Do one quick stroke on a desired area, and after that offer a treat. Stroke again if all body language indicates no stress—and then offer another treat.

Pay attention to your cat's cues. I have one cat who adores being petted on the head, under the chin, and around her shoulders. She doesn't like long strokes down the back or any petting near her tail so I avoid that totally. She let me know what she preferred and I paid attention. As a result, she never has to worry that I might break the rules, and I don't have to worry about being scratched.

Rubbing a cat's belly is another common mistake owners make when petting their cats. Rubbing this most vulnerable area often provokes a defensive response where he'll go on his back and expose all four sets of claws. A cat who exposes his belly isn't asking for a tummy rub. If you test this theory, you will always lose.

It's important to do the behavior modification to stop petting-induced aggression, because once the cat becomes confident that biting is the most effective way to stop unwanted interaction he may start using that more frequently.

Redirected Aggression

Redirected aggression occurs when an aroused and reactive cat, unable to gain access to an intended target, directs his aggression toward an unintended target instead. This can happen under various circumstances. For example, your cat may be looking out the window peacefully when suddenly a strange cat appears in the yard. You walk over to see what the fuss is about and as soon as you get close to your cat, he lashes out and attacks you. Although you weren't the intended target of his aggression, in such an excited state he vented on you because he was unable to get to the primary stimulus.

In addition, it's not unusual for a cat prone to redirected aggression to strike out toward the owner when the owner is trying to soothe him during a veterinarian visit, or attempting to pick him up when he's meowing to go outside.

Leave your cat alone until he has calmed down. If the cause is the appearance of an outdoor cat, block your cat's access to that window for a while, even if it means taping an opaque film or poster board over the bottom half of the window. Also, do your best to keep unfamiliar cats out of the yard. Easier said than done, I realize. But if you block viewing access at the windows you may reduce an outdoor intruder cat's interest in coming around. If you set up a bird feeder for your indoor cat's viewing pleasure, you may have to remove it for a while until the outdoor cat moves on to other areas. Another way to keep outdoor animals from coming close to the house or garden is through the use of the ScareCrow Sprinkler by Contech. This is a motion-activated sprinkler to deter unwanted animals from digging in gardens. Just make sure you don't position it in a way that is prone to false triggering such as near sidewalks, driveways, or entrances. The product is available online.

In a multicat household, it may not be you who is the victim of redirected aggression but a companion cat who is on the receiving end. If, instead of you walking over to your agitated cat, his companion comes by—*bam!* The poor cat is struck without warning. Now the two friends are engaged in a fight. They may now avoid each other all day unless it is unavoidable, such as at mealtime, and even then there may be hissing, growling, and a high degree of tension.

Unfortunately, redirected aggression can put their whole relationship at risk long after the appearance of an intruder. If the innocent "victim" cat starts acting tentative or defensive in the presence of the cat who attacked him, this may keep the aggressive cat in a reactive state. They no longer trust each other. The best thing to do is to separate the cats as soon as possible after a redirected aggression episode. Keep them in separate rooms for the rest of the day. If they don't see each other, they stand a better chance of calming down and not associating this episode with each other. After they're separated and calmed down, give treats and conduct low-intensity, stress-relieving individual play sessions with each kitty. By the following day, the episode will most likely have been forgotten. How long cats may need to be separated will depend on the severity of the aggression. Don't attempt a reintroduction until both cats appear totally calm and relaxed. There's no set timetable so if the cats don't seem ready, let more time go by. Rushing a reintroduction after an aggressive episode will always end in disaster.

If redirected aggression has caused an ongoing feud in your multicat household, separate your cats and start from scratch. Keep them apart for several days, or even weeks, and slowly do a reintroduction as if you were introducing two new cats.

Redirected aggression is one of the most misdiagnosed forms of aggression. Many times it's identified as unprovoked aggression because it appears to come out of the blue. Keep in mind that a cat can stay highly reactive for hours after the initial episode, so you may not actually see any evidence to explain why your cat is acting this way.

If you know your cat has a history of displaying redirected aggression it's important for you to pay attention to changes in his body posture or vocalizations that could indicate he's getting aroused.

If possible, use desensitization and counterconditioning to help your cat become less anxious to particular triggers (such as the appearance of animals outdoors). What's most important, though, is that you keep yourself and other family members and pets safe.

Territorial Aggression

Territorial aggression is crucial for a cat in the outdoor feline world. Your indoor cat can display that same behavior if he feels his territory is being threatened. Cats often display territorial aggression when a new cat is introduced into the environment. It's also not uncommon for a cat to exhibit this type of aggression toward a companion cat who has returned from a veterinarian visit.

Territorial aggression can be displayed toward anyone—human, feline, or canine—but other cats are most commonly the targets.

Turf wars can even occur within your home between companion cats. Indoor territorial disputes can occur over a large area of your house or they can happen over smaller areas within the home. For instance, cats may feud over territorial rights to the owner's bed. Choice spots by a sunny window, a comfy chair, the litter box, or food bowl can also be continually in negotiation. Territorial aggression can be displayed in overt ways or it can be as subtle as one cat guarding an area.

If there is a territorial battle going on in your household, try to create some breathing room in the disputed areas. For instance, make sure there's more than one litter box so the cats don't have to come face-to-face with each other at such a vulnerable time. Each cat should have his own food bowl, and if one cat is bullying another during meals feed them in separate rooms. Put a collar with a bell on the aggressor to give any victim cats some advanced warning of his presence.

Use interactive playtime to help dissolve built-up tension. Be observant of your cats' body language and the times of day or areas of the house that cause territorial rumbles. When you see trouble is brewing beneath the surface, distract the aggressor. For example, if you see one cat is sleeping in a chair and the other cat is walking over to knock him out of there, redirect the aggressive cat with an interactive toy. This will arouse his prey-drive. If you divert his attention before he actually gets to the sleeping cat, you can often lure him away with the toy. If your timing is right, the more times you do this, the quicker that *seek-and-attack* pattern between the two cats will fade.

When the two cats are in a room together and begin staring each other down, distract them with something positive. Toss a couple of toys in various directions so the cats don't collide as they go for them. By using something positive instead of a reprimand they'll begin to associate each other with more positive experiences.

In some cases, the cats will need to be completely separated and then reintroduced using food and treats for positive association. Clicker training can also help here. Click and reward any posture that indicates relaxation or nonaggression.

If you're not making any progress, do short sessions where the aggressor is in a carrier or crate, and the victim cat is able to roam free. This way they can start to get used to each other in a safe, controlled way. This method works well when you're worried that the aggressor will instantly ambush the victim, which would cause the victim to simply remain hidden. Offer treats when doing this exposure session.

You can use your environment in ways that complement your cats' relationship with each other. Make sure there are various elevated perches for the more assertive cats, middle areas and some hiding places for less assertive cats.

If territorial aggression is due to a visit to the veterinarian, keep the returning cat separated until he has had a chance to self-groom and take on the familiar scents of home again.

Pain-Induced Aggression

If you inflict pain on an animal, common sense will tell you that the animal is going to defend himself. It's another reason why physical punishment only worsens the situation you're trying to correct.

This aggression may also surface if you accidentally cause him pain while grooming him by yanking a tail or a mat, for example. A cat's body is very sensitive and if you cause pain, he's going to react.

Another occasion where pain-induced aggression may occur is if a cat has an abscess from a cat fight and the owner accidentally pets that area, unaware of it. When you touch that extremely painful area of his body, he may lash out at you. If a cat who normally enjoys petting and handling suddenly reacts violently, run—don't walk—to the veterinarian because there's a good chance he may have an abscess or other injury.

Rough handling, such as when a child pulls a tail or grabs an ear, may lead to pain-induced aggression.

Older cats who used to enjoy being handled and now show aggression when picked up may have discomfort due to arthritis.

Be sure and have your cat examined by the veterinarian to rule out an underlying medical cause for the aggression.

Unprovoked or Idiopathic Aggression

If your cat becomes aggressive for absolutely no reason that you can figure out, consult your veterinarian. There may be an underlying medical cause. In addition to determining if there is a medical cause, all other potential types of aggression need to be ruled out. Don't attempt to diagnose this yourself. Take your cat to the veterinarian right away. This type of aggression is rare. Your veterinarian may refer you to a certified behavior specialist. Because a cat can stay aroused for hours after a redirected aggression episode, it can sometimes get misdiagnosed as idiopathic aggression.

When You Need Outside Help

Chances are you'll never have to deal with a cat who goes over the edge with aggression for unknown reasons, but if you do, get the help of a certified behavior specialist. Unless you're prepared to handle the problem of an aggressive cat and know what you're doing, attempting to resolve this behavior on your own can result in serious consequences.

Don't battle with your cat, don't try to bully him and—for goodness' sake—don't resign yourself to living in fear of your own pet. Start by consulting with your veterinarian. Once all medical causes have been ruled out, your veterinarian can refer you to a certified behavior professional.

Almost all of the cases of aggression that I've been called in for have been triggered by something that can be identified. The owner may not be able to see it, but based on a veterinary exam, the environment, the circumstances, and the history I get from the owners, the cat's aggression can usually be traced. Don't resign yourself, or your cat, to living with aggressive behavior.

Beware of So-Called Cat Whisperers

With increased awareness of the study of animal behavior and the popularity of the TV show *The Dog Whisperer*, more and more people are calling themselves cat whisperers, cat behavior experts, cat behaviorists, and cat psychology professionals. The problem is that in this unregulated field anyone can put up a Web site and claim to be an expert, or *whisperer*, but how do you know their expertise is valid? You won't know unless you do your homework and find out more about them. If you're having a behavior problem with your pet, and your family life is in crisis because of it, you may be enticed by claims of "guaranteed results," but if you don't choose wisely you could be putting your cat's health and welfare at risk.

If you're in a position where you feel you need professional help with a cat behavior problem, how do you go about choosing the right expert? As I've stated before, start with your veterinarian.

When you visit your veterinarian, be specific and honest about the behavior the cat has been displaying. Sometimes when the veterinarian asks how often the litter box is cleaned or what the circumstances are when the cat bites, the client may be embarrassed to tell the truth. That won't help the owner or the cat, so when the veterinarian asks questions, give as honest and complete of an answer as you can.

Behavior modification is a powerful tool and, if done correctly, an effective way to change unwanted behavior. Behavior modification is science-based; there's no magic involved. A certified expert can explain to you how and why the process works and the science behind it. A certified expert will not "guarantee" results because much of the success of behavior modification depends on client compliance and the specifics of the case.

The best way to protect yourself from the multitude of so-called experts and self-proclaimed cat whisperers is to ask your veterinarian for a referral to a certified behavior expert. "Certified Applied Animal Behaviorists" are certified through the Animal Behavior Society. "Veterinary Behaviorists" are certified through the American College of Veterinary Behaviorists. "Certified Animal Behavior Consultants" are certified through the International Association of Animal Behavior Consultants. You can visit their Web sites for more information and for the location of a certified professional near you. If there isn't one in your area, many certified professionals will do telephone consultations. Refer to the Resource Guide for contact information.

Since anyone can put up a sign or a Web site with all kinds of too-good-to-be-true claims and show "testimonials" which may or may not be true, the best way to protect yourself is to choose someone who has proven that they have met the educational, experiential, and ethical standards in their field.

Drug Therapy for Behavior Problems

We are fortunate to have available today several effective psychoactive drugs for use in behavior modification. Far superior to the drugs used years ago to treat behavior problems, these medications have fewer side effects and are more appropriate in treating specific problems. If your impression of a medicated cat is one who sleeps all day or walks around in a daze, you haven't been keeping up with veterinary medicine.

That said, I caution you that drug therapy is not magic and won't make the problem instantly disappear. It's to be used in combination with behavior modification and under the close supervision of your veterinarian. Psychoactive drugs are not one-size-fits-all nor are they a way to avoid behavior modification. It's critical that your veterinarian and/or veterinary behaviorist get a complete behavioral history along with a medical history to determine which drug, if any, is appropriate. Psychoactive drugs are considered "extra-label" in veterinary medicine. This means the drug was not FDA approved for use in animals; or it was approved for use in one species but is being used in another; or it is being used to treat a condition for which it wasn't FDA approved. Even though behavioral drugs can be extremely beneficial and in some cases an absolute necessity, your veterinarian must be well-informed about the use of the drug. Make sure you are also informed about possible side effects, how the drug works, what changes to look for, and how long the cat will need to be medicated.

Should You Ever Euthanize an Aggressive Cat?

As a certified cat behavior consultant, I'm often the last call before many owners reach their tolerance limit and decide the cat will be relinquished to the shelter. Many cats are put to death for behavior problems that could have been solved. Don't be in a hurry to give up on your cat. He's a member of the family and deserves every chance. So many of the owners I've worked with now have their relationship with their cats back on track—cats who were one phone call away from death.

In the many years I've been doing this, I have come across a couple of cats who had to be euthanized due to severe aggression (the cause in those cases was an untreatable medical condition). It's not a decision to be rushed into. Your cat's life depends on your sound judgment. Make an appointment with your veterinarian, sit down and have an honest discussion about your feelings and fears. Years ago, the option of consulting with a behavior expert wasn't so readily available to the average cat owner, but now there are many more options for getting the professional help needed.

Turning an Outdoor Cat Into an Indoor Cat

Whether you've moved to a busier street, your cat's getting old, the weather's getting bad, or you just don't want to risk outdoor dangers anymore, you'll have to help your outdoor cat through a lifestyle change to become an indoor cat. While you may imagine this to be a difficult task, it's really easier than you think—if you can *think like a cat*.

The first thing to do is look around and reevaluate the environment. Go through your house and try to view it from your cat's perspective. Since he is now going to lose access to all the fun things such as catching live prey, watching insects, scratching trees, and lounging in the sun what will he get in return? Will his indoor environment be as stimulating as the outdoors? With your help, it can be.

Outdoors, he had access to the best places to scratch, courtesy of Mother Nature. What will he have indoors? Provide him with a tall, sturdy, rough-textured post that will meet both his scratching and stretching needs (see Chapter 9). If you've noticed the types of surfaces he has scratched on when outside, you can replicate that with his indoor post. For instance, did he prefer the bark of the tree or the wooden railing of your backyard deck?

Give your cat an indoor version of a tree to climb by purchasing a multitiered cat tree. If you're handy (unlike me), you can even make one for your cat. Depending on how much room you have and how limited your budget, you can create a feline jungle gym. You don't have to get fancy, though, a simple two-post tree with a perch on top of each post will do. One post should be higher than the other to allow a less agile cat to climb to the top. The trees in my house have bare-wood posts and rope-wrapped posts to accommodate the different scratching preferences of each cat. Put the tree by a sunny window and your cat will not only be able to watch the birds, he can curl up and take a nap.

Unlimited prey (or at least potential prey for the less than top-notch hunter) and the other perks of a dynamic outdoor environment can make your newly indoor cat feel as if he has just been sentenced to Kitty Alcatraz. A regular schedule of interactive playtime will not only provide exercise and fun, but will also thwart undesirable, destructive behavior. A cat who is used to being active all day won't instantly take to daintily sitting by the window hour after hour.

If your cat was used to being let out at specific times during the day, he's not going to understand why you've suddenly stopped playing by the rules. He may stand by the door, staring at the doorknob as if willing it to open. If the subtle reminders don't rouse you, he'll probably follow you around, meowing at regular intervals in an attempt to snap you back to reality. Finally, he may just give up on you totally and decide to break out of jail on his own. Digging at the carpet and scratching at the door are the most common escape plans. The very clever cat may act as if he has given up the fight and resigned to being an indoor pet, but in reality, he's planning to make a mad dash the minute someone opens the door. To keep your home from sustaining damage and you from going nuts, you'll need to incorporate redirection techniques to lure kitty away from the door. See the section in this chapter called "Charging the Door."

Use activity toys to keep your cat busy while you're at work or unable to engage in an interactive session. Cats who were used to the changing environment of the outdoors will appreciate coming across unexpected food-dispensing toys, an open paper bag or box to play in, homemade box or bag tunnels, food hidden in unexpected places, and other creative diversions designed by his loving owner.

If your cat was never trained to a litter box because he'd take care of all of his personal duties outdoors, keep him confined to a small area until you're sure he has mastered his litter box lessons. Use an uncovered box with unscented litter. The soft, scoopable litter will be better than clay litter or one of the alternative litters because its texture will more closely resemble the soil or sand he's used to.

8

Litter Box Survival Guide

Everything You Need to Know, from
Setup to Troubleshooting

There is no subject more misunderstood by cat owners than the litter box. When kitty faithfully uses it, all is peaceful in the house. Should kitty begin rejecting his box, though, life in the household is dramatically turned upside down. Tension runs high, punishment is often inflicted, and in many instances the cat is given away to a shelter and/or euthanized. A once loving cat/owner relationship transforms into a stressful day-to-day battle that nobody wins.

You'll never "win" if you think of it as a *battle*—what it takes is understanding the litter box from his point of view and the role it plays in his life. If the thought has ever entered your head that your cat wasn't using the litter box deliberately, to spite you, then you haven't been looking at it through his eyes. Stop thinking like an owner. If you thought it was just a plastic box filled with litter that you stick in the corner of the laundry room, you're underestimating the power that it has over your cat's emotions.

By knowing how to set up the box in the correct location, provide proper maintenance, and understand signals that your cat may be sending regarding it, you stand a good chance of avoiding future problems.

There are no secret tricks. Owners keep trying to find ways to prevent litter box odor from permeating the house and unfortunately they fall victim to quick-fix temporary solutions. The best and only way to reduce litter box odor is to keep it clean.

One of the things we find so appealing about cats is the fact that they do use a litter box, but many owners don't understand the origins of this basic instinct. The cat's instinct to bury his waste is based on a need far more important than his owner's convenience. *Survival* is the motivation behind the ritual of burying waste. A cat's urine is very concentrated and has a strong odor that can be detected by predators in the wild. Cats in the wild urinate and defecate away from their nest and cover their waste so they don't attract predators back to their young. For safety, cats don't eliminate where they eat, sleep, play, or raise young. Your indoor cat has those same instincts.

Which Litter Box?

I find it amazing how complex and elaborate some litter boxes have become. I'm sure you've seen the ads on TV and in magazines for boxes that are sifted and cleaned simply by rolling them over, or better yet, boxes that clean themselves electronically. Manufacturers continue to knock themselves out trying to come up with a litter box so maintenance-free that an owner will hardly know it's there. The problems I have with those are:

1. If owners aren't maintaining the boxes as often, they also won't be *monitoring* their cat's elimination habits as often. For example, if you aren't sifting the box every day, you may be unaware that your cat has diarrhea.
2. It has been my experience through the years that the more complicated the litter box setup is, the less likely the cat will use it faithfully.

A simple, basic box is all you need. As you stand in the store aisle staring at the dozens of boxes, consider your cat's age, size, and health. If you have a tiny kitten, you don't want to start out with a jumbo box that might be too high-sided for him to climb into. You may need to purchase a small box initially and then switch to a larger one as your cat grows. On the other hand, if you have a rather large cat, the litter box needs to be of an adequate size for him to move around comfortably.

The basic litter box is a rectangular plastic pan. It comes in sizes ranging from a small cage-sized box to a jumbo multicat model. I find that owners commonly make the mistake of buying too small of a box in order to have it fit in a corner somewhere. Look at the size of your cat and pick a box that would give him enough room to eliminate in a couple of areas and still have clean spots to stand on. As a general guideline, the length of the box should be 1½–2 times the length of an adult cat, and the width of the box should be the cat's approximate length. If you have more than one cat and they vary greatly in size, base your measurement on the largest cat. It's a major part of your cat's life, so don't skimp on size just so it'll fit under the vanity. Keep your cat's needs in mind when shopping for a litter box. If, after looking through the displays at pet supply stores, you still don't see one that fits your cat's needs (for instance, if he sprays urine over the sides of an ordinary box), go to the discount store and check out plastic storage containers. Sterilite makes containers in a wide variety of sizes. The higher sides of a storage box may just do the trick.

Wouldn't it be easier to simply get a covered litter box? Read on.

Covered Boxes

Covered boxes have two functions: to contain the smell and to ensure that urine and litter stay within the confines of the box. In theory, that sounds very appealing and practical. The problem is it appeals to you, not the cat. A covered box really *does* contain the smell—by keeping it trapped inside so that your cat must endure the concentrated odor each time he enters. The cover on the box also reduces the amount of air circulating so the litter takes longer to dry, creating a perfect environment for odor.

A covered box can also be uncomfortable for a cat. He may feel cramped as he tries to find a comfortable position. A tall cat may have to duck his head to avoid touching the ceiling of the box. If you're considering a covered box to reduce litter scatter or urine spray, you will do just as well getting a taller, open box instead. The effect is the same and your cat will be more comfortable.

A covered box in a multicat household may also cause a cat to feel trapped should another cat show up. More on this later.

Litter

If you thought there were many varieties of litter boxes, wait until you start shopping for litter. The number of choices can be overwhelming for a new owner. Heck, it's overwhelming for seasoned owners.

Every single type of litter on the market claims to have the solution to a cat owner's ultimate quest: *odor control.* Some litters tout their virtually dust-free properties. Others highlight their super-strong clumping ability. Which should you choose? What's a cat owner to do? Here are the fundamentals: The first decision to make is whether you want regular nonclumping clay, scoopable, or one of the many alternative types. Clay litter is the most basic and not very good at odor control. It was the first commercial litter, introduced by Edward Lowe, back when owners were just using ordinary sand. Scoopable litter is sandlike in texture, only when it becomes wet it clumps into a ball. This makes it easy for you to scoop out, leaving the rest of the litter dry and odor-free.

There are also multiple brands of alternative litters such as wheat, corn, or newspaper, just to name a few. Some are scoopable and some aren't. Some are flushable, some aren't.

When you choose a litter, go for unscented or if you must choose scent, pick minimally scented brands. The scented kinds that smell so wonderful to us are often too perfumed for a cat's nose. Cats want to be able to identify their own scent in the litter and the heavy perfume can actually drive him away. If you regularly scoop out the waste, you'll have an odor-free box without all the extra perfume.

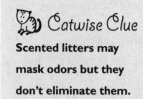

Catwise Clue

Scented litters may mask odors but they don't eliminate them.

Basically, from a cat's point of view, litter should meet three requirements:

1. It has to be a substrate that he doesn't mind standing on.
2. It has to be loose enough for him to dig a hole and cover afterward.
3. It shouldn't have a strong odor.

If you have just adopted or purchased a new kitten or cat, it's best to start out using whatever the previous owner or breeder used. If you decide to switch later, you should do it gradually so the cat won't reject it.

My philosophy on litter is to stick to what a cat would naturally seek out in the wild (with a few modifications, of course). I recommend a scoopable litter with a texture similar to the sandy type of soil a cat would naturally choose. The scoopable aspect makes it easy for you to clean and greatly reduces odor since you'll be removing the soaked ball of soiled litter.

Many cats seem to prefer this substrate and for some cats who have been declawed the soft texture can be more comfortable.

Another advantage to scoopable litter is that it can help you monitor changes in your cat's urine output because you'll be able to see an increase or decrease in the size of the hardened clumps.

There has always been somewhat of a controversy surrounding scoopable litter. Some people continue to have concerns over whether the litter, if ingested by a cat, will turn cementlike in the intestines. There have been no documented veterinarian reports of cases of intestinal damage due to ingestion of litter. If you have any questions, discuss this with your veterinarian.

You'll find several variations of scoopable litters. There are low tracking formulas, unscented, super-scented, and heavy-duty formulas guaranteeing rock hard clumps that won't fall apart. If you have more than one cat sharing a box then consider one of the stronger multicat formulas.

There are also numerous alternative litters. Each cat is individual in his preferences and needs, as is each owner. So if you have a specific situation where the more commonly used litters won't work for you, look among the wide variety of alternatives.

Deodorizers

These products aren't usually beneficial to the cat. They tend to have a very strong fragrance that can drive a cat away from the box, which is not quite the effect you want.

How Much Litter to Use

An important aspect of odor control is how much litter is in the box. Doing my in-home consultations, I've found many owners go to the extremes, using either way too much or not nearly enough. If you use too much scoopable litter, it's just a waste and ends up being kicked over the side of the box. On the other hand, not using enough litter results in a very smelly box because urine hits the bottom of the box and forms puddles where there are not enough granules for adequate absorption.

A good guideline is to spread about a three to five-inch layer of litter in the box. This gives your cat enough for digging and covering. Watch your cat's digging habits and adjust the amount of litter accordingly. In multicat households, you don't need more litter in the box, you need more boxes.

Maintain a consistent litter level by topping off the litter every few days as you remove urine clumps.

Where to Put the Box

Location, location, location. It applies to real estate and it most definitely applies to litter boxes. *Where* you put the litter box is more important than many owners realize. You can have the perfect box, filled with the best litter in the world, but if it's put in an area that the cat finds unacceptable, it may be rejected.

There is one rule that cat owners should never ever break under any circumstances: Don't put the litter box near the cat's food and water. Many owners mistakenly believe that having the box right next to the cat's food will serve as a reminder to him. Unfortunately, this plan can only backfire and you lay the groundwork for litter box rejection. Remember, cats eliminate *away* from the nest. If you put his food and box together it sends him a very confusing message. He'll be forced to make a decision about whether to designate the area as a feeding station or an elimination spot. Since the food is only available in that one area, he'll search for another location for his litter box needs. If you have no choice but to keep his food bowl and litter box in the same room, at least put them as far apart as possible.

The most common place owners put the box is in the bathroom. This is a good spot provided you have the room. It makes cleanup easy and it's convenient in terms of your being able to regularly scoop it. Keep in mind, though, that if lots of steamy hot showers are taken in the bathroom it will be humid in there and that may cause the litter to take longer to dry.

Another popular location is the laundry room. Like the bathroom, the laundry room is usually not carpeted, making for easy cleanup. The downside is that if the washer goes into the spin cycle while the cat is in the box, the sudden noise could cause him to become frightened of using it again.

Pick a spot in your home away from heavy traffic to provide your cat with a feeling of privacy and safety. However, don't choose an area too remote or you'll forget to check it daily. I met one owner who put the box in the "junk" room on the second floor of the house. No one routinely went in there, so the box was forgotten and became so full and dirty that the cat couldn't stand to use it any longer and began urinating on the carpet in the den. Wherever you locate the box, be sure you'll remember to check it twice a day.

A two-story home should have a box on each floor. If your indoor/outdoor cat doesn't use a litter box and prefers to eliminate outside, keep a litter box indoors anyway in case he chooses not to go out in bad weather or becomes ill.

In a multicat household, more than one box will be needed. This is not just because one box gets dirty too quickly (although it does), but also because some cats object to sharing and one cat may be too intimidated to pass another cat in order to get to the cat's area. The litter box rule: have the same number of boxes as you have cats.

Multicat households can create litter box placement problems. If there are any territorial disputes going on or if your cats don't especially care for each other, the boxes should be placed far enough apart so that if one is being guarded, there is easy access to another. It's worth taking the time to pay attention to the areas of your home where each cat seems to spend the most time. You may be able to avoid future problems by placing boxes in rooms within each cat's general preferred locations. Boxes spread throughout the house are better than ones grouped together in one location. It may not initially seem very convenient as far as you're concerned, but trust me, there is tremendous convenience in not having to deal with location-aversion litter box problems.

There is another potential problem to consider when setting up a litter box for multicat households in which there is some feline animosity. A litter box wedged in a corner can make a cat feel trapped. If a cat thinks he doesn't have enough avenues of escape and fears being attacked, he could reject his box. This problem is covered more specifically later in this chapter.

Cleaning the Litter Box

You will need a slotted scoop or shovel to sift through the litter for solid waste. It will also enable you to separate the soiled urine clumps from the dry, clean litter if you're using clumping litter.

If you use nonclumping litter, you'll also want to use a slotted shovel to remove solid waste. A long-handled unslotted spoon is good for removing mounds of wet litter. Saturated litter left sitting in the box is what will create an odor. Don't stir the wet litter around or you'll just end up soiling the whole box. I hope you'll reconsider the use of nonscoopable litter and will gradually switch your cat over to the more convenient scoopable kind. You'll find the box will have much less odor and you'll be able to do a more efficient job when it comes to cleanup.

Keep the litter scoop in a container by the litter box for convenience. There are several companies that make scoop and holder combinations. This will make it much easier and cleaner. Scooping and sifting should be done at least twice a day. It only takes seconds and will make a significant difference in odor control. Scoopable litter will be worth nothing if your cat has to climb over old clumps from days ago in order to find one corner of unsoiled substrate.

Most scoopable litters, especially the heavy-duty formulas, aren't flushable. Clay litter should never be flushed down the toilet. The most convenient method I've come up with for disposal of soiled litter clumps is to keep a small plastic storage container with a sealable lid lined with a plastic grocery bag right next to the box. I scoop first thing in the morning, depositing all the clumps into the container, then I snap the lid shut until the evening's scooping when I'll tie up the plastic bag and dispose of it in the outside trash can. There are also commercial litter-disposal products. These products are available through pet supply retailers and online. They're similar to the diaper disposal systems that have been on the market for years. It doesn't matter what method you come up with as long as it's convenient enough so no one will have an excuse for letting litter box mainte-nance slide. And remember, always wash your hands after scooping out the litter box.

Scooping twice daily will not only keep the litter box clean but it will alert you to po-tential health problems. Routine scooping will help you become familiar with your cat's litter box habits. I know it doesn't sound like a thrilling job, but it can mean the difference between a happy, pain-free cat or one who has to endure a painful medical condition because it has gone undetected by his owner. You'll soon be familiar with your cat's habits: how often he goes, his daily urine output, the for-mation and consistency of his stool. Should any of that change, you'll be aware of it right away and able to get prompt medical care.

In addition to daily scooping, the box it-self will also need routine cleaning. If you use regular clay litter or one of the nonscoopable varieties, you should do a thorough cleaning at least once a week. This involves disposing of the litter, then scrubbing the box and all

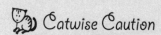 **Catwise Caution**

Pregnant women should ex-ercise caution when cleaning the litter box because of the danger of toxoplasmosis. This is a condition caused by a protozoan parasite called Toxoplasma gondii that can infect a fetus and cause birth defects. Cats spread this parasite through egg spores in their feces. If possible, have someone else do the litter duties for the pregnant owner. Their daily scooping of waste will greatly reduce the risk because the egg spores of Toxoplasma gondii must incubate for several days before they reach the infective state. If you're pregnant and must attend to the litter, keep a box of disposable gloves near the box. Wash your hands after scooping the litter box and instruct your family to do the same.

related utensils. If you use scoopable litter, you can go longer than one week between cleanings. Don't be fooled by the ads for scoopable litter claiming that because the waste is being sifted out you'll never have to scrub the box. Not true. Urine will still come in contact with the plastic. Boxes containing scoopable litter should be completely scrubbed and replaced with fresh litter about twice a month.

When you clean the box, don't use harsh cleansers that can leave a smell. I use bleach that I've diluted with water (¾ water to ¼ bleach). I also scrub all of the utensils and their plastic container. Then everything gets thoroughly dried before the box is refilled with fresh litter.

Plastic Liners

The idea of a plastic liner in the litter box seems wonderful in theory. In reality, the animals who step into the box have *claws* so the liners often end up being more of a nuisance than a help. When you lift up the liner to throw it away, you may find litter escaping through holes that your cat has scratched in the bottom of the liner. Plastic liners can also make litter box odor worse because urine can pool in creases and folds, and urine that leaks through any tears or holes will sit on the bottom and become very smelly.

Your objective is to make the litter box as inviting and comfortable as possible for your cat, so you certainly don't want him struggling to dig or cover because his claws keep catching on the liner.

The Facts About Toilet Training Your Cat

You've probably heard about people who can toilet train their cats. There are videos all over YouTube by people who claim that kitty can use the same toilet as the human family. Perhaps you've been considering the idea of teaching your own cat to use the toilet so you won't ever have to deal with the mess of scooping and cleaning a litter box. In theory, toilet training may seem mess-free but there are things to consider before you attempt this route. There are serious downsides to the toilet training option that many owners don't take into consideration until problems have already taken hold. I've done many consultations with clients because of cat behavior problems stemming from disastrous toilet-training attempts. The cats end up with anxiety-related elimination problems and the owners end up very frustrated.

You might be interested in the idea of toilet training because you hate dealing with litter box mess and odor. The truth is, litter boxes don't have to be messy and smelly. They end up that way because they don't get scooped and cleaned often enough. Litter granules can only hold so much liquid, so if you haven't been scooping regularly, the box will, of course, start to stink. So rethink the idea of toilet training to avoid litter box odor—instead, get on a better maintenance schedule.

Here's a list of reasons why toilet training isn't something I recommend owners attempt with their cats:

- When kitty eliminates in the toilet you won't be able to accurately see whether there has been a change in urine volume or frequency. If the urine is going in the toilet instead of a litter box, you really can't accurately judge whether volume has increased or decreased. A change in urine output is an important clue to potential underlying medical problems. Whenever you scoop the box, you're alerted to changes in urine clumps.

- Toilet training is counterintuitive to the cat's natural survival instinct to dig, eliminate, and then cover his waste. Although many cats won't have a problem with that change, many won't make the adjustment very smoothly.

- The toilet lid must always be up when you have a cat who uses the toilet instead of a litter box. The first time someone accidentally closes the lid, kitty has no option but to eliminate elsewhere. Imagine how confusing and stressful it must be when the cat goes to use the toilet and finds it inaccessible.

- Unless you teach your cat to flush the toilet, the odor from solid waste will linger until someone does flush. So, if you're thinking toilet training causes fewer odors than a litter box, it doesn't. And, if you attempt to teach your cat to flush, keep in mind that he may end up enjoying the "game" of watching the swirling water go down, and might flush repeatedly throughout the day just for entertainment purposes.

- In a multicat home, cats may not want to share the same toilet.

- Even though you can buy toilet-training kits, eventually you have to do away with the kit and have kitty straddle the actual toilet seat. For a young cat, one who is ill, has arthritis, or limited mobility this may not be comfortable or even possible.

- Toilet seats can be slippery for the cat.

- If your cat falls in the toilet, although he may be able to get out, the panic and stress may cause him to not want to eliminate in the toilet again. Should he fall into a dirty toilet, then you'll have the added anxiety of having to bathe him. If he's home by himself, he'll have to remain wet and soiled until you get home.

- If your cat is ever hospitalized or boarded he'll be put in a cage with a traditional litter box. Once back home, you may end up having to retrain him to the toilet.

Introducing Your Cat to the Litter Box

The first step is to make sure your cat knows where the box is. If dealing with a kitten, confine him to a small area until he's using the box successfully and comfortable with his new surroundings. If he doesn't get the idea, then after he has eaten, place him in the box and scratch in the litter with your finger. Don't force him to stay in the litter box, though.

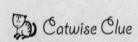 Catwise Clue

Both male and female cats squat to eliminate. The standing posture is reserved for spraying behavior. Male cats, unlike male dogs, don't lift a leg to urinate.

If you're planning to use a covered box, don't put the cover on during this orientation process. You want to make the learning process as easy as possible. And, while you're waiting for your cat to get used to his new box, go back and reread the section in this chapter on covered boxes so you'll fully understand why they're not as good for your cat.

If your kitten doesn't appear to grasp the concept of the litter box and he urinates or defecates on the floor, collect it as well as you can and deposit it in the box. The scent of his own waste should direct him there next time.

Litter Box Aversion

It's high noon. The place is deserted. A few hair balls roll around lazily. There's an eerie ghost-town stillness in the air. The only sound is the lonely echo of your footsteps as you enter the room. It all looks innocent enough but you know that somewhere in this room *that thing* awaits. Suddenly you see it in the corner, covered in dust. The cobwebs laced over it glisten in the sun. It is the *litter box* that your cat refuses to use.

LITTER BOX CHECKLIST

- the right box
- proper location
- appealing litter substrate
- slotted litter shovel
- large unslotted spoon to collect wet litter (for nonclumping litter users)
- washable container to hold litter shovel
- washable container with lid to collect soiled clumps
- plastic bags
- small broom and dust pan or small vacuum and/or litter tracking mat (to control litter scatter)
- Scrub brush or sponge designated for litter box cleaning
- Enzymatic pet stain/odor cleaner (for accidents)

"He's doing it out of spite!"

"He knows he's being bad!"

"He's too lazy to go to his box!"

"My cat is so stupid, he pees on the carpet!"

"He did it because he's mad at me!"

The above is a small sample of the sorts of things I hear on my answering machine. While I certainly can understand an owner's sense of frustration, none of the above statements are at all true about cats. It's only when you stop interpreting your cat's behavior as mean, spiteful, stupid, deliberate, or lazy that you stand a chance of correcting the problem.

Understanding what type of behavior your cat is displaying is crucial. *Indiscriminate urination* is usually done on a horizontal surface such as the floor, carpet, or tub. *Spraying* is usually done against vertical surfaces such as walls, furniture, or drapes. There are some cats, though, who do display horizontal spray-marking behavior. These cats may not feel confident enough to engage in vertical spraying.

You must first identify whether your cat is indiscriminately urinating or spraying. A cat may also defecate outside of the litter box, which we will discuss later in this chapter.

If your cat is spraying and he hasn't been neutered, now would be a really good time to make an appointment for the surgery. A male cat reaches sexual maturity at about seven months of age, and spraying can begin at that time. Neutering will eliminate the spraying behavior in almost all cases.

Spray-Marking: Kitty's Calling Card

If your cat has already been neutered and is still spraying, he either feels that his territory is in danger, is anxious about something and trying to self-soothe, or is trying to exchange information with another cat in a safe way. Many things can prompt a cat to spray, such as the appearance of another cat outside or the arrival of a new cat in the household. If a turf war is being waged in your home, the cats should be separated and individual behavior modification begun (covered in this chapter). Then the cats can gradually be reintroduced. You do this the same way you'd introduce two unacquainted cats for the first time. For specific instructions on this, refer to Chapter 11.

When marking, the cat stands stiff-legged with his hindquarters facing the target. His tail is upright and quivers as he marks. He may close his eyes halfway or completely. Some cats tread in place with their front paws while in the act of spraying.

Some cats will also spray horizontally on items such as bedding or clothing. The urine will be in a thin stream as opposed to the puddle associated with indiscriminate urination.

The key to correcting spraying behavior is to find the cause of the cat's fear/anxiety, and either remove it or modify it by working on changing your cat's association. Spray-marking is an important form of communication in the feline world so if you have a sprayer in your house, he's trying to say something to somebody! Spraying can be performed by confident and nonconfident cats alike, so if you have a multicat environment, don't automatically assume a culprit.

If the spraying is happening near doors or windows, there's a good chance the cat is reacting to the presence of an outdoor cat. Spraying on new items such as bags or boxes brought into the house, or a new piece of furniture, could be a reaction to the unfamiliar scents on those items in the cat's territory. And of course, the most common reason a cat sprays is usually due to the arrival of a new cat in the home or because of intercat conflict with a companion cat.

The first step you should take if your cat stops using the litter box is to take your cat to the veterinarian. Indiscriminate urination is a common sign of a medical condition known as *feline lower*

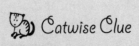

Catwise Clue

Many people assume that cats spray exclusively to mark territory. Spray-marking is far more complicated than that. It's a complex form of communication used for many purposes.

POTENTIAL REASONS FOR A CAT TO SPRAY

- sexual maturity
- the appearance of a strange cat in the yard
- the addition of a new pet or family member
- to patrol territory
- scent of unfamiliar cat on owner's clothing or shoes
- tension or aggression between companion animals

- too dense of a cat population in the household
- renovation or remodeling
- move to a new home
- to calm and self-soothe
- unfamiliar visitors
- to relay information
- victory display after a confrontation
- covert aggression

urinary tract disease (FLUTD). It's not unusual for a cat suffering from FLUTD to make frequent trips to the box but only void small amounts of urine. As the condition worsens, the irritated bladder creates an urgent need in the cat to urinate immediately in order to relieve the discomfort. Sometimes a cat begins to associate the pain he feels upon urination with the litter box itself. FLUTD is very serious and can be fatal if crystals form and block the passage of urine through the urethra. Have your cat checked immediately should he stop using the litter box. For more on FLUTD, refer to the Medical Appendix.

Feces Marking

Known as *middening*, this is where a cat will deposit a fecal marker. Sometimes it's deposited on a pathway frequented by other cats. It may be a way of leaving a visual as well as an olfactory sign. This behavior is exhibited more in outdoor cats. Middening is not common behavior with indoor cats. If a cat is defecating outside of the litter box it's usually not a marking behavior.

There are other medical conditions that could cause your cat to change his litter box habits, such as diabetes or kidney disease, just to name two. Any change in your cat's litter box habits or food/water consumption should be checked by the veterinarian.

If you have a multicat household, you may have difficulty figuring out which cat is the perpetrator. If there is indiscriminate urination and FLUTD

POTENTIAL REASONS FOR INDISCRIMINATE URINATION

- medical condition
- dirty litter box
- covered or inappropriately sized litter box
- unacceptable litter substrate
- abrupt change in litter or litter box location
- unacceptable litter box location
- aversion to scent of product used to clean litter box or perfumed litter
- anxiety/fear
- negative association with litter box
- punishment by owner so a fear of being near the box develops
- increase in owner's absence from cat
- tension or aggression between companion pets
- inadequate number of boxes for multicat home
- need for more escape potential so cat has more option for existing box
- inconsistent litter levels
- geriatric-related problems

SOME SIGNS OF FLUTD

- frequent trips to litter box
- voiding little or no urine
- blood in urine
- urinating outside of litter box
- crying while in litter box
- little or no appetite
- appearing depressed or irritable
- frequent licking of genitals
- spending longer amount of time in box

could be the cause, don't waste time waiting to catch a cat in the act. If you notice any suspicious signs (see above), take the most likely suspect to the veterinary clinic first.

In a multicat household you can separate and isolate cats to try to determine which one isn't using the litter box. The problem with that method is one cat may be eliminating outside of the box because of a tense relationship with another cat. If the cats aren't together, there may not be a display of inappropriate elimination. The most reliable way to determine which cat is eliminating outside of the box is to use video.

Beginning at the Source (the Litter Box)

Take a long, hard, critical look at the litter box. I mean now, this very minute. How does it really look? Have you been keeping it clean? Have you been reliably sticking to your twice daily scooping and routine cleaning? If you haven't, then chances are the poor conditions of the box are driving your cat to find cleaner, less smelly places. Even if you've been scooping twice daily and routinely cleaning, that might not be enough for your particular cat. Some cats want a pristine box every time they step into it.

In certain weather when there's increased humidity (especially if you don't have air conditioning), the litter box cleaning schedule may have to be adjusted. Also, if you keep the box in a bathroom frequently used for steamy hot showers, that will raise the humidity level, and litter will take longer to dry. If you've been using a covered box and you keep it in a bathroom with a high humidity level, remove the cover at the very least. Also, keep the bathroom exhaust fan running during showers to reduce humidity.

Check the amount of litter that you're putting in the box. Make sure there's at least a three- to five-inch layer to permit sufficient digging and covering. If you use scoopable litter, you should periodically be refilling the box with clean litter to maintain a consistent level as you remove the soiled clumps.

An abrupt change in litter can also be enough to make a cat stop using his box. A cat takes comfort in knowing that when he steps into the box, he'll feel the same texture under his paws and the same scent (or lack of scent) he's used to. A change in litter texture or a drastic change in scent can be confusing. Keep in mind how sensitive a cat's senses are; a change in brand may seem subtle to you but may be offensive to your cat. Your kitty is also a very tactile creature and the feel of the litter against his paws can be of extreme importance. A sudden change from a soft, sandy texture to a pelletized litter can be off-putting enough to drive a cat to seek a softer substrate—and that choice might be your bathroom rug or the lush carpet in your bedroom.

If you plan on changing litter brands or types, do it in a way that allows the cat time to adjust. Start by adding a little of the new litter into the box containing the current brand, gradually increasing the amount of new litter while decreasing the old, over the course of about five days.

If you feel your cat may have come to dislike his current brand of litter, or maybe dislikes the texture, you can do a test by placing a second litter box near his current one. In the second box, place a different litter. When I've done such experiments, I've found that if it's a choice between clay, crystals, alternative litters, or scoopable many cats seem to prefer the soft texture of the scoopable. Cats are individuals, though, so if you feel puzzled by what type of litter to buy, experiment by setting out different types—cafeteria style—and let your cat make the decision. You don't have to spend lots of money on litter boxes for this experiment: buy disposable boxes for the short-term. This litter box "buffet" allows the cat to make his own choice. In a multicat household you may find that one cat likes one type of litter and another cat prefers a different type or texture. This way, you'll know to set up litter boxes in each cat's area with their own preferred litter.

If you aren't sure whether your cat actually dislikes his litter or not, there are some clues he may give you. He might stand with his front legs on the rim of the box or he may perch on the very edge. In order to minimize his contact with the litter he may also scratch the area outside of the litter box when attempting to cover his waste. He may not even attempt to cover at all and just bolt out of the box after eliminating (though not all cats cover their waste). The cat may even eliminate on the floor or carpet right next to the box. All of these behaviors can also be associated with an underlying medical condition (such as FLUTD) or it can be simply the result of a too-dirty box. The bottom line is that the cat is telling you something needs to be addressed immediately.

Some people have no problem placing a litter box on carpet and others feel it's a recipe for disaster. Some kitties mistake the soft feel of carpet for litter. Sometimes a little kicked out soiled litter can create an odor problem if left sitting on carpeted surfaces. Also, if the box doesn't meet your cat's standards for cleanliness, the carpet will begin to look especially attractive to him. If you decide to put the litter box on carpet, put a litter scatter mat or piece of sturdy plastic under the box. The litter scatter mat will help control those tossed out litter granules while also protecting your carpet. Litter scatter mats are a good idea even if the litter box is placed on a hard surface to prevent litter from going everywhere. When choosing a litter scatter mat, though, be aware that your cat may have a texture preference. A mat with pointy nubs on the surface may trap litter effectively but your cat may not like the feel on his paws.

There are some cats who, no matter how diligently you clean, won't use the litter box once it has been soiled. If you have this type of cat, invest in two litter boxes for the room so he'll always have a clean one should you be unable to

scoop up the waste before his return visit. You may also be one of the lucky owners of a cat who refuses to defecate in the same box he uses for urination. Put a
second box down for His Highness so he can designate one for urination and
one for his princely poop. It may seem inconvenient to clean two boxes, but I'd
rather scrub an extra litter box than clean urine out of my carpet. In many cases
the boxes can be relatively close together, but not so close that your cat views
them as one big box (otherwise you'll defeat the purpose of having two). With
some cats, the boxes will have to be farther apart—maybe on opposite sides of
the room.

The Disappearing Litter Box
In an effort to find a location that will meet with the approval of all family
members, sometimes the litter box gets moved around too much. This is where
planning ahead proves very helpful. Think about the pros and cons of the area
you have chosen before you start playing musical litter boxes. The harder you
make it for your cat to find the box, the more inviting your oriental carpet will
look to him when his bladder is full.

If you need to change a litter box's location, place a second box in the pro-
posed spot before moving the original one to make sure it's an acceptable area.
Then you can gradually move the first box a few feet a day toward the new location. Once they're in the same location you can then dispose of one of the boxes.
If you don't want to go to the expense of using a temporary second box, you'll
have to relocate the box VERY gradually—no more than a couple of feet a
day—but make sure the final location is one that your cat will find acceptable.

Monitoring A Recently Relocated Litter Box
I was called in for a consultation because Sparkles, a four-year-old female cat,
suddenly refused to use her litter box. The owners also had dogs. The history I
received was that the cat, who was in perfect health, had a very outgoing,
friendly personality, loved being around the dogs, and up until two months
before, when she stopped using her litter box, had been the perfect cat.

Upon further investigation, I learned that the box had recently been moved.
Originally it had been situated in an unused extra room, but now was in the
bathroom because the owners were planning to convert the extra room into an
office. For six months, Sparkles handled the relocation just fine. Then she began
eliminating in the old location. Why the change in her behavior after six
months? Eventually, I learned that during those first six spring/summer months,

the dogs had been kept outside, as usual. However, they'd started sleeping indoors two months ago since the weather got colder.

The dogs had never been allowed in the section of the house where the extra room was located. The owners had installed a baby gate to keep them out. Sparkles, however, was free to roam anywhere, and had just hopped the gate to get to her box. But the dogs now had access to the new litter box location in the central area of the house, and they'd discovered the fun game of following Sparkles to the litter box and crowding her while she was trying to conduct her private business. Apparently, since moving indoors, the dogs had been anxiously awaiting the deposit of feces so they could "snack." No owner wants to believe his or her dog would display this behavior but it is, nevertheless, a relatively common one among canines.

I figured it out when the owners told me that they often saw the dogs hanging around the bathroom door. Because all of the pets got along, they never imagined there was a problem. When pressed, neither owner recalled scooping feces out of the box for the last two months. Each just assumed that the other had already cleaned it.

Understandably, Sparkles was upset at the intrusion upon her privacy, so she went back to eliminating in the old area, which felt much safer. Perfectly logical from a *think like a cat* perspective.

The solution to the problem was for Sparkles's owners to relocate the box back to the section of the house that was off limits to the dogs, or to install a hinged baby gate at the entrance to the bathroom with a small elevated landing box on the bathroom-side of the gate so Sparkles could manage the gate easily.

If you plan to relocate the litter box, think carefully beforehand about what potential problems and obstacles your cat could encounter in the new place. Also, will the new location be convenient for you to maintain your scooping schedule? If you locate the box in the basement, for example, because you don't like the look of a litter box on the main floor of the house, will you remember to go down there twice a day to do box maintenance?

After you've moved the box to a new location, monitor everyone's reactions and behavior to catch any early warning signals (in the case of Sparkles's owners, it was noticing the dogs at the bathroom door).

If Your Cat Has Been Declawed

The first ten days after declawing surgery are painful for the cat. For some cats, the wounds on their paws remain sensitive long after the usual healing period.

He'll need a special litter in his box while he's healing to keep the wounds clean. Your veterinarian will probably recommend shredded newspaper or a pelleted litter. Try not to use shredded newspaper because it's terrible at odor control and is very messy.

Not only can the pain cause the cat to not want to deal with the litter box, the sudden shock of encountering a strange litter substrate can bother any cat. Either circumstance can cause litter box aversion.

If you're set on having your cat declawed (refer to Chapter 9 before making that decision), plan ahead and mix a little of the pelleted litter in with his regular litter before the surgery. Then, after the ten-day healing period, you can reintroduce his regular litter again. If you were previously using regular clay litter and it now seems to cause discomfort, do a gradual switch from the pelleted to scoopable litter. A soft, sandlike texture will be gentler to his paws.

New House

The first time I moved to a new house was an overwhelming and traumatic experience for me. I can understand exactly what a cat must feel at such a time. Everything familiar was suddenly gone and I was faced with the task of establishing new territory. Because I remembered how it had felt, I planned enough in advance to make transitions much easier for my cats when it came time for future moves. If only someone had pampered me the way I pampered my cats.

If you've recently moved and your cat has stopped using his litter box, it might be because of the unfamiliar surroundings. Remember that he's a creature of habit and was used to his comfortable, familiar territory. The best way to prevent pussycat panic is to set up a small area for him while he gets his bearings.

Renovation/New Furniture/New Carpets

The frightening sounds of renovation and all of the unfamiliar faces of construction workers can be perceived as a threat to a cat's territory and cause him to spray. A cat may also urinate away from the litter box if it's located too close to the noise or if he feels too frightened to venture near it.

The addition of new carpet or even a new piece of furniture can be threatening for some cats. They may feel that it doesn't belong in their territory until it has been sprayed with their scent.

It is best to keep a cat as far away from construction noises as possible. If there's a quiet room in your home (preferably not one with new furniture or new carpeting), set him up in there with his litter box. Play soft music to block out some of the distant hammering and drilling.

When you bring in a new piece of furniture and you're concerned about how your cat will react, rub it down with a towel that you've rubbed your cat with. Another option is to keep the piece covered with a sheet or blanket for a day. Using a sheet that you've slept on can speed up the acceptance process because the cat will detect your comforting scent. Always try to initiate new furniture as quickly as possible with the familiar scent of your home.

The Comings and Goings of Family

Whether it's the new sofa cushions or the new spouse, change is change, and most cats don't care for it! Even though down the road it may be wonderful, any change in the family status can cause litter box aversion.

A common worry that owners have is how their cat will react to a new baby. The answer is, if you haven't prepared him for the change, there is a good chance he might not like it.

A new marriage may be the cause of a lapse in good litter box etiquette especially if your new family includes another cat or even a dog.

Remember to ease your cat through the very confusing changes of an addition to your family. Forethought can make the difference between a smooth, incident-free transition and a full-blown family crisis.

For specific information on cats and their relationships with family members, refer to Chapter 11.

Peeping Toms (the Feline Version)

The peaceful sight of your cat looking out the window to watch the birds could turn ugly if he spots another cat in the yard. At best, your cat may perk his ears up and thump his tail. Maybe he'll even issue a hiss or two. At worst, he may view that cat's presence as a territorial threat and become concerned with marking his turf and/or finding an outlet for his anxiety. If your cat is allowed outdoors and he confines his spraying to backyard trees, bushes, or fence posts, you're okay. If your *indoor* cat feels threatened enough to spray, then *Houston, we have a problem.* You may notice streaks of urine on the walls under windows. Another common area to spray is around the front door. If your cat saw the uninvited feline on the patio or deck, then there's a good chance that the doors or any nearby drapes have been marked.

169 • LITTER BOX SURVIVAL GUIDE

A cat with a spraying problem may or may not continue to use his box or he may only defecate in the box.

If the unwanted visitor makes frequent appearances, try to find out if he has an owner. If he's a stray, do your best to catch him because he probably isn't vaccinated or neutered and could pose a serious health risk to other cats. You can contact a local feline rescue group in your area for guidance and assistance.

If you know the cat has an owner and you're unable to convince him/her to keep the kitty indoors, you may need to set up a deterrent. ScareCrow by Contech is a motion-activated sprinkler that may do the trick, depending upon your situation. You can find this through online retailers.

Check around the outside of your doors and windows to see if the feline stranger has been spraying. If so, your indoor cat may be picking up on the scent so clean away any urine odor close to the house.

Block off your cat's view through any windows from which he might be able to see the outdoor cat. You can use poster board, opaque film, or anything else that can be securely fastened. You need only cover the bottom half of the windows. I know it's going to look strange but I'd rather have an opaque film on my windows than cat urine on my walls.

Follow the instructions in this chapter under "The Three-Step Retraining Program."

Hostile Takeovers

In a multicat household, if you isolate a new cat in a separate room before integrating him into the cat family, it will help ease litter box disputes. Refer to Chapter 11 for more on new cat introductions. Now, what if you've followed all of the correct introduction procedures and you still notice someone not using the litter box? This could happen even if there isn't a new cat in the house. One of your three longtime companion cats might suddenly begin eliminating outside of the box.

By now you know that in a multicat household it's essential to have enough litter boxes (the *think like a cat* rule: have the same number of boxes as cats). The boxes must also:

1. Be kept clean
2. Be the right size
3. Be filled with an appealing substrate
4. Be in appropriate locations
5. Have escape routes

Wait a minute . . . an *escape route for a litter box*? Most definitely! Look at it from your cat's point of view. He goes into the litter box, which is probably wedged in the corner of the bathroom. Perhaps it's even a covered box. Let's say the opening to the box doesn't face the entrance to the bathroom. If another cat comes into the room and approaches the box—whether it's with trouble on his agenda or just a routine pit stop—the cat inside the box is taken by surprise. He truly is trapped because there's only one way out and his potential enemy is blocking that route. If the encounter at the litter box is between feuding felines, the fellow trapped inside feels a great sense of threat. Even an open box, if wedged in a corner, may only allow for one way out.

The escape potential from the litter box is important in any cat household but it's of the utmost importance if you're in the midst of trying to resolve an indiscriminate urination or spraying problem.

Look at the box from a cat's point of view and adjust it to avoid the possibility of him getting cornered. If the box is covered, remove the top. If it's in a corner, slide it out a little. If there's a more open area in the room, relocate the box there.

Another way to create an escape route is to afford your cat more warning time. Do this by making sure the box gives him a vantage point from which to view the entrance of the room. If the litter box occupant can see another cat coming, that may give him a few more seconds' warning—enough time to get out of the line of fire. I often recommend that a client place the box opposite the room's entrance so kitty has maximum warning time. That way he can see the length of the room and the room's entrance. Based on your furniture layout this may not be possible but the farther from the door you can place the box, the better.

More than one litter box in different areas of the house is a must to reduce anxiety. It ensures kitty has an alternative in case one box is being guarded. This also means a cat won't have to pass another cat's area in order to access the litter box. So, while you may like the fact that the litter box is well hidden and out of the way, a cat may feel the location is setting him up for an ambush.

If you're dealing with a feline inappropriate elimination problem in your multicat household, look at the places chosen for urination or defecation. You may find that targeted areas offer a cat what the litter box can't: *escape*. Perhaps the cat is eliminating behind the chair in the living room. The cat has privacy and cover but the openness of the area allows him to view the room and offers several escape routes should he perceive a threat. I've found that very often, if the target spot is in a room with only one entrance, the spot will be by the far wall so the cat can have a good view of the doorway.

Pay attention to the route a cat must take to get to the litter box. The journey can be tense and harrowing in a household where there's a turf war. If a more assertive cat stations himself in the long narrow hallway that leads to the litter box, a low-ranking cat will want to avoid an encounter.

Within a hostile household you may encounter both spraying and indiscriminate urination. Spraying may be done by the new cat to establish a territorial space of his own or to leave information about himself in such an unsure environment. It may also be done by the resident higher-ranking cat either as a reminder to others of his status or as a victory display after a confrontation. Unfamiliar cats who are trying to gather information about one another without having an actual confrontation may spray-mark. Find out who is displaying the behavior and what kind of behavior it is (spraying or indiscriminate urination), because that's crucial for solving the problem. Remember, it could be more than one cat and it might be the one you least suspect.

The Three-Step Retraining Program

Let's start with what *not* to do. Don't punish your cat in any way for eliminating or spraying outside of the litter box. If anyone has ever advised you to rub your cat's nose in his mess, DON'T follow it under any circumstances. This method doesn't work and is actually inhumane. By rubbing his nose in his mess you only manage to communicate that the very act of urination and defecation are bad and he'll be punished every time he goes. He won't make the connection that you're displeased only with his choice of location. He'll assume that whenever he has to eliminate, he'll be punished. This only adds to the anxiety he already feels. For whatever reason, his litter box isn't a comfortable place so

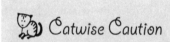

Catwise Caution

Any form of punishment will only make a cat more secretive in his location choice for inappropriate elimination due to the added fear of the owner.

he'll soon find more secluded hiding spots to avoid your reprimand. He may also become afraid of you or defensive in your presence.

The next big *don't* on the list: don't hit your cat. Once again, he'll associate the act of elimination with being punished and he'll become afraid of you or even react defensively.

Another common but counterproductive retraining method is to grab the cat while he's in the act of spraying and forcibly whisk him off to his litter box. If you think that transporting your cat to the box mid-pee will work, you're sadly mistaken. Trust me, he hasn't forgotten where his box is.

Confinement is a method sometimes suggested, but it won't help you to determine the underlying cause of the behavior. If you haven't addressed the true cause for the behavior then the inappropriate elimination will resume once confinement ends. This method is good for cats who are in an unfamiliar environment or are just learning what the litter box is actually for.

Now, what should you do? First you want to reduce the appeal of your carpet or furniture as a litter box alternative. Begin with cleaning, odor neutralizing, and making the area seem less attractive as an elimination choice. Regular household cleansers may get rid of stains but they only mask the odor. The scent of urine on the carpet or along the baseboard of the wall can trigger the cat to soil that same spot repeatedly. Completely get rid of the odor so that your cat's sensitive nose doesn't lead him back there again and again. Pet stain and odor neutralizing products are what you need.

I have outlined below a basic three-step program for retraining your cat to the box. Even if your veterinarian determines that your cat has been urinating because of FLUTD or another medical condition, you may still need to follow the steps listed below. The cat may have formed negative associations with the box from the pain he felt during urination, so you may also need to use behavior modification. At the very least you'll need to clean and neutralize all soiled spots.

Step 1: The Cleanup

Before you can clean and neutralize stains and odors you have to identify where they are all located. There may be obvious ones that you can see, but there may also be ones that are hidden or old. You also want to make sure you clean the entire stain. That's when a special detection light becomes a necessary tool. A *black light* can be held a few inches away from a surface and will cause urine stains to fluoresce. If you think your cat has hit several locations, the light will be a very worthwhile investment. Get a roll of painter's tape so you can mark the soiled areas for cleanup. There are several brands of black lights available at pet supply stores and online.

You'll also need a *pet stain and odor neutralizing product*. When you shop for these products, make sure the label says that it is specifically for pet urine/feces stain and odors. Don't use regular household cleansers.

Read the instructions before using. The cleanup technique isn't the same for all products. Also, it may recommend testing an inconspicuous area first.

If the spot is fresh, start by gently blotting up the urine with paper towels. Be careful not to force the liquid deeper into the pile of carpet or the fabric of upholstered furniture. After you've blotted up as much as possible, you can press down to absorb the rest of the moisture. Keep replacing wet towels with dry ones. Next, use a pet stain and odor neutralizer on the spot.

If you're cleaning carpet, leave the pet stain and odor remover on long enough so it can reach all soiled areas. If the urine has seeped through to the padding, the pet stain and odor remover needs to soak that far down also. Follow the product's instructions for how long to let the product sit and then blot with towels until you can't get up any more liquid. Some products have to be rinsed with water, so make sure to read the label carefully. Then, if needed, you can set up a small fan to help accelerate drying time.

If you're using the pet stain and odor remover on an area of the carpet that's been sprayed repeatedly, you may need to dilute the old urine residue before you use the product. All that built-up urine may be too much for some products. First treat the stain with plain water and then blot with paper towels. Now you can treat the area with the product just as you would a fresh urine stain. The instructions on the product you're using will indicate whether this step is necessary. If in doubt about how to use a product, call the manufacturer's toll-free number.

To clean feces from carpet, slip a plastic sandwich bag over your hand and carefully remove the solid stool. If the stool is well formed, you should be able to lift it off the carpet easily. I don't advise using newspaper to pick it up because you run the risk of pushing it deeper into the carpet. If you decide to use paper towel or toilet paper, be very light handed. Once you've removed the stool, treat the area with the pet stain and odor remover, following label instructions.

If the stool is very watery, you can avoid causing more of a stain if you carefully scoop it up along the top of the carpet with a spoon or thin metal spatula. Diarrhea that is pure liquid should be blotted up with paper towels and the area cleaned as previously described for urine stains. Remember, try not to force the stain down deeper into the carpet.

Never use ammonia or ammonia-based products because urine contains ammonia and the smell could trigger your cat to revisit the cleaned spot.

Step 2: Protection

This step applies to your carpets and furniture. If your cat has targeted specific areas of the home, limit access to these spots during the retraining phase. If he's

targeting a specific area of the carpet, cover it with a piece of plastic carpet protector. If it's the bed that's getting peed on, put a plastic shower curtain on top
of the comforter or use a water-proof pet coverlet. Cover targeted pieces of furniture with sections of plastic carpet protector, pieces of plastic shower curtains,
or water-proof pet throws/quilts.

If the cat is targeting an entire room, block his access to it when you aren't
there to supervise or when you're not retraining (see Step 3).

Step 3: New Associations

If you've been reading this book carefully, you know that in order to resolve litter
box problems, you have to uncover the underlying cause. If you're still unsure of
what could be causing your cat to eliminate outside of the box, go back and reread the beginning of the chapter for clues. You'll never fix the problem just by
cleaning the area with a pet stain and odor remover if you haven't figured out
why kitty is displaying the particular behavior. He'll just find a new spot for
every spot you clean. Take the time to look at the environment from your cat's
point of view. The answers are there.

If you're thinking like a cat, you understand the power of changing a cat's
association with a particular location or behavior. Playtime is a great way to
switch a negative association to a positive one. When a cat is in prey-drive, those
"feel good" brain chemicals are flowing. Do interactive play sessions in the areas
where your cat has eliminated in the past. The more often you do them the more
he'll associate the spots with good experiences.

You can also help change a cat's association with a targeted area through
clicker training. Click and reward the cat when he walks over to an area he has
previously soiled, just sniffs it, and walks away.

Feeding your cat in previously soiled areas (once they've been cleaned) is
another technique for changing association. Cats will not eliminate by their
food. If he's urinating in only one area, you can feed him his entire meal there.
If he's urinating in various spots, place a small bowl of food at each spot. Don't
pile on the food because you don't want to increase his daily portion. Just divide
up his normal amount.

Address any intercat conflict by following the behavior modification techniques previously outlined in this chapter. The cats need to be segregated for a
while and then reintroduced. Each cat needs to feel comfortable in the home
and have safe and unthreatened access to resources—feeding stations, litter
boxes, sleeping areas, and playtime opportunities—then you can gradually re-

introduce them using positive association. Reintroduction won't work, however, if you haven't addressed the resources issue. Having to share a litter box and risk ambush or feeling intimidated at the food bowl will trump all your good reintroduction progress. It's a package deal and you can't take shortcuts if you want a spraying cat to feel spraying is no longer necessary or a cat exhibiting inappropriate elimination to feel safe in his box again.

There is a product called Feliway, by Ceva, that contains synthetic feline facial pheromones. It's based on the theory that cats don't spray-mark where they facially mark. Feliway comes in a spray bottle to use on specifically targeted areas or can be used as a plug-in diffuser. It should not be used as a replacement for behavior modification, though. Some people report excellent results with Feliway and others notice no effect.

Another Litter Option

A product that has been very useful for many cats who display indiscriminate urination is a unique litter called Dr. Elsey's Cat Attract made by Precious Cat. It contains a special combination of herbs that encourages the cat to return to the correct substrate for elimination. Developed by a veterinarian, it's 99 percent dust-free and clumps very well for easy scooping. The product is available through pet supply retailers and online.

Give It Time

If your cat has had prior negative experiences in an area, go slowly, and let him set the pace. Say for example, the narrow hallway leading to the litter box has been a scary place because that's where an intimidating cat would lie in wait to attack. Put the intimidator in another room and then begin a low-intensity interactive play session with the victim of intimidation. Stay within his comfort zone by letting him set the pace of how far into the hallway he wants to go. It may take several sessions of playtime and clicker training to raise his confidence level. If ongoing intimidation or hostility is the cause of litter box problems, you'll probably need to separate the cats and then do a reintroduction in order to permanently resolve the litter box issue. Refer to Chapter 11.

When attempting to retrain a cat to a litter box there is another very important aspect of behavior modification. It's the one aspect we tend to be short on when the going gets tough: *patience*. Many indiscriminate elimination or spraying problems didn't happen overnight, so they won't be solved overnight either. Some of the clients I've seen had been living with a spraying cat for several years before contacting me. Those are not problems that can be corrected in forty-eight hours. Quick fixes don't work.

Data Tracking

Put a calendar on your refrigerator and keep track of when your cat inappropriately eliminates or sprays and note the locations. Note the time of day (if known) and what the potential antecedent might have been.

Data tracking will help you to see any pattern and will give you a better idea of how behavior modification is progressing.

Contacting a Certified Behavior Expert

As you've read this chapter you've become aware of how complex, stressful, and sad litter box problems can be. It can be a deal-breaker when it comes to whether the cat stays with the family or is sent outside, abandoned, relinquished to a shelter, or euthanized. If you're dealing with a litter box problem without success, there are options available for you. Talk to your veterinarian about a referral to a certified behavior expert. For more on this, refer to Chapter 7.

Behavioral Drug Therapy for Litter Box Problems

There are times when behavior modification won't be enough to counteract all the problems that a cat may have. The serious nature of the problem, the length of time the problem has been going on, or the extreme level of fear or stress in the cat may preclude the use of modification techniques at this time.

There are now drugs used in animal behavior therapy that are very effective with few side effects. If there is an accurate diagnosis and the appropriate drug is used, it could save a cat with a behavior problem from being euthanized. A word of caution, though: do not, under any circumstances, take it upon yourself to medicate your cat with any drugs you may be taking. An accurate diagnosis must be made by your veterinarian or veterinary behaviorist and then the appropriate drug and dosage must be prescribed.

Although psychoactive drugs can be extremely beneficial for cats with behavior problems, they're not one-size-fits-all nor are they a quick fix. Before you and your veterinarian decide to go the route of drug therapy, you need to have a thorough discussion about all aspects of this treatment, including how it might affect the medical health of your cat, the cost of the drug, potential side effects, and the type of monitoring required to ensure the cat's safety. No drug therapy should begin without a complete medical workup on the cat. Be sure you know

POINTS TO CONSIDER BEFORE BEGINNING DRUG THERAPY

- the medical health of the cat
- the accuracy of the diagnosis
- inefficacy of behavior modification so far
- inefficacy of environmental modifications so far
- possible side effects of the drug
- cost
- ability of owner to administer medication
- how the drug affects the behavior
- how long the cat will need to be on the drug

the expected duration of drug therapy as well as instructions for how the cat should be weaned off the drug at the end of therapy.

Drug therapy must always be used concurrently with behavior modification or else you stand a very good chance of seeing the problem resurface after the drug has been stopped. It's *part* of the complete behavior modification program, and not a way to avoid doing the work necessary to help your cat.

If you feel drug therapy is needed, make an appointment with your veterinarian to discuss the options thoroughly. A referral to a certified behavior expert may be needed before your veterinarian feels drug therapy is appropriate. Don't take shortcuts. Be an informed owner—your cat's life depends on it.

Unusual Elimination Preferences

Cats mostly prefer a soft substrate that enables them to scratch, dig, and cover. Every now and then, though, a cat comes along who prefers to eliminate on hard surfaces and turns his nose up at litter of any kind. Because urinating in tubs, sinks, or on floors is a common sign of FLUTD, make sure such a cat has been checked by the veterinarian. If in fact the problem is behavioral, then it's time to figure out just what kind of substrate he would prefer.

If your cat only eliminates on smooth, flat surfaces, put an empty, low-sided litter box where he is currently eliminating. If he starts eliminating in there you can gradually start to add soft-textured scoopable litter in there. If he eliminates on the floor again then it usually means you've put too much litter in too soon. If, no matter what you've tried, he doesn't want any type of litter whatsoever, place an absorbent sheet in there (similar to puppy pee pads). The absorbent material will have to be changed quite often but it's better than having your cat pee on the floor.

Another preference of some cats is to eliminate only on rugs, towels, or clothing. If you've gone through the medical checkup, tried the behavior modification, and offered your cat a variety of litters (buffet style), provide a litter box with a soft material inside instead of litter. This can be a towel or scrap of carpet, depending upon the type of material your cat has been using for urination. If he uses the box, keep replacing the soiled material with clean, then gradually begin to add small amounts of scoopable litter on top. As you replace the carpet or material piece make it a bit smaller each time. If you do this gradually enough, you should be able to acclimate him to litter again.

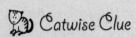 Catwise Clue

Remember to use your *think-like-a-cat* detective skills before assuming the cat is eliminating on the floor because of a texture preference. Make sure the cause isn't due to a medical issue, a need for more escape potential, or an aversion to the size of box, type of box, or cleanliness of litter. Also, make sure you've offered a variety of litters, buffet style, to see if there's a more appealing substrate texture for him.

Plants and Cat Pee

Eliminating in the potted plants happens more often if the cat has spent much of his life outdoors. It can also happen if a cat discovers he prefers the texture of soil to that of the substrate currently in his litter box. If you're using traditional clay litter or another litter that doesn't have a soft texture, place a second box out with soft, scoopable litter to see if that texture is what the cat is seeking.

Set up deterrents in the pots to discourage your cat from using them as a litter box. Sticky Paws for Plants, made by Fe-Lines, is a product that can be placed over the pots in a tic-tac-toe pattern. For large floor planters, cover the soil with rocks. The rocks need to be heavy enough so the cat can't push them away. Another option is to cover the soil with garden netting. All of the above-mentioned methods will allow you to continue to water your plants easily.

Geriatric-Related Litter Box Problems

As your cat ages, physical and/or mental deterioration may result in house-soiling behavior. Arthritis can make it difficult for him to get in and out of the box. Climbing and descending stairs might be too painful. Some cats can become disoriented as they age and may have trouble remembering the location of the litter box. Diabetes, kidney disease, and other medical conditions that create increased water intake and urine output can also make it difficult for a cat to reach the box in time.

Provide several low-sided litter boxes that are easy for your cat to get to. If the lowest litter box is still too high, use plastic serving trays. If your cat eliminates in his sleep, put absorbent pads on top of his bed. Be tolerant of accidents and make life as convenient as possible by providing multiple litter boxes throughout the house. For more on geriatric-related issues, refer to Chapter 16.

9

Scratching Posts, Sofas, Antique Chairs . . . Which One Will Your Cat Choose?

Yes, You Can Have a Cat and Nice Furniture Too

During visits to cat-owning friends' homes, you've seen the tattered remains of what once were drapes. You've tried not to notice the shredded sofa that looked as if it had been the victim of a tiny chain saw. Now you have your own cute little kitten back at home. Is he capable of inflicting this much damage? Is this the end of your nice furniture? Should you have him declawed?

Before you decide to declaw, go back to those friends' homes and really take a closer look at things. Do you see scratching posts anywhere? If so, are they short and wobbly? What methods did your friends use to try and redirect the scratching behavior to this more appropriate object? Was punishment the only way your friends thought they could train their cats? If you've read the previous chapters in this book, how successful do you think punishment would be? Based on what you've read so far, wouldn't it make sense to you that if a cat was scratching the furniture, it might mean that either the scratching post wasn't meeting his requirements or, worse yet, that there wasn't a post available?

You have the opportunity to become an informed owner of your little kitten and use productive training methods.

Having a cat declawed is extremely serious and permanent, so please read this entire chapter and make sure you understand why cats scratch, why they choose certain textures over others, and the training methods I've successfully used for years.

The Need to Scratch

Scratching is an innate behavior and serves many functions in a cat's life. The most obvious one is to maintain the health of his nails. A cat discards the outer nail sheath on his forefeet by raking them down a rough surface. As he pulls his nails along the material, the dead outer sheath comes off exposing the new growth underneath.

Scratching also serves as a visual and olfactory marker. When a cat rakes his nails down a surface, a visual mark is left that can be seen by other cats at a safe distance. This can greatly reduce physical confrontations because an approaching cat may see the mark and decide not to come any closer. When the cat scratches, he also leaves an olfactory mark through scent glands in the paw pads. So if an approaching cat decides to advance further, he'll get more information about who left the scratch mark through scent communication. Even though scratching serves as a territory marker, it also probably plays an even more important role in providing security and familiarity for the cat.

If you've ever seen a cat run to his post to scratch when his owner arrives home, you've witnessed how scratching can serve as an emotional outlet as well. A cat will also use scratching to displace the frustration he may feel after being reprimanded or being unable to do something that he wants to do (for example, capturing the bird he sees through the window).

Scratching enables the cat to stretch out the muscles in his shoulders and back. A cat often enjoys a full stretch after napping in a curled-up position or after eating.

The Impact of Declawing

Many owners rush into the decision to declaw without understanding the consequences. Luckily, more veterinarians are educating owners that declawing should be a last-resort surgery.

Declawing, also known as Onychectomy, surgically removes an animal's claws by amputating the end bones of the animal's toes. It is the equivalent of having the top joint of all your fingers removed. After the joints of the cat's toes are amputated, a pressure bandage is put on the legs and remains in place overnight. The cat is in pain upon waking and will continue to feel pain for many days afterward. If the cat isn't given pain relievers, it's an even more difficult recovery.

The wounds need a week or more to heal and during the recovery time, regular litter can't be used because it's painful to the sensitive paws and can get stuck in the wounds.

A declawed cat is almost totally defenseless if he can't slash his enemy with his claws. Therefore, a declawed cat can never be allowed outdoors. A cat without front nails would have severe difficulty climbing a tree or fence in order to escape an attacker.

Declawing can sometimes affect a cat's sense of balance and if surgery was improperly performed, one or more of the nails could grow back in a way that causes the cat discomfort.

There has been an ongoing controversy as to whether declawed cats are more inclined to become biters. Many experts will argue that there's no supporting evidence to prove that a declawed cat is more likely to bite. I have seen some cats become biters and/or go through a personality change. I've also seen cats who remained just as good-natured as they were before being declawed. What is so unfortunate, though, is that these good-natured cats might have been the easiest to train to a post had the proper method been used. Declawing is extremely painful, causes the cat unnecessary suffering, and denies him the natural ability to scratch—something that's vital to his physical and emotional well being. Declawing, in my opinion, is nothing more than mutilation. It is considered an act of animal cruelty and is illegal in many countries such as Australia, Brazil, Austria, United Kingdom, Finland, Switzerland, many other European countries, and most recently West Hollywood, California.

If you have a kitten, wait until you've tried training him to a post before considering declawing. I know it seems as if his claws are always exposed, but in time he'll learn more about how his body works and he'll figure out that he can keep his nails sheathed more often than he's doing now.

Getting your kitten used to regular nail trims will help him accept having his paws handled when he is an adult. Keeping his nails trimmed will lessen damage to furniture, which is something that will benefit both of you.

The Average Scratching Post

The cat owner tries to do the right thing by purchasing a scratching post at the local pet supply store. The post is usually covered in a colorful carpet material and may even have a cute little toy dangling from the top. Home the owner goes with the best of intentions to provide for kitty's needs. The post gets placed in the corner of the living room. The cat, ever curious when it comes to anything new in the home, goes over to check it out. Sniffing the post, the cat even gives the dangling toy a little swat with his paw. The owner smiles. Satisfied that this new addition to the home is harmless, the cat turns his back to it and trots over to the sofa where he proceeds to sink his nails in and scratch. The owner frowns.

Is the cat being stubborn and destructive? Willfully disobedient? Not at all. He just knows that the post won't satisfy him when it comes to his natural, normal, and healthy need to scratch.

So what's wrong with the average post? Let's start with the cover material. Most posts are covered with carpet that's too soft and plush. A cat needs a rough textured material that he can sink his nails into to help discard the dead sheaths. If you have a cat who is scratching on furniture instead of the post, compare the two textures. Run your hand along the post and then along the furniture. The furniture wins.

Moving on down the list, the next problem with the average post is that it's usually not sturdy enough. Many have a small base so when a cat leans his weight on it while scratching, it topples over. Some poorly constructed posts aren't connected to the base securely so they wobble. Because furniture is sturdy the cat has another incentive to use your sofa. He knows that it won't wobble.

Most posts are also too short. The act of scratching is also a way for a cat to get a full back stretch. Look at how your cat's body elongates when he engages in a full stretch. Stretching out feels so wonderful that he's going to return to the place he knows will provide that—your furniture.

Choosing the Right Scratching Post

When you go out shopping, keep three rules in mind. A scratching post must be:

1. Covered in the right material
2. Sturdy and well constructed
3. Tall enough for a full stretch

For most cats, you can't go wrong if the cover material is sisal. It's rough texture is very appealing. As you run your hand along the post, the rougher it feels, the better. Think of a nail file. You wouldn't want to use a dull, smooth file, right? Neither does your cat.

Some carpet-covered posts are acceptable if the material is rough enough and the loops of the carpet don't catch the cat's claws.

If you're unable to find a sisal-covered post, you can order one online. There are several companies that make tall, sturdy, good quality, sisal-covered posts.

Making Your Own Scratching Post

You'll need a 4" × 4" piece of wood (actually, it really measures 3½" × 3½" but it's called 4 × 4 for some odd reason. Perhaps it's a carpenter's joke on the rest of us). It should be 30" in length. For the base, a 16" × 16" square ¾" piece of plywood will work. Select cedar, redwood, fir, or pine for the post. Oak, which is a hardwood, will be more difficult to drill.

At the store, you'll probably find both *treated* and *untreated* wood. Don't choose the treated kind because it has an obvious odor that neither you nor your cat will like. If your local lumber company or home improvement store only has treated 4" × 4" posts, then get a regular untreated 2" × 4" × 8". Cut two 30" pieces and screw them together to form a 4" × 4" × 30" long post.

If you plan on leaving the base uncovered be sure to sand it well so you won't get splinters should you stub your toe on it while on your way to the bathroom in the middle of the night.

To fasten the post to the base, you'll need five #8 2½" drywall screws. Mark on top of the base where the post will sit. Draw two diagonal lines from the opposing corners. At the center of the "x" place your post and mark a square. Drill one hole in the center and one hole on each diagonal line, one inch from the center. Coat the screws with bar soap or wax from an old candle so they'll go in more easily. Turn the base upside down and run the center screw through the bottom of the base into the positioned post. Double-check the location of the post with the marks you made on the top of the base before running the rest of the screws. When you've finished, if you still think the post isn't sturdy enough, attach a small metal angle iron on each side of the post bottom where it meets the base.

There's one common mistake that many owners make about cover material: they hunt down that carpeting they had left over. As with what is on most store-bought posts, that carpeting is usually too plush and soft. Even if your cat, for some reason, decided that the fluffy soft carpet was an acceptable cover material for the post, it will send a mixed message to him. He won't understand why scratching the carpeted post is acceptable but scratching the carpet that covers the floor isn't.

I've found the easiest covering for a post is rope. When you purchase it, get more than you think you're going to need because it'll be wound very tightly around the post. You can also use rope to cover a carpeted post that your cat has been ignoring. Secure it at the top and bottom with heavy-duty carpet staples or carpet tacks. To protect your hands, wear work gloves when winding the rope.

Some cats prefer to scratch on plain old wood. You may have noticed this if your cat scratches on the logs stacked by the fireplace. If that's the case, the

SUPPLIES NEEDED FOR MAKING A POST

- 4" × 4" × 30" piece of wood
- 16" × 16" square of ¾" thick plywood
- cover material for post
- cover material for base (optional)
- sandpaper (to smooth base)
- five #8 × 2½" drywall screws (more if using a 2" × 4")
- four small metal angle irons (optional)
- carpet staples or carpet tacks
- drill
- bar soap or wax
- safety glasses
- catnip (to rub on finished post)

easiest thing to do is make an upright log post. Nature has already supplied the ideal cover material for you in that case. If your cat scratches on bare wood, you can strip the bark off the log or use a plain 4" × 4" piece of wood.

Cats can have such individual and unique preferences for scratching, so use creativity to come up with the ideal post. Don't give up!

Where to Put the Scratching Post

Don't make the mistake of trying to hide the scratching post. It may not be the greatest-looking addition to your décor, but your cat needs to know that it's there. The post, conveniently located, can be a visual reminder to scratch in the right place.

Many cats enjoy scratching and stretching after a nap or after they've eaten. Because scratching is also an emotional outlet, many cats will want to use the post when their owner comes home or as they anxiously wait for dinner.

If the post is for a kitten, keep it right in the middle of his room or area so he can't miss it. If your kitten has access to the entire house, invest in more than one post. You can't expect him to keep a lid on his desire to scratch while he searches from room to room for his post. Make it easy for the youngster.

In a multicat home, provide scratching posts in the areas each cat spends the most time. Some cats may not feel comfortable sharing one post.

Training Your Cat to Use the Scratching Post

Scratching, for a kitten, is actually a means of climbing to higher ground. To a new cat owner, it may appear that your kitten has Velcro paws, as you watch him scale furniture, drapes, beds, and the clothes hanging in the closets. Take a deep breath and be patient. This phase will pass. Even though your kitten may do nothing with the post other than climb up and over the top, very soon he'll discover scratching behavior and you'll want to be ready.

The training method is the same for a kitten or an adult cat: make it a game. Dangle a peacock feather or other enticing toy right next to the post. As your cat goes for the toy he'll feel the irresistible texture of the post. With your own nails, gently scratch up and down the post. Often, that scratching sound can inspire him to join in.

If your cat doesn't have a clue about what to do with the post, lay it on its side and dangle the toy all around it. As he jumps on the post or paws at the toy, he'll discover the texture. He may then begin scratching the post in earnest. Once he has discovered its true purpose, you can stand the post upright again.

Never force your cat to scratch by taking his paws and putting them on the post. No matter how gently you do it, your cat won't like the experience and it'll just cause confusion. His attention will be focused on getting out of your grasp and you'll have done nothing but create a negative association with the post.

Make the games around the scratching post a regularly scheduled event for a kitten.

Keep your training methods consistent so you don't confuse your kitten. Don't drag the toy under fabrics such as comforters, clothing, or behind drapes. That could encourage him to scratch there as he claws at the toy. Don't run the toy up and along upholstered furniture. That will cause your kitten to extend his claws and climb. Never send mixed messages.

Retraining a Cat to the Post
After He Has Discovered Your Furniture

It can be done. First, though, you must have the right kind of post. Make sure you've followed my instructions and purchased or constructed an appropriate one. If you already have a post in your home that has sat for years gathering dust, don't even attempt to retrain your cat to it, unless it's tall and sturdy, in which case you may try recovering it with a better material. Chances are, though, you should probably just get rid of the relic.

Next, look at the areas where he's currently scratching. If it's the sofa or chair, you'll have to make it unappealing. If the scratched area of the furniture is limited to certain sections, lay strips of Sticky Paws (a double-sided transparent tape made especially for this purpose) across them. Plain masking tape can leave a residue behind. According to the manufacturer, Sticky Paws has an acrylic base so it won't leave any reside when removed from the furniture. The product is also water-soluble. Don't use on leather or vinyl, though, and don't keep Sticky Paws on upholstery indefinitely.

If the cat has been working on the entire chair, cover it with a sheet. Carefully tuck it all around and tape the bottom so he can't climb up underneath it. Place strips of Sticky Paws at several locations. If you need to cover large areas of your upholstery, Sticky Paws also comes in extra-large strips. Now you've turned this great scratching surface into an unacceptable one. The next step is to put the new post next to the covered furniture. That way, when he goes over for his routine scratch and realizes his usual spot has disappeared, he'll discover something even better. You can further entice him by using a toy around the post to get his attention. Also, rub the post with catnip to ensure his approval (adult cats only).

If you catch your cat attempting to scratch the furniture during retraining, don't punish, hit, or yell at him. Increase the amount of double-sided tape. You can even attach pieces of plastic carpet protectors over the top (nubby side out).

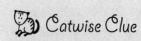 Catwise Clue

Get your clicker out and click-and-treat your cat when he scratches on his post. Reward him to let him know he's done something good.

Keep the furniture covered until your cat has been using the post routinely and no longer attempts to get at the furniture. Then gradually move the post over to where you want it permanently located. I recommend that you keep it relatively close to the same area, though, to remind him. When you feel he's retrained and goes right for the post without so much as looking at the furniture, go ahead and remove the sheet or double-sided tape.

If your cat is scratching by the front door or around entrances to rooms, it may have more to do with marking than nail maintenance. Put a scratching post near the doorway and cover the scratched area with Sticky Paws. In narrow hallways or anywhere else it would be impossible to put a post, use sisal covered pads that can be attached to the wall or a doorknob. You can find them in many pet supply stores and online. You can even make your own.

Once you have your post(s) in place, you can monitor how successful it is by looking at the base. If your cat is using it, you should probably begin to see small crescent-shaped nail sheaths there.

Once a week during retraining, rub a little catnip on the post as a little hint (adult cats only). When retraining is complete, use catnip on the post periodically as a treat.

Should You Ever Surrender?

It's one of the most common things I hear from owners. In desperation, they decide to give up and let the cat destroy a chair because they plan on buying a new one eventually. The problem with that logic is that the cat won't understand why he isn't allowed to scratch the new piece when he was allowed to scratch the old one. Don't send mixed messages to your kitty. Invest in a great scratching post, put it in the right location, and do the training to entice your cat to use it.

Horizontal Scratching

Not every cat reaches up and scratches vertically. There are some who prefer scratching flat surfaces. You may notice your cat scratching on the carpet, welcome mat, outdoor deck flooring, or on the arms of furniture. There are also many cats who enjoy both horizontal and vertical scratching. If you notice that all of the scratched surfaces are horizontal, that may be why attempts at training your cat to a vertical post have been unsuccessful.

There are many commercial scratching pads available for horizontal scratchers. Many inexpensive pads made of corrugated cardboard are available. There are terrific corrugated-cardboard scratching pads made on an incline as well, in case you think your cat would prefer that type of position.

Feline False Nails

These are little plastic nail caps that can be placed over your cat's existing nails. Permanent glue is squeezed into the cap and then it's fitted over the nail. The caps last from one to two months. Your cat's nails grow, so any caps that don't fall off or aren't chewed off will have to be removed.

The cat will still attempt to scratch with these nail caps in place but obviously won't be able to penetrate anything.

For owners who are totally unable to train their cats to a post but also don't want to declaw, these nail caps are an option.

I'm not a fan of this product because once the caps are in place, the cat is unable to retract his nails fully. I'm not sure how comfortable that would be over the long term. Also, the caps prevent the cat from enjoying natural scratching behavior. Even though I don't like the nail caps, I'd prefer you use these instead of declawing.

The first time the caps are applied, it should be done by your veterinarian or veterinary technician in case your cat has any negative reaction.

Nail kits are available for at-home application and come in various sizes. Don't attempt to do this at home if your cat is aggressive. Even if he isn't, you'll need an assistant to hold the cat while you apply the caps.

I've found that many cats manage to chew at least one or two of the caps off shortly after application. So you can't just put the caps on and forget them. Check periodically to make sure they're all still in place because two or three exposed nails will still cause damage to your furniture.

If you're interested in nail caps, speak with your veterinarian.

Indoor Trees

Every home should have at least one. Not only do they provide a tall, sturdy scratching surface, they enable a cat to climb and perch on his very own furniture. There are a wide variety of trees available. You can get multitiered ones so that two or three cats can share, and they come in many different configurations and heights.

The support posts on the trees can be covered in rope, bark, sisal, or left as bare wood. Multitiered trees with two or three posts can have several coverings. It's pure paradise for a cat!

The tree needs to be sturdy with a wide base because your cat may decide to do a flying leap from the top perch to the floor. Invest in a well-made post.

Choose a tree with U-shaped perches as opposed to flat ones. Cats like to feel their backs up against something so they don't feel so vulnerable.

Should You Replace That Well-Used, Worn-Out Old Post?

Your cat has been faithfully using his scratching post for years. So much so that it's now just shredded rope hanging from a mangled post. You throw the thing away and lovingly surprise your kitty with a brand new one. Guess what? There's a good chance he's not going to like it. He'd gotten that post just the way he wanted it, complete with visual and olfactory marks. It was truly his! Then suddenly, to his horror, his post is gone . . . vanished.

Don't get rid of a post that your cat is strongly attached to. Instead, get an additional post and place it nearby so he'll have a great new scratching option. Remember, scratching isn't just for maintaining the health of the nails, but also for marking and emotional release. If he truly abandons the worn-out post for the new one, then you can dispose of the old one.

In our house, we have three large scratching posts and two cat trees. All are well-used, so I know my cats are happy with them. The most popular post is actually ten years old.

10

The Kitty Chef

Finicky Eaters Aren't Born—They're Created

As a new cat owner, you are no doubt very concerned with providing the best possible nutrition for your growing youngster. *What* you put the food in and *where* you place it can have a surprising impact on whether your cat runs in delight to the bowl at mealtime or sits and stares at it (and you) in disgust. It's about presentation.

There are several options when choosing your kitty's food and water bowls. Before you go out and spend big bucks for a jewel-encrusted, personalized dish or dig through the attic for that old water bowl you've saved from the German shepherd you had eight years ago, evaluate your cat's needs.

A bowl is a bowl, you say? This is true, but what you're looking for is the *best* bowl for *your* cat. Bowls are generally made of plastic, glass, ceramic, or stainless steel. The following are some things to consider when making your choice.

Plastic: Probably more bowls are made of plastic than anything else. It's inexpensive, lightweight, and unbreakable. Some cats can develop allergies from eating out of plastic bowls. The allergy will show up as hair loss or acne on the chin. Some cats can even develop quite serious lesions. No matter how hard you clean it, the dish still retains odors. Plastic bowls are also easily scratched, which can lead to food residue and bacteria collecting in the scratches. A scratched plastic surface can also be abrasive to a cat's sensitive tongue. A scratched bowl must be replaced, so even though you may initially feel as if plastic is inexpensive, the repeated cost of replacement bowls make them not such a bargain.

Finally, I dislike plastic bowls because they're too lightweight. My cats don't enjoy having to follow their bowl all around the kitchen as it slides along the floor. While you may think it's kind of cute and funny, in hostile multicat households, *distance* during meals is critical. A food bowl sliding in the enemy's direction can lead to big trouble.

Glass and Ceramic: A good choice because they're heavier than plastic, so they won't go on trips around the kitchen. They're breakable, though, so you have to take care when washing because chips or cracks can injure a cat's tongue. Additionally, some ceramic bowls have imperfections that create a rough texture. This can be irritating to the tongue. When choosing ceramic, look for manufacturers who state their products are "lead-free."

Stainless Steel: Virtually indestructible. This is a great choice. Because they can be lightweight, though, look for bowls that have nonskid rims on the bottom. To maintain cleanliness, if the rubber nonskid rim is removable, don't forget to wash underneath where bacteria can hide.

Food Bowl Size and Shape

Choose the size appropriate for your cat. With a tiny kitten, if you give him a large bowl, guess what's going to happen? He'll end up stepping in his food. You can save the larger bowl for when he has grown a bit more.

Deep, narrow food bowls that severely crowd the cat's whiskers aren't a good idea. With long-haired cats, deep bowls will cause the fur around his face to become soiled. This type of bowl is also not recommended for short-nosed breeds such as Persians or Himalayans. They need a wide, shallow dish.

Community Feeding Bowls

If you have two or more cats and you purchase one large bowl, you may be creating a problem. Some cats require a greater space around them as they dine. Making the cats eat so close to each other may encourage the more assertive one to intimidate others. A less assertive cat may be too intimidated to approach the bowl until the first cat has finished eating, and by then, all of the food may be gone. Give them at least a few feet between bowls, if possible. In some cases the food bowls may need to be placed on opposite sides of the room or an additional feeding station may even have to be placed in another room.

Double Feeding Dishes

Some people use a double bowl to hold food on one side and water on the other. There are a couple of reasons why I'd recommend you not do that. Some cats don't like their food that close to the water. The result may be a cat with a finicky appetite or a cat who gets his water from other sources (such as the toilet bowl). The other reason why I dislike food and water in one double bowl is that pieces of food usually end up falling into the water and contaminating it, which can be very unappealing to a cat.

Automatic Food and Water Dispensers

Automatic gravity-feed water dispensers are a good idea if your cat drinks lots of water and you're concerned that the bowl will run dry before you get home at the end of the day. They can also be good for multicat homes to ensure adequate water supply. The only thing you have to be careful of is that the water can taste stale if it sits in the gravity-feed bottle for too long. So even if the dispenser has adequate water and you know you filled it a few days ago, empty the container and refill with fresh water often.

Gravity-feed dry-food dispensers are popular in homes where the owners may spend a night or two away or if there is more than one cat in the household. Keep in mind, though, that if you're using the food dispenser for convenience when you travel, you still need someone to come into the home to check on the cats and scoop the litter.

Automatic food and water dispensers don't get cleaned as often as they should and that might discourage a cat from eating or drinking. Be sure to thoroughly empty the dispensers and give them a good cleaning on a regular basis.

There are also automatic feeding dispensers that can release a specified amount of dry food at preselected times on a timer. This is a good way to keep your cat on scheduled meals even when you're gone all day at work. If your cat eats wet food there are timed dispensers with cooling packs inside to keep the food fresh. At the preselected time, the lid opens to reveal a fresh meal for kitty.

Don't depend on automatic feeders (or automatic litter boxes for that matter) to do your job if you are going to be away from home for several days. Electronic products malfunction, get knocked over, and their batteries can go dead.

Washing Food and Water Bowls

No matter what type of bowls you decide on, keep them clean on a daily basis. Wash with dishwashing liquid by hand or in the dishwasher, following the bowl manufacturer's instructions. If washing by hand, be certain to rinse off all traces of soap. Any residue can be irritating to the cat's mouth and tongue. Sometimes, in homes where cats are free-fed, the bowl gets refilled routinely but not washed.

This causes the food to eventually taste stale and the bowl also becomes covered in bacteria. The same applies to water bowls.

Food and Water Placement

As previously stated in this book, the one place in the house you should *never* put the food is near the litter box. I can hear the footsteps now as some of you run to the litter box to see just how close . . . uh-oh, there it is—the food bowl and the litter box side by side. Why is this so bad? To understand, let's go back to the cat's survival instinct. In an outdoor environment, a cat eliminates away from his nest area to avoid attracting predators back to where he lives. By having the food so close to the litter, the cat feels conflicted. The behavior problem that may develop is that the cat chooses to eat the food at that location, since it's the only place the food can be found, and then chooses somewhere else to eliminate. I promise you, his choice of location for elimination won't be one you'll like very much.

Other bad choices for food placement are areas that are noisy, scary, or unpredictable. If you have a timid, jumpy cat and you put the food in the laundry room, guess what's going to happen when the washer goes from *rinse* to *spin*? Your cat is going to bolt out of there. If you have a dog and the cat's food is very appealing to him, then placing the bowls on the floor where the dog can get to them may not be the best choice.

The most obvious place for the food and water is in the kitchen, but based on your particular circumstances, that may not be possible. If your cat is timid and the activity in the kitchen is overwhelming, then put his food in a quieter area of the house. Owners can get very creative to meet their cats' needs. Just remember, mealtime should be a time when the cat feels safe so he can enjoy his dinner.

Once you've settled on the best spot for the food, don't switch locations if the cat is happy. Being such creatures of habit, cats don't like it when they go to their usual feeding spot only to discover it has disappeared.

Elderly cats may require adjustments in their usual feeding routine or location. If you've always kept your cat's food in an elevated spot, be sure he's still able to make that leap up and down. You may have to lower his food to the floor or create a way for him to easily climb to the spot, such as a small carpeted stairway or pet ramp.

Pet Place Mats

For seriously messy eaters or cats who love to spill their water bowls, you can find place mats with raised edges that contain the water and prevent damage to your floor or carpet. These place mats are available at pet supply stores and online.

The Confusing World of Pet Food

Unless you've been living under a rock you've probably noticed how much shelf space in stores is devoted to pet food. The variety is mind-boggling. Then there are the therapeutic and prescription foods sold through veterinarians, specialty and organic foods sold in organic food stores and the Internet, and finally, there's raw food as well.

The pet-food industry is a big, big business. Pet-food advertising can be very misleading by appealing to *our* impression of food. Some companies create food that looks as if we ourselves could eat it—slices of beef, smooth gravy, peas, tiny carrots, etc. Do you think those things really matter to a cat? If your kitty took over the duties of chef at your house, you'd be sitting down to a plate of one small mouse with a side dish of butterflies and grasshoppers. Tomorrow's menu would probably include Bird a la Felix, seasoned to perfection with a hint of catnip. Oh, and one other important ingredient in both of the menus . . . the main dish would still be breathing. Hungry yet? Me neither, but cats would be lined up for miles.

This chapter will help guide you toward understanding what your cat's nutritional requirements are and how to supply them. I don't want you paying more than you should for food just because it's well advertised, but I also don't want you loading up the trunk of your car with forty pounds of some economy brand that won't help your kitty grow and thrive. Sound nutrition will give your cat optimal health, a glorious coat, and increased energy. He'll have higher resistance to disease, fewer behavior problems, and will be more likely to live to a ripe old age.

Understanding the Basics

Protein

Cats need protein for growth, energy, and to allow the body's tissues to function. Cats require a higher amount of protein in their diet than dogs. A kitten requires even more protein than that of an adult cat.

Protein is made up of *amino acids*. There are two kinds: *essential* and *nonessential*. The nonessential amino acids can be synthesized by the body. Of the approximately twenty-two amino acids, eleven are referred to as *essential* because they can't be synthesized by the cat and must come from food sources.

One of the amino acids, *taurine*, is of particular importance to the cat. Many years ago, cat foods lacked sufficient amounts of this, and health problems arose from the taurine deficiency. Blindness and heart disease are two extremely serious conditions that can result from an inadequate supply of taurine in the diet. Luckily, pet-food manufacturers responded to the need by supplementing food with more taurine. The taurine supplementation by manufacturers was necessary because canned food requires higher taurine levels due to changes that occur during the canning process. Since taurine supplementation, deficiencies are seen less frequently. Cats who are fed dog food are still at risk because dogs don't have the same need for taurine. A cat fed a diet meant for a dog may develop deficiencies.

Why Cats Can't Be Vegetarians

Cats are carnivores, period. They must get their vitamin A, along with other *essential* nutrients, from meat. Unlike us, a cat's body is unable to convert beta carotene into usable vitamin A.

You may be on an exclusively vegetarian diet and might even be strongly against the consumption of meat under any conditions. With all due respect to your beliefs, your cat must have meat or his health will rapidly decline.

Fats

The very word *fat* strikes fear in most of us these days. We spend so much effort trying to eliminate it from our diet. Cats, on the other hand, have a higher need for fat than humans. Here's another case where, as with their need for meat, we have to understand the differences between our nutritional requirements and our cats'.

Fat is a concentrated source of energy, and animal-source fats provide the body with essential fatty acids. Fatty acids group together to form fat. Fat soluble vitamins (A, D, E, and K) require fat for proper absorption and delivery throughout the body.

Even though cats require more dietary fat than we do, not any fat will do. *Polyunsaturated* fat (from vegetable oil) can't be converted by the cat, so the essential fatty acid, *arachidonic acid*, must be obtained from animal sources.

Fat also adds to the food's palatability. That much we do have in common with cats—we both like the way fat makes our food taste.

Carbohydrates

Carbohydrates are comprised of sugars, starches, and cellulose. Besides being a source of energy and fiber, carbohydrates assist in the digestion of fats. The cellulose in carbohydrates is not digested and acts as fiber, which helps to promote normal fecal elimination by absorbing water in the intestine.

Vitamins

Vitamins are either *water soluble* (such as vitamin B complex, niacin, folic acid, pantothenic acid, biotin, choline, and vitamin C) or *fat soluble* (A, D, E, and K).

As long as you're feeding your cat a high-quality, well-balanced food that's appropriate for his age, there's no need to supplement with additional vitamins. To do so without the advice of your veterinarian could cause possible toxicity. Unused water-soluble vitamins are excreted in the urine, but the fat-soluble vitamins can build up in the body to dangerous levels. Some cats, due to age or illness, require additional vitamins—your veterinarian will determine if that's necessary.

As I mentioned previously, cats are unable to convert beta carotene into a useable form of vitamin A, so they must obtain it from meat sources—save the carrot sticks for your own lunch.

Mineral oil or petroleum jelly-based hair-ball-prevention products can interfere with proper absorption of fat-soluble vitamins. If you have a cat who suffers from frequent hair balls, be careful not to overuse the prevention product. This also applies to the excessive use of mineral oil or petroleum jelly. For more on hair-ball prevention, refer to Chapter 12.

Minerals

As with vitamins, your cat requires minerals in the proper amount to maintain health. The minerals *calcium* and *phosphorus* must be maintained at a certain ratio. If the balance shifts significantly, the cat can experience debilitating medical complications. Cats who are fed an all-meat diet, which is deficient in calcium, can develop bone disease. A diet too high in calcium can interfere with normal thyroid function.

The best way to be certain your cat is getting all of the minerals he needs, in the proper amounts, is to feed him a high-quality, well-balanced food that's appropriate for his stage of life.

Water—The Underappreciated Nutrient

Every process of life depends on water. A cat's body is made up of almost 70 percent water. So when thinking about how to supply your cat with the best nutrition, don't forget that overlooked essential nutrient: *water.*

Your cat needs to have access to clean, fresh water at all times. Your responsibility doesn't end with just filling up the water bowl every time it's empty, though. Your responsibility includes monitoring how *much* or how *little* your cat drinks. Note any changes in water consumption, as it could indicate a medical problem (such as diabetes or kidney disease).

The water in your cat's bowl should be changed daily and the bowl itself washed to avoid contaminating any fresh water you refill. Don't get a huge bowl thinking that you'll only have to refill it once a week. Water gets stale, and cats can taste that.

If you notice food particles or dirt in the water, clean the bowl and refill with fresh water. Make the water your cat drinks as appealing as possible.

Some cats are particular about the shape and size of their bowl. Your cat may prefer a shallower bowl over a deep one. If that's the case, be aware of the more frequent need to refill.

If you share your life with not only a cat but also a dog (especially a big one), the cat may not want to share one large community water bowl. To a tiny cat, your big dog's water bowl may look more like a swimming pool. If that's the case, place another, smaller bowl in an elevated spot for kitty's exclusive use.

A number of cats prefer to combine two activities at once: playtime and water drinking. They enjoy, and sometimes insist on, drinking the dripping water from faucets. While you may initially view this as cute, take my word for it, the cuteness of it wears thin in no time. You'll soon find yourself trained by your cat to either turn on the faucet whenever he sits and cries near it, or worse yet, you'll give up and just leave the faucets dripping. Neither option is a good one. If you have a kitten, don't even put the idea in his fuzzy little head that a dripping faucet is a great game. If your cat has already developed a faucet fixation, there are products available that will meet his running water requirements and keep him away from your sink. There are several brands available through pet supply stores and online.

It can be a challenge to get some cats to drink enough water so the pet water fountain may be a good option. Cats with certain medical conditions such as feline lower urinary tract disease or cats in renal failure need to drink larger quantities of water. For those cats, the fountain becomes more than a source of entertainment—it becomes a valuable tool.

To keep your cat from drinking the toilet water, always keep the lid down. The detergents and chemicals used to clean toilets can be deadly to pets.

If your cat goes outside, make sure he always has access to clean, fresh water out there.

Cats who eat a diet of dry food exclusively need to drink more water. Canned food contains approximately 70 percent water, so a cat on wet food will be getting more water through his diet.

Your Cat Isn't a Dog, so Don't Feed Him Dog Food

Sounds pretty basic, right? Yet many owners are under the misconception that dog and cat foods are interchangeable. How many times have you seen the cat with his nose in Fido's food or the dog pushing the kitty out of the way to steal a few of his tasty morsels? This practice, unfortunately, can cause serious health complications for both pets.

If your cat eats dog food, he's at serious risk of developing health problems because of vitamin and mineral deficiencies. On the other hand, a dog who is allowed to eat cat food will be consuming far more protein than he requires, which can cause health problems for him. Additionally, the higher fat content in cat food can lead to obesity in your dog. I know it's difficult to play referee at mealtime to make sure everyone keeps their nose in their own bowl, but the consequences of not monitoring it are far too great. Unfortunately for dogs, the high fat content in cat food tends to make it taste more appealing, so once Fido gets a taste of Fluffy's dinner, he'll become even more determined to switch the bowls when you're not looking.

Which Foods Are Right for Your Cat

There are a frightening number of choices out there. Every company, from the small mom-and-pop ones to the large well-known corporations, claim to meet your cat's nutritional needs. How do you decide? Organic? Supermarket brand? Frozen? Raw? Premium? Homemade? It's enough to give an owner a headache.

Here are some basic guidelines to help you:

- Learn to read labels. Although you won't be able to identify every last ingredient, you'll at least be better able to make comparisons between brands. You'll learn more about this later in this chapter. Labels can be misleading, though, so if you're unsure of a brand's nutritional claims, call the company and talk to your veterinarian.

- Feed your cat the diet that's intended for his stage of life. Growing kittens need a *growth formula* food. Pregnant or lactating cats are generally put on a growth formula as well due to the increased nutritional demands placed on them. Be aware of what dietary adjustments may be needed as your cat goes through life. Consult your veterinarian if you're uncertain about whether your cat needs to be on a specific formula. For example, your overweight cat may need to be placed on a calorie-restricted formula. There are many different formulas out there that can address specific issues such as dull haircoat, hair balls, weight control, sensitive stomach, food allergy, etc.

- Whether to feed one food exclusively will depend on what type of food your cat is eating. If he's on a diet for a specific issue, he'll need to stay exclusively on that. For a cat with no health issues, feed a variety of foods so you don't end up with a finicky eater. Vary the diet with different flavors. You may also want to alternate between a couple of manufacturers. If you vary the diet from the beginning, you're more likely to raise a cat who won't become *addicted* to one kind of food. When you first begin alternating, mix in the new food with the old gradually. This way, you'll avoid rejection of the food and potential intestinal trouble. If you switch between more than one flavor and more than one manufacturer, you avoid going into sheer panic should a flavor be discontinued or your regular brand out of stock.

- Follow your veterinarian's instructions concerning prescription food. If your cat needs to eat a special food, make sure you understand *why* and *how long* he should stay on it. Many times, I've found that owners don't really understand the reason why their veterinarian has prescribed a specific food, so they don't understand the *risks* of not complying with the diet. If your cat is on a diet for renal failure, it won't help if you're supplementing his meals with leftover ham. Don't leave the veterinarian's office with those cans or that bag of food until you understand your instructions completely.

- If you decide to feed a homemade diet, follow a recipe approved by your veterinarian.

Wet Food (canned and pouch)

Canned food has a longer shelf life than dry food. Cats usually love the taste of wet food and, depending upon the manufacturer, the flavor combinations are almost endless.

Wet food is lower in carbohydrates than dry food and much higher in water content. On the average, wet food contains about 70–76 percent water. The low-carb diet of wet food is beneficial to a cat as a carnivore. The cat gets more bang for the buck, so to speak.

Wet food is often more expensive than dry food. If you have several cats, the large cans are more economical as long as everyone agrees on the same flavor.

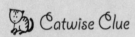

Catwise Clue

Your cat needs a diet that:

1. Is high in protein (animal based)
2. Has a moderate amount of fat
3. Has a low amount of carbs

If you decide on free-choice feeding then wet food isn't a good idea. It'll dry up and become extremely unappetizing in about twenty minutes. I'm sure the last thing you want to do when you come home from work is scrape rock-hard cat food out of the bowl.

Allow leftover canned food that has been refrigerated to come to room temperature before serving it to your kitty. Not only could the chilled food upset his stomach, but a lump of cold, day-old food stands a good chance of feline rejection. Always keep food tightly covered when storing. Once opened, a can of food should be used within a couple of days.

Dry Food

Dry food is higher in carbohydrates than canned food. The moisture content of dry food is somewhere around 10 percent.

Dry food is a better choice if you're going to feed free-choice. You can fill the bowl in the morning and it'll still be appetizing by evening. However, the high carbohydrate content of dry food can sometimes lead to obesity and other health issues. Don't feed a particular type of food based on convenience; choose a type of food because it's what's best for your cat.

Usually less expensive than canned, dry food comes in various sized bags and boxes. Once opened, if stored in an airtight container, a bag will stay fresh for several months.

Semimoist Food

This is sort of a cross between canned and dry. This food is shaped like dry food but has a soft consistency. Semimoist food is higher in sugar than other foods. I think these foods were created to appeal to us more than to cats. The kibble comes in cute little shapes, is often multicolored (even though I have yet to meet a cat who chose his food based on color), and has less of an odor than canned food.

Read Labels

The Association of American Feed Control Officials (AAFCO) was started to develop and maintain consistent standards in the pet-food industry. An advisory board of feed control officials from every state establishes guidelines regarding the nutritional claims of pet-food manufacturers. AAFCO defines the product labeling guidelines based on their testing requirements.

Although AAFCO has no power to enforce these guidelines, its rules are accepted by the FDA, and the better pet-food companies comply with them. Those companies will state on their labels whether the food has met or surpassed AAFCO standards and by which method. There are two ways a manufacturer can substantiate their claims. They can conduct feeding trials based on AAFCO protocols or they can do it based on nutrient analysis (also based on AAFCO protocols). Feeding trials are preferable because you know that cats were actually fed the food and it met the nutritional claims stated by the manufacturer.

When shopping for cat food, always look for the AAFCO feeding trial statement on the label.

If you want to learn more about AAFCO guidelines, you can contact them directly. See the Resource Guide.

Ash

Ash refers to what's left of a food's mineral components after protein, water, fat, fiber, and carbohydrates are burned away to determine the food's nutritional analysis. The higher the ash content, the less usable food there is, and the more minerals are present. Excessive amounts of minerals are not necessarily good for the cat's health and may contribute to urinary problems in cats.

Product Name

AAFCO rules dictate how an ingredient can be used in the product's name. For example, in order for the food to be named "Chicken Cat Food," chicken must constitute at least 95 percent of the total weight of all ingredients (minus water used for processing). If chicken isn't at 95 percent, it can still be used in the name, according to AAFCO, providing it constitutes at least 25 percent, but it must then be referred to as *dinner, grill,* or another descriptive term. So the name of the product might then be "Cat Food Chicken Dinner." If there's more than one ingredient in the name, they must appear in order of weight. Also, if a combination of ingredients are used in the name, each ingredient must constitute a minimum of 3 percent of the product weight (less water used for processing).

Ingredient List

Ingredients are listed in order of their proportions. The first few ingredients on the list are the main protein sources. In canned food, water is the first ingredient listed.

As you look at the ingredient list you may see the term *by-product*. AAFCO guidelines exclude certain ingredients for use as by-products. They include feathers, feet, teeth, heads, hair, hooves, horns, contents of stomach, or intestines.

Vitamin and mineral supplements as well as preservatives are also listed.

Nutritional Adequacy Claim

This tells you what stage of life the food is intended for. The manufacturer must show how the "complete and balanced" statement made on the label can be guaranteed. This is where it's explained that the claim is based on feeding trials or nutrient analysis using AAFCO protocols. Remember, feeding trials are better than nutrient analysis alone.

Feeding Instructions

The amount to feed per pounds of body weight is usually listed in this format. Remember, these are *general* guidelines.

Guaranteed Analysis

This is shown as either guaranteed minimum or maximum quantities. For example, minimum guarantee means there's a limit to how little of that ingredient is in the food but no upper limit to the amount.

Manufacturer's Name and Contact Information

The label must include this information to identify the company responsible for the product. Most manufacturers include a toll-free number and Web site address for consumer questions or comments. If you have a question, comment, or complaint concerning the product or its ingredients, don't hesitate to contact them. Manufacturers want to please you, so let them know what you think by contacting them.

Premium, Regular, All-Natural/Organic, and Generic Cat Food

Premium

Premium food is sold in pet supply stores and veterinary clinics and is, in general, of consistent quality, and usually has higher amounts of protein and fat. Premium food is more *nutrient dense*, meaning the cat won't have to eat as much as he would of regular or generic food in order to receive the same amount of nutrition. Several formulas are available in canned or dry, and for various life stages, and most cats find the taste of premium food very palatable.

Premium foods make their nutritional claims based on AAFCO feeding trial protocols.

Regular/Standard

Regular or standard cat food is the kind you find in pet supply stores and super-markets. Manufactured by the major pet-food companies you're used to seeing in advertisements, these foods also come in several formulas for the various life stages and have seemingly endless flavors. With canned foods, many manufac-turers offer choices between the consistencies and textures of entrees such as sliced, in gravy, stewed, shredded, flaked, or bite sized.

Less expensive than premium food, regular/standard cat food still provides the nutrients needed for your cat to live a long, healthy life.

When feeding standard cat food, vary flavors and brands to keep from de-veloping a finicky eater.

All-Natural/Organic

Sold in organic food stores, pet supply stores, and online, these products are made without any unnatural ingredients and use natural-fat preservatives. All natural or organic cat food may come in a variety of types: canned, dry, and even frozen.

All natural products may seem very appealing but be sure of what you're get-ting. Just because it's natural doesn't mean it meets your cat's nutritional require-ments. Read the label and talk to your veterinarian if you have questions about whether a particular brand is right for your cat. Also, check the label for how the nutritional guarantee is substantiated.

Generic

This is available in supermarkets, warehouse clubs, and discount stores. I would be *very* cautious when evaluating generic food. Nutrient quality and consistency can vary greatly. Remember, the quality of your cat's nutrition plays a vital role in whether he lives a long, healthy life.

Very often, low-priced generic food seems alluring because you think you're getting more for less, but you may notice that you're cleaning more waste out of the litter box. That means much of the food going into the cat is ending up as waste. So you *paid* less but also *got* less. Your cat would also have to eat much larger quantities of the generic food to get the same amount of nutrients he would get in a higher quality food. That adds up to lots of empty calories because he'll be eating more of what he doesn't need. Not such a bargain.

Storing Cat Food (Out of Kitty's Reach)

A cat on a diet can be one determined kitty, so make sure you've stored unused portions of food safely away.

Dry food should be placed in airtight containers. I prefer the plastic containers with snap-on lids. I also keep a little measuring cup in there so it's convenient for anyone in charge of feeding duty. They can easily dispense the proper amount.

Once you open a bag of dry food, don't just fold over the top and shove the bag in the cabinet. That's a sure way of: 1) accelerating spoilage, 2) tempting your cat (or dog) into thievery, and 3) attracting ants and rodents.

Canned food, once opened, should be stored in the refrigerator. Remove it from the can and store it in an airtight container. If you decide to store the food in the can, get a snap-on lid. Don't just cover the can top with plastic wrap because the contents will spoil faster not to mention the aroma of the food will be detectable every time you open the refrigerator.

How Much to Feed

Owners often ask me this, but more often than not, the ones who never ask are the ones who should. They're the ones who have been stuffing their kitty like a Thanksgiving turkey. I'll look at that mass of fur waddling into the room and be shocked that the cat's owner considers it normal. When I ask them about it, very often their reply is that they're just following the instructions on the bag of food. Just because the label says to feed a half cup doesn't mean *your* cat needs that exact amount. Individual adjustments have to be made based on the specific factors concerning your own cat.

When trying to decide how much food your cat needs, there are several things to take into consideration:

- age

- health

- body type

- body weight

- activity level

- type of food

- whether the cat is pregnant or nursing

The instructions on the bag or can are *general guidelines*. Your individual cat may need more or less based on the above factors. Your veterinarian will be able to advise you on whether the quantity needs to be adjusted. By looking at and examining your cat, you should also be able to tell if you're on the right track. You should know what your cat's ideal weight range is and periodically weigh him. To do this at home, weigh yourself first, and then weigh yourself while holding your cat. Subtract the difference to get your cat's weight. If you have any questions concerning how much to feed, the best person to ask is your veterinarian. You can also take your cat to the veterinarian to be accurately weighed.

If you still believe that old myth that a cat will never overeat, you apparently haven't looked around lately—there are a lot of fat cats out there.

Dinner Is Served

Free-Choice Feeding

The most popular method of feeding a cat is called *free-choice* or *free-feeding*. You just leave dry food in the bowl at all times so kitty can nibble whenever he's hungry. This works well if you're gone for long hours. It doesn't work with wet food, though, because the food dries out too quickly and becomes unappealing.

Although this is the most popular feeding method, the high number of obese cats leads me to believe it's not necessarily the best for all cats. If your cat is the correct weight and thriving on free-choice feeding then by all means, continue with what works. If you have an overweight kitty, scheduled feeding may be the way to go.

Scheduled Feeding

This method works best for wet-food eaters, cats who tend to eat too much, and multicat households where one cat is on a special diet. It's also the best way to go for training purposes. If food isn't readily available 24/7 then you're able to use it as a primary reinforcer. This can be a valuable asset when dealing with behavior problems or trying to prevent potential behavior problems.

If you're trying to get a hesitant or troubled cat to trust or bond with you, scheduled meals allow you to be identified as the *provider* of the food, which can accelerate the acceptance process.

With scheduled meals, you'll need to provide a few meals per day. Once-a-day or twice-a-day feedings aren't recommended because the cat gets too hungry and may start gulping his food. Twelve hours between meals is a long time for a cat to wait. Cats have small stomachs and do better with several small meals as opposed to one or two large meals. If you're away from the house all day and wonder how you can provide several small meals, this is where timed food dispensers and food-dispensing puzzle toys are helpful.

Scheduled feeding allows you to better monitor how much your cat is eating. In a multicat household, it's often the only way to make sure everyone gets their fair share.

Home-Cooked Meals

Even if you don't mind the time-consuming job of cooking for your cat and would lovingly chop every vegetable and each piece of meat into bite-sized chunks, from a nutritional standpoint you could be doing more harm than good if you don't know what you're doing.

If you decide to provide home-cooked meals, work with your veterinarian to make sure the recipes you've chosen are well-researched and nutritionally balanced for your cat's life stage.

Raw-Food Diets

This is a hot topic for sure these days. Proponents say it's the closest to what a cat would naturally eat in the wild: meat-based, high moisture content, low carbohydrate, and appropriate amount of fat. Critics argue that a raw diet is unsafe and puts the cat at risk for salmonella and E. coli, among other diseases. Proponents claim to have used raw foods to not only maintain excellent health but supposedly cure many health issues through diet alone. Critics argue that a raw-food diet is often unbalanced. You can find experts on either side of this argument.

If you're considering switching your cat to a raw-food diet, consult with your veterinarian. He/she will be able to provide guidelines and resources to help you ensure you meet your cat's nutritional needs. Also, do extensive research before you go down this path to make sure you fully know what will be expected of you.

When feeding raw meat you'll have to take precautions to ensure everyone's safety.

- Buy meat directly from a respected and trusted butcher and not from the meat case at your local supermarket.

- Have a separate cutting board used only to cut and prepare the raw meat.

- Thoroughly clean and disinfect the cutting board, utensils, and food bowls.

- Thoroughly clean the cat's water bowl at least once a day.

- Follow a trusted, well-researched regimen so you'll know what supplements must be added, such as probiotics for intestinal health.

- Freeze individual portions of meat for storage so you don't risk feeding your cat meat that has been sitting in the refrigerator too long.

Treats

For initial training, most cats respond to treats. I often use treats to reward my cats for positive behavior especially when they could have easily opted for an unwanted behavior. In our house, treats aren't just arbitrarily given out. Treats are an earned reward, and as such, they are powerfully effective training aids.

Even though treats can help with behavior, remember that they are *treats* and not *meals*. Your cat doesn't need a mouthful of them to feel rewarded (although he'll probably try to convince you otherwise). Depending upon the size of the treat, I often break them in half. My cat doesn't realize she only received a half or a quarter of the treat. What registers in her head is, "Treat, I got treat!"

Foods to Stay Away From
Milk

Once weaned, a cat no longer produces a sufficient amount of the enzyme *lactase* that is necessary to digest the *lactose* in milk. Cats

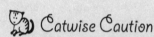

Catwise Caution

Don't get in the habit of giving treats to your cat like clockwork. He'll soon figure out that he doesn't have to do anything for them, which means you've lost a powerful behavior modification tool. He may even sit by the drawer or cabinet where the treats are stored and begin begging for them. That's exactly the time **NOT** to offer a reward. Never give a treat to your cat just to stop his meowing or other unwanted behavior. What will happen as a result is that you will have reinforced the very behavior you didn't want.

are ironically—given the myth—lactose intolerant. Feeding milk to your cat could result in diarrhea. If you want to give your cat a little milk as an occasional treat, watch carefully for any digestive problems.

The milk fed to kittens is different from the cow's milk we drink. The milk from the queen (mother cat) is higher in protein and *arachidonic acid* (which kittens need). If you're hand-raising a kitten, consult with your veterinarian concerning the appropriate kitten formula to feed.

Tuna

Cats love it. The tuna meant for humans, though, is not a good food for your cat. Tuna is high in polyunsaturated fats that cats don't metabolize well. A steady diet of tuna depletes the body of vitamin E and can lead to a very painful condition called *steatitis*. Tuna-flavored cat foods are supplemented with extra vitamin E to prevent this, but straight tuna is not.

Cats can quickly become addicted to the strong taste of tuna. No matter what food you place before him, your cat will only want his tuna. To get him off of it, you have to gradually mix in other food. It's not easy to reform a tuna junkie, so try not to create one.

Raw Eggs

Raw egg whites contain an enzyme called *avidin* that destroys biotin in the body. Biotin helps convert food into energy.

Chocolate

Mere ounces can kill a cat. Chocolate contains an ingredient known as *theobromine* that is deadly to cats. Theobromine affects the cat's heart, gastrointestinal tract, nervous system, and can also cause the cat to lose body fluid since it is a diuretic.

If your cat has ingested chocolate, contact your veterinarian immediately or, if it is after-hours, call the emergency clinic. The size of your cat, the type of chocolate ingested (for example, baking chocolate is more lethal than other forms), and how much was ingested will be important information for the veterinarian to know.

Onions and Garlic

Onions, whether raw, cooked, or dehydrated, are toxic because they contain a substance that can destroy a cat's red blood cells. The result is a type of anemia known as *Heinz body anemia*.

Garlic can also cause the formation of Heinz bodies, but is not as toxic as onions.

If you're ever instructed by your veterinarian to coax your cat into eating by using baby food (a very popular method), read the label to make sure the food doesn't contain onion or garlic powder.

Tablescraps

Feeding tablescraps to your cat can seriously upset his nutritional balance. The good-quality cat food that you feed him is well balanced with the precise amount of protein and fat, along with the correct ratio of vitamins and minerals. Adding your leftover turkey, unfinished hamburger, or piece of bacon causes that scale to tip. While your cast-iron stomach may look forward to those spicy dishes and rich desserts, they're certainly not good for a cat. By allowing your cat to nibble on your burrito or sample your spaghetti sauce, you risk causing him intestinal upset and perhaps a nasty case of diarrhea.

Feeding from the table also encourages begging, which is only cute for about five seconds—then the novelty of your cat clawing repeatedly at your leg while you're trying to eat wears off very rapidly. The begging behavior can escalate into jumping on the table, which your company won't find appetizing (especially the ones who aren't cat lovers). When the cat is allowed to eat tablescraps, it also becomes more difficult to keep him off the kitchen counters when food is present. You may also find yourself with a little feline dumpster diver. Basically, everything becomes fair game at that point as he decides there's no reason to wait for you to hand him the food when he can just serve himself.

Not feeding tablescraps can be a more difficult rule to enforce in a family with children. If they're old enough to understand, explain the dangers of sharing people food with the family cat. If they're not old enough, then you'll have to make use of those eyes in the back of your head—which is standard equipment in parents, especially mothers.

If you absolutely can't resist the urge to treat your cat to the occasional tiny piece of cooked chicken, do it *away* from the table and do it as a reward for a particular behavior, so the cat doesn't make the connection that whenever the family sits down to dinner, there'll be something in it for him. Also, never give your cat food when he begs—otherwise you've just show him the way to train *you*. Veterinary nutritionists advise that tablescraps comprise no more than 10 percent of the cat's daily diet.

Finicky Eaters

We actually cause this problem ourselves. When our cat shows a preference for a particular food, we buy a truckload of it. If that flavor or brand becomes unavailable, after years of eating the same food, the cat may refuse to even taste anything else. Finicky eaters are also created when we repeatedly spruce up the cat food with tablescraps or strong-tasting foods. Then, when faced with plain ordinary cat food again, he feels cheated. If he knows that by holding out and turning his back to the food he'll get something much tastier, thus is born the *finicky* eater.

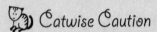 Catwise Caution

If your cat refuses to eat, don't get tough by taking the attitude that he'll eventually eat when he gets hungry enough. A cat who refuses to eat for more than two days could have serious health complications. Don't play "chicken" with your cat by trying to wait him out—the result could be deadly. If your cat has stopped eating for more than two days, he needs to be seen by the veterinarian.

To avoid raising a finicky eater and spending your days opening countless cans or bags of food for your cat's inspection, feed a variety of flavors from a couple of manufacturers. Feed both dry and canned food so your cat is comfortable with different tastes, scents, and textures. How I do this in my home is to feed canned-food meals and use dry food in the puzzle feeders.

Taste is not the only consideration in your cat's decision to accept or reject a food. *Smell, texture, size,* and even the *shape* of the food are important issues to him. In terms of dry food, some cats prefer the way a triangular shape feels in their mouth, while others will accept only round pieces of kibble. Don't laugh, it's true. What's more, pet-food manufacturers have spent lots of money evaluating which shapes, sizes, tastes, aromas, and textures are preferred by cats.

Tipping the Scales

I don't know about you, but whenever I watch one of those nature shows on television, I never see any fat lions or overweight leopards. Looking around me, I also don't see fat stray or feral cats. But in homes all over, I see fat house cats. Some are so fat that any slight movement requires great effort. We're killing our cats with kindness. The overabundance of food that we endlessly offer our kitties is shortening their lives. We need to take a lesson from nature. Let's examine the situation.

Cats in the wild have to *work* for their food. A stray cat, if he's lucky, may catch a number of prey in one day but I can assure you that they don't march up to him and offer themselves up as a meal. He has to *hunt* before he can *feast*. Then there are our beloved, doted on, spoiled cats. All they have to do for a meal is basically *show up*. And even then I've seen owners go and track down their sleeping cats in order to bring them meals—kitty room service. The cats don't have to hunt—they can skip that part and go right to the feast. What's even worse is that it usually is truly a *feast*. We simply feed our cats too much. Unless your cat has found a way to sneak into the cabinet and open the container of food himself, then *you* must take responsibility for his condition.

As owners, we've taken away a vital part of our cats' lives—*activity*. It all boils down to this: too many incoming calories + not enough calories burned off = a fat cat.

Another common mistake owners make is not adjusting the amount of food needed as the cat matures from a revved-up kitten to a more sedentary adult. Overfeeding commonly occurs with cats once they've been neutered or spayed as well. Many owners blame the procedure for the cat's weight gain, but in reality the cat simply doesn't require as many calories due to his maturing and consequent reduced metabolic needs.

Many owners follow feeding instructions on the pet-food label without making adjustments for their particular cat's physical shape. This contributes to weight problems because the owner continues to feed the suggested amount despite the fact that the cat may be gaining weight.

An obese cat is more susceptible to heart disease, diabetes, and arthritis. As your cat gets older, if he does develop arthritis, the extra weight on those joints will cause even more pain. Obese cats undergoing surgery are more at risk from anesthesia as well.

Feeding tablescraps and offering too many treats contribute greatly to obesity. You may not realize how many calories your cat is consuming because it's happening gradually over the course of the day. Perhaps you share bacon with him at breakfast, cat treats later that morning, then refill his empty food bowl. Then maybe you treat him to the remains of your sandwich at lunch, more cat treats throughout the afternoon, some samples from dinner, a few more cat treats in the evening and a large sampling of your unwanted ice cream at night, and then you wonder why he's not losing weight, even though you've put him on a reduced-calorie cat food!

How to Determine If Your Cat Is Overweight

The first place to start is at your veterinarian's office. A physical exam will be done, possibly along with additional diagnostic testing.

Certain purebred cats have very different body types. A Persian's ideal cobby body is very different from a Siamese's ideal slender body. If you aren't sure what your cat's ideal body weight should be consult your veterinarian.

Stand over your cat and look down at him. How do his sides look? Can you make out any kind of waistline above his hips? A cat of ideal weight has a little fat over his ribs (remember, I said a *little*) and a detectable slight indentation just behind the ribs, above the hips. If he looks more like a furry football than a cat, he's overweight.

Put one hand on either side of him. By firmly stroking his sides, you should be able to feel his ribs (if you can actually see his ribs, then he's underweight). If you can't feel his ribs without applying very firm pressure then he's overweight.

If you're unable to feel his ribs, his chest feels soft and padded with fat, or you can feel fat pads along the backbone then he's not just overweight, he's *obese*.

Look at your cat in profile. Does his underside hang down in a pouch of fat? If so, he's overweight.

Lift up your cat's tail and check his anal area. Does it look clean and well groomed or dirty and neglected? Some cats become so obese that they can no longer reach back there to do normal grooming.

Does your cat snore? Sometimes obese cats wheeze and snore in their sleep due to the increased fat putting more pressure against their lungs.

Putting Kitty on a Diet

Your veterinarian will be able to give you an idea of what your cat's ideal weight should be and how to *safely* reach it. The reason I emphasize the word *safely* is because if you attempt to put your cat on a crash diet or restrict his calories too severely, it can result in serious health complications. That's why you'll want to do this under the veterinarian's supervision. The cat's liver can't handle severe calorie restrictions; there's a risk of *hepatic lipidosis*. When a cat misses too many meals, fat gets deposited in the liver, which results in liver failure.

Your veterinarian will determine how much to feed your cat and what type of food is best to use. Depending on how overweight he is and how much food he has been getting, you may be instructed to simply cut down the portions of his regular food. Reducing the diet by no more than a quarter is usually medically safe and less upsetting for kitty. In other cases, a changeover to a prescription food may be necessary. Whatever option your veterinarian decides is necessary will be successful only if *you* comply. That means no sneaking treats to your cat because you feel guilty. You have to be strong. Being the owner of a cat on a diet isn't fun, in fact, it'll be one of the hardest things you do. Be forewarned, your cat is going to pull out all the stops. He's going to sit on your lap and stare into your eyes with the most pitiful look. He'll lay by his empty food bowl as if in mourning over those long lost meals. He'll cry, meow, and maybe even follow you from room to room, convinced that surely you've lost your mind and forgotten the way to the kitchen. To avoid the "poor, pitiful me" behavior, use puzzle feeders so it takes longer for your cat to eat.

Another trap that you'll have to avoid is attempting to make your cat's diet food more appealing. Sometimes when the veterinarian prescribes a prescription diet food and the cat doesn't care much for it, the owner tries to entice him by adding little goodies into the food. Don't sabotage his diet in the name of love.

Free-feeding should be ceased when you have a cat on a diet. Stick to scheduled meals so you can monitor his daily intake. Feed smaller meals more often so your cat is fooled into thinking he's getting more than his restricted amount. It'll also prevent your cat from gulping down the day's portion in one sitting and then complaining about the empty food bowl.

The "Catkins" Diet

Humorously referred to in the veterinary community as the "catkins" diet, this way of eating is based on the famous human diet introduced by Dr. Robert Atkins. Dr. Atkins claimed that obesity is mostly the result of an overconsumption of refined sugar and carbohydrates. Some veterinary nutritionists are making the recommendation that cats, obligate carnivores that rely on protein, don't need such a high level of carbohydrates.

Carbohydrates are abundant in pet food, most especially dry food, as fillers and binders. Cats don't rely on carbohydrates as an energy source rather, as carnivores, they use protein and fat for their energy needs. As a result of the excessive carbohydrate intake, the cat becomes obese. But keep in mind that carbohydrates alone are not the sole culprits—portion control is a huge factor as well. Calories do count.

Don't Forget the Importance of Exercise

It's true for humans and it's true for cats: exercise and activity are crucial to a successful weight-loss program. Now, if the vision of putting your cat on a treadmill or signing him up for kitty aerobics is worrying you, relax. The best exercise for your cat is based on what he loves to do—*play*. Of course in the case of some cats, it's based on what he used to love to do before he got so fat. Use your cat's natural instinct as a predator to engage him in daily interactive playtime. For more specifics, refer to Chapter 6.

Use Those Puzzle Feeders

Leave these around the house for your cat's enjoyment. Divide up your cat's daily food portion so you're not actually increasing his normal amount. With the puzzle feeders, the cat will have to work for the food, which will keep him occupied, and then he'll enjoy the food as a reward.

The hollow balls designed to dispense dry food, such as the Play-N-Treat ball and the Egg-Cersizer (to name just two), are not only a source of entertainment for a cat, but they're valuable tools for weight loss. Snap the puzzler feeder apart and fill it half full with dry food. When you snap it back together, you'll see how food can randomly fall out through the holes. The Play-N-Treat has one hole but the Egg-Cersizer has several and you can change the degree of difficulty. My cats love the Egg-Cersizer and I think they secretly look forward to when I leave for the day, because they know all the Egg-Cersizers will be filled and ready for them.

Feed Smaller Meals More Often

The free-choice feeding method usually doesn't work if you have an overweight cat. He may eat everything in his bowl the minute you put it down and then go hungry the rest of the day. This isn't a good plan. Instead, control his diet by feeding him several small meals on a scheduled basis throughout the day. Don't give him an increased amount of food, just divide his prescribed portion. He won't go as hungry and you'll get him out of the habit of gorging himself.

Using the puzzle feeders is a great way to feed him smaller, more frequent meals, but you can also just simply put the food in the bowl. The purpose of the feeders is to get the cat used to a smaller amount in a timelier manner.

Food Allergies

Food allergy reactions may show up in several forms including diarrhea, vomiting, or other digestive problems. Food allergies can also appear as an itchy skin rash any place on the body. Food allergies can cause behavioral changes as well, such as anxiety, restlessness, or aggression.

What's so ironic about a food allergy is that it may be caused by a specific food that your cat has been eating for years.

If your veterinarian suspects a food allergy, he or she may prescribe a hypoallergenic diet. This diet contains food sources not normally found in cat food and won't contain the usual ingredients such as beef or chicken. If the rash clears up, the normal diet may be reinstated to confirm diagnosis. If the rash returns, it's a pretty sure bet that it's one or more of the ingredients in the cat's food. Determining which ingredient is the specific cause can be difficult and costly, involving skin sensitivity testing. Very often, the cat is maintained on the hypoallergenic diet.

Changing Over to a Better Nutritional Program

If you've been reading this chapter and realize that you've been compromising your cat's nutrition by feeding lower-quality foods or ones that are inappropriate for his stage of life, don't make an abrupt change. The transition needs to be gradual for two reasons: 1) to avoid digestive upset, and 2) to avoid rejection. If you've been feeding a low-quality food and are now going to switch to a high-quality one, you have to allow the cat's body time to adjust. Make the change-over gradually by adding a little of the new food in with the old diet. Gradually increase the amount of new food while decreasing the old food over the course of about five days. If your cat begins to reject the new food, go even slower. Be patient, no matter how long it takes. It'll all be worth it when you see the difference in your cat's health, physical appearance, and disposition.

Feeding Kittens

Good quality protein and nutrients will play a vital role in your kitten's development since his body is going to undergo major transformations. He will double in size several times in a short period of time (just mere months).

After weaning, kittens should be eating four meals a day until they're four or five months old. At that time you can reduce it to three meals. If you're doing free-choice feeding then just provide access to growth-formula food at all times until the kitten reaches one year of age. At that time, you'll switch to an adult formula. If you're free-choice feeding, make sure all kittens (if you have more than one) are eating successfully without any problems and are gaining the appropriate amount of weight. Replace food often and wash the bowl to keep food fresh and appealing.

Feeding a Geriatric Cat

See Chapter 16.

11

Relationships: Other Cats, Dogs, Kids, and Your Grumpy Aunt Esther

Does Your Cat Hate Your Spouse?
Will He Be Jealous of the New Baby? Should You
Get a Second Cat? How About a Dog?

Cats have been inaccurately labeled as asocial, but the truth is they *do* enjoy companionship and *are* social creatures. In outdoor life, it's not unusual for female cats to nurse and care for each others' kittens. Cats are routinely referred to as solitary creatures but that misconception probably comes from the fact that cats tend to hunt alone because of the size of the prey they go after.

To most dog owners, the idea of introducing a second dog into the household brings to mind images of the two pets playfully romping as they get to know each other. For cat owners, though, any initial images of playful romping when introducing a second cat into the home are quickly squashed by the reality of hissing, growling, and the feline version of a nuclear war. Does that mean you shouldn't risk bringing in a second cat? Absolutely not. Many single cats benefit from the addition of a companion although they may raise quite a considerable fuss initially. Being prepared beforehand and knowing how to do the introduction in the least stressful way will do wonders for getting the two cats to give each other a chance. By understanding their need for territorial security and individual comfort zones, you can make this process go more smoothly.

Will every cat like it? No way. There are some cats who are so territorial that they could never accept any competition. Unfortunately, though, when many owners see their resident cat's initial hostile reaction to a new cat in the house, they interpret it to mean that the cat could never share her home with another and they give up. On the flip side, there are some cats who are forced to share territory in the name of companionship, and they spend day after day terrorizing each other. Call it bad chemistry or mismatched personalities, but they just get under each other's skin day after day after day. Some owners don't pay enough attention to the personality and temperament of their cat and then they bring in a second cat who creates competition instead of companionship.

What kind of a cat would benefit from a feline companion? If your cat is lonely, spending long hours by herself due to your work schedule, another cat might be a wonderful friend. If you travel often and leave your cat at home in the care of a pet sitter, two cats would provide comfort for each other in your absence. A very active cat who never seems to wind down would most likely enjoy being able to run around with a friend. The addition of another cat into the household may put the spark back into the life of a sedentary or overweight cat. There are many reasons to provide your kitty with a companion.

When *shouldn't* you consider a second cat? Never try to introduce a new cat when your current cat is in the middle of a crisis. For example, if your cat just lost her longtime companion, don't try to take her mind off things with the sudden appearance of a kitten. When she has just begun grieving isn't the time to confuse her with such an overwhelming experience. I advise cat owners to avoid compounding one already stressful situation with another. Make sure your cat is in the right frame of mind to handle the process of a new cat introduction.

If your cat is ill, the addition of another cat could compromise her recovery due to the added stress.

In general, know your cat's temperament. Some cats just won't tolerate any other cats. Look at things from her side and use that insight to do what's best for her when it comes to choosing her buddies.

Bringing a Second Cat into the Home

How well you handle the introduction can make or break the relationship the two cats have. Yes, it all rests on your shoulders. Talk about pressure! So, let's get it all planned out in advance so everything goes smoothly (well, relatively speaking, that is).

The first thing I want you to keep in mind is that you're going to be introducing one animal into another animal's established territory. Plopping the new cat down in the middle of the living room is guaranteed to create hostility, panic, terror, aggression, and maybe even injury. So, let's just cross that method off the list, shall we? How should you do a new cat introduction? *One sense at a time.* Introducing two cats one sense at a time allows them to process each step and avoid overreacting, and gives you the opportunity to adjust the speed of each phase. Head off a feline circuit overload; one sense at a time is far less threatening for both cats. Not only do you have to concern yourself with how your *resident* cat is feeling, but the *new* cat as well. Remember, he'll be in unfamiliar territory.

Remember to have any new cat checked by the veterinarian. Never bring an unvaccinated cat into your household with existing cats. Have the cat checked for parasites as well. You certainly won't want to bring home uninvited guests such as fleas or ear mites.

Before you bring the newcomer in, set up a sanctuary room for him. In it should be several hiding places (they can be boxes lined with towels), a litter box, some toys, and a bowl of water. Whether food is left out depends on if you plan on feeding free-choice or on a schedule. Put a scratching post or a corrugated cardboard scratch pad in the room. For an adult cat, it may help if he feels he can mark some territory. For a kitten, it's a good way to start proper training right off the bat. Keep the door to the sanctuary room closed.

Bring the new cat into the house in a carrier. Just casually take him right into his room. Set the carrier in the corner of the room, open the door, place a treat on the floor just outside the carrier, then leave. The new cat may or may not choose to leave the safety of his carrier. After you leave the room, he'll be able to do an initial investigation and choose his own hiding place.

Your immediate concern needs to be your resident cat, who may be completely unaware of what has just taken place in her home or may be right outside the door with a look of disgust. Act casual as you shut the door and walk past your cat. If you have another treat, you can drop it behind you.

At this point you can conduct an interactive play session with your resident cat, feed her, or leave an activity toy or puzzle feeder out for distraction. Don't be surprised, though, if she shows little interest in anything but what's beyond that closed door. She may sniff around the door, camp out in front of it, even hiss and growl. Don't be alarmed—those are all normal reactions. The good thing about having the newcomer out of sight is that only a portion of your resident cat's turf is violated.

Pay lots of attention to your cat but in a casual, nonclingy way. Don't try to comfort her by holding and clutching her. Keep the tone of your voice and your body language very normal—casual and soothing.

Let your cat get used to the idea that somebody's behind the door. Depending on your individual cat, that could take anywhere from a day to a week.

When you go in to feed or visit the new cat, try to do it on the sly so your resident cat doesn't sit outside the door feeling upset. Visit with the newcomer when your other cat is eating, sleeping, or in another room.

Getting the new cat to bond with you and come out from hiding places may take time depending upon whether he's a kitten or an adult, what kind of socialization he had, and the type of environment he recently came from. Use treats, food, and interactive playtime to win him over. With a kitten, it won't take much convincing—he'll be eager to be with you—but an adult may be a little more skeptical. Refer to Chapter 6 for tips on how to begin the bonding process and build trust.

The next step toward introduction of the two cats will involve *scent*. For this you'll need a pair of socks. Put one sock on your hand and rub the new cat down to get his scent all over it. Rub around his face, being sure to go along the sides of the mouth. Leave the scent-filled sock in your resident cat's territory. Use the other sock to rub down your resident cat and then leave that one in the newcomer's room. This enables the cats to begin getting familiar with each other's scents in a controlled, nonthreatening way. You can do this several times, using a few socks.

As your resident cat sniffs the sock, reward her with a treat if she doesn't show any signs of aggression. If you're using clicker training, click and treat when the cat approaches the sock (before she has a chance to hiss or growl).

If your cat reacts negatively to the scented sock, just ignore her. If you shoo her away or reprimand her it won't help her learn to make a positive association with the new kitty. It's better to just ignore her reaction. After she has moved away from the sock you can engage in an interactive play session so she doesn't stay reactive.

When the scented sock exchange has been going well, you can then move on to incorporating more of the newcomer's scent into the environment. Place your resident cat in another room and then let the newcomer do a little investigating. As he investigates beyond his sanctuary room he'll be spreading his scent as he walks and rubs against objects.

Now, if everything is going well and your resident cat hasn't declared World

War III, you can open the door to the sanctuary room a little and feed the cats within sight of each other but at a far distance. This is a good reason to feed on a schedule so you can keep the cats more focused on the food and less on each other. Food can be a very valuable tool during this crucial time so take every advantage you can.

Keep the sessions short and sweet. It's better to have the session end before the food runs out. Always go slower than you think you need to in order to increase your chances of success and reduce the risk of a session ending negatively.

Do several of these short mealtime training sessions a day, if possible. Gradually, you should be able to inch the food dishes closer together. Always go at the pace of the most stressed-out cat. If one cat feels more secure being partially hidden or even totally hidden when the sanctuary room is opened, then start at that level. This isn't a race and you're not on a schedule.

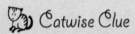

Catwise Clue

If you have no window of opportunity when it comes to having the cats see each other before one or both immediately go into attack mode, you can place a cat in a carrier. If needed, put each cat in a carrier and place the carriers on opposite sides of the room. It's extremely important, if using the carrier method, to be sure that the cats are far apart so they don't feel trapped in the carriers.

If either your resident cat or the newcomer seems dangerously aggressive, you can stack two or three baby gates up to cover the open doorway during the mealtime sessions. That way, the cats can see each other but no one can ambush.

When I do these sessions I sit right at the doorway so I can close the door immediately, if needed. I also keep a thick towel on my lap so I can either cover the gate to prevent the cats from seeing each other or toss it over an ambushing cat. Another option is to install a temporary screen door. A breeder I know came up with the idea of using plastic-coated wire shelving placed vertically. Get a piece the size of the door and install it with a few hook-and-eye closures.

If you are clicker training, click and treat (and this is when you want to use totally irresistible treats) for a break in any negative behavior. For example, if the cats are staring each other down and one cat looks away, click and treat the cat who looked away.

If you've taught your resident cat to come when called, this can be beneficial during the introduction of a new cat. When a tense situation starts to develop between the cats, if you have one or both trained to a recall cue, you can call someone to you to break the hostility.

Target training can help ease tension as well. Train the cats to go to a certain spot to chill out. You'll need a clicker and a target stick (you can use a chopstick, eraser end of a pencil, or target training stick). Start target training by holding the target stick an inch or two away from the cat. Click and reward when she touches it with her nose. Move the target out of sight and wait for the cat to look at you (to help her associate YOU with the reward). Now reintroduce the target stick an inch or two away from her and then click and reward again when she touches it with her nose. Continue to move the target stick around but make sure she looks at you in between. Once she is consistently touching it with her nose, you can give the behavior a verbal cue such as "touch" or "target." Just be sure you're consistent with whatever verbal cue you use.

Once kitty is proficient in target training, use the stick to direct her to a particular spot. Place a small mat or bed out and hold the target stick over it. Click and reward when your cat puts a paw on the mat. Toss the treat away from the mat so the cat moves off it. Pick up the mat and put it down again, close to her. Set up the target stick again. What you're doing with the target stick is luring the cat and you only want to use the target stick a couple of times to give her the initial idea of where you want her to go. After that, just place the mat down near her and wait for her to put a paw on it. After the cat has consistently put a paw on the mat, start to delay the click until she puts two paws on the mat, then work up to three, and then four paws on the mat. Each time you reward her, be sure you toss the treat off the mat so she'll have to move to retrieve her reward. Then reset the mat.

If your cat isn't getting the idea when you place the mat near her, you can go back to using the target stick to lure her there but only do it a couple of times. Fade the lure so the cat focuses on the fact that going on the mat is the objective and not just following the target stick.

When the cat understands the behavior and is consistently stepping on the mat, give this behavior a cue. It can be anything as long as it is consistent. I use "go to mat" but some of my clients use "go to bed" or even "go chill."

The "go to mat" cue must be consistently trained for each cat individually before attempting to use it to diffuse a tense situation.

For this to work as well, the mat or bed must be located where the cat likes to be. With some clients the cat is cued to go to a perch or cat tree, or the mat is placed on a chair or other favored place. It doesn't have to be located on the floor or carpet if your cat prefers an elevated spot.

Once the cats begin sharing space in the house, keep the sanctuary room set up for a while so the newcomer has a safe place of his own during initial tense encounters. Continue to click and treat when they show tolerance. If one cat passes another and would usually hiss, but doesn't do it this time, click and treat her for showing tolerant behavior.

Keep two litter boxes set up in different locations—not next to each other. This way one cat will always have another option. Having litter boxes spread out in the house is also a way of helping the cats maintain peace because one cat won't have to cross over another cat's area in case they have established clear-cut turf divisions.

Take a close look at your home and be certain that the cats will have enough spaces to call their own. For instance, is there only one window perch? One food bowl? Don't put the cats in the position of having to compete. When a new cat enters the environment, it causes the feline residents to have to renegotiate on some space issues. You can ease the stress and increase the chances of a peaceful coexistence by increasing vertical space. Use your *think like a cat* approach when modifying the environment for a multicat home.

Enemies Under One Roof: Easing the Tension in a Multicat Household

Now that the cats are out and about the house, there are bound to be some tense moments and unfriendly encounters as they renegotiate and establish personal space.

Whether they're two cats just beginning the tentative process of getting to know each other or longtime companions barely coexisting year after year, there are things you can do to ease the hostility.

The first rule is to make sure there's enough of everything for everybody. No one should have to share a litter box, food bowl, scratching post, bed, or toy if they don't want to. Ideally, there should be an equal number of litter boxes to cats and several safe sleeping retreats available.

If you don't have a cat tree, I strongly recommend you invest in one now. It's not a luxury, it's a necessity in a multicat home. By adding *levels* you increase territory. A multitiered tree can allow two or more cats to occupy the same area without anyone feeling their personal space has been encroached upon. It allows any status issues to remain intact so a more assertive cat and a lower-ranking one don't stress over having to share one level.

If you're trying to get two cats to like each other, help them see that in the presence of their "opponent" they get more treats, more playtime, etc. They'll eventually begin to develop a more positive association with each other.

Distraction and Redirection

Redirection tactics usually involve toys. An interactive toy such as the Cat Dancer is easy to curl up and store anywhere. The scenario: you're sitting on the sofa watching TV, one cat is peacefully sleeping in his cat tree, and suddenly, out of the corner of your eye, you spot your other kitty walking into the room. She has the look of a gunslinger at high noon. She's staring at the sleeping cat and you just know she's about to launch an attack. Quietly and very quickly pull out your interactive toy and distract the aggressive cat. Being a predator, she'll very likely prefer to go after the toy. Then she will get her aggression out in a positive way and forget what her original intent was. The more cat-to-cat attacks you can prevent through redirection, the more likely they'll begin to tolerate each other. Tolerance may then progress toward actually liking each other. In a hostile household, keep interactive toys in each room so you'll always have one handy.

When you use redirection, it's important to get in there *before* an actual attack. Even if you only suspect that something is about to happen, use diversion. Since you're using a positive method, even if you're wrong, what's the worst that happens? Your cat gets an unexpected play session. Another important reason to time your use of redirection just before the aggression is so you aren't reinforcing unwanted behavior. When I'm working with clients, I make sure they keep one special interactive toy reserved exclusively for redirection. If you know it's a toy your cat can't resist, it increases your chance of a successful diversion.

If both cats are staring each other down from across the room but a fight hasn't taken place yet, divert their attention with something fun to avoid a continual buildup of hostility. Here's a little scenario from your own childhood that may help to put it in perspective: you and your new friend (whom you aren't sure you even like yet) are playing in the yard when you begin fighting over a toy or the rules to a game. Your mother comes out and orders your friend to go home and you to go to your room. You march into your room where you sit on the bed and proceed to stew in anger over how your friend got you in trouble. Boy, are you mad! So even though your mother put a stop to the fighting, you're left with a negative feeling toward your friend. Let's go back to the beginning of the scenario where you and your friend are just starting to build up some tension, only this time your mother comes out and announces that she just made a batch of cookies, or maybe she's standing there with two ice cream cones in her hands.

You and your friend put the game (and your potential fight) on hold as your attention is redirected to something fun. By using a positive approach, your wise mother stopped the escalating tension and no damage was done to the blossoming relationship.

If a fight has already broken out, you don't want to reward the behavior by offering a treat or toy. The chances of a cat even noticing a treat while in the middle of a fight would be rather slim anyway. In the case of an actual fight, make a noise such as clanging a pot, clapping two lids together, or just clapping your hands loudly. Whatever you have, use it to make a noise to startle the cats. Don't attempt to physically break up the fight because you'll most likely get injured.

Once you've startled the cats, they'll likely head off in opposite directions. Don't try to cuddle or pet anyone because they'll still be highly agitated. Make sure they stay separated for a while so they can calm back down.

Introducing a Dog to Your Cat

Despite what you may have believed in the past, cats and dogs can get along. Some cats who are unable to tolerate the addition of another cat into their territory may more easily accept the introduction of a dog. The upside of bringing a cat and dog together is that their views on territorial rules usually don't compete with each other the way a cat-to-cat introduction can. The downside of bringing a cat and dog together is that they speak two different languages and you need to help them find common ground.

Dogs and cats make wonderful companions. In order to make a good match and keep both the cat and dog safe, it's important to do your homework so you can try to create a compatible match. Once you've picked a companion you'll then need to do a careful and gradual introduction. If you attempt to merely put a cat and dog together in the house you'll be creating a dangerous and potentially deadly situation.

Making a Good Match

Think about the personality and disposition of your cat. If you're adopting a dog from a shelter or from another family and the dog has been allowed to chase squirrels, cats, birds, rabbits, etc., and has a high prey-drive, then adding him to your household would not be a wise idea. If you're in doubt as to whether it could be a potentially good match even after proper training, consult with a qualified, certified dog trainer or behaviorist for a professional evaluation. If you know from past experience that the dog has displayed very aggressive behavior toward cats then that is also a sign that the match would be too dangerous.

If you know from past experience that your cat has displayed very aggressive behavior toward dogs or has displayed extreme fear when a dog is in sight, you might be adding too much stress to her life by adding a dog. If in doubt, consult a certified animal behavior expert. See Resource Guide in the back of this book or start by getting your veterinarian's recommendation.

Try to match complementary personalities. Don't match a timid cat with a rambunctious dog. Don't match a nervous dog with a revved up kitten.

Even though the dog is a social creature, be aware of the fact that excitement and playful intentions can get out of control in certain situations. A dog who has a history of rough play or is too stimulated can not only frighten a cat but can pose a very serious danger to her. If more than one dog will be coming into the cat's life, one dog's excitement can feed the other's, creating a highly charged situation. You must be aware of any potential for danger.

Preparations

With a dog coming into your home, some environmental changes may need to be made in order to safeguard your cat's territory. Doing so gradually, before the pup's arrival will enable your cat to make a comfortable, easy adjustment. For example, if your cat's food bowl is normally left out on the floor for her to nibble free-choice, you may have to relocate it to an elevated feeding station or transition her to scheduled meals.

Think carefully about the litter box. The last thing a kitty needs is to be suddenly ambushed by a playful dog while trying to attend to her business in the litter box. Prevent the dog from having access to the box to keep him from eating cat poop as well, which is viewed as a delicacy by many dogs. Because the cat's diet is higher in fat, dogs tend to find those little litter box nuggets very tasty. Using a covered litter box may not stop a determined dog (and limits the cat's escape potential) so the best setup is to keep the box in an off-limits area. If the dog is small, you can put a baby gate in the doorway of the room that houses the litter box. Place a chair, box, or small stool just inside the room by the gate so the cat has something to jump off or land on. If the dog is large, use a tall, hinged baby gate with a small pet opening at the bottom. These types of gates are available in pet supply stores and online.

If you'll be changing the location of the litter box, move it gradually until it's in the final spot, well in advance of the dog's arrival. Don't make abrupt changes, because your cat won't tolerate that well. Move the box a little each day if necessary so your cat doesn't have to deal with the "now you see it, now you don't" disappearing box.

Provide your cat with safe retreats when there will be a dog in the house. A cat tree can be a real haven for a kitty being chased around by the new pup. The bigger the dog, the taller the tree should be (if it's in your budget), so your cat will have a place she can climb to for an undisturbed nap. Even if the dog chases only in play it can be disconcerting to the cat. The dog should also be trained that the cat tree is off limits.

Before the introduction takes place, make sure everyone is healthy and free of parasites. You certainly don't want your indoor cat infested with fleas from the new dog. Take care of any problems before the introduction. For more on fleas, refer to Chapter 13.

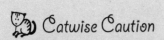 Catwise Caution

Don't attempt to introduce an untrained dog to your cat. If you don't have verbal control over the dog, enroll in a training course or work with a qualified private trainer. Work on clicker training your dog so you'll have a better ability to shift his focus during the actual introduction.

If you and your cat will be moving into the dog's environment, a sanctuary room will need to be set up for the cat so she'll have time to adjust to the new surroundings. Don't introduce her to a new home and a new dog all at once. When she has adjusted to her new surroundings in the sanctuary room, let her out to explore the new house and become familiar with everything before you attempt the dog's introduction. If it's possible to bring the dog over to the cat's home for a gradual introduction before you move, that may help her to accept him more easily. She'll be in familiar territory and will know where she can go to feel safe.

The Introduction

Depending on the ages of the animals you're introducing, there should be some slight modifications to the process.

Introducing an Adult Dog to a Cat

Allow the dog to work off energy before attempting an introduction. Take him for a good walk or out to play. Trim your cat's nails beforehand to reduce any damage should the unthinkable happen.

The dog needs to be on the leash. Place the cat in a room with a baby gate to prevent the dog from gaining access should he slip out of your grasp. Sit outside the room with your dog and reward him with treats and praise when he focuses on you and not on the cat. You can have toys for him as well. Clicker training works well in this situation so you can click and treat the dog for a relaxed body posture or for turning his attention to you. If the dog gets tense and starts staring at the cat, divert his attention, and when he breaks the stare, click and reward.

It's best to train your dog to turn his attention to you on command using a "watch me" cue. Put your finger to your nose (holding a treat the first several times), and when the dog looks at you, click and reward. Add the verbal "watch me" cue. This refocusing behavior can help him relax and put his attention back where it needs to be.

If the dog isn't comfortable, move farther away from the cat's safe room. As the dog gets more relaxed you can then move a few inches closer.

Start at a distance that's comfortable for the animal who is most stressed out. If the cat is too afraid to be in sight of the dog, put her in a carrier in her sanctuary room and partially cover the carrier so she'll feel hidden. This way, she can watch the dog's relaxed body language. Under no circumstances should you or anyone else attempt to hold the cat in your arms. Not only will she feel more threatened and confined, the person holding her stands a very good chance of becoming injured.

Let the animals get used to the sight of each other at this very safe distance. You can also walk your dog around the room and click and treat him as he walks by the gate without focusing on the cat. Do this at a comfortable distance for the cat, though—not right next to the gate. As the dog's body posture relaxes you can then walk closer to the gate.

Use a soothing tone of voice as you talk to the dog: stretch out your words ("goooood doooog") and dip your voice down at the end. Don't talk in an excited tone or use baby talk. The dog will take his cues from you, so if you're excited, the dog is going to get excited too, and that might panic the cat.

Once the two pets have seen each other for a while, separate them. Continue this gradual introduction several times a day as the two get used to each other. If they appear comfortable, you can let them get closer. With the dog on the leash, allow the cat to have full access to the area. Take down the baby gate so your cat can go wherever she wants. If the dog attempts to run or pulls against the leash, move him in the opposite direction so he'll learn that pulling only gets him farther away from where he wants to be. He needs to learn that his approach to the cat must be slow and relaxed and that as long as he moves that way, he'll have slack on the leash and get rewards and praise.

Cats have a larger personal zone than dogs, so the pup will have to learn to respect that. If he goes rocketing up to the cat, he'll more than likely encounter a series of paw smacks and hisses. The cat needs to set the pace for how much personal space she's willing to share.

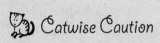 *Catwise Caution*

Don't let the dog off the leash until you're sure both pets are comfortable with each other. Don't rush this step because a mistake could have tragic results.

Keep a baby gate across the cat's room so she can go in and out of her sanctuary as needed to have some time away from the dog. Even with a large dog, you can train him not to jump or push over the baby gate, which may give your cat a sense of security knowing that one room in the house is exclusively hers. When you aren't there to supervise, don't depend on the baby gate to keep both pets separated. Put the cat or the dog in a separate room with a closed and latched door.

Introducing a Puppy to a Cat

Allow the cat to have free access through the house. Confine the puppy to one room so the cat doesn't get ambushed by the exuberant youngster. It will help the process if the kitty feels only a portion of her environment has been invaded by this little alien.

Once the cat is comfortable with the fact that there's a puppy in the house, you can start the introduction with the puppy in a crate. The worst thing you can do is let a playful, energized puppy chase the cat. The pup may be engaging in play but the cat will interpret it as a hostile behavior.

When kitty is comfortable being in the room with the crated pup, begin the basic introduction technique previously described in this chapter.

Introducing a Kitten to an Adult Dog

Start with the kitten in a carrier or crate, or confine him in a room with a baby gate. This will allow the dog to safely view the kitten. Keep the dog on a leash and begin the basic introduction process previously described in this chapter.

Making Progress

As the two pets begin to settle in and get comfortable with each other, continue to watch for any potential trouble. Observe them during meals to be alerted for any signs of aggression or intimidation. Also, since play methods differ (dogs chase and cats stalk), make sure there's no miscommunication happening.

If you haven't done adequate environmental modifications, be sure to do them now before the cat and dog spend any unsupervised time together. This includes providing cat trees, elevated areas, and hiding places.

During the introduction sessions (and this will take many training sessions), if at any time the dog tries to aggressively go after the cat then this isn't a safe match. If you feel uncertain as to whether the situation might improve, contact a professional trainer or certified behavior expert to work with you.

Even after you're sure everyone has made friends, continue to monitor to ensure safety and peace.

Overcoming Fear of Strangers

The doorbell rings and your cat vanishes right before your eyes. To help her overcome this common fear, refer to Chapter 7.

Why Your Cat Insists on Sitting in the Lap of the One Guest Who *Hates* Cats!

It never fails. You invite four or five friends over, and your kitty ignores all the cat lovers and focuses her attention on the guest who doesn't just *dislike* cats, but absolutely *detests* them. If you look at it from the cat's point of view, though, it makes perfect sense. Cats are territorial animals who primarily use scent as a way of investigating and recognizing others. So if the cat is suddenly faced with a bunch of unfamiliar-smelling strangers in her domain, she needs to check them out and make sure they're okay. The cat *lovers* will usually walk right over to her, reach out to pet, or—even worse—try to hold her before she's had time to evaluate them. The only one who makes no overture to her is the cat *hater*. That person sits on the couch and completely ignores your kitty. That behavior allows the cat to conduct her investigation. She's able to get close, sniff the guest's shoes, maybe even jump up on the sofa and conduct a closer inspection. The cat is able to do all of this without so much as a glance in her direction. So it's not a big mystery—it's just a cat using common sense.

What to Do When Your Cat Hates Your New Partner

I find this subject so interesting. Over the years, I've come across quite a few owners who would just as soon get rid of the spouse if they didn't meet with the cat's approval. When I was single, I had a cat, Albie, who was my "date barometer." I found that if Albie didn't care for my date, he'd sit on the coffee table directly in front of the guy and stare him down. If my date attempted to pet him, Albie would bob and weave to stay out of range. I soon found out that the men Albie sat and stared at usually did turn out to be jerks. I learned to trust Albie's assessment and breathed a sigh of relief when he didn't engage in a staring contest with my future husband.

From a cat's point of view, the unexpected addition of a new person to the home can be very alarming. If the new spouse is moving into your home, the cat is faced with not only the intrusion of a new person, but their strange belongings as well. The cat, a territorial creature of habit, watches as her environment is turned upside down. Furniture usually gets rearranged, schedules get disrupted, and worst of all, her usual sleeping spot on the bed may become off limits to her. Now add to that the lack of attention she may receive due to the hectic activity surrounding a wedding and honeymoon. Poor kitty can easily get lost in the shuffle.

If you and your kitty move from your home into your spouse's home, or even to a new home, imagine how much of an adjustment that becomes. It's an anxious time for you, but *you* entered into this willingly, whereas your cat had no choice. So here she is, in a new home, with a stranger (and maybe other pets or even children), and the only thing familiar to her is *you*. The techniques in Chapter 14 will help her adjust to this new environment.

When you talk about a cat hating your spouse or appearing jealous, it's really that she's anxious, confused, and fearful. She has to make many overwhelming adjustments in a short amount of time.

If your cat seems uncomfortable or even aggressive toward your new spouse, you need to slow down and give her the opportunity to adjust at a more comfortable pace. She needs as much of her familiar routine as possible during the transition. Banishing her from her usual spot on the bed will only heighten her confusion and anxiety. She needs to be an included family member—not an excluded pet. So as you all make the transition, continue to look at the situation from the cat's point of view.

One thing that can cause anxiety in a cat is the unfamiliar sound and movement of a new spouse. A cat who has only been exposed to a female owner may need time to adjust to the heavier sounds of a man's footsteps as well as his deeper voice or broader movements. It will help if you can ask your spouse to try to walk and talk a bit softer for the first few days. The same adjustment will be needed for the cat of a male owner who must now adjust to quicker movements and high-pitched sounds. The new female in the house will need to try to avoid sounding too high pitched or moving too fast.

One of the best ways to help a cat to bond with her owner's new spouse is through playtime. Using an interactive toy, the spouse can help the cat develop a positive association. Teach your spouse how to use the toys and let him or her conduct play sessions. It's important that your spouse remain still and nonthreatening throughout the game. If your cat refuses to play, *you* can start the interactive session and eventually hand the toy to your spouse. Watch to make sure that your spouse conducts playtime in the way your cat is used to—with lots of successes and captures. Even if your spouse isn't a cat lover, I've found that much of that feeling comes from not being around cats, which prevents getting to know them. Through play sessions, both your cat and your spouse will begin to relax around each other. Your spouse will also start to view your cat in a different light while watching how graceful, fast, and comical she can be during play.

Your spouse should also take over feeding duties. Even if you normally put food out free-choice, your spouse should be the one to do it, leaving the scent of their hands on the food bowl. Treats should also come from the spouse.

Let the cat set the pace of things and offer her plenty of opportunities to investigate your spouse without the fear of being picked up, petted, or held. Your spouse may be dying to hold or pet your cat in a show of friendship, but the cat may not be ready for that. If your spouse rushes the trust-building process, it'll just set everything back. It's amazing how well the relationship will progress once the cat feels secure enough to proceed.

One little inside feline etiquette tip to offer your spouse is to do a human/cat version of nose-to-nose sniffing. Don't worry, your spouse won't actually have to go nose-to-nose with your kitty. I'm sure both your spouse and the cat will be very relieved to hear that. Actually, it's a modified version where the human uses an index finger as a makeshift kitty nose. If you extend your index finger down to the cat's level when she's approaching, she may come over and do a little sniffing. In the cat world, a nose-to-nose greeting is the feline version of a handshake. If the cat wants further interaction, she may rub the finger with the side of her face and/or continue to advance toward you. If she doesn't feel comfortable enough for further interaction, she'll back away or just stand there waiting to see what your next move will be.

It's important to resist the urge to pet or even wiggle your finger when doing this exercise. If the cat makes it clear that she's not ready, casually and slowly withdraw the finger and try again another time. Give these instructions to your spouse and hopefully the *feline handshake* will aid in the trust-building process.

Eventually, through positive association surrounding playtime, meals, and treats your cat will very likely see the same wonderful qualities in your spouse that you do.

Preparing Your Cat for the Arrival of a Baby

When the wife finds out that she's expecting a baby, all too often, she starts to panic about what to do with the cat. Well-meaning friends and neighbors warn her about how dangerous cats are. Many cats, once beloved family members, soon find themselves living in a cage at the shelter, never to see their owners again. Some cats, while not relinquished to a shelter, may become banished to the outdoors—something horribly traumatic and potentially deadly for a once indoor-only cat.

By now, I'm sure you don't believe that cats suck the breath from babies. Perhaps what we now know as SIDS was once blamed on innocent cats for lack of any other explanation. The one concern a pregnant woman should have, though, has to do with *toxoplasmosis*. With proper litter box maintenance and a little education on your part, you can avoid this danger. IT IN NO WAY MEANS YOU MUST GET RID OF YOUR CAT! Refer to the Medical Appendix, which will explain what toxoplasmosis is and how to avoid it.

Some cats handle the arrival of a new baby without so much as a whisker getting out of place. Some others, though, appear to view it as the ultimate invasion of a hairless, foul-smelling, ear-shattering alien. Realize that it's *anxiety* and not *jealousy* that may cause your cat to hiss or act less than friendly. Don't punish your cat or banish her to the garage for being apprehensive. Instead, use patience, love, and positive reinforcement to help her through this so you can all be one happy family.

Unless, due to some unforeseen circumstances, you suddenly have a child in your home, you'll have plenty of time during pregnancy or adoption to prepare your cat for the arrival. By taking the time to ease your kitty through the transition, you'll have a calm cat well-equipped for the changes the new baby will create in the family.

If you're planning to redecorate a room into a nursery, complete with new paint, wallpaper, carpet, and furniture, do it gradually. Start early and do a little bit at a time to give your cat a chance to adequately adjust. Remember, a cat is a creature of habit, so if one room in the house is suddenly transformed in a whirlwind of activity, she may be a little concerned. Do one or two things at a time and allow your cat the opportunity to investigate. If you're remodeling, take breaks to play with the cat if she seems anxious about the goings-on. If workers are in the house, take time after they've finished to interact with your cat to help her adjust to the changes. Conduct play sessions in the new areas or offer her some treats.

Buy the crib enough in advance of the baby's arrival so you have time to train your cat to stay out of it. My favorite method is to fill the crib with lots of shake cans or plastic bottles. A shake can is an empty soda can or bottle with a few pennies sealed inside. Fill the crib with the shake cans so she won't be able to find a quiet, comfortable spot to nap in there. Keep the shake cans in there until the baby's arrival. If the cat attempts to climb the crib once the baby comes you can buy a crib tent to place over the crib. If you do decide to use a crib tent, choose a sturdy one that won't end up becoming a hammock for the cat.

The sounds a baby makes can be disconcerting to a cat (and to parents as well). You can find crying-baby sound effects on the Internet or you can record the crying sounds of a friend's baby and play it at a low volume while you conduct play sessions with your cat.

If you have musical mobiles or any other sound-generating baby toys, play them while the cat engages in a game or is eating so that by the time the baby arrives, all of these noises are old news to the kitty. This especially applies to any large toys, high chairs, motion swings, exersaucers, or anything else that may cause a cat to raise an eyebrow.

If you have a friend with a baby, invite them for a visit so you can gradually get your cat used to the sight and smell of a baby. When the friend and the baby visit, conduct a play session with your cat. Click and treat the cat for showing relaxed behavior around the baby.

Scent is very important to cats, so before your baby is born, the mother-to-be should start wearing baby powder, lotion, or whatever other products will be used on the newborn. This will help the cat associate those scents with her owner so they'll be familiar when she smells them on the baby.

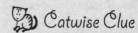

Catwise Clue

Don't lavish an overabundance of attention on your cat before the baby arrives, because chances are you won't be able to maintain that schedule when the baby is home.

If your cat gets used to this seemingly endless amount of affection for nine months and then becomes all but forgotten after the delivery, it'll cause her even more anxiety. Maintain a normal schedule before the baby's arrival.

Keep the cat's schedule as normal as possible. Don't skip her play sessions even if it means that one family member plays with her while the mother tends to the baby. Allow the cat to be a part of things. If the mother is nursing the baby, there's no reason why the cat can't be sleeping by her side.

One thing to be aware of is that the increase in visitors to your home to see the baby can be a bit overwhelming. Conduct play sessions and click and treat your cat for displaying relaxed behavior.

If you find that your cat is too fascinated with the baby and you'd prefer that she stay out of the nursery completely, you may want to install a screen door at the room's entrance.

My best piece of advice to you is to relax. Cats and babies can be wonderful together. I loved watching my cats and my children discover each other. I prepared in advance, kept a watchful eye, and made sure my demeanor around my cats and kids was calm and relaxed.

Small Children

One of the scariest sights your cat may encounter is a toddler coming down the hallway in her direction with fingers ready to grab a fistful of fur. Ouch! Always supervise small children around the cat. It's so easy for a tail to be grabbed or an ear pulled. A cat who feels trapped by a toddler may react by scratching or biting.

Teach children that the cat is a member of the family who should be treated with gentleness and respect. The cat is not a toy to be teased, dressed up, or restrained. Show your children how to pet with an open hand. Instruct them to pet with one hand only to avoid making the cat feel confined. As soon as the children are old enough, teach them how to interpret the cat's body language and means of communication so they'll begin to learn when the cat prefers to be left alone.

I taught my children the cats' names as soon as possible and repeatedly shared with them what loved members of the family the cats were. I also modeled the gentle behavior I wanted from my children. If any adult or older child in your family inappropriately handles the cat or speaks in a derogatory manner, that will quickly be picked up by a young child.

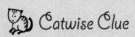 Catwise Clue

Use a stuffed animal as a teaching tool to show small children how to pet and also demonstrate what areas are off limits and sensitive. This is especially helpful if your young children tend to be too enthusiastic or if kitty is timid or nervous.

The litter box, feeding station, and where the cat sleeps are three places that should be off limits to young children. You may want to install a baby gate across the doorway to the room where the litter box is kept. There are gates available with small openings to allow the cat to go through. The other option is to put a chair, box, or stool on the other side of the gate so the cat has something to land on or jump from when hopping over the gate. If the cat is older or not as athletic, use the gate that comes with the small opening.

When your children want to play with the cat, provide them with safe interactive toys, such as the Cat Dancer. Don't allow them to use laser lights. Interactive toys on long poles should only be used by children old enough to understand how to avoid poking the cat in the face. Children, no matter how responsible, should be supervised by an adult when using an interactive cat toy. Instruct children on the toy's proper use. In addition to watching that children don't accidentally poke the cat in the face with the toy, you also don't want the cat to be teased by having the toy constantly kept out of reach. Explain to your children how it makes the cat feel good to have successful captures, just as they themselves feel happier when they do well at a sport or game.

I often see the family cat being hauled around by a child with only a small portion of the body supported. She ends up hanging from the child's arms, barely supported under the armpits with her front paws almost straight up in the air. Teach your children how to properly lift and carry the cat. If they aren't big enough to support the cat's full weight they shouldn't carry her at all.

You're Responsible for the Cat's Welfare

When your children are old enough, it's certainly a good idea to have them help with the responsibilities of caring for the cat. They can fill the food and water bowl, you can show them how to brush the cat, or they can scoop the litter, but a child can't possibly handle the total responsibility of an animal. You must monitor to make sure the cat is getting everything she needs. A child won't notice if the cat hasn't been urinating in the box or eating regularly. A child also may not notice if the cat has diarrhea or is constipated. Neglecting the cat because she belongs to your child will not teach anyone any lessons—it only causes the cat to suffer.

Unfortunately, in some families, animal abuse by children occurs. Do not tolerate any mishandling of the cat and be alert for signs of "accidents" that may have been intentional. If you suspect abuse, move the cat to a safe environment immediately and contact your child's doctor.

Supervise your cat and/or provide her with a sanctuary room when unfamiliar children come over and want to play with her. Even if children don't mean any harm, they're often unable to read a cat's warning signs. Events such as birthday parties are fun for the children but not necessarily for the family cat. As a responsible owner, use your good judgment and always provide for your cat's safety.

12

Glamour Puss

How to Make Grooming a Pleasurable Experience (Really, It Can Be Done)

Hardly an activity goes by in a cat's life that won't end with him doing a grooming touch-up or full-scale coat maintenance. Cats are master groomers.

Grooming serves many important functions in a cat's life. Although the people who dislike cats will tell you that a cat grooms solely for the purpose of being able to throw up a hair ball on the bed, that's far from true.

As the cat runs his raspy tongue over his coat, he's able to pull out the dead hair. His tongue also cleans dust, traces of his meal, dirt, and other particles from the coat. He does his best to remove parasites such as fleas by biting and licking. Spreading his toes, he cleans between them, under and around each nail. When he's satisfied that he's done an adequate bathing job, his tongue smoothes out each hair to provide maximum insulation from cold or heat. Licking helps evenly distribute the natural oils in his coat, which affords him some waterproofing and imparts a glorious sheen.

After being petted, you'll often notice your cat groom himself right at the spot where you touched him. He's reinforcing his own scent on his coat and also enjoying yours as well. On the other hand, after a negative encounter (such as being handled by the veterinarian), the cat will go through an elaborate grooming ritual once he gets home. He'll want to wash away the "bad" scent and redistribute his own comforting scent.

After a hunt, the cat will end his meal by grooming to remove all traces of the prey's scent as well as any leftover debris. This helps him to not alert other prey or predators of his presence.

Social grooming among companion cats is another way in which they bond by mixing their scents.

Grooming is also used as a displacement behavior. When a cat wants to do something and is prevented from it, he often will groom himself to relieve his anxiety. You may notice this when your cat watches the birds outside. He can't get to them and needs to do something with his energy.

Why You Need to Groom Your Cat

Even though cats are so meticulous about their personal hygiene, your cat still needs your help in maintaining his glorious coat. The coats of long-haired cats are glorious to look at but an unfortunate side effect of breeding to enhance the coat is an inability of the cat to maintain the coat by himself. Even your short-haired cat will benefit from being brushed. Although you don't have to brush a short-haired as often as you would a long-haired cat, the more meticulous you are about grooming your cat, the more beautiful and healthy his coat and skin will be.

Cats have two major shedding seasons each year: one in preparation for winter and one for summer. A cat exposed to the dry indoor heat sheds consistently year-round (but at a more moderate rate) so he really benefits from regular brushing. Grooming your cat helps tremendously. If you brush your cat not only will it cut down on the amount of hair that ends up on your furniture, it will reduce the amount of hair that your cat ingests during self-grooming. And this in turn will lessen the likelihood of hair balls, which can be a serious problem for cats who ingest too much hair. They're also a problem for owners who walk around in bare feet because cats always manage to vomit hair balls where you're sure to step on them. Regular brushing, along with other routine feline maintenance, may also help those in your family with allergies.

Grooming your cat on a regular basis also allows you the opportunity to do a health check. When I groom, my hands go over every inch of the cat's body and I can catch any lump, bump, sore, or rash early. I can feel if there's been any weight loss or gain. I check for fleas and when I clean the cat's ears, I also look for any sign of infection or irritation. When I brush the cat's teeth, I look for signs of gum swelling or redness. Owners who don't groom may not notice that small lump or wound on their cat until it has advanced. Grooming lets owners of outdoor cats check for ticks that can hide in places where you wouldn't detect them otherwise—such as between the toes, in the ear folds, or under the tail.

Finally, if you don't get your cat comfortable with being groomed, you'll probably have trouble medicating him should it ever become necessary. Trying to put ear drops in a cat who isn't used to having his ears touched often results in more medicine getting on your clothes or the walls than in his ears.

The Tools You Need

Have everything in one convenient case so it'll be easier for you. This way, you won't have to leave your cat in the middle of the grooming session to go get something you left in another location. The tools you'll need will depend on the type of coat your cat has. The instructions provided are meant as general grooming guidelines for keeping your cat's coat clean, healthy, and free of mats. If you're grooming for show competitions or have a cat with specific care requirements, work with a top-notch professional groomer or get instructions from a breeder who will be knowledgeable on show requirements.

Long-Haired Cats

A pin brush, which resembles a pin cushion with a handle, works best. The bristles are straight and get through the dense, fine coat. You'll also need wide, medium, and fine-toothed combs. When your cat gets tangles you can't brush or comb out, you can buy a special detangling spray made for cat hair or you can sprinkle a little cornstarch into the coat. The spray is less messy. Some long-haired breeds tend to stain under their eyes. To remove this, use a tear stain remover that's safe for cats. I also finish off the session by polishing the coat with a soft bristle brush.

Short-Haired Cats

A *slicker* brush, a small gentle brush with thin wire bristles bent at the tips, works well on short coats. If your cat has very short, dense hair, you can use a soft bristle brush instead of the slicker brush. To loosen dead hair and give your cat an enjoyable massage, you'll start off with a rubber currycomb—a brush with rubber nubs instead of actual bristles. If your cat objects to being brushed, you can start with a grooming glove to help him get used to the procedure. The glove has little rubber nubs that trap the hair as you pet your cat. It's not as effective as the currycomb but if that's all the cat will let you do for now, it's better than nothing. A very fine-toothed comb, such as a flea comb, will enable you to run through the hair and trap not only fleas, but their excrement (dried blood), and their eggs. It really keeps the coat clean. And nothing finishes the grooming process on a short-haired cat like a piece of chamois or velvet rubbed in the direction of the hair growth.

The FURminator, made by Furminator, Inc., is another good grooming tool for effectively getting out the loose, dead hair. You have to use a very light touch with this product and don't rake over bony or sensitive areas.

Kittens

No matter whether he's long haired or short haired, start familiarizing him with being groomed by using a baby brush.

Special Coats

If you have a wirehaired or crimped-haired cat, you'll need the same tools that you'd use for a short-haired cat. If your cat's hair is very sparse, use a soft baby brush instead. You'll also need a flea comb. For a Sphinx cat, a rubber currycomb works to massage and remove the fine down that covers the skin. The skin on the Sphinx can get oily, which attracts dirt in the folds.

Tools of the Trade Needed for All Cats

A rubber bath mat, which you'll put on the table, prevents your cat from slipping. You can also use it if you bathe your kitty.

You'll need nail trimmers even if your cat has been declawed (the nails on the hind feet will need a trim). Buy nail trimmers designed for a cat's nails. Dog trimmers are too big and you risk injuring your cat with them. Regular human fingernail clippers aren't designed for the shape of a cat's nail so if you use them the end result could be ragged. You'll also need some styptic powder on hand just in case you cut too much and cause the nail to bleed.

Keep a supply of cotton balls to protect your cat's ears while you're bathing him. They can also be used for ear and undereye cleaning. Gauze pads are handy for wrapping around your finger to brush the cat's teeth in case you aren't comfortable using a toothbrush. Gauze pads can also be used for ear cleaning. A cat-safe ear cleanser should be part of your grooming supplies. Your veterinarian can give you a recommendation on what type to use.

Keep a supply of cotton swabs on hand to apply the styptic powder. I don't recommend using cotton swabs for ear cleaning, though, because you could easily puncture the cat's delicate eardrum.

To clean teeth, you can either use the gauze, a pet toothbrush, finger toothbrush, or even a baby toothbrush. You'll also need toothpaste designed especially for pets. Don't use toothpaste for humans because it'll burn the throat, esophagus, and stomach.

Getting Started

When you first get your cat is the time to begin getting him used to being groomed. Start by getting him comfortable with being touched. If he's normally uncomfortable with being petted, click and treat him when you touch him.

Start by introducing grooming tools slowly. Sit with your cat and pet him and leave the brush next to you. Click and treat the cat if he sniffs the brush. Do the same with other brushes and grooming tools.

Before you actually start brushing your cat, gently go over his body with your hands so you'll be alerted to any sores, scabs, or bumps. This way you'll know in advance to be careful around those areas. This also lets the cat get comfortable with being touched.

When the cat is comfortable with the above steps, take the brush and gently stroke behind his head (that's usually a cat's favorite spot to be petted or brushed). Click and treat. Make brushing an extension of petting. Keep the experience positive, casual, and short. Once your cat makes the connection that grooming is enjoyable, the process will be a pleasure for both of you.

There are some grooming rules that you'll need to follow. The first rule: *don't hurt your cat.* One reason so many cats hate to be groomed is that it truly becomes a torture session. Don't pull, yank, or be rough in any way. A cat's body is *very* sensitive. His skin can easily tear. Also, because the skin is thin, taking a comb or brush over the spine or various other bony parts will be very painful. The moment you hurt your cat, he'll tense up and begin to dislike being groomed. My cats don't struggle to get away when they're being groomed because they trust me—I make sure I never hurt them. Before you use any brush or comb, run it along the inside of your forearm to get a feel for how lightly you should brush.

Another reason cats hate grooming is that often it goes on for an intolerably long time. The owners of long-haired cats who brush only when they remember or when they feel a mat, end up subjecting the cat to thirty minutes or more of grooming. Owners who brush daily can get the whole thing done in less than three minutes. If you have a long-haired cat, you must brush him daily. That's the only way to prevent tangles and mats. Even if you have a long-haired cat whose hair doesn't mat, daily brushing keeps the coat in good shape and reduces shedding and the risk of hair balls. Daily brushing for short periods keeps it a familiar, comfortable routine in the cat's life.

Brushing short-haired cats once or twice a week is enough to keep the coat looking nice. If your cat has a problem with hair balls, you may want to brush more often.

You won't have to do ear cleaning and nail trimming every time. Nails usually need a trim about once a month. Your cat's ears may be very clean and only need to be wiped out every few weeks. Some cats need it weekly. The point is, by checking the ears every time, you can catch problems early.

Teeth should be brushed daily. It's a quick process (described later in this chapter) and once you get the hang of it, you can do it in ten seconds. But, now that I've said that it should be done daily, I'll tell you that most owners don't follow that rule. Unfortunately, many owners don't brush their cats' teeth at all. That's a big mistake because if you do preventive maintenance, your cat may not have to go under anesthesia to have his teeth professionally cleaned by the veterinarian as often. You can also, in many cases, prevent gingivitis and periodontal disease. Your cat's breath will also stay very sweet. Brushing daily would be best, but if you can't, do it at least three times a week. Don't neglect your cat's teeth.

Where to Groom

If you groom on a table or elevated surface, it'll certainly be much kinder for your back. Place a rubber mat on the table or counter so your cat will have something to grip. He'll feel more secure than if he's sliding all over the place and scrambling to keep his footing. The table or counter has to be a surface that your cat is normally allowed on so that you don't send mixed messages. If you have a long-haired cat, it's worth checking into purchasing a grooming table.

If you're more comfortable with the cat on your lap, just place a thick towel across your legs to catch the hairs and prevent injury to you should he dig his nails in. I found that cats get more impatient being groomed on the owner's lap because they get hot. It's also more difficult to reach all areas of the coat when the cat is curled up in your lap.

Brushing Techniques
Short-Haired Cats

Start by using the rubber currycomb in a circular motion to loosen the dander and dead hairs. Your cat will most likely enjoy this. Then take the slicker brush and gently do long strokes from the back of the head, down the length of the body on either side of the spine. Don't rake the brush over the bumpy spine. On the parts of the body where you need to do shorter strokes, be very gentle each time you lower and lift the brush.

Doing the cat's chest and tummy can be very tricky. One way is to raise your cat up so that he's standing on his hind legs. I do it by having my cat face away from me while I lean over him a bit so he has the extra support of feeling me close to his back. I hold him up by gently supporting him under the front legs. If your cat prefers to sit, gently lift one leg at a time to reach the armpit and underneath areas. Don't twist your cat's leg, just hold it high enough to reach the area beneath.

During flea season, take the fine-toothed comb and pull it through the coat to trap fleas and their debris (comb in the direction of the hair). Then, when you've finished brushing, polish the coat by rubbing him down with a chamois or piece of velvet to bring out the coat's sheen. Go in the direction that the hair grows.

If your cat has a very short coat that lies close to the skin, go from the rubber currycomb to a soft bristle brush. Don't use the slicker brush. Finish with the chamois. The fine-toothed comb will still be needed to search for fleas.

Long-Haired Cats

Start with the wide-tooth comb. Begin at the tail base and do one section of the coat at a time. Lift a section of fur to comb the area underneath. This is the best way to get all the way through a dense coat and check for hidden mats. Work your way up to the cat's head. Pay close attention to trouble spots such as armpits, behind the ears, and the groin area because mats here can be easy to miss. Be very gentle because you may reach a tangle. If you come across a tangle or mat, gently work it apart with your fingers. Don't pull on the cat's skin. If you have trouble separating a mat, use the detangling spray or sprinkle cornstarch into the hair and keep combing it out. Don't forget to comb the neck ruff, chest,

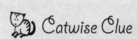 Catwise Clue

Start combing the tips of the hairs and gradually work your way closer to the skin so you don't yank on potential tangles or mats on long-haired cats.

and tummy. Hold the cat up as described in the section on short-haired cats. Some owners find it easier to groom the underside when the cat is stretched out on his side. You and your cat will learn what works best as you go. When you have finished with the wide-tooth comb, use your medium-tooth comb, again moving slowly and gently. This comb will help test for mats that you may have missed.

As you groom you may notice your cat's tail in motion. This could indicate that he's losing patience with the whole procedure. Work quickly and gently. Oh, and speaking of tails in motion, when you attempt to brush his, again, be gentle and quick. Cats don't appreciate having their tails restrained.

Hairless Cats

If your Sphinx has oily skin, you'll probably need to bathe him every seven to ten days. This cat needs to be kept warm, though, so make sure the bathroom is a comfortable temperature. Wrap the cat in warm towels and keep replacing the wet one with a warm, dry one. The towels can be warmed in the dryer beforehand.

If oil buildup is a problem between baths, use wipes to clean in the folds of the skin.

If your Sphinx develops clogged pores from an overproduction of oil, you can ask your veterinarian to recommend a safe astringent to use on those areas.

Nail Trimming

Start by touching your cat's paw and then click and treat. Do this to each paw. Work up to stroking the paw then holding the paw briefly. Be patient, as this will take several sessions depending on your cat's comfort level. It's worth going through this training in order to have your cat cooperate during future nail-trimming sessions.

Next, put your thumb on top of the paw and your fingers underneath for support, then gently press and the nails will extend. Clip only the very tip of the nail, which is the nonliving cuticle. If your cat has light nails, by looking closely you can see where the pink area starts. This is the vein and accidentally cutting it will cause pain and bleeding. If your cat has dark nails it'll be impossible to see the vein so only trim the tip of the nail. Don't go beyond the start of the curve. If you're at all unsure of how to do it, ask your veterinarian for a demonstration. Don't forget to trim the dewclaws on the front paws. They look like little thumbs.

If you do accidentally cause the nail to bleed, apply the styptic powder to the end of the nail. If you don't have styptic powder, gently dab the toe

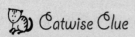 **Catwise Clue**

If you have a kitten, he may feel more secure if you hold him against you. Using your arm to support him puts you in a perfect position to hold the paw and extend the nails with the hand of the supporting arm. Your other hand can work the trimmers.

with a little cornstarch. Remember, trim less than you think you should. If you continue to cut the quick of the nail, your cat will resist having his nails trimmed due to the pain you cause him each time. It also puts the toe at risk for infection.

At first, don't try to get all of the nails done at one time. It's not worth wearing out his patience and possibly getting scratched by the very nail you just worked so hard to trim. Do one nail and then click and treat. Later, do another nail and then click and treat. Gradually work up to doing several nails at a time.

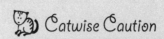

Catwise Caution

When holding the clippers with the claw positioned, double-check to make sure the blades aren't near the *quick*. If the cat is struggling, don't continue.

To keep your cat familiar and comfortable with the process, do nail trimming every two or three weeks initially. Not every nail will need trimming but this way you'll just have to clip the very tip on just a few. You'll keep kitty comfortable with the procedure and that will make life easier for both of you in the future. Once he's okay with having his nails trimmed, you may be able to switch to a monthly schedule depending on how fast your cat's nails grow.

Polydactyls are cats with extra toes. If you have one of these cats, don't forget to trim the nails on those extra tootsies.

Brushing Your Cat's Teeth

To brush your cat's teeth, you can use a finger toothbrush, pet toothbrush, or even a baby toothbrush. You can even wrap a piece of gauze around your finger if you're not comfortable using the toothbrush (if using gauze, don't rub too hard or you risk irritating the gums). As for toothpaste, use one specifically made for pets. They come in flavors appealing to pets. Never use toothpaste meant for humans as it'll burn their mouth, throat, and stomach.

The first time you attempt to clean your cat's teeth should be a short training session to get him used to having his mouth manipulated.

Touch him along the sides of the mouth. Gradually work up to gently placing a toothbrush just inside his lips, against his teeth. If he allows this, use your clicker to click and treat him. If you're not clicker training, just reward him with a treat, praise, petting, or play session.

Make the brushing sessions quick and comfortable. The faster you are, the less he'll object to the process.

If you're unable to brush your cat's teeth no matter how you've tried, there are plaque-reducing products available that can be squirted in the mouth. They're not as effective as brushing but they're better than not doing anything. If you have trouble with brushing, ask your veterinarian for one of the liquid or spray products. In order for them to be effective, be sure to follow the directions on the label carefully. For instance, you shouldn't feed your cat for at least one half hour after using the dental rinse.

Ear Cleaning

Look inside your cat's ears before you start to clean them to check for signs of infection, sores, or ear mites. If a blackish-brown crumbly material is visible in the ears, that's a sign of ear mites. Your cat will need to go to the veterinarian and will require ear medication (for more on ear mites, see the Medical Appendix).

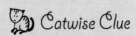 Catwise Clue

To help your cat get comfortable with ear cleaning, gently touch his ear and then click and treat. Gradually build up to more ear touching.

If the ears look inflamed, are sensitive to the touch, or have an odor the cat needs to be examined by the veterinarian. Don't clean the ears in that case, just get him checked out. If you attempt to clean inflamed or sore ears you'll make them more irritated.

If the cat's ears are healthy but have dirt or wax in them, pour a little ear cleaner on a cotton ball and wipe the inside of the ear. Don't use a cotton swab because you could injure the delicate eardrum.

Do ear cleaning last because it makes your cat's ears itchy and he might become a little impatient if he has to then sit still for other procedures.

Fleas and Other Itchy Things

Scratch . . . scratch . . . scratch. You hear it in the night when you're trying to sleep. During the day you notice your cat is about to pounce on a toy when suddenly he stops, sits down, and scratches frantically at his neck. It could be something as simple as being uncomfortable with his collar, or it could be any number of skin problems that can plague a cat at any age. Allergies, fungal disease, and parasites can drive a cat crazy. One of the most common causes of skin scratching is the pesky little flea. If your cat has an allergy to fleas it just takes one to cause him (and you) sleepless nights.

If your cat appears to have skin problems such as a rash, inflammation, oily or dry skin, bumps, or anything else that looks or feels suspicious get it checked by the veterinarian. In addition to any oral or topical prescription, a special medicated shampoo may be needed.

With fleas and ticks, because cats are such dedicated groomers, you may never actually see the parasite but you may be able to see the excrement they leave behind on the cat's skin.

With the availability of effective topical flea-control products, your cat really doesn't have to suffer the discomfort of flea infestation. To learn more about total flea and tick control for your cat and his environment, refer to Chapter 13.

Overactive Oil Glands

Stud tail is an overproduction of oil that usually appears as a greasy spot on the end of the tail of males (mostly unneutered). You can control the greasiness by cleansing the tip of the tail with an oil-cutting shampoo. If the condition worsens, creating hair loss or inflammation, see your veterinarian.

Feline acne, the result of those oil glands working overtime on the chin, shows up as dark, crusty blackheads. It can also cause more serious pustules. To clean mild acne, use a gauze pad or washcloth and warm water. If it continues to be a problem, your veterinarian will recommend more specific treatment.

Refer to the Medical Appendix for more on stud tail and feline acne.

Hair Balls

Due to the backward-facing barbs on the cat's tongue, the hair he grooms must be swallowed. Some of this swallowed hair passes through the digestive system without a problem. If he swallows too much hair, the cat may vomit up a tubular-shaped glob of wet hair known to those of us who end up stepping on them as hair balls. Not all hair balls get vomited up or passed with the stool, though. Some swallowed hair ends up trapped in the intestines, causing a blockage. If your notice your cat passing rock-hard feces or no feces at all, it could be due to a partial or complete hair-ball blockage. Call your veterinarian immediately.

Some cats never have a problem with them. But hair balls aren't just reserved for long-haired cats; short-haired cats do get their share of them too.

Solution? Brushing.

For cats who have a problem with hair balls despite your diligence, there are hair-ball-prevention products available. Basically a laxative, the gel products come in a tube and are usually malt-flavored. They're mineral oil–based so they aren't absorbed by the body and just work as a lubricant. They shouldn't be used more than twice a week, though (unless advised to do so by your veterinarian), because mineral oil inhibits the body's absorption of fat-soluble vitamins. Squeeze out a one-inch strip onto your finger and offer it to your cat. Many cats like the taste and will lick the gel off your finger. If your cat doesn't, you can open his mouth and slide your finger along the edge of his upper teeth to deposit the gel onto the roof of his mouth. Some owners of reluctant cats try rubbing the laxative onto the paw, knowing that the cat will ingest it when he grooms himself. I've seen more hair-ball laxative splashed across walls because the cats decided to shake the stuff off rather than use their tongues. It can also be very messy on the fur, so if you feel you must resort to this method, place only a small amount on your cat's paw until you're sure he'll lick it off. If a dose of hair-ball laxative once or twice a week isn't sufficient, talk to your veterinarian about increasing the amount of fiber in your cat's diet.

There are commercial hair-ball-control-formula foods available. Your veterinarian may recommend changing your cat over to this diet. There are hair-ball-control treats as well.

Bathing Your Cat

I must be kidding, right? Perhaps the very idea of it brings on hysterical laughter. You're sitting there, shaking your head thinking, *no way, not me, I'm not bathing my cat!* Do you imagine a soaking wet cat covered in suds, racing through the house shrieking, with you in hot pursuit?

You most likely will never need to bathe your cat. Is it my imagination, or did I just hear you breathe a sigh of relief? Some long-haired cats require frequent baths because their coats get oily, and short-haired cats may need an occasional bath depending on their coat condition or what they may have gotten into. It can be a relatively easy procedure, or it can be an exhausting battle, where you end up wetter than the cat and he ends up shredding the shower curtain before escaping from your grasp and racing out of the bathroom. Doing it the easy way is better for you, your cat, your bathroom, your home furnishings, and your relationship with your spouse.

Start by having everything you'll need all in one place. After the cat is wet isn't the time to remember that you forgot the shampoo. Choose a shampoo made for cats. Base your choice on your cat's individual needs; there are specific shampoos designed to enhance whiteness, reduce oil, etc. Don't use dish detergent because it's too drying. Even if you never need to bathe your cat, keep a shampoo on hand just in case. Long-haired cats will need a conditioner as well to help detangle them. You'll also need a shower attachment or portable sprayer that slips over the faucet, a baby washcloth, and plenty of towels to bathe your cat. If your hair dryer runs at industrial power and volume, purchase a quiet one with low settings.

REMINDER LIST:

shampoo meant for cats
conditioner (for long-haired cats)
several absorbent towels
cotton balls
brush
rubber bath mat
shower attachment
plain eye ointment
baby washcloth
hair dryer

Before one drop of water ever hits the cat's coat, you must brush him to get all the tangles and mats out. If you bathe the cat with mats in his coat they'll tighten so much you'll have to cut them out. Take the time before the bath to do a good brushing.

You can bathe your cat in the sink, using the hose attachment, or in the tub, using the shower attachment. If you don't have a shower attachment, you can get a portable hose attachment that slides over the faucet. Bathing your cat in the kitchen sink or laundry tub is easier on your back but you may feel as if you have more control by being able to close the bathroom door. It's also easier to keep the smaller bathroom warmer. I make such a mess when I bathe my cats that I have no choice but to do it in the bathroom or else there'd be puddles everywhere.

Lay the rubber bath mat in the bottom of the sink or tub. This gives your cat something to dig into, which will make him feel more secure. Some groomers lay a small window screen in the tub or along the side of the sink for the cat to claw. Use whatever makes your cat feel more secure so you can get the job done without too much anxiety.

Before bringing the cat in, I run the water to warm up the tub and the room. Open your shampoo bottle so you won't have to fumble with it later. I also hold the shampoo bottle under the warm running water to warm it up. Gently place a half or a quarter of a cotton ball in each of the cat's ears. Don't shove it down into the ear—just place it securely in there to prevent water from running into the ear. I keep a couple of extra ones nearby also, in case my cat manages to shake one loose.

Put a drop of plain eye ointment in each eye for protection from shampoo. Even with the ointment, though, be extra careful to avoid getting shampoo in your cat's eyes.

When you place the cat in the tub, be certain to keep a secure hold on him. Don't restrain him more than necessary but if you loosen your grip, I promise you, the cat will be out of there in a flash.

Wet the coat completely by using the hose attachment. Don't dunk your cat under the water. The water should be comfortably warm. Check it against your inner forearm to be sure it's not too hot or too cold. Never pour water over the cat's head. If you have to clean or wet the hair on the head, wipe it with a damp washcloth. You want to avoid getting any water in the cat's ears, eyes, nose, or mouth.

Soap the cat all around the neck first. If you do the back first and there are any fleas on the cat, they'll race up to his head and crawl into his ears, eyes, nose, and mouth. Shampoo around the neck to prevent this. If there are fleas around his face, use the baby washcloth to wipe the area—don't douse him with water. Suds the body and legs. Don't forget to do under the tail and completely down the legs. Don't vigorously scrub the coat, especially with long-haired cats, or you'll create knots and tangles.

Using a damp washcloth, wipe all around the face. For cats with tear stains, pay close attention to the undereye area.

Rinse the coat thoroughly. Hold the sprayer right against the skin to lift the hair, which will help remove traces of soap underneath. If the cat is very dirty, you can do a second sudsing.

Rinse, rinse, rinse. Any shampoo residue left on the cat's skin after he dries will cause itching and possible irritation.

When you've finished rinsing, gently press the coat with your hands to remove the bulk of the water. Then remove the cotton balls from the cat's ears.

Wrap your cat in a towel and pat him dry to absorb the water. Don't rub the cat down. With long-haired cats, rubbing will create knots. Cats aren't too fond of vigorous rubdowns anyway.

Continue patting, replace the wet towel with a dry one, and keep doing that until you've absorbed most of the water. If you're going to use the hair dryer, it must be set on *low* and be sure to keep the dryer in motion. Don't hold it in one place on the cat's body because it can easily burn him. Never aim the air flow at the cat's face. And don't feel as if you have to dry every last hair, especially if your cat's patience is wearing out. He'll finish drying on his own.

Use a soft-bristle brush as you dry to fluff and lift the hair. With a long-haired cat, be careful when drying so you don't create tangles.

If your cat doesn't tolerate the hair dryer, keep him in a warm room until he's dry. Watch him to make sure he doesn't get chilled. Turn up the heat temporarily if necessary until he's dry.

Reward your cat when you've finished, then while he goes off to groom himself in order to get his coat back to the way *he* likes it, you can go clean the hair out of the drain.

Waterless Baths

If your cat won't tolerate a bath or is not well enough, you can use a waterless bath. There are several products available. Powders have been around a long time. There are also foam products, which I think work better. While these products certainly aren't as effective as a bath, they can come in handy when a bath isn't possible.

My Cat Has Been Skunked!

My best suggestion is to put him in his carrier so he doesn't run all over the house.

You can either bathe your cat yourself or call your veterinary hospital. They often have someone on staff who will do the bath for you. I strongly recommend you have the cat bathed at the clinic or grooming salon because they have the skunk odor-neutralizing shampoo on hand.

If you're bathing your cat at home, wear old clothes that you won't mind throwing away because the smell won't come out of them. You'll need old towels as well. Bathe the cat first in his regular shampoo, then in tomato juice or de-skunk solutions (available at pet supply stores or from your veterinarian). Follow that with another sudsing in his regular shampoo. By the way, you're going to need a bath yourself.

When You Need Professional Help

No, I'm not referring to a psychiatrist, although after attempting to bathe an uncooperative cat you may feel as if you need one. The type of professional I'm talking about is a *groomer*.

If you have a long-haired cat and are unable to keep the coat mat-free, you'll need the services of a professional groomer. If the cat is very matted, he may have to be clipped.

Some owners schedule regular grooming sessions with a professional groomer to do bathing.

Ask your veterinarian and other cat owners for a recommendation on which groomers are best. Before leaving your cat with a groomer, check them out carefully. Make sure your cat won't be caged near dogs. What does the groomer use to clean the tables and equipment? Does the groomer require cats to be up-to-date on vaccinations? If not, that puts all the cats at risk. Do you see pet hair everywhere? If the groomer doesn't appear to enjoy his or her work or seems impatient around cats, grab your kitty and get the heck out of there. Cats require a gentle touch, so go in search of a groomer who practices that.

13

The Pest Patrol

Taking the Bite Out of Fleas and Ticks

Fleas are the most common parasite found on cats and these little creatures can cause big trouble. Adult fleas are fast and jump high, making it very difficult to trap one in your fingers. Cats, because they're such lightning-fast groomers, often lick away evidence of fleas before an owner even knows that there's an infestation.

Fleas live by feeding on the blood of the host. They spend their entire life on the cat, in a constant cycle of eating, eliminating, and reproducing. Females lay their eggs on the cat, the eggs soon fall off the animal and settle in the carpet, bedding, ground, or furniture to complete their incubation. In ten days, the eggs hatch into larvae, where they settle deep into the carpet pile or under your furniture. There, they feed on debris, mainly adult flea feces.

After about a week, the larvae spin a cocoon and enter the pupal stage. It is from these cocoons that adult fleas emerge. Depending on the environment, the adult can stay in the cocoon until conditions are favorable to emerge (even if it takes months). As soon as the adults emerge, they begin their search for a host.

Some cats have a sensitivity to the antigens in flea saliva and develop an allergic reaction. Red, irritated skin, scabs, and bald patches (usually on the rump, near the base of the tail) are a few telltale signs of *flea allergy dermatitis*. For a cat with a flea allergy, it only takes one to start the reaction.

Fleas are the intermediate host for tapeworms, so as the cat attempts to rid herself of the fleas, she may swallow one containing a tapeworm.

Heavy flea infestation can cause anemia in some cats because of the significant blood loss. Kittens, cats weakened by illness, and older cats are especially susceptible.

How to check for fleas: separate the hairs of your cat's coat and look for signs of the small, brownish-black fleas. Because they move so fast, you may not actually see a flea itself, but you may see their feces. Flea excrement, which is digested blood, looks like specks of pepper. You may even see some white specks that are flea eggs. Check your cat around the rump, tail, neck, and groin area.

For a cat with dark fur, place him on a white towel or white piece of paper. Brush him and you may find lots of dark specks on the white towel or paper. If using a flea comb you'll probably find trapped fleas and debris.

Treatment: To effectively treat for fleas, you have to do all of the pets in your house. A mistake that some owners frequently make is to only treat the pet who goes outdoors, not realizing that the fleas will just as easily infest any indoor cats.

The secret to avoiding flea infestation altogether is to start early, *before* the fleas have a chance to get on your cat or in your house. Fortunately, we now have truly effective flea-control products. They won't work, though, if you don't use them correctly.

When beginning a flea treatment program, I urge you to first contact your veterinary clinic to discuss all of the available options and what would be best for your individual cat. Your veterinarian or veterinary technician will make suggestions based upon your cat's age, health, the severity of the infestation, your financial concerns, and his or her experience with particular products. Don't just run to your local grocery, pet, or discount store and buy products you aren't familiar with. Toxicity levels of products vary, and you may end up doing more harm than good. If you have a kitten, you must be especially careful with what products you choose. Remember, anything you put *on* your cat will also end up *in* your cat due to self-grooming. There are also products on the market that do absolutely nothing and are a waste of money. The staff at the veterinary clinic can help you plan an effective and safe flea-treatment program.

Another aspect of successful flea control is treatment duration. Depending upon the type of climate you live in, you may need to practice flea control year-round. In areas where winters are warmer, fleas thrive all year. Even in areas that experience cold winters, if you haven't eradicated the flea infestation inside of your house, they'll set up camp in your nice warm home no matter how low the outdoor temperature drops.

Topical Flea Control Products

There are many topical flea-control products available. Before you choose a product ask your veterinarian's advice. A product that you purchase over-the-counter may not be safe for your cat. Your veterinarian will advise you on the appropriate product for your cat specifically. Some products also control ticks and internal parasites.

The long-term topical products (they last about one month) are very effective and are easy to apply—something both you and your cat will appreciate. The products come in vials that are opened and squeezed onto the back of the cat's neck. Over the course of twenty-four hours, the flea-control product will spread over the cat. You just have to remember not to pet the cat on the back of the neck for twenty-four hours.

The efficacy of good quality topical products have pretty much reduced the need for messy shampoos, sprays, or powders.

Flea Combs

These are an excellent way to remove fleas, their excrement, and their eggs from the coat. As you comb, the fleas become trapped in the tiny, narrowly spaced teeth. Flea combing alone is not effective flea-control treatment, though. It's a way to check if your cat has fleas and a way to clean the fur of flea debris.

Treating the Indoor Environment
Plug in the Vacuum

Unless you have a serious infestation, using the topical flea control products may be all you need to do. With a heavy infestation, vacuuming is necessary after the topical flea products have first been applied as a way to cut down on the number of fleas in the environment.

I hate to vacuum and usually look for any excuse to get out of the task, but it's a good step in environmental flea control. The more eggs and pupae you can suck up out of the carpet, under the furniture, and off the chair cushions, the better. Frequent vacuuming will help reduce the flea numbers. Be merciless and suck up those little creatures, then afterward toss the bag in the *outdoor* trash can. If you vacuum and neglect to toss the bag, all those sucked-up eggs will hatch inside the vacuum cleaner.

When vacuuming, do a thorough job *under* the furniture (I sound like your mother, right?) and also under any cushions, because fleas and their pupae can hide deep down in chairs and sofas. Don't forget pet bedding, cat trees, and windowsills. Vacuum as if your mother-in-law is coming for a visit, wearing her white gloves.

Ticks

Because of the cat's frequent grooming, you may not actually see a tick on her. If you do see one, it's usually on the head, neck, or in the ears because of the cat's inability to access those areas. Ticks can even be found between the toes.

Ticks attach themselves to the skin and burrow their head underneath. Before feeding, when they aren't attached to the skin, they resemble tiny spiders. When attached, though, a tick often resembles a wart on the skin. As it feeds on blood, the tick's body becomes bloated. That's usually the time an owner first sees or feels the parasite on the cat.

To remove a tick, cover it with a drop of alcohol or mineral oil. Wait a few seconds for the tick to release its hold and then grasp it carefully with a tick removal tool. These products are available at pet supply stores. They look like plastic spoons with a notch cut out in the center. You can also use tweezers but be very careful because it's easy to detach the tick's body from its head, which will end up still embedded under the skin. If using tweezers, position them close to the *head* of the tick.

After removing the tick, drop it into a small cup containing alcohol to ensure that it dies and then give the little creep a proper send-off by flushing him down the toilet.

Never use a hot match to remove a tick because the chance of injuring your cat is too great. If you have trouble removing a tick or feel that the head is still embedded, see your veterinarian.

If you have a cat who goes outdoors she needs to be protected with a topical flea/tick preventative.

14

Fasten Your Seat Belt

Traveling Without Trauma

Travel is a four-letter word in the feline dictionary. If cats ruled the world, vacations would consist of: unlimited countertop access, first dibs on the bird feeders, an endless supply of mice, seven days of not having their teeth brushed or ears cleaned, and of course, eighteen hours of beauty sleep in the comfort of the master bed. Nowhere in this vacation plan would *travel* ever be considered. Most cats prefer staying home. They'd also prefer it if *you* stayed home as well. We love adventure—cats love routine. We love exotic new locations—cats love familiar locations.

If you have a kitten, spare yourself much trauma by getting her comfortable with travel at an early age. That's not to say that as an adult she still won't play hide-and-seek when she sees your suitcase come out of the closet, but it'll be a heck of a lot easier than if you only venture out with the cat once a year for that dreaded trip to the veterinary clinic when it's time for her annual vaccinations.

With an adult cat, it's still not too late to make the travel experience less frightening. She may never learn to appreciate the adventure of travel but you can hopefully greatly reduce the anxiety and avoid long-term negative results.

Like it or not, travel is necessary for cats—whether it's the trip to the veterinarian, a move to a new home, or even an appointment with the groomer.

Why Every Cat Needs a Carrier

No matter how well-trained and comfortable with travel your cat becomes, she needs a carrier. Transporting a cat in a carrier is the only way to ensure her safety. Whether you're taking her across the country or just across the street, she must be in a carrier. It provides her with a feeling of security by allowing her to have a hiding place. If she becomes frightened or aggressive, you won't want to hold a growling, struggling cat in your arms. Attempting car travel with a loose cat running around inside the vehicle is extremely dangerous (for you and her) and can cause an accident.

Think of the carrier as one of the most important safety items for your cat. Even if you never plan on going anywhere, your veterinarian makes house calls, and you happen to hate vacations as well, you still need to own one.

Having a carrier enables you to safely get your cat out of the house in the event of an emergency. Should I have to quickly evacuate my home in a fire I would never be able to handle my three cats, who would undoubtedly be extremely frightened, unless they were in their carriers. I keep the carriers set up and ready to go, so I'll always be prepared. I live in a part of the country where tornadoes are relatively common so having the cat carriers already set up is part of my standard disaster preparation plan (for more on creating a disaster preparation plan, see Chapter 18).

Choosing a Carrier

A carrier should give your cat a sense of security, provide safety, be easy to clean, and enable you to get your kitty in and out without anyone getting injured.

Wire

This is about the most frightening way for a cat to travel. She's trapped in a cage, yet feels totally exposed. By the time you reach your destination and attempt to remove her from the carrier, she'll very likely be quite upset. *Upset* cats are not easy to handle.

Soft-Sided

They resemble the kind of soft-sided luggage you might use for yourself.

Soft-sided carriers are lightweight and most are approved for airline travel if you're taking your cat in the flight cabin with you. The downside to these carriers, though, is that if something should fall on them during travel, there's little protection. They're also more difficult to clean if your cat has an accident.

If you do choose a soft-sided carrier, look for one that's sturdy, has a firm floor, and is well constructed so the sides won't end up caving in on the cat.

Wicker

It may look cute but it's a horrible choice. Just try cleaning urine or feces out of a wicker carrier. I also think the wicker carriers are probably less comfortable for cats and more prone to damage from claws.

Plastic Kennel Carrier

The all-around best choice. They're sturdy, easy to clean, and come in many different sizes. Most come with a grill-front entry door made of metal or plastic. Some carriers have top entry doors as well. Many are airline-approved and the smaller carriers are usually approved for in-cabin travel (the only way to go). Virtually indestructible, the plastic carrier will probably last the lifetime of your cat.

Even though you want your cat to be comfortable during travel, don't buy a carrier that's too large. She won't need to move around much in there, and in fact, cats feel more secure when they can feel the sides of the carrier around them. A large carrier for general use is awkward for you to handle and the cat will end up being jostled from one side to the other. For lengthy travel, though, more room will be appreciated by the cat.

The plastic kennel is also a beneficial tool for creating more security for a frightened cat during veterinary visits. Instead of dragging or dumping the cat out of the carrier you simply detach the top so she can remain in the bottom half. Line the bottom with a towel for extra comfort. In many cases, the entire veterinary exam can take place with the cat remaining in the bottom half of the carrier.

With a cat who is acting aggressively at the veterinary clinic, this carrier may work better than others: after the top is taken off the technician or veterinarian can cover the cat with a towel.

Cardboard

They're very inexpensive and sometimes even free. If you adopt a shelter cat, you'll probably be given one to take her home in. A cardboard carrier is okay when you have a kitten but it's not durable enough for an adult cat. A determined cat can claw or chew her way out of a cardboard carrier in the blink of an eye. Even though the cardboard is coated on the inside of the carrier, once a cat urinates or vomits, the box is pretty much useless. It scares me when I see an owner trying to contain a large, very unhappy cat in what's left of a cardboard carrier that's falling apart. In the animal hospital, I've seen the bottoms of dilapidated carriers give way as owners struggled to keep the box intact, only to have the cat go crashing to the floor—or worse—the *parking lot*.

There are a couple of things I *do* like about cardboard carriers, though. Because they can be disassembled and stored completely flat, they make great extra emergency carriers. If you have ten cats and can't afford ten carriers, or don't have the room, keep a few plastic ones and the rest cardboard. That way, if you ever had to remove all of your cats from the house, everyone would have a carrier.

Getting Your Cat Used to the Carrier

Not training a cat to be comfortable in a carrier will result in having to retrieve your hissing, growling cat from under the bed and attempting to fold four out-stretched, scrambling limbs into the carrier while trying to avoid the unsheathed claws moving at lightning speed in your direction. Loosen your grip for just a fraction of a second and the cat crawls up over your head, leaps to the floor, and dashes back under the bed. Bleeding, covered in cat hair, wearing clothes that now sport countless pulls and holes, you tiptoe back to the bedroom to begin the adventure all over again. Your other option is to train your cat; that way you can easily place her in the carrier without having to change your clothes, bandage your wounds, and pick tufts of cat hair out of your mouth.

Begin the training process by placing the carrier in a corner of the room. Remove the grill door or at least secure it so it stays in the open position. Line the bottom of the carrier with a towel. If your cat is extremely suspicious of this setup, just go about your normal business and leave the carrier set up for a couple of days without proceeding to the next step. Eventually, she'll get used to the presence of the carrier even though she may not venture anywhere near it. Conduct an interactive play session in the areas around the carrier but don't bring the toy too close to it.

Now place a couple of treats in front of the carrier but still at a safe enough distance away from it so your cat feels comfortable (do this a couple times a day for a few days if kitty is nervous). When she's comfortable eating the treats near the carrier, place the next round a little closer. You can break up the treats in small pieces so you won't be interfering with your cat's normal nutritional program, or you can use pieces of her dry food. If you feed wet food, place a tiny amount in a small dish here. Put a treat on each side of the carrier and a couple in front. Don't be in a rush to put them too close to the carrier. By going slowly, your cat won't become suspicious or feel threatened. If your cat chooses not to eat the treats at this time, just leave them there because she may go back to the spot when you aren't around. If she still seems very nervous, even when you aren't close by, then you may have taken the next step too soon—just move the treats farther away from the carrier.

When your cat is comfortable taking treats directly in front of the carrier, place them on the edge of the carrier entrance next. Each time, move the treats a little bit farther into the carrier. For now, make the carrier the only place your cat receives treats, or a portion of her meal.

Now that your cat freely goes in and out of the carrier and realizes that it's no big deal, you can put the door back on but secure it in the open position. Then, when she goes in to eat a treat, close the door, count to five, and then open it up. Have a toy ready to engage her in an interactive play session as soon as she emerges from the carrier. Do this a few times so she gets used to the closed door.

Another training option is to have her eat her meal in the open carrier. Place the dish at the front of the carrier at first. When she's comfortable with that, start placing the dish at the back of the carrier. Eventually, you should be able to close the door (unlatched) while she eats.

After your cat is comfortable being inside of the carrier, the next step is to toss a treat in the carrier and when the cat goes in, close the door, pick up the carrier, walk a few steps, then place it back down. Open the door, let the cat come out, and engage in a play session.

Practice the above step every day or so. Keep the experience positive, talk soothingly to your cat and hold the carrier as still as you can. She'll be picking up her cues from you so be calm and casual about the whole procedure. If you need to backtrack a little and go back to just tossing the treats near the carrier, don't worry about it. Just move at the pace most comfortable for your cat. Some cats will take to the carrier in a very short time but others may need more adjustment time.

Work up to teaching your cat to go into the carrier using a verbal cue. Just say the word *kennel* every time you toss the treat in the carrier. Make your voice upbeat and positive. Give her the treat when she steps inside the carrier. You can also use clicker training to help the cat quickly associate the word *kennel* with the desired behavior and the payoff of the food reward.

The next step is to have your cat in the carrier in the parked car. Do multiple sessions so kitty gets very comfortable. Reward her for calm behavior in the car. Next try having the engine turned on. At this point, the car hasn't even left the garage or driveway yet.

When it's time for the actual traveling part begin by taking her in the car for short rides. Start by just going around the block and don't go any farther than that on your first try. It's much better to ease through this by gradually increasing the distance in subsequent sessions.

To prevent your cat from solely associating her carrier with the less-than-thrilling experience of going to the veterinarian, take her there for purely social visits so she can see that something bad doesn't always happen every time she goes there. With a kitten, bring her to the veterinary clinic regularly as she grows just to be petted and greeted by the staff. This helps her to become less afraid of the hospital's or clinic's smells, sights, and sounds.

Emergency Procedure for Getting the Most Uncooperative Cat in a Carrier

What if you haven't carrier-trained your cat and you need to get her in one NOW. What do you do? Based on previous experience, you know she'll fight you tooth and nail. The following is the quickest and least traumatic method.

Stand the plastic kennel carrier on its end so the end opening is now on top. Scruff your cat with one hand and hold her hind legs with the other (scruffing refers to holding a cat by the loose skin on the back of the neck). Quickly and carefully lower her into the carrier, hind end first. As soon as she's in, quickly let go and close the door. Be careful not to slam it on her paws or ears. Latch the door quickly, before your cat has an opportunity to lunge at it. Slowly lower the carrier back to its normal position. Whew, mission accomplished—cat in carrier and no injury to human.

🐱 Catwise Caution

Don't scruff your cat without supporting her weight by holding her hind legs. NEVER dangle her by the scruff alone. Also, this scruffing method of getting her in the carrier is for an emergency where she isn't injured. This isn't a substitute for proper carrier-acceptance training.

Should Your Cat Travel?

Even if you've carrier-trained your cat, it doesn't mean she should travel everywhere with you. Take into consideration her temperament, health, age, the type of travel you'll be doing and the time of year. Cats who are easily stressed will be much better off staying at home while the family vacations at a favorite theme park. Take into consideration whether your destination would actually be good for your cat. Just because you like to go to the beach every weekend doesn't mean your cat wants to also. Dragging kitty to cat-hating Aunt Esther's house for a holiday with the entire family would most likely be extremely stressful for everyone, from the cat to Aunt Esther.

If you're traveling by plane, I'd leave the cat at home unless she can ride in the flight cabin with you (see "Air Travel" later in this chapter). The experience of riding in the cargo hold can be terrifying and possibly life-threatening.

Persians, Himalayans, exotic shorthairs, and other short-nosed breeds shouldn't travel in hot weather unless you'll be in an air-conditioned environment.

If you're in doubt as to whether your cat is up for the trip and are considering using a sedative on her, please discuss this carefully with your veterinarian. Most cats travel much better without sedation. If you've never given a particular drug to your cat, being on the road or in the sky isn't the time to find out she has an adverse reaction to the medication. If it turns out that your veterinarian recommends a mild drug for your cat, consult with your veterinarian about medicating her once in advance of your trip so that you will be alerted to any adverse reaction and can get her immediate medical help if needed. The last place you want to be dealing with a crisis is on the road or in the plane.

Traveling by Car

When traveling by car, if you're going to be staying in motels or hotels, find out ahead of time which accommodations accept pets. To prevent the housekeeping staff from opening the door to your room and letting the cat out while you're gone, make sure the front desk knows there's a pet in there. They can arrange for housekeeping to be done while you are present. In addition, put the DO NOT DISTURB sign on the door. If you have doubts as to whether the cat will still be safe, close her in the bathroom with a big note on the bathroom door for the housekeeper not to enter there.

Many hotels have signs for you to post on your door to alert housekeeping that there's a pet inside. If not, leave your own note on the door as an extra precaution.

Carrier

Your cat will need to be in her carrier throughout the trip. For long trips you may want to get a large crate so you can place a small litter box in the back. If you can't fit a small litter box in her crate, whenever you stop to stretch your legs, let your cat have access to a litter box but be sure that car doors and windows are closed and that she is harnessed and leashed.

Don't place your cat carrier in the front seat. Airbags are designed for adults, not pets.

Don't hold your cat in your lap. Inside of a carrier is the safest place for her during car travel.

When using a carrier, secure it in place with the seatbelt. If you're using a crate in the back of the car, secure it with a bungee cord. This will reduce the risk of your cat being thrown around in an accident and will also limit jostling and motion sickness during turns and sudden stops.

Harness, ID, Leash

Even if you never plan on taking your cat outside to walk on a leash, you should leash and harness train for added safety when traveling. Keep the harness on your cat during the trip and make sure she has an ID tag attached. When you take her out of the carrier, put the leash on her. When you get to your hotel or other destination, remove the harness and put her collar on (with ID). Make sure she's always wearing an ID tag that has both your home and cell number as well as your vacation number.

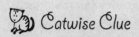 **Catwise Clue**

As an added precaution, have your cat microchipped before your trip if you haven't already done so. Your veterinarian can perform this quick and easy procedure. If you're moving to a new home, be sure to provide the updated information to the registration company.

Litter Box and Litter

You can buy a package of disposable litter boxes that are made of coated cardboard. It's much easier than having to wash out a plastic box. If you have room in the car and will be at your vacation destination for a while, bring along a regular litter box. It'll probably be more comfortable for the cat, especially if she's on the larger side.

Bring your cat's usual brand of litter because you may not be able to find it at your destination location. If your litter comes packaged in a bag, you may want to transfer it to a plastic storage container with a tight-fitting lid. I've had to vacuum litter out of the car after an opened bag fell over and it's not fun. Bring along a plastic cup to fill the litter box with litter.

Don't forget the all-important litter shovel. If you're using a reduced-size box you'll need to be very diligent about frequent scooping. Pack the shovel in a sealable plastic bag. Bring a box of plastic trash bags so you have somewhere to empty the dirty litter that you've scooped. If you're staying in a motel or hotel, you'll need to empty the dirty litter into the sealable trash bags because you can't just dump the litter right into the room's wastebasket. Be courteous of the housekeeping staff as well and take the bag of soiled litter to the outside trash container so the person cleaning your room doesn't have to handle anything to do with soiled litter.

When traveling by car, bring along a small bottle of hand sanitizer so you can clean your hands after scooping the litter.

Extra towels are needed in case of spills and accidents. Wipes come in handy in case the cat messes on herself during the trip.

Food

If you feed wet food, buy the smallest sizes. If the cans aren't pop-top, remember to bring a can opener and plastic spoons. For larger cans, you'll need to pack a cooler for storage after the can is opened. Bring a plastic lid for the can or a separate container with a lid for storage of leftover food.

Bring a bottle of water so you can offer some to your cat periodically during the ride. To prevent any stomach upsets due to a change in water, bring along a plastic jug filled with your regular water from home or offer your cat bottled spring water. When you reach your destination, fill the cat's bowl with the water from home and gradually add the new water. Don't forget to pack her bowls and, while you're at it, toss a package of treats and your clicker into the suitcase as well in case you need to do some clicker training to help her over any rough spots.

Other Necessities

If your cat is on prescription medication, be sure and bring it along. Check the amount in advance just in case you're running low so you can refill the prescription before the trip.

If you're traveling during a time when your veterinary clinic will be closed (and as such, you'd be unable to have records faxed to a temporary clinic), bring along a copy of your cat's medical record.

If you have a long-haired cat you'll need to pack your grooming supplies.

Don't forget to pack some toys or it certainly won't be a vacation for your cat. I also pack a little catnip, a couple of puzzle feeders, and a corrugated cardboard scratching pad whenever we travel.

Bring along a photo of your cat just in case something happens and she gets lost. This way, you'll be able to make flyers and posters.

Don't Leave Your Cat Unattended

Don't leave your cat alone in the car in warm weather. Even just a quick restaurant stop can put your cat's life in danger. Temperatures can reach life-threatening levels in just a few minutes.

Air Travel

Airlines have always had restrictions concerning air travel for animals flying as cargo during extreme hot or cold weather, but now those restrictions have become even stricter to help ensure the safety of the animals. Each airline has its own rules regarding whether animals are permitted at all during certain months of the year. For flying cargo, there are also specific outdoor temperature restrictions so you'll need to know what the temperature is going to be the day of your flight. Some airlines don't allow pet air travel at all.

Some airlines allow small animals to fly as carry-on but the cat must be in an airline-approved carrier. You can either use a plastic carrier (make sure it states that it's airline-approved) or a soft-sided one. Some airlines only permit one pet in the entire cabin so you must call well in advance and make your cat's reservation when you make your own. Very often there's a fee to have your cat travel onboard with you. If at all possible, have your cat fly as carry-on.

Find out from the airline what documentation will be needed, such as a health certificate. Health certificates must be issued within ten days of the departure date. Don't pack your cat's health papers in the checked luggage—keep it with you so you'll be able to present it when needed. Animals must be at least eight weeks old in order to travel by air.

Put identification on the carrier as well as on your cat. The carrier should have a sign that says LIVE ANIMAL. Even though she'll be with you during the trip, the label is in case some unexpected crisis occurs and you get separated. The identification tags on the carrier and on your cat should have your mobile phone number.

At home, before you place your cat in the carrier, check it out to be sure it's in good condition. With a plastic carrier, tighten all the bolts. With a soft-sided carrier, check the seams and mesh for any tears and double-check all zippers.

When packing for air travel, look over the section on traveling by car, which lists packing essentials. Although you certainly won't be able to pack as heavily as you would for a road trip, many important items shouldn't be forgotten.

If you must fly your cat as cargo, she must be in an airline-approved kennel. There must be a LIVE ANIMAL sign on the crate as well as directional arrows pointing up, indicating the upright position of the crate. Your name, address, and phone number must be firmly affixed or written on the crate. There must also be food and water bowls attached to the grill door. Confirm your reservation twenty-four hours before departure and get to the airport early enough to allow for all the procedures you'll need to go through. Check with your airline to find out how early you need to arrive at the airport for your flight.

For international travel, contact your destination country months in advance to find out if pets are allowed, and if so, what the quarantine period is and what additional documentation is required. Contact the country officials again four–six weeks before departure to confirm that nothing has changed.

Leaving Your Cat at Home
Pet Sitters

By far, the ideal arrangement for your cat is for her to stay in her own home while you travel. Pet sitters can be a dream come true or the ultimate nightmare if you haven't checked them out carefully.

A pet sitting arrangement can range from having your neighbor come over twice a day to feed your cat and clean the litter, to hiring a professional pet sitter, to getting someone to actually move into your home while you're away.

If you have a cat-owning friend who would be willing to come over twice a day, I think this works out well because you know you can trust them and they'll be comfortable with the required duties. Your cat will probably be more comfortable as well since it'll be someone she's familiar with.

Show your friend where the interactive toys are kept and demonstrate how you play with your cat. Offer to return this favor whenever your friend needs it, and this could end up being a very convenient arrangement.

A professional pet-sitting service is also an option. Besides caring for your pet, they will get your mail, turn lights on and off, and water plants. If you know of pet owners who've used them, ask for names and reviews on the quality of the services. You can additionally get referrals from your veterinarian. Check reviews on prospective pet sitters that are posted on the Internet. Check the Resource Guide for more petting sitting information.

Before hiring a professional pet-sitting service, ask them the following questions:

- *How long have you been in business?* You don't want to be one of their first clients.

- *Do you have references?* If they don't provide any, look for another sitter. Be sure to check all references.

- *Are you bonded and insured?* A professional pet sitter should be.

- *What plans do you have in case of bad weather?* (As a safeguard, give a nearby neighbor an extra key just in case). Find out what kind of vehicle they have and what their bad weather contingency plan is. This is where hiring a pet sitter who lives nearby is a good idea.

- *Are you the one who will be making all of the visits?* Some larger services send different sitters depending on who's working that day. The person you interview should be the one who makes the visits.

- *Do you provide a written agreement or contract?* Get everything in writing.

- *What is provided during a visit?* Again, get it in writing.

- *Are you able to administer medication?* This is important if your cat is on prescription medicine. Find out what training the sitter has had and if he or she is capable of making sure your cat gets all necessary medication.

Check out the pet-sitting service thoroughly. After all, you'll be entrusting them with your pets and your home. You should interview the pet sitter in person by having him/her come to your home. That way you can show the sitter exactly what would need to be done. You can also get a feel for how your cat reacts to that individual. If the pet sitter needs to be warned about anything, be forthcoming. For instance, if your cat bites, has a habit of bolting out the door, etc.

Most pet sitters make one or two visits a day to the home. They charge per visit so be sure you know exactly how many visits you'll need.

Leave the pet sitter all necessary information in case of an emergency. In addition to your mobile number, write down all other contact information regarding where you'll be staying, as well as the number of a trusted neighbor in case the sitter needs immediate help with something. Write your veterinarian's name, address, and number as well. Ask the sitter if they know the location of your veterinarian. Additionally, call the veterinary clinic and inform them that a sitter will be caring for your cat and provide permission to do any necessary medical treatment. Give the veterinarian your mobile number as well. Show the sitter where the cat carrier is in case they need to take your cat to the veterinary clinic.

If you'll be going out of town for an extended period be sure you leave an adequate supply of food and litter, as well as any prescriptions your cat takes.

Take the pet sitter's phone number with you in case you get delayed on your trip. I've spent enough overnights in airports to learn that I need to always have a back-up plan. Make sure your pet sitter will be able to extend his/her services should you not arrive home on time. Call the sitter when you do get back so he/she will know you've arrived home safely.

Boarding Your Cat

Even being in the best boarding facility may create anxiety for a cat, so if you have a frightened or highly reactive cat, she would be better off in her own familiar surrounds. For some owners, though, the only option is to place their cats in a boarding facility. I don't know about boarding facilities in your area but where I live, we have several truly cat-friendly facilities. Some kennel owners understand how to make the cats feel as comfortable as possible when it comes to be being away from home. Some, unfortunately, view cats as small dogs and don't create any special surroundings to address emotional security issues.

Inspect the boarding facility personally. There should be proper ventilation in the boarding room. When you walk in, if the odor makes you feel as if you've stepped into a giant litter box, imagine how horrible it must smell to the cats.

All boarding facilities should require you to show proof of vaccinations. Any facility that doesn't require your cat to be up-to-date on its shots means it's not requiring it of other cats as well. That puts all the cats at risk. Kittens who are not yet fully vaccinated shouldn't be boarded.

Boarding facilities range from simple rows of cages to luxurious multitiered individual rooms, complete with televisions or scenic window views. Although it may seem silly at first, placing your cat in one of these deluxe facilities that resemble a fancy hotel room definitely has advantages. The staff often provide more personalized care, the cats have more hiding places, and there are scheduled individual play periods. If you have one of these special boarding facilities in your area, I urge you to check it out. They may be surprisingly affordable.

When you bring your cat to the boarding facility, bring her regular food, litter, and medications. Don't bring your cat's litter box, though. It won't fit in the cage and you don't want your cat developing a negative association with it once she gets back home. Provide your cat with a T-shirt that you've worn as well, for its comforting scent.

One of the most frightening aspects of being boarded is that cats have no hiding place, so very often they sit hunkered down in, of all places, the *litter box*. How stressful for a poor terrified kitty to have to seek refuge there. An open paper bag on its side can create enough of a hiding place for your cat to feel secure (bring along a supply of paper bags). A staff member can place a towel in the bag for extra comfort. For a very frightened cat, the bag should be placed at an angle so the cat doesn't feel on display. To help keep the bag from collapsing, roll a one-inch cuff around it.

If your cat still becomes too stressed out, a sheet of newspaper can be taped over the front of the cage by one of the staff.

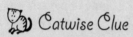 **Catwise Clue**

Boarding facilities get booked up early for the holidays, so make your reservations well in advance.

Moving to a New Home

From a cat's perspective, it probably doesn't get much worse than this. First, out comes the dreaded carrier, then a car ride, and it's all topped off by the arrival at an unfamiliar location that her owners keep referring to as "home." *Home? Are you crazy? We left our home hours ago, so turn around and let's head back there. I have birds to watch, mice to keep away, and a nap to take.*

Once again, if cats ruled the world (and I know many people think they already do), you'd never go anywhere, not to work, not on vacation, and certainly not to the veterinarian. A move to a new house? Don't even mention it.

Since moving to a new house is something that most owners will have to do at some point, making it as painless for your cat as possible will also make it a little less painful for you as well.

If you have a cat who goes outdoors, about a week before the move, stop letting her outside. The week before the move is usually crunch time for people: their packing becomes more intense, they're sleep deprived, and the stress level rockets off the scale. Your cat, ever the observant one, will sense something is afoot and may choose to lay low for a while by not returning home at night. The last thing you need is to have to spend the day of the move searching outdoors for your kitty. There are many sad cases of owners who have had to give up and leave their cats because the movers had already left and schedules had to be kept or there'd be no one to let them in at the new location. It's tragic to think about the fear and confusion that the cat must feel when she does head back home and finds no one there for her. Unless a neighbor recognizes her and can capture her, she'll go from being a loved family member to a homeless stray. If I'm sounding a bit dramatic, it's because owners often overlook this plan-ahead precaution and their cats *do* disappear before the move. It's worth all the complaining you may have to endure from your cat during the week in order to ensure her safety.

The process of packing is drudgery. For cats, though, it's an intense experience. They often love it, choosing to dive in and out of boxes, thinking you've created this indoor playland just for their amusement—or they hide in fear over the chaos taking place in their once-peaceful territory. Whichever reaction your cat has, precautions have to be taken to be sure she doesn't get packed in a box. Don't laugh—it happens. A cat playing in the boxes may decide to take a little nap in one. She burrows down into the linens that you've placed in there. You don't realize that she's in there, you close up the box, and into the moving van it goes. Whenever you pack, put your cat into a separate room or at least make sure you know where she is before you close any boxes.

The week before your move, get a copy of your cat's medical records from your veterinarian (if you'll be changing veterinary clinics). If you already have a veterinarian selected in your new location, have your current veterinary clinic forward the records there. Also, the week before the move is a good time to have an ID tag made with your new address and phone number for your cat's collar. You'll put it on your cat the day of the move.

On moving day, have all of the cat's food, medications, etc., in a separate box that will go with you in your vehicle. You don't want to get to the new home and realize you packed the food in some unknown box. The day of the move will be a hectic, stressful time, so either keep your cat confined in one little room or have her boarded for the day. If you have an extra bathroom, put her in there with her litter box, a bowl of water, and a bed. Put a little radio in there and set it to a classical or soft music station to filter out some of the commotion occurring just beyond her door. Place a big sign on the door warning people not to enter.

I also place the cat carrier in the bathroom so it doesn't get placed in the moving van.

When you get to your new home, your cat should have a little sanctuary room. A bedroom is ideal. Set up her litter box, scratching post, bed, water, and food. Toss a few toys in there as well. Unless you've had to choose the bathroom as a sanctuary room, set up some of the furniture (even if it's not in the permanent location) so she'll have a place to hide. Having the comfort of the furniture she's familiar with will be helpful to her.

Some cats will make the adjustment in a few minutes but others may need anywhere from a day to a week in the sanctuary room. Don't rush things. Your cat will let you know when she's ready to check out the rest of the house.

Take time out from your unpacking to visit and play with your cat. Fifteen-minute play sessions here or there throughout the day won't wreck your schedule and you'll be providing a world of comfort for your cat. Break open the catnip as well so you and your cat can celebrate your new home in style. Her confinement in the sanctuary room shouldn't be a jail sentence. Remember, she's a little emotional sponge so if you keep your attitude positive and casual, she'll pick up on that and it could help in reducing some of the apprehension she may be feeling about this unfamiliar environment.

You'll know your cat is ready to be let out of the room when she resumes normal behavior, i.e., eating, using the litter box, venturing out of the closet, not hiding, etc. When you open the door to her room, don't force her to come out. Let her decide at what pace she feels most comfortable. You can leave a few treats scattered just outside the door.

Keep her sanctuary room set up for her because she may choose to go back there if she gets too anxious.

If your cat was allowed outdoors in your previous home, this is an excellent opportunity for you to make her an indoor cat. There's a whole new territory right inside the house for her. It's more than enough to keep her busy. The territory outdoors is unfamiliar, and you don't know what other cats are out there who may feel there isn't room enough in the neighborhood for a new cat.

If you're absolutely set on allowing your cat outdoors, wait at least a month so she has a chance to firmly establish comfort in her indoor territory and to fully adjust to the move. When you do begin letting her out, do it with a leash and harness. After all, there's no connection to this yard for her so you stand a good chance of her running away. Take her out daily for walks close to the house so she repeatedly makes the connection. If the weather is nice, sit outside with her on the deck or porch and feed her dinner there so this starts to become her home base. Let her walk in and out of the door so she makes the connection of where the entrance to the home is. She needs to know where to stay while waiting to be let inside.

Don't allow your cat outdoors unless she's fully vaccinated, has ID on, and is trained to come when called. I know the last one may be a stretch for many owners but it can be done (see Chapter 5).

Once again, seriously reconsider making her an indoor cat. With all you've learned so far in this book about environmental enrichment, playtime, and safety you can create an indoor environment that is stimulating, fun, secure, and comfortable.

Lost Cat

It does unfortunately happen despite an owner's best efforts. Here are some guidelines in case you're faced with this crisis.

Create Flyers

LOST INDOOR CAT should be at the top of the flyer. Below that should be a clear picture of your cat. Make color copies of the flyer (not black and white) so the picture stands out and the cat's coloring/markings are easy to distinguish. Below the picture include a description, noting any unusual or identifying marks. Write the date lost, where the cat was last seen, plus your daytime and evening, or mobile, number. Offer a reward to create even more incentive. Make it substantial enough so every kid in the neighborhood will go out looking for your cat.

Create the flyer using bold, easy-to-read type. If you have to handwrite it, make sure your phone number is clearly readable.

Post the flyers *everywhere* you can: veterinary clinics, intersections, supermarkets, and pet supply stores. Wherever a flyer can legally be put up, attach yours there.

Make the Rounds

Immediately call the local shelter to let them know your cat is lost. Follow that up with an in-person visit to leave a flyer there.

Bring flyers to as many veterinary clinics as you can. Most veterinary clinics have a "lost pet" bulletin board. If they don't have room for the flyer, you can at least post the picture with the information written on an index card.

Internet/Publications

Place an ad on *Craigslist* and use your local newspaper or neighborhood publication to post a "lost cat" notice.

Inform Your Neighbors

Go around to the neighbors in your area with your pictures or your flyer. There's a good chance your scared cat could be hiding in someone's bushes or garage.

If you find your cat, go around and remove all the flyers. Call the shelters, veterinary clinics, etc., to let them know so they can take down the pictures. Remove your ad from *Craigslist*. You don't want people spending time looking for a cat who has already been found.

If the person who finds your cat refuses the reward, consider donating the money to your local shelter in their name. That way, some other lost kitty may be able to find her home again.

15

And Baby Makes Three . . .
Four . . . Five

What to Do If Your Cat Makes
You a Grandparent

It's not exactly the stuff of romance novels. Feline mating is a violent and dangerous process. In the presence of a female in heat, any tomcats in the area will fight with each other for the chance to mate with her.

The male paces back and forth nervously, waiting for the signal from the female that it's okay to approach. He then grasps the nape of her neck with his teeth and straddles her. The female arches her back, flips her tail over to one side, then the tomcat begins thrusting.

Once ejaculation has occurred, the female lets out a scream and struggles to break free of the male's grip. If the male isn't fast enough in retreating, the female may attack him quite aggressively. She then begins rolling, stretching, and genital licking.

The pair may mate again immediately or it may take a while before the female is ready to accept the male again. They may mate many times over the next several hours. As he waits for her to become receptive again he remains on guard to prevent other toms from attempting to claim his female. If other males are present, they may challenge him for a chance to mate with her as well. The result is often a violent fight that ends up with one or more cats getting bitten or slashed. Tomcat fights can result in very serious injuries and sometimes even death. If more win a chance to mate with the female, the kittens born to her can have more than one father.

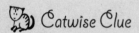

Catwise Clue

Unaltered females generally have three or more heat cycles per year. Males are capable of mating any time throughout the year.

If you're under the worn-out illusion that having your children witness the miracle of birth will be a learning experience—you're missing the boat. The message they should be learning is how to be a responsible pet owner, which means spaying or neutering the cat. Responsibly caring for and loving a pet for many years will be a far more valuable lesson for their lives than watching four more kittens come into an already overpopulated pet world.

Why Your Cat Should Be Spayed or Neutered

If you have a mixed-breed cat and you're considering breeding, please think again. I know you love your cat and you think she'll have beautiful kittens, but the truth is, millions of "beautiful" kittens become homeless or are put to death simply because there are too many of them. People end up standing outside of supermarkets with a box full of kittens in a desperate attempt to give them away because homes are hard to come by.

Don't become a backyard breeder. Just because you have a purebred cat doesn't mean you can make money by mating her with a male of the same breed. Experienced, reputable breeders are very knowledgeable about breed genetics. Attempting to breed your cat without this knowledge can result in kittens with congenital deformities.

If you believe you'll make money from breeding your cat, you're in for a big surprise. It's an expensive proposition as any breeder will tell you. Good breeders spend a lot of time and money creating a good environment, caring for the adult cats, and raising the kittens. Good breeders are in this because they love the breed and they want to maintain the standard—not to get rich quick.

Even if you hadn't planned on breeding your cat, it can happen "accidentally" if you let your intact cat outdoors. You may have intentions of getting her spayed but she may come home pregnant before you get the chance. And if you have an intact male cat, don't think you're at an advantage because you won't have kittens to take care of. Instead, you'll be taking care of an injured cat, time and time again as he fights with other males. You also have a responsibility as a cat owner to not contribute to overpopulation by letting your intact male roam to randomly mate.

Beside the overpopulation issue, there are medical and behavioral reasons to have your cat spayed and neutered. Spaying prior to a cat's first heat will virtually eliminate the risk of mammary cancer. Neutering your male cat will eliminate the risk of him developing prostate cancer later in life.

The difference between an altered and an intact cat is like night and day. Neutering before a cat reaches sexual maturity will virtually eliminate urine spraying and roaming. Even if your cat is already an adult, having him neutered can greatly reduce those undesirable behaviors. With a female, not spaying her will doom you to endure her endless vocalization and restlessness. It will also attract every tomcat in the neighborhood. I don't know about you, but I'd rather not have the local toms urine-spraying the bushes around my front door.

Contrary to what you've probably heard, altering a cat won't make her fat. *Overfeeding* is what leads to obesity.

Male cats are neutered. This surgery involves the removal of the cat's testicles by way of an incision in the scrotum. No sutures are required and post-op care consists of monitoring to make certain the healing incision stays clean and dry. If your cat is allowed outdoors, keep him inside for several days until he's completely healed.

Female cats are spayed. More involved than neutering, this surgery consists of removing the uterus, tubes, and ovaries through an abdominal incision. The few sutures across your cat's shaved tummy will be removed in about ten days.

Your veterinarian will give you specific instructions regarding post-op care. You'll need to monitor the sutures to be sure they stay clean and dry. You'll also need to make sure your cat doesn't chew at her sutures. If you regularly bathe your cat, that will have to wait until the sutures are removed.

Limit your cat's activity during the healing process by keeping her indoors and discouraging jumping and strenuous activity.

Even though neuter and spay surgeries are probably performed more often than any other procedures, do your homework before choosing to go to a low-cost spay/neuter clinic. A surgery, regardless of how "routine," still involves risk. If you plan on using a low-cost clinic instead of your regular veterinarian, investigate the place carefully. Find out all you can regarding how their procedures are done, what anesthesia is used, whether the cats are monitored by a surgical assistant during and after the procedure, and not only what kind of sutures are used but how many the veterinarian routinely puts in.

If you have confidence in your veterinarian, don't go price shopping when it comes to surgery. Your veterinarian has a serious interest in the long-term health of your cat.

Caring for a Mother-to-Be

While you may not have planned it, you might find yourself with a pregnant cat. Maybe you waited just a little too long in deciding when to have her spayed or maybe a pregnant stray found her way into your life.

Gestation in a cat is about sixty-five days. During the first few weeks, you may not be able to detect pregnancy except for an increase in weight.

Some cats experience morning sickness somewhere around the third week of pregnancy. She may vomit and not eat well. This usually only lasts a few days.

If you suspect your cat may be pregnant, take her to the veterinarian so that if it's confirmed you can begin prenatal care. Your veterinarian will provide you with a recommended schedule of how many visits you'll need based on your individual cat's health concerns, as well as make recommendations regarding nutritional changes. Don't give any supplements unless advised to do so by your veterinarian. Usually, you'll be instructed to feed a *growth*-formula food due to the extra need for protein and calcium among other nutrients. During the last half of the pregnancy, your veterinarian may advise an increase in the amount of food being fed. This will depend upon your cat's weight and health. You want to avoid creating an over-weight cat during her pregnancy, which could make her delivery more difficult.

As the cat gets to within a week or so of delivery, she may need to be fed several smaller meals. Due to her large abdomen, she may not be able to eat her regular meal-size portion. Also, at this time, you'll probably make another visit to the veterinarian for a final prenatal exam. You'll be given instructions on how to prepare for delivery, what to expect, and how to care for newborn kittens.

Preparing for the Big Day

About a week before delivery, the cat will appear restless and you may notice an increase in the amount of grooming she does to her abdomen and genitals. She may begin scratching in clothing piles or digging around in closets as she prepares a nest.

Despite the most elaborate accommodations you may create for the cat to give birth, she'll prefer someplace dark, quiet, and warm. Take a sturdy cardboard box, cut an opening in one side of it, then line it with clean newspaper or towels. You may want to use a box with a lid to offer a nervous queen more privacy, yet still be able to have easy access to clean it and monitor the activities inside. The box should be tall enough so the cat can stand up and move around and large enough so she can recline to comfortably nurse.

Place the food and water bowls near the box. The litter box should be within easy reach as well, but not too close.

Don't allow your cat outdoors toward the end of her pregnancy because she may go into labor and deliver her kittens in someone's garage. It's a good idea to keep her in the room you've selected for delivery so she doesn't go off and choose a different location in the house.

About a day before she's ready to deliver, the cat's temperature drops two or three degrees. If you're experienced at taking your cat's temperature and she's comfortable with having it done (use an ear thermometer), you can take a reading. Don't create more anxiety, though.

You cat will, in most cases, deliver her kittens just fine without human interference. You can help a long-haired cat out by trimming the hair around her nipples and the area beneath her tail or have the veterinarian do it. Additionally, have a few supplies at hand just in case assistance is needed:

Extra newspaper
Clean towels
Scissors
Antiseptic
Dental floss or a spool of thread
Infant syringe

Your veterinarian will instruct you on how to use the above, if needed, but he or she may also have a different list of products to have on hand. Always follow your veterinarian's instructions.

Hello, World! (The Delivery)

In the first stage of labor, the cat will pant and begin straining. This can last several hours. She may cry out and almost attempt to bite at her backside. It's not unusual for her to hiss at you if you get too close. Some cats have been known to eat their kittens if people interfere too much.

In active labor, you may notice a light-colored discharge followed by a darker-colored one. Contractions will begin and then the first kitten is usually delivered within thirty minutes. The newborn kitten will be surrounded in a membrane that the mother will bite open; then she'll begin licking the kitten's face to clear the nose and mouth to start his breathing. She'll also sever the umbilical cord and roughly lick the kitten all over to stimulate circulation.

Unless another kitten starts coming before the mother can stimulate the kitten's breathing, DON'T INTERFERE. If she doesn't care for the kitten you can gently tear open the membrane and rub the kitten down with a towel to stimulate breathing. With the dental floss or thread, tie off the umbilical cord about one inch from the kitten, cut it with the scissors, then swab the stump of the cord with antiseptic. Make sure the kitten is breathing before you place him near his mother. If he isn't, use the infant syringe to clear any fluids from the mouth. If he still isn't breathing, hold him securely in your hands and, supporting his head, turn him downward and swing him in an arc very gently to clear additional fluid from his nose or mouth. As soon as he's breathing, present him to his mother so she can continue licking him.

Delivery intervals between kittens range from thirty minutes to an hour. A *placenta* for each kitten should be passed after each delivery. The mother instinctively eats the placentas (and sometimes any stillborn kittens as well). If she eats several placentas, it can result in diarrhea so you should remove them before she can eat them as well as any stillborn kittens. Be sure to count the number of placentas, though, to make sure there is one for every kitten delivered as any left undelivered can cause serious infection.

If delivery isn't going well or you're concerned that the mother is having trouble, you'll need to contact your veterinarian. Call immediately if:

- The cat has had strong contractions or is straining for an hour without delivery of a kitten

- The cat appears weak or in pain

- There is vomiting

- A placenta for each kitten isn't delivered

- There's a discharge of fresh blood

- Above or below normal temperature

- The cat remains restless

- The kittens continually cry

(Note: Refer to the Medical Appendix for information on reproductive and neonatal disorders.)

Once the kittens are born, they'll immediately begin nursing. The first milk, called *colostrum*, is vital because it'll provide antibodies that temporarily protect the kittens against disease until their own immune systems begin functioning.

If everything seems to be going well, leave the family alone. Let the mother take care of her kittens without disturbance for the first two weeks, except for any necessary cleaning, feeding of the mother, or general monitoring.

If the kittens aren't doing well or the mother is not allowing them to nurse, contact your veterinarian immediately because they may need to be tube-fed. If tube feeding and bottle feeding need to be done your veterinarian will give you specific instructions.

The next morning after delivery, contact your veterinarian even if everything went smoothly because an examination of the cat should be performed to be sure there are no retained fetuses. The veterinarian may also check to make sure milk production is adequate and healthy. Bring the kittens along as well so that they won't be separated from their mother.

Newborn kittens are deaf and blind. They locate their mother by her warmth and through the vibration of her purrs. They'll spend much time suckling and often develop a preference for a specific nipple. Newborn kittens exhibit rooting behavior as they locate the mother's teats. It resembles a swimming pattern of the front feet and a pushing pattern of the hind feet.

Many changes happen in the first two weeks. A couple days after birth the umbilical cords fall off. The kittens will double their weight in a week, and their eyes and ears will open somewhere around seven to ten days.

The mother remains constantly attentive to her babies. After nursing, she licks them with her warm tongue to stimulate their elimination of waste, which she ingests. A cat's devotion to her kittens involves maintaining a clean nest to keep them all safe from predators.

By three weeks of age, you can begin handling the kittens to start their socialization process. Frequent gentle handling by humans can help them grow to become more comfortable and sociable around people. Don't overdo it, though, because you can make the mother anxious.

Also at three weeks is when you can begin the weaning process by providing the kittens access to solid food. A gradual weaning process is healthiest for both mother and her kittens. By providing food, the kittens will nurse less and less as each week

🐱 *Catwise Clue*

While nursing, kittens knead with their front paws. This action stimulates milk flow.

passes. Remember, it *must* be gradual. Use a kitten formula of either canned or dry food that has been softened with warm water. Put a tiny bit of food on your finger and place it on the kitten's lips or under his nose.

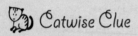 Catwise Clue

Kittens are excellent *observational learners*. By watching the mother cat perform a function or behavior, the kittens are able to learn it.

Litter box training will pretty much be conducted by the mother. Provide a litter box with low sides for easy access. Because the kittens can't travel through the house to find the litter box, keep everyone confined to one room to make it easy for the youngsters to get to the box in time.

At eight weeks of age, the kittens should begin receiving their vaccination series.

Continue your frequent handling of and playing with the kittens to help socialize them. They'll also be continuing to develop their skills through littermate playtime and interaction.

You may be tempted to start finding homes for the kittens at this stage, but this is still valuable time for them to remain with the mother and littermates. This time is important because it will determine how well they'll interact with other cats as adults. Don't separate the litter until they're twelve weeks old.

Feeding Schedule for Weaned Kittens
Refer to Chapter 10.

Caring for Orphaned Kittens
It may happen that you come across an orphaned kitten or an entire litter. The mother may have died, or perhaps she rejected her kittens, or became ill or unable to nurse due to a mammary infection.

Orphaned kittens, since they don't have the advantage of the mother's body heat, need to be kept warm in an environment with a temperature of 85–90 degrees Fahrenheit for the first two weeks of their lives. By the third week, you can lower the temperature by a few degrees and continue to gradually lower it each week after. Your veterinarian can instruct you on how to create a homemade incubator using a lamp and a cardboard box, or advise you on how to use a heating pad on the lowest setting.

Orphaned kittens should be taken to the veterinarian immediately where you'll be shown how to administer a proper kitten replacement formula. It's a

SOME OF THE IMPORTANT STAGES IN KITTEN DEVELOPMENT

The First Two Weeks

- blind and deaf at birth
- weight at birth will be approximately 3½–4 ounces
- mother will stay with kittens around the clock for the first twenty-four hours
- umbilical cord will drop off after two or three days
- inability to regulate body temperature
- highly developed sense of smell
- weight will double in the first week
- mother must stimulate each kitten's elimination process by licking

Two Weeks–Four Weeks

- eyes and ears open at about ten to fourteen days
- milk teeth start appearing
- at three weeks the kittens are able to eliminate on their own
- the mother shows her kittens how to cover their waste
- social play begins between three to four weeks of age
- important socialization time
- righting reflex develops
- weaning starts, consumption of solid food begins

Four Weeks–Eight Weeks

- able to groom themselves at five weeks
- weaning generally completed by eight weeks
- all baby teeth are in by eight weeks
- continued important socialization time
- play behavior gets rougher as weeks progress
- skill at prey-killing behavior increases

Eight Weeks–Fourteen Weeks

- kittens engage more frequently in object play
- senses will be fully developed by twelve weeks
- adult eye color established around twelve weeks
- adult teeth begin to erupt at fourteen weeks
- adult sleep patterns will begin to develop

Six Months–Twelve Months

- kittens reach sexual maturity
- continued growth (but at a slower pace)

full-time job to keep kittens fed around the clock. Every two or four hours is usually the schedule in the beginning. Tube feeding (in which a tube goes down the esophagus and directly into the stomach) is the preferable method before switching over to bottle feeding. A kitten replacement formula must be used because ordinary cow's milk lacks the protein and other nutrients kittens need. Feeding has to be done with the kitten in an upright position (the same position he'd be in if nursing from his mother), and if bottle feeding the kitten must be burped. This is done by holding the kitten up to your shoulder and rubbing his back. You have to be careful not to overfeed because their stomachs are small and the kidneys can't handle an oversupply. Underfeeding is also dangerous, so make certain you have received instructions from the veterinarian and are comfortable with what you need to do. Your veterinarian can give you a demonstration on how to hold and feed the kitten as well as how to tell when he's full.

Since kittens can't eliminate on their own, they'll need your help to stimulate the process. A warm, moist cotton ball can be used to massage the abdomen and anal area to stimulate urination and defecation. This will need to be done after each feeding until they're three weeks old, at which time you'll begin to teach them how to use the litter box. That's done by placing them in the box after meals. Massaging their abdomens with a warm water-moistened finger will help if they need a little extra assistance. Use your fingers to scratch around in the litter to help give them the idea as well. Leave a little of their waste in the litter box to help them make the connection of what the box is for. If any kitten eliminates outside of the litter box, scoop up the waste, and place it in the box. The scent will help direct them to the correct place next time.

Keep the kittens clean because they're going to get very sticky and messy during feedings. Use a soft washcloth moistened with warm water (don't immerse kittens in water). They can get chilled easily, so dry immediately with a towel. If needed, you can use a hair dryer set on the lowest setting. Keep the dryer far away from the kitten to prevent burning.

Orphaned kittens won't have the protection of the mother's colostrum, so they'll have to be vaccinated at about three or four weeks of age.

Since caring for orphaned kittens is very involved, your best bet is to get all the guidance you can from the veterinarian. Some clinics have technicians who specialize in fostering orphaned kittens and will take them home until they're eating on their own. Some shelters as well have volunteers who are experienced in orphaned care. Call before showing up at a clinic or shelter with orphaned kittens.

A single orphaned kitten who doesn't have the benefit of interacting with littermates may have trouble relating to other cats as he grows. If at all possible, all attempts should be made to locate another nursing mother with a litter. Nursing mothers are very accepting of an orphaned kitten added to the litter. Mothers have even accepted orphans of another species.

Finding Homes for the Kittens

When the kittens reach twelve weeks of age, if you aren't planning on keeping them, you'll need to find good homes for them.

Whether this was a planned pregnancy or an accidental random mating, your responsibility extends beyond caring for the kittens until they reach an adoptable age. These precious little lives are totally dependent upon how much effort you place on making certain they get adopted into loving homes.

By taking the easy way out and "getting rid" of them by holding up a sign outside of the supermarket offering free kittens (or placing an ad on *Craigslist*), you have no way of knowing whether they'll get a good home. You should take the time to screen potential adoptive parents. After all, this is a life you've been entrusted with—not a piece of furniture.

Find out if the prospective owners have had pets before. If so, what happened to them? I certainly wouldn't adopt out a kitten to a family with a history of pets being hit by cars. How about any current pets? Do they already have cats? Dogs? Any children? If so, what ages?

Depending upon your views on declawing and whether or not a cat should be let outdoors, these are issues you'll need to discuss.

You'll want to find out about their lifestyle, how much time they can devote to a cat, and how prepared they are for the responsibility. Do they know what a cat needs?

Come to an agreement regarding vaccinations and spaying or neutering as well. You may agree to cover certain expenses as long as they show proof of compliance. Work all of this out in advance and get it in writing.

If you don't screen prospective owners by asking questions and checking references, it may mean a death sentence for the kitten. I have known several people who didn't investigate a prospective owner enough and ended up assuming the kittens were going to good homes—only to discover they were being used as bait to train fighting dogs or were fed to snakes. There are truly sick people in this world who answer "free pet" ads in order to acquire victims for many horrible purposes.

Responsible, caring people don't mind being asked questions concerning their suitability to own a pet. By your thoroughness and concern, the prospective owners know they're getting a kitten that was obviously well cared for and had a healthy start in life.

16

Getting Gray Around the Whiskers

What You Need to Know About Your Geriatric Cat

When is your cat considered old? Well, what kind of life does your cat lead? You can look at the chart in Chapter 2 to get a general idea of how a cat's years compare to ours, but as with our life span, many factors can have an influence on how accurate those numbers are. An intact, unvaccinated outdoor cat who lives to be four is, in my opinion, an old cat. Compare that to the altered, vaccinated cat kept indoors and given good quality food and veterinary care. At four, that cat is in the prime of his life and may well live another fifteen years or more. You have a great influence over how well your cat ages by providing him with love, good care, a safe environment, proper nutrition, regular health exams, and appropriate vaccinations, and having him altered.

Behavior

This is interesting because you may notice that your once short-tempered, untouchable cat has begun to mellow. On the other hand, your sweet-natured, tolerant kitty may now seem irritable.

The cat who used to tear through the house at the speed of light may now restrict his activity to sleeping, stretching, and eating.

The scratching post that was once the center

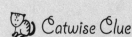 Catwise Clue

In general, a cat is considered geriatric at about ten years of age. Of course, you must factor in lifestyle, nutrition, genetics, and health.

SOME SIGNS OF AGE-RELATED COGNITIVE DYSFUNCTION

- excessive vocalization (especially at night)
- disorientation
- anxiety
- nonrecognition of family members
- elimination outside of the litter box
- change in normal sleeping patterns
- changes in relationships with other pets in the home
- pacing/restlessness

- uncharacteristic avoidance or dislike of physical interaction
- loss of appetite
- irritability
- constipation
- changes in litter box habits
- incontinence
- loss of interest in play
- loss of interest in grooming

of activity in your home may now be used less frequently. Some cats who in their younger years didn't use posts very much may now regularly seek them out for purposes of stretching and relieving stiff muscles. A cat who knew every nook and cranny of his environment may now have trouble finding his way through the house without getting lost.

Another change to be aware of is *aged-related cognitive dysfunction*. Similar to human Alzheimer's disease, this is more serious than just the normal brain deterioration of age. This doesn't affect every cat but if you suspect your cat's behavior change is not just normal aging, talk to your veterinarian. The cause of age-related cognitive dysfunction isn't exactly known but some cats may be genetically predisposed.

Age-related cognitive dysfunction needs to be accurately diagnosed because your cat's behavioral changes may be due to another underlying medical condition. For example, a sudden dislike of being touched may be due to arthritis, and a change in litter box habits may be due to renal failure or hyperthyroidism. A change in personality could have hyperthyroidism as the underlying cause as well.

The disease will, unfortunately, progress. Medication may help slow the progression and your veterinarian will guide you as to what is appropriate for your cat. He/she may put your cat on a therapeutic diet containing ingredients known for maintaining cognitive function, such as vitamin E, selenium, antioxidants, etc. Don't supplement on your own, though. Your veterinarian will customize a plan specifically for your cat.

To help your cat during this time, keep the environment familiar. Don't rearrange furniture or make major changes in your cat's life (no new pets, renovation, new furniture, etc.) if at all possible. Increase the number of litter box locations in case your cat has trouble remembering where his box is.

The cat may need to be confined at night. At the very least, make sure doors are closed to rooms where he may hurt himself.

Continue to provide stimulation for your aging cat through interactive playtime and environmental enrichment to help slow the progression of cognitive dysfunction. Increase your cat's visits to the veterinarian to at least twice yearly for regular checkups. Age-related cognitive dysfunction can't be cured but you may be able to slow your cat's rate of decline.

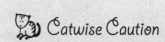 **Catwise Caution**

An elderly cat often doesn't handle stressful situations as well as a younger cat. Be very mindful of how less tolerant your elderly kitty may be.

Physical Changes

Your cat's weight may begin changing as he enters his golden years. He may appear thin or he may gain weight. Often older cats become thin. Others lose muscle tone as they age and seem thin and flabby. You may notice his spine to be more prominent along his back nowadays. An older cat is more vulnerable to fractures because the bones become brittle and less dense. Your cat's skin may have lost some of its elasticity and may become dry. Your veterinarian may recommend a fatty acid supplement.

The cat's coat may no longer be as glorious as it once was. Some cats develop gray hair as they age, especially around the muzzle. He may also not be as fastidious with his grooming.

The older cat's nails become more brittle and the paw pads thicken. If your cat no longer uses his scratching post regularly you may have to trim his nails more often.

When you look in your cat's eyes, you may notice they're no longer bright but now have a slight cloudiness to them. A cat of any age can develop cataracts but the chances certainly increase for a senior kitty.

His gait may be slow, his limbs stiff, and it may take longer for him to get up from his afternoon nap.

Cold may bother him more now and you might find him curled up by the heating vent or in the sun every chance he gets.

Declining Senses

Some cats suffer a deterioration of senses with old age. It may be a slight decrease in vision or hearing or it could be as severe as total blindness or deafness.

A gradual decrease in hearing may not be apparent to you but take note of any behavioral change that could be connected to hearing loss. For example, a once friendly cat who now bolts when you reach for him may be getting startled by a sudden pair of hands on him. He may also show uncharacteristic aggression when touched. The aggression could also be due to pain, so a veterinary checkup is always needed. If it turns out that he's getting startled by a sudden approach, make your footsteps heavier as you come near because the cat will still be able to feel the vibrations. If the room is dim or dark, flick the light on before reaching for your cat. Always give advanced warning of your approach.

Any changes in vision or the look of the eyes should be brought to the attention of your veterinarian. This includes any mobility changes you may notice as well, such as the cat seeming to have difficulty navigating around the room, bumping into objects, or having trouble following the movements of an interactive toy.

A cat's sense of smell has a strong influence on his appetite. If your cat has lost interest in food, it may be that he can't smell it as well.

A cat with declining senses is at a severe disadvantage outdoors, so if you haven't already started keeping him inside, you should begin as soon as you feel any of his senses are deteriorating or he is displaying any physical decline. A cat with decreased sight or hearing won't have warning before a car approaches or if a dangerous dog is barking around the corner. If you still want him to be able to enjoy the outdoors, on nice days you can bring him out on a leash so he can lounge with you in the sun.

Consult your veterinarian regarding any physical changes or medical symptoms you observe. Don't assume it's just old age—there could be a medical problem that needs to be addressed.

As your cat ages, it's important to have him checked regularly and appropriately vaccinated as advised by your veterinarian. The doctor may change your cat's vaccination protocol. It's also essential to do more in-depth troubleshooting. As part of the exam, your veterinarian may recommend routine blood and urine tests. If you start early and do them on a regular basis, you'll be able to catch many problems in their initial stages. You'll also be able to more accurately gauge how fast a problem is progressing. As part of a geriatric profile, your veterinarian may also feel that a blood pressure reading, ECG, and X-ray of the chest should be done. Some clinics offer geriatric-pet physical packages that include various procedures at a reduced fee.

For older cats, I think it's a good idea to have a checkup every six months instead of just once a year. You stand a much better chance of catching problems earlier. A year is a long time in a cat's life and a medical condition can progress a great deal in a matter of months.

Have You Neglected Your Cat's Teeth?

If so, by the time he enters old age, he could be in serious trouble. Periodontal disease can make it painful for your cat to eat. He could even stop eating totally. Should the bacteria enter the bloodstream, it can travel to internal organs and lead to infection.

If you've been faithfully brushing your cat's teeth all these years and having professional cleanings when needed then your cat probably has nothing more than the usual signs of dental wear and tear. His teeth may not be as white as they once were, but at least they're in good shape with no signs of gingivitis. On the other hand, if you've neglected his teeth, there's a good chance that not only will his breath stop a train in its tracks, but there's probably gum inflammation or loose teeth as well.

On a regular basis, lift up your cat's upper lip along the side of his mouth and check the condition of his teeth. Do they look very yellow or even brown? Do the gums look puffy and inflamed? These are signs of gingivitis or periodontal disease (refer to the Medical Appendix for a more specific description). If you aren't comfortable looking in your cat's mouth or if he won't let you, have your veterinarian check him.

Because your cat is getting up there in years, you may be hesitant about putting him under anesthesia for a professional teeth cleaning. However, the risk of letting periodontal disease advance is more dangerous than the anesthesia. If your veterinarian feels your cat should have his teeth cleaned, he'll undergo diagnostic tests to determine his anesthesia risk factors.

If you've ever had a toothache or an abscessed tooth, you know how painful it is. Imagine your poor cat enduring a mouth full of sore, infected gums and painful teeth—all at a time in his life when he needs to keep his immune system up and maintain a healthy appetite.

COMMON AGING CAT HEALTH CONCERNS

anorexia	diabetes
arthritis	glaucoma
blindness	heart disease
cancer	hyperthyroidism
cataracts	liver disease
cognitive dysfunction	obesity
constipation	periodontal disease
deafness	renal failure

If your cat does undergo a professional cleaning, keep up a regular schedule of at-home care. Brush his teeth daily (or at least three times a week). If you just can't do it, ask your veterinarian about using an oral hygiene spray.

Making Day-to-Day Life Easier for an Elderly Kitty

My cat, Albie, lived to be just shy of twenty-one years old and he spent all of those years, minus the first few weeks of his life, with me. I watched him grow from an awkward kitten to graceful, stealthy adult, and finally, to a lover of sun-drenched naps. I remember when Albie was the fastest thing on four feet in our house. He made leaps that didn't seem possible and could run through our obstacle course of furniture without losing any speed. In his geriatric years, his main activity was napping on the bed in the sun—so much so that it became commonplace for me to just make the bed around him when I woke up in the morning rather than disturb him. His once daring, carefree leaps turned into carefully planned ones that were limited to low-level elevations. Every once in a while, though, when he was feeling great, he would show off some skillful and stealthy moves, but for the most part, he lived life a whole lot slower.

As he aged, I made adjustments so he could continue to be as comfortable as possible and still enjoy all of the pleasures of his environment. Albie has passed but I have two other geriatric cats now. The litter boxes have lower sides, there are heated pet beds stationed around the house, and we've increased the number of scratching posts. To help Mary still be able to enjoy elevated areas, we've created steps so she can reach her favorite napping areas. Interactive play sessions are still frequent but they're now at a much lower intensity. The meal schedule has changed as well. Mary, who has some intestinal issues, is fed many small meals per day because her stomach can't be empty for too long but can only handle a small amount of food at a time.

Look around your home and see what environmental modifications you can make to create a more comfortable living arrangement for your geriatric cat. Talk to your veterinarian about any nutritional changes. And don't forget the playtime—your cat may or may not be able to engage in lots of physical activity but any amount of playtime is beneficial.

Easy Access

To enable your cat to still reach those high places he loves, you can use a multi-tiered cat tree so he can make a series of little jumps. If he has trouble even getting up into a chair, you can place a ramp or pet stairs in front of it. You can either make your own or purchase commercial ones. There are several brands available and they're easily found in most pet supply stores and online.

Temperature Tolerance

Drafts, cold floors, and unheated garages or basements can make a cat's aches and pains seem much worse. An elderly cat may also have a reduced tolerance for cold. If your cat sleeps on a bed on the floor, line it with a fleece pad. To protect him from drafts, use a high-sided round bed. If your cat seeks out the warmest spots in the house, you may want to use a heated pet bed.

Litter Box Habits

Your aging cat may not have the greatest bladder control now, especially if he's diabetic or in renal failure. Provide additional litter boxes so that he doesn't have a long way to walk when the need arises. There should be at least one litter box on every floor. If the box is usually in the basement or garage, it may be too difficult for him to negotiate stairs. He may also not want to go out into the cold. Cats who don't use litter boxes and are used to doing their eliminating outdoors should have litter boxes made available indoors now.

Check on how well your cat can get in and out of the box. It may be time to switch to low-sided boxes. Monitor his litter box habits very carefully now. If you notice a change in urine output or if he eliminates outside of the box, a trip to the veterinarian is needed. Constipation is also a common occurrence in elderly cats. The cause could be due to decreased mobility, not drinking enough water, discomfort in walking, or just the fact that the intestinal tract functions slowly now. It could also be due to an underlying medical cause, though, so be sure to check with your veterinarian. If you notice your cat having difficulty with stool elimination, or if he hasn't had a bowel movement recently, he needs to be checked.

Food and Water

If your cat has difficulty getting around, move his food and water closer to his bed. If he drinks larger quantities of water now (maybe as a result of a medical condition), provide a bowl in each of his favorite locations. Some cats have the opposite problem, and they don't drink enough water. Always have fresh clean water available. Don't let it get stale and make sure you clean the bowl daily. If your cat appears dehydrated or you don't think he's drinking enough, consult your veterinarian. Dehydration can be checked by gently lifting the loose skin on the cat's back (at the shoulders). If it doesn't spring back into position right away, he's probably dehydrated. If you're in doubt, consult your veterinarian.

If your cat has a problem with chronic constipation, adding ¼–½ teaspoon of canned pumpkin may help as it's rich in fiber. Ask your veterinarian first, though.

Don't allow your cat to become obese, which is a danger as he gets less active. An obese cat is more prone to diabetes. Arthritis will be more intolerable as well, if he's carrying around extra weight on those sore joints.

Keeping weight *on* the cat may be a problem for some owners. As a cat ages, the number of taste buds are reduced. That, in combination with a declining sense of smell, can cause a decreased appetite. If his lack of appetite is caused by fading senses, ask your veterinarian about ways to make the food more enticing. If you're feeding dry food, you may want to offer a little canned food as well, which has more of an aroma. Warming the food slightly will also release more of an aroma. Sometimes it helps to add a little warmed unsalted chicken broth over the food. Ask your veterinarian about what would be best for your cat's specific condition. Don't make any dietary changes for an older cat without consulting with the veterinarian.

If you've always fed your cat on a schedule, you may find that his stomach can't handle his normal-size meal now. Feeding smaller meals more frequently may be more comfortable.

As for changing his diet, there are multiple senior formulas on the market. A senior diet isn't one-size-fits-all, though. Senior formulas have reduced calories as well as added antioxidants. They're also designed to be more digestible. Many have increased fiber to help with motility. Whether a cat needs a senior formula should be determined on a case-by-case basis. An inactive geriatric cat has different caloric needs than a nonstop senior kitty who doesn't know the meaning of the words *old age*. This is where you should get your veterinarian's guidance on which food is right for your cat. If you decide to switch formulas, remember to do it gradually.

Grooming

Your cat may have been a stunner in his prime, but now grooming may be low on his list of priorities. Maintain a regular schedule of brushing to keep his coat in good shape. The massage of the brush will also feel especially good. If your cat has sensitive skin, has become bony, or his hair has become thin, switch to a soft brush. You may need to reevaluate the grooming tools you've used in the past.

Use your grooming sessions as a chance to do a health check as well, especially when it comes to detecting any lumps or bumps.

Keep in mind that a cat who suffers from arthritis may experience discomfort when attempting to self-groom. Help him out by increasing your grooming schedule and assisting in keeping his anal area clean.

MONITORING YOUR OLDER CAT

- watch for changes in litter box habits
- watch for changes in urine amounts and color of urine
- watch for changes in stool (constipation, mucous, color change, etc.)
- make sure your cat can comfortably get in and out of the litter box
- monitor your cat's food intake and be alert to any weight loss or gain
- monitor sleep pattern changes
- monitor water intake
- check for lumps, bumps, and sores during grooming sessions
- monitor behavior changes
- brush your cat's teeth regularly and check for swollen gums, excessive drooling, and bad mouth odor
- monitor your cat's mobility for potential signs of arthritis, lameness
- make regular visits to the veterinarian

Other Pets in the House

Even though all the pets in your home may be the best of buddies, watch for signs of increasing irritation on the part of your elderly cat. Also, make sure his companions aren't bullying the once "king of the house" now that he's moving a bit slower. In multicat homes where there had been ongoing tension between companion cats, it's not unusual for the younger ones to seize the opportunity of an older cat slowing down as their chance to rev up their agitation toward him. Make sure your senior cat doesn't become the victim of aggression or get nosed out of his favorite sleeping areas.

Should you get your cat a new kitten? I'd think long and hard before doing this. A playful, "in your face" kitten may not be what your elderly cat had in mind for his golden years.

At a time when he is least able to cope with added stress and confusion, a kitten may cause your cat to display some behavior problems, such as litter box avoidance.

You also don't want a playful little kitten to have to endure the constant rejection from a cantankerous old feline.

Some elderly cats do great when a kitten is introduced. I've seen it put the sparkle back in the eyes of an aging kitty. I've also seen it cause constant tension and create stressful last years for the cat. Don't add a kitten to your household if your older cat's mobility is greatly decreased. The cat needs to be able to easily move away from a kitten. A cat with limited mobility may try to leap onto an elevated surface to escape the kitten and risk injury.

Use your judgment, based on what your cat seems to need. If he appears bored and has lost interest in life, playtime with *you* may be all he needs. He may not be able to do the incredible leaps that were once his trademark in his youth, but I'll bet he still has a few good moves left.

Playtime and Exercise

If you don't have interactive toys (shame on you), go out and get some right this minute. Earlier in this book, I discussed how playtime and hunting are *mental* exercises as well as *physical*. So no matter how limited he is physically, he'll still enjoy the success of a victorious hunt thanks to your interactive playtime skills. Though he may not be able to move as fast, some form of physical exercise is extremely beneficial. Certainly you don't want him to overdo it and risk pain or injury, but a customized play session tailored to his specific health state will do wonders.

Your cat's mind will benefit from these play sessions as well as they may help keep his brain active and healthy. In addition to using your fishing pole toy, set up a few puzzle feeders.

Don't forget the catnip when it comes to your old cat. What a great Sunday afternoon treat or a good way to kick-start a play session.

Be Tolerant

He has been a wonderful cat all these years, so be tolerant of fumbled attempts at jumping on the table that result in something being knocked over. Be tolerant as well of the occasional litter box mishap—but don't neglect having him checked by the veterinarian. He's still a handsome guy even though he no longer grooms himself and is unaware of the food on his chin. Just discreetly wipe his face and help him with the grooming duties. Don't be insulted or impatient if he doesn't come when you call him or if he acts grumpy when his nap is disturbed. Finally, if the mice in your home feel a little safer these days, don't let on to your cat.

If you're having concerns about the quality of your cat's life and need guidance on issues such as if or when your cat appears to be suffering too much, talk to your veterinarian (see Chapter 17 as well).

17

Legacy of Love

The Good-bye We're Never Prepared to Say

We gently call it "putting the pet to sleep." As a pet owner, it's the hardest decision you'll ever make. We always hope that should we have to face this situation, we'll simply know *when it's time*—that our cat will give us a clear signal that she's in pain or her quality of life has badly deteriorated.

For many owners there's no clear-cut signal from the cat, and not every owner uses the same guidelines. Some watch for a lack of appetite, feeling that as long as she's eating, she still has a will to live. Others gauge it by their cat's inability to move around or a decline in litter box habits. And of course, no owner ever wants to see their pet in pain. Every day you'll find yourself studying your cat, looking in her eyes, almost willing her to give you the answer. Is she in too much pain? Just when you think that she is, doubt will creep into your mind and you'll second-guess yourself. Some owners don't want their pet to experience any discomfort, so they choose to euthanize in the earlier stages of terminal disease.

For some owners, unfortunately, *money* is also a major factor when deciding whether *it's time*. The cost of long-term care is beyond the budget of some families.

Catwise Clue

Some veterinary clinics offer in-home hospice care for animals.

With the advancements in veterinary medicine, the cost of a breakthrough life-extending procedure could be out of reach financially. Every responsible pet owner wishes they could spare no expense in doing everything possible to prolong the life of their beloved pet, but in reality, for many that's just not possible.

Your ability to provide long-term care for an ill cat is also a major consideration. Some owners aren't able to medicate their cats, give injections, or perform other necessary nursing duties.

For most owners, there is never a clear sign. You can never know *for sure*. You do the very best that you can for your cat and make your decision based on her condition, spirit, your abilities, the guidance of the veterinarian, and your endless soul-searching. You can seek advice from friends, family, other pet owners in similar situations and veterinarians, but when it comes down to it—the decision is truly yours.

Euthanasia is the last act of love that an owner gives to a beloved but suffering pet. Humanely ending a pet's pain by allowing her to leave this world in peace and with dignity is a truly unselfish act of love.

Euthanasia

Once you've made the decision, there are other difficult questions that need to be addressed. Do you plan on being there with your cat? What are your options in dealing with the remains? What is right for one owner isn't necessarily right for another. Take time to talk with your veterinarian and discuss the options.

Call ahead to the veterinarian's office and make the appointment. Inform the receptionist of the purpose for the appointment so that you don't have to sit in the waiting room. When you get to the hospital you'll immediately be brought into the privacy of an exam room. Many clinics also have a dedicated room for this very sensitive and difficult time—a room with a chair or sofa and an atmosphere that feels less like a hospital.

If you don't feel that you can remain with your cat, inform the receptionist when you call. Don't feel you have to be there through the process if you're not comfortable with that. It's a personal decision and there's no right or wrong. I've accompanied many owners to the hospital during these times and some were unable to watch their pets die. Those owners didn't love their pets any less than the owners who stayed. The goal is to keep the cat calm and make this time as peaceful for her as possible.

When I worked at an animal hospital, I had to be present for the euthanizing of many homeless animals who had been brought to us from the shelter. The animals were either too injured or too sick to be in the shelter. Many of the animals had probably never been loved, cared for, or even touched. I would hold each one, tell them they were loved. I would also give thanks to the animals for having graced our world with their spirits. Ironically, the process of dying was probably the most peaceful moment of their brief, lonely lives.

The actual euthanasia procedure is very quick. The euthanizing solution is basically an overdose of an anesthetic, so the procedure does very much resemble putting the pet to *sleep*. If your cat normally gets very stressed or agitated when at the veterinary clinic, a sedative can be administered before the procedure to calm her. After the sedative, the veterinarian will clip the fur on the cat's foreleg to make the vein more visible. Often a catheter is inserted in the vein to make it easier when it comes time for the solution to be injected. The solution is administered by injection. Your veterinarian will explain to you that sometimes animals may vocalize a bit, but it's not due to experiencing pain. The only pain will be the initial stick of the needle used for catheter insertion. Once the solution is injected the cat will immediately become unconscious, and in a matter of seconds a peaceful death will occur.

The veterinarian may ask you afterward if you'd like a few minutes alone. Don't be embarrassed about needing time alone with your cat after the euthanasia. It's an overwhelming experience and you need time to collect yourself. It can also be helpful to see your cat resting peacefully, especially if she'd been in a lot of pain.

Some veterinarians will come to your home to perform the euthanasia. If your cat gets too upset at the veterinary clinic, or if you'd rather she spend her last moments in the familiar surroundings of her home, discuss this option with your veterinarian.

Another important decision you'll have to make is in terms of the arrangements for your cat's remains. Discuss the options with your veterinarian beforehand. There are full service pet cemeteries that offer everything from individual burials to cremation. Depending upon the laws in your local area, you may want to bury your cat on your property.

Coping with Grief

Almost anyone who has ever shared life with a pet will understand the sense of loss you feel. Be prepared, though, for the people who will inevitably say, "It's only a cat," and won't be able to relate to the depth of your pain. Even if your cat had been a member of your family for twenty years, there will always be those people who don't understand the deep connection between humans and their cherished pets. My advice is to surround yourself with the friends and family who *do* understand.

Until you actually experience the loss, you don't know how you're going to react. I've known owners who were shocked at how deeply they grieved. The emotions experienced over the loss of a pet can equal those for the loss of a human.

Don't try to rush the grieving process. Your cat was a beloved member of the family, a cherished friend, a constant companion who gave unconditional love. It will take time to heal, but believe me, healing does indeed happen. Eventually, you'll be able to think of the memories without them being so raw and overpowering. In time, those memories will bring warm feelings and smiles as you fondly remember that very special friend.

If you feel unable to cope or just need a sympathetic ear, there are various pet loss support lines available. I've listed some in the back of this book. Many veterinary universities offer this service. If you'd rather confine your communication to the computer, you can find online groups where people feeling the same depth of pain can come together.

There are also several books available on coping with pet loss. You'll find books for your children as well as for yourself.

Helping Your Children

One thing that disturbs me when it comes to how some people help their children through this process is when they immediately get a "replacement" pet. Instead of teaching children that pets are disposable and easily replaceable, we should be helping them through this difficult time without trivializing the value of an animal's life.

If your children are old enough to understand, offer clear, honest explanations of what has happened to the pet. Don't go into graphic detail but don't say things such as "the cat ran away" or "the cat went to sleep." Don't tell a child that the cat was sick or injured and died without going on to explain that not all sickness and injury result in death.

Have children plan a memorial for the cat to help them deal with their grief and any unanswered questions. Provide support for your children and explain that crying and grief are normal. For a lot of children, this will be their first experience with loss and death.

IDEAS FOR HELPING CHILDREN GRIEVE

- Ask your children to write a tribute to the cat. It can be a poem, essay, favorite memory, etc. They can work on one piece together or write individual tributes. Place the written tribute in a double frame that contains a favorite picture of the cat.

- If your children like to draw, have them paint a picture of the cat. Talk to them about their picture and what a special tribute it is.

- Frame a favorite picture of each child with the cat. Each child can pick out their own special frame or they can decorate their own frames.

- Donate money in your cat's name to a favorite charity or animal welfare organization. Have your children choose the organization. If your chil-

dren have piggy banks, they may want to donate some of their own money.

- Plant a special tree or garden plant in honor of the cat. Place a memorial stepping stone there as well. Your children can help in the selection of the plant and the stone.

- There are several books published for children on the subject of losing a pet. Find one that is age-appropriate for your children and set aside some quiet time to read the book together and then have a discussion afterward.

- In the case of a deceased pet who belonged to a relative, neighbor, or friend your children can draw or write a sympathy card. You can also find pet sympathy cards at your local card store.

When Your Cat Dies Suddenly

It's difficult enough to prepare ourselves for euthanizing an old or terminally ill pet—the thought of dealing with a sudden death can be unbearable. No one wants to think about it, but sudden, unexpected deaths happen. Cats slip out the door and get hit by cars, attacked by other animals, or killed by cruel people. Cats also fall out of windows. When the death is unexpected, you experience shock, denial, and anger. You may find yourself blaming the people you hold responsible (the veterinarian, the driver of the car, yourself). In the case of negligence, seek advice and take the correct course of action. Don't let your emotions get the best of you in a situation where you run the risk of doing something you will regret. When in a highly emotional state, taking matters into your own hands will only make a tragedy even worse. Speak to a lawyer if you feel legal action is warranted.

Sometimes pets die accidentally and it's not anybody's fault. As careful as you try to be, the cat may bolt out the door when a visitor comes in. She may run out in the road and get hit by a car. It's a horrible accident and you may blame yourself more than anyone else involved, but even accidents happen to the most watchful, careful people.

Helping Your Surviving Pets Deal with Loss

The family members who often get overlooked when a death occurs in the family are the other pets. Although it's not something we can positively verify, animals most likely experience the loss and mourn the absence of their companions. In fact, it's probably even more difficult for them because they're confused by *your* behavior. A pet who sees their owner grieving, crying, and not interacting with them as usual can create anxiety and even depression for them.

Even if the cats weren't close, the loss can create an unstable environment. You may notice anxiety-related behavior; the cat may seem needy and follow you around. The surviving cat may be restless and not as tolerant. He may also show less interest in family interactions. Every cat is an individual, so the important thing is to watch for behavioral changes.

To help your surviving pets through this difficult time, try to balance affection with casual, light interaction. The cats need to know that much of their normal lives remain intact. They will get through the mourning period much more easily if you display as close to your normal behavior as possible. Although you may not feel much like playing with your cats and acting happy, that's just what they need. Animals are little emotional sponges and they easily tune into and absorb the way we're feeling and acting. They also need their familiar routine. If you normally played with your cats at particular times of the day, maintain that schedule for the cat who is left behind. Provide affection and comfort in a gentle, soothing way. Try to avoid clutching, clinging, and sobbing because those are stress-trigger red flags for the cat. Your touch should be soothing and not stressful.

Signs of mourning can include: irritability, loss of appetite, increased vocalizations, withdrawal from family, anxiety-related behaviors, inappropriate elimination, and increase in sleeping patterns.

Don't overlook your pets during this difficult crisis. They need you. For more information on depression, see Chapter 7.

Should You Get Another Pet?

This is another one of those personal decisions that only you can answer. If you've dealt with the loss of your pet and feel ready to open your heart again, there will certainly be a pet out there in need of a loving home.

When is the right time to get another pet? Only you can answer that. My advice, though, is to not try to replace the cat who died. Searching for another cat with the same looks or personality isn't fair to the memory of your beloved cat and it certainly isn't fair to the new cat. The newcomer will never be able to live up to your expectations as you compare her to the loving companion you had for so many years.

If you have pets at home, make sure they've dealt with the loss before trying to introduce another pet. If they're still in crisis, they're likely to be more hostile toward any new additions.

Providing for a Cat in the Event of Your Death

Even though in your eyes your cat is a bona fide member of the family, in the eyes of the legal system she's merely personal property. As much as she may be far more deserving than any of your relatives, you can't leave your estate to your cat. That doesn't mean you can't provide for her—in fact, you should. Although we don't think of our pets in terms of outliving us, it can and does happen.

You can leave your cat and money to care for her to someone as specified in your will. Because of the chance that the person chosen could take advantage of this situation, it obviously needs to be someone you truly trust. Talk it over with that person and be sure you're both comfortable with this, then discuss it with your lawyer. It has to be arranged so the person will be able to immediately get possession of the cat after your death without having to wait for the will to be read.

You may decide to have two caregivers—one immediate short-term one (who may be geographically close) and then one long-term one. This way, if the long-term caregiver needs time to make arrangements to come and get the cat, your kitty will be taken care of right away.

Work with a lawyer who does estate planning. If you don't have formal instructions for the care of your cat, she will become the property of an heir who inherits your belongings. This may not be the person you want taking care of your cat. That's why it's so important to make these arrangements formal and legal.

Don't arrange for one lump monetary sum to be given to the caregiver. Instead arrange for regular payments. This way, if something happens to the caregiver, there will be money left for the next caregiver of your cat. Make sure that when you set this up, you have at least two trusted people who are willing to be caregivers because an individual's personal circumstances can change and the desire to care for your cat may no longer exist.

Something to also think about is whether you might be able to be a caregiver for someone else's cat. It might be a good arrangement to mutually make with a trusted cat-owning friend. If you have a friend who hasn't yet thought of a plan for his/her cat, it would be helpful to offer some guidelines. I've seen so many sad situations where an owner didn't plan for the unexpected and a beloved cat has ended up euthanized, in a shelter, or passed along to an inappropriate relative.

Also, discuss with your lawyer how to set it up so someone will be able to legally come in and care for your cat in case you're hospitalized. Once all the legal aspects have been taken care of, you should take the time to make sure your cat's emotional needs will be met as well. Sit down and write out instructions for the person who would be caring for your cat. Besides the usual things such as what kind of food, how much to feed, how often, litter preferences, veterinarian's contact information, etc., include the more personal things. What games does your cat like? How does she like to be petted? Is she afraid of certain things? Does she love to sit in the window all day? How do you groom her? Write down all the things that will not only help the new owner but will also help your cat make a less traumatic transition.

Keep the letter with your cat's supplies as well as provide a copy to the person. Periodically update the information as needed.

18

Emergencies and First Aid

Keeping Your Cool in a Medical Crisis

I've included this chapter on first aid, handling emergencies, and how to stock a general first-aid kit, but keep in mind that the *most important* part of emergency care is getting the cat to the veterinary hospital immediately. Unfortunately, situations may arise where treatment in seconds is crucial—for example: a cat who isn't breathing or is choking—and how you handle the crisis could mean the difference between life and death.

Be able to act immediately when your cat has been injured, poisoned, or becomes ill because it may save his life and reduce the amount of pain and suffering he endures.

You should prepare for emergency situations and *plan ahead*. Now, I know that as you sit there with your cute little kitten on your lap, the last thing you want to think about is the possibility of him being poisoned, hit by a car, or attacked by another animal—but it does happen. Have a plan so you don't waste precious seconds.

First and foremost, know where to take your cat for emergency treatment *after hours*. If there isn't a pet emergency clinic in your area, ask your veterinarian what the emergency procedure is. If there is an emergency clinic in your town, make sure you know how to get there. Take a drive and map out the shortest route. Make sure all family members who are of driving age know how to get there as well. Some emergency clinics are only open in the evenings, so find out what the hours of operation are.

The plan should also include having a first-aid kit and being familiar with all of the contents.

Keep an assembled cat carrier on hand. Many owners dismantle the carrier for storage, which makes it too time-consuming to use in emergencies. Keep at least one carrier out with a towel in it and maybe your cat will use it as an extra place for midday naps.

A cat in pain is scared and often reacts defensively. Your sweet, docile cat when severely injured may bite or scratch when you attempt to help him. Have a blanket on hand for protection or keep a pair of wildlife gloves.

Be familiar with your cat's temperature, pulse, and respiration under normal conditions to help you to evaluate his condition during illness or in a crisis.

First-Aid Kit

Nothing replaces immediate medical care from a veterinarian, but having an organized first-aid kit can make a difference when it comes down to *seconds* in a life-threatening situation. Having a well-stocked kit and knowledge of emergency procedures can enable you to prevent further damage or blood loss while you transport your cat to the hospital.

Familiarize family members with first-aid procedures and locate your kit in a convenient place. Besides having a first-aid kit, keep a hot water bottle, heating pad, blanket, towels, and a flat board.

Your veterinarian's phone number and that of the nearest emergency clinic should be posted near the phone. You should also post the number of the ASPCA Animal Poison Control Center (see Resource Guide).

You can purchase equipped first-aid kits or you can stock your own. I prefer to stock my own, using things that my veterinarian recommends.

For a container, a fishing tackle box or tiered tool box work great. All of the contents can be neatly organized when the box is open and everything is instantly displayed so you don't have to go digging around in search of smaller items. Keep your first-aid kit well supplied, and replenish items before they run low. Check expiration dates and replace medicines before they get old.

The following is a general list of first-aid contents. Check with your veterinarian concerning use of specific items if you're unsure of anything. He/she will also be able to guide you on special items you should stock based on your cat's individual needs and the location in which you live.

FIRST-AID CONTENTS

- phone number of veterinarian and emergency clinic
- phone number of poison control center
- first-aid manual
- ear cleaning solution
- water-based lubricant
- plastic eyedropper
- activated charcoal
- antiseptic cleaner (one that's safe for cats)
- thermometer
- tweezers
- small, blunt-edged scissors

- sterile, plain eyewash solution
- hydrogen peroxide
- sterile saline solution
- ice pack
- cotton balls
- roll of gauze
- gauze pads
- pen light (with fresh batteries)
- adhesive tape
- tongue depressors
- towels
- latex gloves
- needle-nose pliers

Handling an Emergency

1. The most important thing is to get to the veterinarian or emergency clinic immediately.
2. To prevent further injury, remove the *cause* if at all possible.
3. Make sure the cat is able to breathe. Watch for rise and fall of the chest. Put your cheek near his nose to feel for air. Clear airways of any obstructions, blood, or fluid.
4. Check for pulse.
5. If you know how, give artificial respiration if cat has a pulse. Give CPR if there's no pulse.
6. Control bleeding.
7. Move the cat as little as possible because the extent of his injury is unknown. When you must move him, support his body to prevent causing further damage and pain. Use whatever you have available for support, such as a blanket, towel, jacket, board, or box.

8. If the cat appears to be unable to swallow or is nonresponsive, position his head lower than his body to prevent aspiration of fluids.

9. Cover the cat to keep him warm.

10. Don't panic. I know this is easier said than done, but you need to stay calm enough to assess the situation, provide appropriate immediate care, and safely transport the cat to the hospital.

Picking Up and Restraining a Cat

How you pick up and restrain a cat greatly depends on how calm, frightened, or aggressive he is and what type of injury he has sustained. Here are some general guidelines:

How to Pick Up a Cat

These instructions are for a cat who isn't severely injured. If you suspect any fractures, extreme care must be taken to avoid further injury or pain. If your cat isn't frightened and is used to being held, you can pick him up in your usual manner to place him in his carrier.

When dealing with a sick or injured cat, you need to use caution to avoid being scratched or bitten. Carrying your cat in your arms could make you vulnerable to being scratched in the face. Remember that an injured, sick, or nervous cat is unpredictable.

If your cat isn't used to being held, approach him from above. Don't go face to face with him because he might react defensively. In a reassuring tone, calmly talk to your cat. Let him first get used to your physical contact by gently petting his head and rubbing his chin. Slide one hand under his chest so that his lower body weight is resting on your forearm. Snuggle the cat in close, toward your body, to immobilize his hind legs. Gently but securely, grasp his front legs with your fingers. Your other hand can either cradle his chin or, if it keeps him calm, you can gently place your hand over his eyes and ears. Carefully place the cat in his carrier. If you don't have a carrier on hand, use whatever you have that will ensure safe transport.

Handling a Fractious Cat

An injured animal is confused and frightened. He doesn't know the reason for his pain; he just knows that he hurts. If at all mobile, his tendency will be to escape. In this crisis situation he most likely won't recognize you or understand that you're trying to help him. You stand a good chance of being scratched or bitten, so take precautions to protect your face, hands, and arms. An injured cat may lash out at your face as you lean in to assess his injuries, so proper restraint is crucial. Most people don't have thick leather or suede gloves handy, but in case you do, use them to protect your hands.

With a cat who may be potentially aggressive, you can grasp him by the scruff of the neck and lift him into the carrier. Offset some of the weight by holding his back legs with your other hand. This also prevents him from thrashing around.

A frightened, fractious cat can usually be handled more easily if you cover him with a thick towel. Give him a minute and he'll relax a bit because he'll feel hidden. Gently gather up the cat and towel, tucking the rest of the towel underneath. Don't let your guard down, though, because a cat under these conditions is still very dangerous. Once you've picked him up, place him in his carrier or in a box. If you don't have a carrier or box and are transporting him in a towel or blanket, make sure his head is exposed enough for him to breathe in order to prevent suffocation.

If your cat is too dangerous to pick up inside the towel or blanket, drop a box over the top of him. Slightly lifting up one corner, slide a flat piece of cardboard underneath. You can now safely transport the cat.

When in a crisis situation, you'll have to use your judgment on how best to handle and transport the cat based on his condition and what you have available. The most important thing is getting to the veterinary hospital quickly, safely, and without causing injury to yourself or the cat.

If attempting to transport the cat is causing too much stress, he may become too exhausted, which could cause shock. Contact your veterinarian or local emergency clinic for instructions. They may be able to send someone to help.

Respiratory Distress

Foreign objects in the nose, mouth, throat, or bronchi can obstruct breathing, as can wounds to the chest or diaphragm, or the collapse of a lung.

Signs to look for that may indicate respiratory distress: pale or blue mucous membranes (check your cat's gums); gasping, open-mouth breathing; shallow breathing; short, rapid breaths; labored breathing using abdominal muscles; unconsciousness.

If the respiratory distress is caused by choking and you can see the object, try to remove it using blunt-nosed tweezers or your fingers. If the obstruction is farther down the throat, place your cat on his side and position the heel of your hand right behind the last rib. Firmly push at a slightly upward angle three or four times to dislodge the object. Don't be too forceful or you'll break his ribs. If you can't free the obstruction, get the cat to the veterinarian immediately.

If the respiratory distress isn't caused by choking, it may be due to injury or illness. Get your cat to the veterinarian immediately.

Artificial Respiration

If the cat isn't breathing *but has a heartbeat*, artificial respiration is needed. **Do not attempt this on a cat who is breathing on his own**.

- Remove the cat's collar.

- Open the mouth and pull the tongue outward to prevent it from blocking the throat, and so you can check for a foreign body.

- Clear the mouth of any excess saliva or mucous. If there's vomitus in the mouth or if the cat was underwater, suspend him upside down by the hips and gently swing his body a couple of times to remove the liquid.

- Lay the cat on his right side with the body slightly higher than his head. The head and neck should be straight to ensure an open air passageway.

- With his tongue pulled forward, place your mouth over his nose only (don't cover his mouth). Blow air into his nostrils for approximately three seconds. You should see the chest expand. Excess air will escape through the mouth. Every two seconds repeat the procedure until the cat begins breathing on his own.

CPR (Cardiopulmonary Resuscitation)

If the cat *has no heartbeat* and *isn't breathing*, CPR must be performed. If the cat *does* have a heartbeat but there's no respiration, then artificial respiration should be performed. **Don't attempt CPR on a cat who is breathing**. If it's at all possible to get to the nearest animal hospital, do so, because CPR is difficult to perform. If you're too far from the nearest hospital, then you'll have to perform the procedure yourself.

- Lay the cat on his right side.

- Continue doing artificial respiration in rhythm with CPR.

- With one hand, place your thumb on the cat's sternum and your fingers on the opposite side, so that your palm is cupping his chest.

- Compress the chest firmly but gently. CPR must be performed gently or the cat's ribs may be broken. The rate is one compression per second. Perform five compressions then administer a breath of artificial respiration without stopping the rhythm of the heart massage.

- Always observe the cat for signs of life and every few minutes check for pulse and spontaneous breathing.

- Stop immediately once you feel a heartbeat.

- Another method of administering CPR is to place one hand on each side of the cat's chest, just behind the elbows. Using both hands, compress the chest five times then perform artificial respiration one time before repeating the chest compression.

- If you've been performing CPR for thirty minutes, it's extremely doubtful that the cat will be revived.

Choking

The symptoms may include: coughing, pawing at the mouth, drooling, difficulty breathing, bulging eyes, unconsciousness.

If your cat is calm enough, attempt to look into his mouth in order to check for a foreign object. You may have to wrap him in a towel for restraint. If possible, remove it using blunt-nosed tweezers or your fingers. With a struggling or panicked cat, don't attempt to remove the object because you could send it deeper into his throat. As long as the cat is not having breathing trouble, just get to the veterinarian immediately. If the cat is unable to breathe, you'll have to administer emergency first aid. Lay the cat on his side with his head lower than his body and pull out the tongue. Place one hand below the sternum, give four quick upward thrusts (press *in* and *up*). Your thrusts should be forceful but not so hard as to break a rib. Immediately check the cat's mouth to see if you've dislodged the object. If unsuccessful, repeat with four more quick thrusts. If you can't dislodge the object, get to the veterinarian, performing artificial respiration in the meantime.

Controlling Bleeding

Applying Pressure

Place a sterile or clean gauze pad over the wound and apply even pressure. You can wrap a gauze bandage over the wound but observe the cat's limb for signs of swelling, which could indicate possible circulation impairment. If that happens, loosen the bandage.

If the gauze pad gets soaked with blood, *leave it in place* and just add another one over top. To remove the gauze may disturb any potential clotting.

Don't apply peroxide to the wound, or it'll become harder to control the bleeding. Once the bleeding stops, don't wipe the wound because you risk disturbing the clots and causing the flow to resume.

Another technique to try if direct pressure isn't working is to firmly press the artery located on the inside of the foreleg (in the armpit) or the inside thigh of the hind leg (at the groin). This may help inhibit the blood loss from a limb while an assistant attempts to pressure bandage.

Tourniquet

The application of a tourniquet is to be used as a last resort to control life-threatening bleeding on a limb when attempts at pressure bandaging have failed. Irreversible damage and the loss of the extremity can result from a tourniquet that has been left on too long or put on too tightly. Don't apply a tourniquet to any part of the body other than a leg or the tail.

Make a tourniquet by looping a piece of gauze, at least one inch wide, around the limb a couple of inches above the wound (the tourniquet goes between the heart and the wound). Tie the gauze once (don't make a knot), place a stick or pencil on top then tie one more time. Twist the pencil slowly until bleeding has been controlled. *IMPORTANT: the tourniquet must be loosened every five minutes (for one minute) to allow blood to flow to the limb.*

It's crucial that you get to the nearest veterinarian immediately to prevent permanent damage to the limb.

Shock

Shock occurs when blood pressure falls, causing inadequate blood flow to organs and tissues, which results in decreased oxygen. Attempting to compensate for the decreased circulation, the body speeds up the heart, diverts blood flow away from nonvital organs, and tries to maintain enough fluid in circulation. Without adequate oxygen, though, the organs have trouble functioning and the heart has an increasingly difficult time pumping.

Shock isn't always easy to recognize or is mistaken for other conditions. If untreated, shock can cause death.

Some common causes of shock include: trauma in general, heat stroke, burns, poisoning, hemorrhaging, serious illness, and dehydration (due to diarrhea or vomiting).

Signs of shock include:

- A drop in body temperature (the cat may feel cold to the touch)

- Shivering

- Pale mucous membranes

- Weak pulse (often rapid)

- Rapid breathing

- Weakness

To treat shock: first stop the bleeding, if any, and administer artificial respiration if breathing stops. If the heart stops, proceed with CPR. Position the cat with his head lower than his body but if he wants to sit, don't force him into a position. Keep him calm and let him settle into the position he finds most comfortable. Don't stress the cat because it'll make breathing more difficult.

Wrap the cat in a blanket and seek emergency veterinary care immediately.

Cleaning Wounds

This applies to less serious wounds. Bleeding wounds should have pressure applied (see "Controlling Bleeding") and immediate emergency veterinary care.

A wound that is less serious should still be treated to prevent infection. It's always best to have the veterinarian check any wounds, regardless of how insignificant they may appear to you.

For home treatment of minor wounds, enlist the aid of an assistant, if possible, to help hold and calm the cat. First, make sure your hands have been washed and that any equipment you'll use is clean. The hair around the wound should be clipped. The easiest way is to put a dab of *K-Y* jelly or antibiotic ointment on the wound itself prior to clipping and flush it out afterward. This helps collect hair and keeps it from sticking down in the wound. Then, using scissors, *carefully* clip the hair around the edges of the wound. If you don't have any *K-Y* jelly or ointment, just be very careful and hold the ends of the hair with your fingers as you clip. Next, with a clean, damp gauze pad, cleanse the edges of the wound. Using clean water, flush the wound to remove dirt and debris. If there is trapped debris in the wound, use a clean, wet cotton swab.

Using a gauze pad, you can clean the wound with antiseptic cleaner. Use the gauze pad to dab the wound only once then replace with a fresh one. Don't contaminate the wound by reusing the same pad.

Keeping a bandage on a cat is often tricky, so if the wound needs to be covered to keep it clean, tape it carefully. Make sure the bandage stays clean and dry; change it daily, or more often, if needed.

Always check with your veterinarian to see whether a particular wound should remain bandaged. Some wounds heal faster when left uncovered, and any that are draining pus should be left open to the air.

Fractures

You may notice your cat walking on three legs, unable to put any pressure on the fourth leg. If he doesn't hold it up, it may just drag uselessly. Another sign of a fracture might be an unusual angle to the leg.

Fractures to the spinal column will cause an inability for the cat to use his legs if the spinal cord is damaged.

Don't waste time trying to splint or treat fractures yourself. In the case of a compound fracture (breaking through the skin), cover the area with a sterile cloth and get the cat to the veterinarian. Don't attempt to push the bone back under the skin.

Be very careful not to move the cat more than needed for safe transport. Using a box that has been padded with towels will be most comfortable.

The tail is an extension of the spine and is very vulnerable to injury or fracture. Some signs to look for: tail held limp; crook in the tail; obvious sign of wound; cat appears to be in pain; or change in bladder or rectal function. If you notice any of these signs, get to the veterinarian immediately.

Heatstroke

Cats are unable to tolerate high temperatures as well as humans do. Heatstroke can happen in minutes if a cat is left in a parked car. Even leaving the windows cracked won't lower the temperature enough. A car parked in the shade will still turn into an oven in a matter of a few brief minutes. Heatstroke is also a risk for cats confined to carriers in hot weather, restricted to sunny decks, porches, or yards without shade or access to water. Cats confined to rooms without air conditioning or any ventilation during hot weather can also suffer heatstroke. Short-nosed breeds such as Persians are especially vulnerable to heatstroke, as are older, overweight, or asthmatic cats. Overexertion on hot days or fever can also cause heatstroke.

Cats can't perspire the way humans do. They must attempt to cool their body temperature through evaporation by rapid breathing and licking their fur. Heat-affected cats drool a lot and lick their coats to spread the saliva in an attempt to cool themselves. As the temperature of the air increases, the cat's system of cooling through evaporation doesn't function sufficiently enough.

With heatstroke, the cat begins panting. The color of the mucous membranes and the tongue turn bright red. Saliva becomes very thick, the cat starts drooling, and often vomits.

Left unchecked, the cat becomes weak, unsteady, and may have diarrhea. The mucous membranes then become pale or gray and the cat collapses into a coma or may even die.

Treatment: remove the cat to a cooler environment immediately. If his body temperature has reached 106 degrees Fahrenheit, wet the cat down with cool (not cold) water and then place him under a fan—this encourages evaporation, which results in cooling. Don't immerse the cat in cold water, because the skin will begin to cool too quickly. Feeling the cold, the vessels to the skin will constrict and blood flow is directed internally. As a result, the core body temperature won't start to drop as rapidly. Provide cool water for him to drink. Massage his skin and legs to regain normal circulation. Take the cat's rectal temperature every five minutes. Once the temperature goes below 103 degrees Fahrenheit, you can cease wetting him down. Because the cat's system is so unsteady, you want to make sure you don't cool him down too much, risking hypothermia.

Get the cat to the veterinarian as soon as possible to check for any internal complications and to provide additional supportive treatment. Very often, a cat suffering from hyperthermia goes into shock.

Observe your cat for several days afterward because not all complications from heatstroke may be immediately apparent. Hemorrhagic diarrhea (due to cell death) and renal failure can appear hours or even days later.

Hypothermia

Hypothermia can occur when there's a fall in body temperature. This can be caused by exposure to cold, wet, shock, after anesthesia, or illness; newborn kittens are also at risk.

Signs include: a rectal temperature below 100 degrees Fahrenheit, being cold to the touch, shivering, depression, stiffness, dilated pupils, and anxiety. Without treatment, the cat will collapse and go into a coma.

Treatment: Wrap the cat in a blanket or towel and dry him off if he's wet. Don't use a hair dryer to warm the cat because you risk causing burns. Fill a hot water bottle with *warm* water and wrap it in a towel before putting it next to the cat's skin. If you use a heating pad it must be set on *low* and place a towel between the pad and the cat's body. To avoid shock, the rewarming process must be slow. Check the cat's rectal temperature every ten minutes. Continue using the warm water-filled bottle until the cat's temperature reaches 100 degrees Fahrenheit.

Hypothermia predisposes a cat to low blood sugar. When he begins moving around again, give him a little honey to raise his blood sugar level.

Take the cat to the veterinarian for follow-up treatment.

If you're unable to get your cat's temperature back to normal within forty-five minutes, get medical attention.

If hypothermia occurs in a kitten, place him under your clothing and use your own body heat to warm him. Don't place him on a heating pad or attempt to feed him. Get him to the veterinarian for immediate medical attention.

Frostbite

This is caused when a cat is exposed to extreme cold. The ears, tail, and feet are the places most usually affected. As circulation is impaired, tissue damage results. At first, the skin will look pale. As thawing occurs, the skin becomes red, swollen, and hot. Later, peeling sometimes occurs. The skin will also be *extremely painful* if touched, so use caution when handling a cat suffering frostbite.

Treatment: Move the cat to a warm area. Either immerse the area affected in warm (never hot) water or apply warm moist packs until the area appears flushed. **DON'T rub or massage the areas because you risk causing further damage.** Apply an antibiotic ointment and seek immediate veterinary attention.

Oral antibiotics may have to be given to prevent infection and your veterinarian may also prescribe a pain reliever.

Frostbitten areas later become more susceptible to cold.

Prevent frostbite by keeping your cat indoors during very cold weather. If you're feeding outdoor strays, provide access to dry shelter.

Burns

Burns can be a particular hazard for cats should they walk across stoves, get too close to a burner, or get splattered with hot oil or boiling water while being underfoot during meal preparation. The paw pads are the most commonly burned areas due to the cat walking on a hot surface (whether that is a hot stove or hot pavement).

For superficial burns, apply a clean, cold, water-soaked cloth over the area for about thirty minutes to relieve the pain. Then, gently pat the area dry. Clip the hair away from the burn. Make sure the burn stays clean and dry. Watch for signs of blistering. **NEVER use ice** because it will damage the tissues underneath. Don't apply butter or ointments. Take your cat to the veterinarian immediately in case further treatment is needed.

Second-degree burns often cause blistering, swelling, and usually some oozing. The skin will be very red. Apply a clean, cold, water-soaked cloth over the burn. Then very gently pat the area dry. Don't rub. Put sterile gauze lightly over the area, being careful to not touch any blisters. Get to the veterinarian right away.

Third-degree burns are the most serious. Underlying tissues are destroyed. The skin will appear charred or it may even look white. The cat will probably be in shock. Soak a clean cloth in cold water and very gently place it over the burn. Gently put a dry cloth over the wet dressing and get immediate emergency veterinary care. Don't waste time trying to administer any treatment at home. It's crucial that you get to the veterinary clinic immediately.

Chemical Burns

Chemicals that splash on the cat's body or in his eyes can result in serious injury. A cat can even make the situation worse by attempting to remove the chemical from his coat by licking. Fast action on your part is critical to prevent further damage.

For burns to the skin, if you don't know what type of chemical it is, flush the area with clear water. If you have rubber gloves, use them because some chemicals can actually eat through the skin. If you know that the chemical is an *acid* (such as bleach), flush the area with a solution of baking soda and water (one teaspoon baking soda in one pint of water). Wash *alkalis* (such as drain cleaner) with a solution of equal parts vinegar and water. If you're at all in doubt, just use clear water. If you have the container, read the label for additional instructions concerning what to put on the burn, and then get to the veterinary clinic right away.

For chemicals splashed in the eyes, place the cat on his side, hold the eyelids open and flush the eyes with lukewarm water. You can also use saline solution. You may need to wrap the cat in a towel for restraint. If only one eye is affected, tilt the cat's head back and rinse *away* from the unaffected eye. Use sterile gauze over the eyes and rush to the veterinarian.

Electric Shock and Electrical Burns

Shocks are usually caused by chewing on electrical cords, contact with downed power lines, or by lightning.

Never touch a cat if he's in contact with an exposed wire. Involuntary muscle contractions may prevent him from releasing his grip on the wire. Turn the current off at the control panel, and then use a wooden broomstick or yardstick to push the cat away from the wire. The cat may be unconscious or in shock. If he isn't breathing, administer artificial respiration. If the cat is in shock, keep him warm. Get to the veterinarian immediately.

Electric shock can cause cardiac arrest. It can also cause pulmonary edema, which is a buildup of fluid in the lungs. Signs of pulmonary edema include: breathing difficulty, open mouth breathing, and preferring to sit or stand instead of lying down. Emergency medical care is needed. Even if your cat appears to have recovered, he needs to be checked by the veterinarian. Pulmonary edema doesn't happen right away.

You may not actually catch your cat chewing on an electrical cord but you might notice signs of electrical burns. The usual places are the corners of the mouth and on the tongue. Any inflammation in these areas, redness, blistering, or gray appearance are strong indications of electrical burns. If you notice any of these signs, seek immediate medical attention. Also, check the cords in your home to locate the one that has been damaged.

Refer to Chapter 3 for information on prevention of electrical burns.

Poisoning

Many products we use every day are poisonous to cats. Very often, these products are easily within a cat's reach. For example, have you left cleaning agents out on the counter? What about pill bottles? Remember that antifreeze leak in the driveway? Do you know which plants are toxic to your cat? Are containers of kerosene, paint, pesticides, etc., safely sealed without drips running down the sides? Even if a cat doesn't intend to ingest a substance, he'll use his tongue to clean it off his fur. So even though cats may be less at risk than dogs for ingesting poisons due to the fact that they don't typically gulp food, being fastidious groomers still puts them in danger. If the substance is toxic, it will only take a small amount to poison him.

Outdoor cats are more at risk than indoor cats. They're in danger of coming in contact with chemicals and solvents improperly stored in garages, fertilizers, pesticides, sidewalk salt, gasoline, intentional poisoning, and antifreeze to name just a few. Antifreeze, for instance, is so toxic that less than a teaspoon can be fatal.

All too often we unintentionally poison our cats by using too many products or inappropriate products on them. In an effort to kill fleas we sometimes overdo it by using too many preparations at once or we don't read caution labels. We also give medicines (such as aspirin) without knowing the dangerous and deadly side effects.

Signs of poisoning: Depending upon the poison, signs can range from anxiety and convulsions to depression and coma. You may notice excessive drooling, weakness, a strange odor on the breath or on the body, vomiting, breathing difficulty, or bright red color to the mouth (sign of carbon monoxide poisoning).

Cats are in danger of ingesting rodent poisons or the poisoned rodents themselves. Many rodent poisons are anticoagulants, which can cause hemorrhaging. Signs may include: blood in vomit and stool, pale mucous membranes, nosebleeds, skin bruising. When you bring your cat to the veterinarian, if possible, bring a sample of the bloody stool or vomitus.

If you suspect that your cat has been poisoned, try to identify the substance. Read the label for instructions or locate chewed leaves on plants. For help, call your local poison control center. There is also the ASPCA Animal Poison Control Center, which is available twenty-four hours a day, seven days a week. See Resource Guide.

Chemical Poisoning

For first aid, whether to induce vomiting depends on the type of poison ingested. An acid or alkali poison such as drain cleaners and solvents will cause more damage, burning the esophagus, throat, and mouth as it comes back up. If the cat vomits kerosene back up, it will cause additional burns. Check with your veterinarian and poison control center, but here are the general guidelines for first aid:

- For *acids*: give a dose of Milk of Magnesia (one teaspoon per five pounds of cat's body weight)

- For *alkalis*: mix equal parts water and vinegar and give up to four teaspoons

Once the acid, alkali, or kerosene poison is in the cat's stomach, your only course of action is to dilute it to reduce the amount of damage. Milk of Magnesia, Kaopectate, or regular milk given orally (by syringe) will help coat the intestines.

For *noncorrosive* poisoning (antifreeze, perfume, pills), you can induce vomiting. You need to do it before the substance gets into the cat's system. Don't attempt this if the cat is convulsing or is unconscious.

If you don't know what kind of poison was ingested or no antidote is indicated, diluting the poison is the safest route. You can purchase activated charcoal as a liquid. There is also a paste form available that comes in a tube. Follow dosing instructions on the label. Activated charcoal helps to prevent absorption of the poison. Don't confuse activated charcoal with the charcoal used for grilling—they're not the same. Activated charcoal is purchased at a pharmacy. Don't give activated charcoal if you've given syrup of ipecac, because they neutralize each other. Even if your cat has vomited, don't give the activated charcoal if you've already given syrup of ipecac.

You can also use Milk of Magnesia or Kaopectate (one teaspoon per five pounds of body weight) to coat the intestines and dilute the poison. If you don't have either of those products just use regular milk. You can feed the cat as much milk as needed but do it gradually.

How to Induce Vomiting

Give ½–1 teaspoon syrup of ipecac (dose is about 1 teaspoon per 10 pounds of body weight). Repeat only once after twenty minutes if cat hasn't vomited. An alternative to syrup of ipecac is to administer 1 teaspoon of hydrogen peroxide. This can be repeated in ten minutes if the cat hasn't vomited, but don't exceed 3 teaspoons.

NO MATTER WHAT KIND OF POISON, GET IMMEDIATE VETERINARY CARE. Bring the bottle of poison with you. If the cat has vomited, bring a sample of the vomitus. During transport to the hospital, keep

SOME POISONOUS HOUSEHOLD SUBSTANCES

acetaminophen	insecticides
antifreeze	kerosene
aspirin	laxatives
bath oil	mothballs
bleach	nail polish
brake fluid	nail polish remover
cosmetics	paint
deodorant	paint remover
detergents	perfume
disinfectant cleansers	plants
drain cleaner	prescription meds
fertilizer	rodenticides
floor polish	shampoo
furniture polish	shaving lotion
gasoline	shoe polish
hair coloring	suntan lotion
ibuprofen	turpentine
weed killer	

the cat warm, watch for signs of shock, and keep his head lower than his body to allow drainage of fluids or vomitus.

Poisons Absorbed Through the Skin

Organophosphate flea or fly spray can be absorbed through the skin and cause metabolic disease in addition to external burning. See section on chemical burns.

Poisoning from Plants

An indoor cat with not a lot to do to keep himself occupied may nibble on houseplants. Some cats just do occasional munching, while others leave nothing but mangled stems sticking out of the soil. Depending on the plant, even a few nibbles can be very toxic. Some, like the *dieffenbachia* (also known as dumb cane), cause intense burning and swelling of the mouth and throat, creating difficulty in breathing. Some plants, including the dieffenbachia, will cause burning and further damage again if you attempt to induce vomiting.

For a list of poisonous plants go to the ASPCA Web site. They also have a Poison Control Hotline. See Resource Guide.

Signs of plant poisoning: Depending on the type of plant ingested, there may be excessive salivation, vomiting, bloody diarrhea, breathing difficulty, fever, abdominal pain, depression, collapse, trembling, irregular heartbeat, mouth and throat ulcers. Things can quickly deteriorate leading to convulsions, coma, cardiac arrest, and death.

Treatment for plant poisoning depends on the type of plant ingested. If you can identify the plant, contact your veterinarian and local poison control center for instructions. If you're instructed to induce vomiting, refer to the previous section on chemical poisoning.

Administering milk will coat and soothe the intestines and will also dilute poisons. If you haven't given syrup of ipecac to induce vomiting, you can give activated charcoal (follow dosing instructions on the label). Don't administer activated charcoal if you have already administered syrup of ipecac because they inactivate each other.

Get the cat to the veterinarian immediately. Keep him warm and watch for signs of shock.

Falls from Windows

If your cat ever falls from a window, however low to the ground it is, get him to the veterinarian for an examination. Even if you don't see any visible signs of injury, he may have sustained internal damage.

Preventing falls: Check all screens to be sure they're secure and not in need of repair. Don't trust a cat with a partially opened, unscreened window, no matter how slight the opening or how big the cat. Don't allow cats out on balconies, even if there are railings. Just because your cat hasn't jumped on top of the railing yet, doesn't mean he won't.

Insect Stings

Cats, with their fascination for anything that moves, can easily end up on the receiving end of a bee sting. Bees, wasps, hornets, and yellow jackets can inflict a painful sting. Stings to the face or mouth can cause dangerous swelling as air passageways may become blocked. Swelling around the throat can result in suffocation.

Aside from the pain and dangerous swelling, some cats, like humans, can have an allergic reaction to insect stings. If swelling persists or the cat shows any signs of breathing difficulty, drooling, seizures or vomiting, seek emergency medical care.

Treatment: Remove the stinger with tweezers. Apply a thin paste of baking soda mixed with water to relieve itching. Use ice packs or a cold compress to reduce swelling and relieve pain. If you use an ice pack, wrap a small towel around it before placing it next to the cat's skin. Observe the cat for signs of shock. Ask your veterinarian about the use of a cortisone cream to relieve itching if the cat is very bothered by it.

For a sting inside of the mouth, seek immediate medical attention so the veterinarian can observe your cat for breathing difficulty.

If your cat is prone to being stung, keep Benadryl on hand—or better yet, keep your cat indoors.

Ticks

See Chapter 13.

Spiders

Brown recluse, tarantulas, and black widow spiders are severely dangerous. The site of the bite may be extremely painful. The cat may develop a fever, have difficulty breathing, and go into shock. Some spider bites will lead to necrosis or abscesses without having acute signs. Get immediate emergency care. If you actually see your cat get bitten, take him right to the veterinarian.

Drowning

Although a cat is able to swim a short distance, drowning often occurs when he's unable to climb up and out of the water. For instance, cats drown in swimming pools because they can't reach the ledge. If you have a pool and there's a possibility that your pets may get near it, install some kind of a ramp so an animal who accidentally falls in will be able to safely climb out.

First aid for drowning involves: getting water out of the cat's lungs. Hold the cat upside down by the hips and gently swing his body for about ten to twenty seconds or until no more water comes out. Lay the cat on his right side and begin administering mouth-to-nose resuscitation. If the heart has stopped, perform CPR.

When the cat is breathing on his own, take him immediately to the veterinarian for medical care. He may be in shock, so keep him warm.

If the cat was in cold water, wrap him in a blanket and turn the heater up in your car as you transport him to the veterinarian.

Dehydration

Dehydration is the loss of body fluids and often the loss of electrolytes (minerals). Causes of dehydration include: illness, fever, prolonged diarrhea, and prolonged vomiting.

You can test for dehydration by gently pulling up on the skin of the upper back. It should snap right back. If the skin falls back into position slowly or stays up in a peak then the cat is dehydrated. The gums are also another indicator of dehydration. Normally wet, gums will look dry and feel tacky when a cat is dehydrated.

Treatment: Prompt veterinary care is needed. IV fluid therapy will be administered to replenish fluids and restore electrolyte balance.

Disaster Preparedness

I live in Tennessee and we face the risk of tornadoes on a fairly regular basis. In fact, a few years ago we actually had a tornado touch down in our neighborhood. Fortunately, the fact that my cats are trained to go into their carriers on cue made preparing for this emergency much easier. Our area also faced a major flood in 2010 and we were ready in case we had to evacuate because our family had a disaster preparedness plan.

Your individual disaster plan should be customized based on the area in which you live and the type of potential disaster risks. View the following information as a general guideline to start you on the road to preparedness.

Your first-aid kit should be handy. Be sure to restock out-of-date supplies.

Here's a list of supplies for your evacuation kit:

- first-aid kit as well as any current medication
- two-week supply of food and water
- hand-held manual can opener and a spoon
- small or disposable litter box, litter, and scoop

- small plastic bags for litter disposal

- trash bags

- brush and comb (to remove debris and also to avoid mats)

- hand sanitizer

- paper towels

- carrier

- emergency cash

- flashlight with extra batteries

- battery-operated radio

- your cat's up-to-date medical records and a current photo of your cat

- blanket and/or bedding

Keep supplies handy so in an evacuation situation everything is convenient to grab. You may have to customize or streamline your kit, depending on your storage limitations, but what's important is to have a plan and basic kit.

Microchip your cat and have an ID tag as well, because during a crisis cats can easily get separated from their owners.

Don't let the gas tank in your car get too low; if you have to evacuate in a hurry, you won't lose precious time having to fill up the tank. In some crisis situations there may be long lines at gas stations.

If you have an outdoor cat, bring him in at the first sign of potential trouble or if severe weather is in the forecast.

In hurricane risk areas, arrange in advance for friends or relatives who are more inland to take you and your cats in.

Don't leave your cat behind when evacuating your home. This is very important because the odds are great that if left behind, your cat could be killed or lost. The cat is at high risk of severe injury or death due to collapsing structures, flooding, fire, and electrical shock. A terrified cat can also be impossible for rescuers to find. Your cat's only chance for safety and survival is if you take him with you or make arrangements ahead of time for him to stay somewhere else. Keep a list of veterinarians in areas outside of the danger zones so you can either keep your cat there, or get him medical attention if needed during or after the disaster. Keep a list of pet-friendly hotels as well. If you can't return to your home after the disaster because it's unsafe or needs extensive repair, your cat may be able to stay at pet-friendly hotels, the veterinary hospital, a boarding facility, or with a friend/relative in an area unaffected by the disaster. The key is to be prepared and have this list of possibilities in advance. Red Cross shelters DO NOT accept pets.

Disasters don't always happen when you're home to care for your cat. Work out a mutual plan with a neighbor so your cat will be taken just in case you aren't able to get home in time. Exchange house keys and work out a disaster plan with a trusted pet-owning neighbor so you can help each other's pets in a crisis.

Place a sticker on your door or window to alert rescuers or firefighters that there are pets inside. These stickers are available through pet retailers and the ASPCA.

For more information on disaster preparation, refer to the Resource Guide.

Medical Appendix

Listed in this Appendix are some of the disorders cats may acquire. Some are very common and others are rare, but being an alert, informed owner can make a big difference in how quickly symptoms get noticed and diagnosed and how fast a cat's pain and suffering will be relieved. The problem could be minor or it could be life-threatening. Your familiarity with your cat and how he normally looks, acts, feels, or sounds enables you to suspect trouble when he just "isn't his usual self." Cats' lives have been saved because of hunches like this.

The purpose of this book is neither to be a complete medical reference nor is it meant to replace the personalized care of your veterinarian. If you'd like to read in more detail about all the disorders that can affect cats, I urge you to add a veterinary medical reference book to your home library.

INTERNAL AND EXTERNAL DISORDERS

INTERNAL PARASITES

Tapeworms
These worms live in the intestines and are probably the most common of the internal parasites in adult cats.

Tapeworms require an intermediate host during the larval stage before transmission to the cat. Fleas are common tapeworm hosts and based on the cat's fastidious grooming behavior, it's very likely that at least one flea that is harboring immature tapeworms will be ingested.

Cats can also acquire tapeworms by eating raw meat or raw freshwater fish. Outdoor cats who routinely hunt can also be exposed through their prey.

The tapeworm attaches itself to the intestinal wall by way of suckers and hooks on the head. The body is comprised of segments, each one containing eggs. These segments break off and pass out of the body in the cat's feces. The segments, which are about a ¼" in length, can wriggle by themselves when freshly separated from the worm. You may notice one or two moving segments clinging to the hair around your cat's anus. As the segments dry, they resemble grains of rice. You may also find these tapeworm segments on your cat's bedding.

The cat may also drag his hindquarters along the carpet or lick his anus frequently due to the itching.

If you notice tapeworm segments, the veterinarian will administer deworming medication specifically for tapeworms, either in oral or injectable form.

If there are tapeworms *in* your cat, most likely there are also fleas *on* your cat. Combine the deworming with a comprehensive flea control program to avoid a reappearance of the parasite. Even if you don't see little tapeworm segments on the cat or in the environment, if he has a significant flea problem, there's a chance that he also has tapeworms.

Roundworms

A common worm found in kittens and puppies. Roundworm larvae are transmitted to nursing kittens by way of the mother's milk. Kittens with roundworms develop a characteristic pot belly appearance while the rest of the body remains thin.

Cats acquire roundworms by coming in contact with egg-contaminated soil, water, feces, or vomit. Roundworm eggs are very hard and can withstand unfriendly conditions in the soil for a long time, until an unsuspecting host comes along.

Roundworms, which grow from four to five inches long, live in the cat's stomach and intestine. You may notice a roundworm in the cat's feces or in vomitus. Roundworms resemble spaghetti (not a pleasant comparison, I know, but it's unfortunately accurate). Symptoms include weight loss, diarrhea, vomiting, pot belly, lethargy, and coughing (coughing occurs when the worms have reached the cat's lungs).

Treatment: deworming medication is given to kill mature worms and larvae. Your veterinarian will also recommend a follow-up visit so the cat's feces can be rechecked to ensure all worms and larvae have been completely killed.

Roundworms are rare in adult cats.

If you've adopted a stray cat, in addition to having him tested for diseases and vaccinated, he should also be checked for worms.

Hookworms

These thin worms attach to the intestinal wall to feed. Hookworms are relatively small, ranging in length from ¼–½".

Transmission occurs through contact with feces or soil containing the larvae. Hookworms are shed through feces and end up contaminating soil or litter. They can then enter another cat's body through the paws as the animal steps on the contaminated soil or litter. Transmission to kittens can occur through nursing contaminated milk from the mother. For kittens, hookworms can be potentially fatal. Transmission doesn't occur in utero. Signs of hookworm can include: diarrhea, constipation, weight loss, weakness, pale nostrils, and pale lips. Hookworm infection can lead to anemia with continual loss of blood from the intestine.

Heartworm

Heartworm is a disease more commonly associated with dogs. Even though it's not as common in cats, it's important to keep your cat protected. Heartworm prevention in cats hasn't received the attention and awareness needed to alert owners to the danger.

Heartworm is spread by mosquitoes carrying the larvae. Once the mosquito bites the cat, it injects the larvae from its saliva. When the larvae mature into worms, they move through the circulatory system and eventually travel to the heart or lungs. Because of a cat's small size, the presence of just a few worms is considered a heavy infection and therefore life-threatening.

Signs of heartworm can include: vomiting and coughing. As the disease progresses, it leads to breathing difficulty. Diagnosis is confirmed through blood tests, urinalysis, X-ray, and ECG. It can be easily misdiagnosed as asthma during a routine exam.

Prevention is the key since there is no medication to kill adult heartworms (usually surgery is the only option).

There are heartworm preventatives that can be administered. Discuss these options with your veterinarian. If your cat goes outdoors and you live in a high-risk area, which is any climate where a mosquito might fly by, it's a good idea to protect your cat. Cats living in warm climates may need to remain on a heartworm preventative year-round. In colder climates the preventative should be given just before the start of mosquito season and continue until the season is well over. Your veterinarian will advise you on whether your cat should remain on a preventative year-round.

Treatment for a heartworm-positive cat is decided on a case-by-case basis. Prednisone may be given. In acute cases, a cat in shock will need to be stabilized using oxygen, IV fluids, bronchodilators, and IV steroids.

Toxoplasmosis

Toxoplasmosis can cause birth defects in humans by infecting the fetus, and as such should be a concern for pregnant women. If you're pregnant or suspect that you

TIPS FOR PREVENTING TOXOPLASMOSIS

- Take care of any fly problems, because they can carry egg spores from infected feces and contaminate food.

- Don't eat raw or undercooked meat.

- Don't use the same cutting board to cut vegetables that you also use to prepare raw meat.

- Bleach cutting boards and clean all work surfaces with disinfectants.

- Wash your hands *often*! Wash them immediately after handling raw meat, cleaning the litter box, or gardening. Instruct children on hand-washing importance.

- Immediately remove feces from litter box. Sift the litter at least twice a day and completely change the litter and disinfect the box once a week (for more on litter box cleaning, refer to Chapter 8).

- Keep your backyard sandbox covered and don't allow children to play in public sandboxes or in any friend's sandboxes that are left exposed. Stray cats may have used them for defecation.

- Wash homegrown vegetables because outdoor cats may have used the soil in the garden.

- Pregnant women and those with suppressed immune systems shouldn't do litter box duties; if it is unavoidable, disposable gloves and a face mask should be worn.

- Wear gloves whenever you do any outside work.

- Keep your cat indoors because he can easily become infected from other cats as well as from digging in contaminated soil.

might be, another family member should take over litter box responsibilities. Refer to Chapter 8 for specific instructions.

Caused by the protozoan parasite *toxoplasma gondii*, toxoplasmosis is acquired by cats ingesting infected prey or coming in contact with contaminated soil. For cats, contaminated soil is dangerous because of their fastidious grooming habits. Paws that touch the soil eventually get licked by the cat's tongue.

People are at risk of acquiring toxoplasmosis by eating raw or undercooked meat that contains the parasite. People who use the same cutting board to prepare raw meat and raw vegetables are putting themselves at great risk.

Cats can carry the parasite and remain asymptomatic. If symptoms are present they may include: fever, poor appetite, vomiting, weight loss, cough, lethargy, diarrhea, enlarged lymph nodes, and irregular breathing. Asymptomatic cats can still shed the disease through their feces.

Tests can indicate whether your cat has been exposed to the parasite. The presence of oocysts (egg spores) in the feces means that the cat is shedding infective organisms.

Note: It takes forty-eight hours for the oocysts to become infective once the cat has defecated. Promptly removing stools from the litter box will greatly reduce the risk of infection. If you're pregnant and must handle litter box duties yourself, invest in a box of disposable gloves and be certain to wash your hands immediately afterward. You should also wear gardening gloves whenever working outdoors.

If you test your cat and find that he hasn't been exposed to the organism and also hasn't built up an immunity, keep him indoors for the duration of your pregnancy (and hopefully, thereafter as well). That way, everybody stays safe.

Treatment involves antibiotic therapy. In some cases the cat may need to be hospitalized and receive IV fluid therapy.

Coccidia

A highly contagious intestinal parasite that mostly affects kittens, coccidia can attack adult cats as well. Transmission occurs through contact with contaminated feces. Signs of infection include: weight loss, dehydration, vomiting, and mucous-coated diarrhea. The diarrhea often contains blood as the infection progresses. If untreated, the cat develops a fever and is at high risk of dehydration.

Stressful situations such as malnutrition, overcrowding, and unsanitary conditions can cause a lowered resistance to coccidiosis. Cats can be reinfected by coming into contact with their own feces, so keeping the litter box very clean is important. Diagnosis is based on microscopic examination of a stool sample.

Treatment involves the use of sulfa-based drugs. Controlling the diarrhea as well as coccidiosis is important to prevent dangerous dehydration. Treatment is usually as an outpatient but if the cat is very dehydrated or weak he may need to be hospitalized. A follow-up fecal exam is needed after treatment to ensure the parasite has been eliminated.

SIGNS OF SKIN AND COAT PROBLEMS

- scratching
- crusts and scabs
- mats
- hair loss
- broken-off hairs
- inflammation
- odor to the skin
- pimples or pustules
- rash

- excessive shedding
- appearance of black or white specks in the fur
- appearance of anything that looks like insects
- lumps
- lesions
- change in skin color
- dandruff

Giardia

This is a protozoan parasite that lives in the cat's small intestine. The cyst stage of giardia gets carried out of the body in the cat's feces, making it infective to any animal that comes in contact with the stool. Beside oral contact with infected feces, giardia can be transmitted by ingestion of contaminated water.

A cat may not show active symptoms of giardiasis but can still shed infective organisms. Signs of giardiasis include: diarrhea that is often yellow in color.

Diagnosis is made by microscopic examination of a stool sample and treatment includes antibiotics.

SKIN DISORDERS

A cat's skin is very sensitive and can be more prone to allergic reactions and injury than ours. Skin problems can show up at any stage in life, and often a condition stays hidden from the owner until a loss of hair or overgrooming by the cat is observed. Disorders can range from parasitism, allergies, stress, nutritional imbalances, bacterial infection, injury, burns, exposure to chemicals or temperature extremes, tumors, and the list goes on.

Regular grooming, control of parasites such as fleas, routine checking by the owners, and prompt veterinary treatment when needed will help keep the largest organ of your cat's body in good shape.

EXTERNAL PARASITES

Fleas and Ticks

These common little pests earned a chapter all their own. Refer to Chapter 13.

Lice

Lice are rarely found on cats. When infestation does occur, it's usually seen in malnourished, debilitated cats living in unsanitary conditions.

Lice appear as pale-colored wingless insects. Their eggs, called *nits*, become attached to hairs. The nits look similar to dandruff, only they aren't easily brushed away. Nits resemble white sand.

Mats on the cat's coat should be clipped away because lice are commonly found beneath them. They can also be found around the ears, head, neck, and genitals.

Treatment includes bathing the cat, followed by an insecticidal dip used for fleas. *Note*: Because a louse-infected cat is probably very debilitated, extreme caution must be used when deciding an appropriate treatment. Consult your veterinarian before treating an infested cat.

Treatment for the environment consists of vacuuming, washing all pet bedding, and thoroughly cleaning all areas where the cat has been.

Maggots and Flies

Botflies lay their eggs in grass where the hatched maggots end up on the animal's fur. They work their way into an orifice and then travel through the cat to end up under the skin.

Symptoms include nodules under the skin (with tiny breathing holes for the maggots), and also may include eye lesions (due to larvae actually in the eye), coughing, fever, difficulty breathing, blindness, and dizziness.

Treatment by your veterinarian involves prescribing a parasite-killing medication, clipping the soiled hair, and if a nodule is present (called a warble), the veterinarian will remove the maggot and cleanse the infected area.

Adult flies lay their eggs near rodent or rabbit burrows. Cats who come in contact with the infested grasses are then at risk of becoming unexpected hosts. Kittens can become infected by coming in contact with the mother's fur.

Prevention: stay on top of parasite control by administering the monthly heartworm, flea, and tick preventatives.

Mites

Resembling spiders, but microscopic in size, mites live on the skin of the cat. The mange caused by the various types of mites can range from patches of hair loss to sores that develop secondary infections.

Demodectic Mange

This form of mange is more commonly found in dogs. The *demodex* mite usually resides on the animal's skin and causes a localized dermatitis. You may notice areas of hair loss and pus-filled lesions on the skin, generally around the head, on the eyelids, ear, or on the neck.

There is also a generalized form of demodicosis that causes lesions, thinning hair, or actual hair loss over much of the body. Cats suffering from generalized demodicosis often have a suppressed immune system due to a separate underlying medical condition such as feline leukemia, diabetes mellitus, or chronic respiratory infection.

Diagnosis is made by taking skin scrapings for identification under a microscope. The treatment for localized demodicosis involves the application of a topical agent. Your veterinarian may also recommend the use of an antibacterial shampoo.

Generalized demodicosis may be treated by the veterinarian with repeated baths in prescription shampoo and the application of mite-killing dips, but the most important treatment involves identifying and treating any underlying medical condition.

Treatment continues for about three weeks after the last skin scraping shows up negative.

Cheyletiella Mange (Walking Dandruff)

The *cheyletiella* mite causes a large amount of scaly buildup on the skin that resembles dandruff. Other symptoms include: hair loss, frequent grooming, frequent scratching, and skin lesions.

Cheyletiellosis is not common in cats, but is very contagious and can be transmitted to humans.

Diagnosis is confirmed through physical examination and skin scrapings. Due to ingestion of the parasite during grooming, microscopic evaluation of a fecal sample may also be done.

Treatment by your veterinarian includes repeated applications of an insecticidal lime sulfur rinse. Oral medication may also be prescribed. Treatment continues for two weeks after the cat is considered cured.

The environment and other animals in the home must also be treated. The cat's bed, combs, brushes, etc., must be disinfected.

Ear Mites

A common problem in cats, ear mites are covered in this chapter under "Ear Disorders."

Skin Allergies

An allergic reaction, also called a *hypersensitivity*, can be a result of exposure to certain substances through the lungs (such as dust or pollen). There are also food allergies that result from eating a particular food that causes a hypersensitive reaction in the digestive tract. Substances absorbed through the skin can cause allergic reactions (such as flea shampoos or sprays). Insect bites and stings can also cause hypersensitivity. Certain medicines and even vaccines can result in an allergic reaction.

Cats tend to have more skin and intestinal tract allergies than humans. We have more difficulty with allergies affecting our air passages.

Flea-Bite Hypersensitivity

This is the most common hypersensitivity in cats. It may only take one flea to cause a reaction resulting in severe itching, patchy hair loss, raw skin, and even infection. Cats who experience flea-bite hypersensitivity are allergic to an allergen in the flea's saliva. When a flea bites the cat, a small amount of saliva is introduced under the skin.

In severe cases, the cat may need antibiotics to treat infection. In some cases, oral or injectable cortisone is used to relieve the itching reaction to allow the sores time to heal. Antihistamines may also be given.

For cats with flea allergy dermatitis, the topical flea-control products are extremely helpful, because many of the fleas won't even get the chance to bite the cat.

The most effective treatment is diligent maintenance of your cat's environment to eliminate fleas, along with keeping up with appropriate flea control on all cats and dogs in your family.

Contact Hypersensitivity

The result of coming in direct contact with a substance or chemical, contact hypersensitivity can even be caused by the use of a plastic food bowl. The areas on the cat most likely to be affected are where hair is the thinnest, such as the abdomen, ears, nose, chin, and paw pads.

Symptoms include hair loss, inflamed skin, itchiness, and small bumps.

Flea-control products (such as shampoos, sprays, or powders) can cause all-over allergic skin reactions. Reactions to the insecticide in flea collars can affect the skin around the neck.

Treatment involves identification of allergen and avoidance of further exposure, if possible. Bathing is important if the allergen is still present. Oral or topical corticosteroids may be prescribed to relieve itching but limited or nonexposure to the allergen is the best therapy.

Inhalant Allergy

This is caused by inhalation of allergens such as house dust, pollen, animal dander, and mold spores. Depending on the allergen, reactions may or may not occur seasonally and can vary in symptoms.

Signs can include dermatitis, itching around the face and neck, and itchy lesions on the head that cause hair loss.

Diagnosis is made through intradermal skin testing.

The best treatment is, of course, elimination of the allergen. Antihistamines or corticosteroids may be administered. Your veterinarian will want to recheck your cat every few weeks to evaluate the effectiveness of prescribed treatment.

Food Hypersensitivity

A cat can become allergic to certain foods despite the fact that he may have eaten that particular food for years. Common food allergens include beef, pork, dairy, fish, wheat, and corn.

Symptoms can include: an itchy rash around the head, hair loss, and possible skin sores due to scratching. Common food allergic reactions include gastrointestinal problems such as vomiting, diarrhea, audible stomach sounds, and excessive gas.

Your veterinarian will do a thorough exam in order to rule out nonfood related causes.

Treatment consists of long-term hypoallergenic dietary management. This will also mean that treats containing possible allergens will have to be eliminated from the diet as well.

FUNGAL INFECTIONS

Ringworm

Despite the name, ringworm is not a worm but a fungal disease. One of the most common skin problems of cats, ringworm invades the hair follicle. The name ringworm comes from the appearance of the skin lesion. A red ring outlines a circular patch of scaly skin and broken-off hairs. Very often on cats, the lesions will appear as crusty skin with patchy hair loss that resembles stubble. Ringworm can be found anywhere on the body but is seen most frequently on the ears, face, and tail.

Transmission occurs by contact with the organism in soil or through contact with another infected animal. It can also be transmitted by contact with the infected hairs of an animal, for example, the hairs on a pet's bedding. Sources of transmission can be a boarding kennel, grooming facility, or anywhere a contaminated animal may have been. Ringworm is highly contagious and can be transmitted to humans. Spores can survive in the environment for over a year. Most adult cats with a healthy immune system will have some degree of resistance to ringworm. Young cats or those with suppressed immune systems are most at risk.

Diagnosis of ringworm is done via a fungal culture and microscopic examination of hair.

Treatment involves antifungal medication.

Treating the environment is essential to stop the spread of ringworm. Discard pet bedding or wash in bleach, and disinfect all grooming supplies and plastic carriers. A thorough vacuuming of the home should be done right away and repeated twice weekly to remove infected pet hairs. Thoroughly clean all areas that the cat frequents and use diluted bleach to clean the litter box, countertops, and nonwood floors.

BACTERIAL INFECTIONS

Abscesses

An abscess is a localized pus-filled pocket of infection in the skin. Unfortunately, abscesses are common occurrences in the cat world due to the bites and scratches resulting from fights. If you have an outdoor cat (especially a male), there's an excellent chance that at some point he'll develop an abscess. Actually, you'll be lucky if he develops only one in his life. Realistically, you'll probably be making numerous trips to the veterinarian for treatment of several abscesses over the course of your outdoor cat's lifetime.

The inside of a cat's mouth is a breeding ground for all kinds of ugly bacteria. What happens is that a puncture wound caused by sharp teeth or claws quickly seals over on the surface, trapping the bacteria beneath. All too often, your outdoor cat will come home and you won't even know that he has been in a fight because the puncture wound is small and disguised by fur. What's happening under his skin, though, is that his immune system is working to fend off the bacteria. It isn't until you notice a painful lump on your cat or the skin feels hot that you become aware of a problem. You may even see your cat limping. Sometimes the abscess ruptures and drains a white or reddish pus accompanied by an odor.

Abscesses can occur anywhere on the body, but they're most often located around the face, neck, legs, and the base of the tail. The face, neck, and legs are prime targets for an opponent during a fight. The base of the tail may get tagged by the attacker's claw or tooth as the victim attempts retreat.

For abscesses that haven't drained, in addition to giving antibiotics, the veterinarian will lance it to allow the pus to escape. Some abscesses require surgery so a drain can be inserted. The drain allows the pus to drip out. The wound is also periodically flushed with an antiseptic solution to keep it open and clean. The goal is to have the wound heal from the inside out so the same problem doesn't recur with skin sealing in the bacteria. The drain is later removed by the doctor (although in some cases, an impatient cat does it for himself).

Neutering your cat isn't a guarantee that he won't get in any more fights, but there's an excellent chance that the frequency will be lessened. Neutering reduces his inclination to roam, thus limiting his exposure to other male cats.

If you notice any puncture wounds, feel a lump, or sense a hot area on the skin get medical care immediately. The sooner a cat-fight wound is treated, the better. It could save your cat a tremendous amount of pain and avoid a lengthy recovery time.

If you have an outdoor cat whom you suspect comes in contact with other cats or who is known for fighting, check him over every day to be sure there are no wounds. Even though cats are notorious groomers, if you see your cat licking one particular area repeatedly, it could be that he's nursing a fight wound. Another sign might be when your normally affectionate cat suddenly cries or becomes agitated when you touch a certain part of his body.

Feline Acne

A fairly common skin condition, acne appears as tiny blackheads, crusts, or pimples on the chin after hair follicles become clogged. In more severe cases, the pimples drain pus, and the chin and bottom lip become swollen. The cause of acne is believed to be lack of grooming to the chin so dirt and oil accumulate. Cats who eat from plastic bowls may also be more prone to this condition due to the fact that plastic is more difficult to keep as clean as ceramic, glass, or stainless steel. Sleeping on the hard ground may also contribute to the development of acne.

Mild feline acne, where there are just blackheads, can be treated by gentle cleansing with a warm washcloth and a little medicated shampoo. Scrubbing can worsen the condition, so care must be taken to not clean too vigorously. Antibiotics may also be prescribed.

Some cats get recurring acne, so a routine cleansing schedule will need to be followed.

Stud Tail

Caused by overproduction of sebaceous glands in the tail, this condition is seen mostly in intact males.

With this disorder, the tail appears dirty and greasy. There is also an accompanying odor. As you look closely you'll see the skin near the base of the tail covered in brown waxy debris. Dirt and dust are easily attracted to the oily part of the tail. In more serious cases, the hair follicles get inflamed and the condition becomes painful to the cat.

Treatment for stud tail involves washing the tail in a medically prescribed shampoo on a regular basis. Antibiotics or even surgery may be required if there's inflammation. Neutering the intact cat is also recommended.

Folliculitis

This inflammation of the hair follicles can occur on its own or be the result of another condition, such as feline acne or flea-bite hypersensitivity.

A deeper and more severe condition involving the hair follicles is called *furunculosis*.

Veterinary treatment includes cleansing and then administering topical and oral antibiotics.

Impetigo

Occurring in newborn kittens, impetico results in pustules and crusts developing on the skin. It's believed to be caused by the mother's mouth as she repeatedly moves her kittens.

Antibiotic treatment is administered for about a week.

Alopecia

Alopecia means baldness and can be complete or partial. There are many causes of alopecia.

Excessive grooming due to a behavior problem can cause baldness. This condition

SIGNS OF RESPIRATORY PROBLEMS

- coughing
- sneezing
- wheezing
- noisy or moist-sounding breathing
- labored breathing
- rapid breathing
- shallow breathing
- open-mouth breathing
- panting
- discharge from eyes and/or nose

- excessive meowing or crying
- loss of voice
- pale or bluish mucous membranes
- hunched posture
- head held in an extended position
- retching
- fever
- rapid pulse
- loss of appetite

is known as *psychogenic alopecia* and is a displacement activity that causes a stressed cat to overgroom.

Alopecia can also result from a hypersensitivity reaction (for instance, fleas or other parasites), infections, or nutritional deficiencies.

Feline symmetrical alopecia (named for its symmetrical pattern on each side of the body) is usually seen on the abdomen, flank, and thighs. Causes of feline symmetrical alopecia can be food sensitivity, parasites, fungal infection, and bacterial infection. Another very common cause is hyperthyroidism. One of the first signs of an overactive thyroid gland is symmetrical hair loss on the cat.

Diagnosis will be based on varying tests to rule out allergies, infection, parasites, thyroid problems, etc. The veterinarian will also closely examine the hair to determine if the hair loss is due to overgrooming (hairs will be broken off). The physical exam and tests will also rule out parasites.

Treatment of alopecia is based on the underlying cause. Cats with psychogenic alopecia usually respond well to behavioral therapy in conjunction with antianxiety medication.

RODENT ULCER

This is not a condition caused by rodents. The rodent ulcer lesions can develop in cats of all ages. They're found most often on the upper lip but occasionally are seen on the lower lip as well. The lesions appear as thick ulcerated areas that don't necessarily cause itching or pain.

Rodent ulcer lesions can potentially be precancerous. They start out as shiny pink lesions. As they advance, they become deeper in color and ulcerate.

Prompt veterinary care is required. If caught early, treatment involves the use of oral or injectable cortisone and antibiotics. In cases that don't respond to cortisone, surgery may be necessary.

The cause of rodent ulcer is not definitely known and may be allergy-related.

SOLAR DERMATITIS

A chronic inflammation of the skin due to repeated exposure to ultraviolet (sun) light, solar dermatitis occurs in white cats. Symptoms include redness of the skin, scaly, crusty skin, or lesions (especially on the ear flaps). Solar dermatitis can develop into cancer if not treated.

Treatment depends on the specifics of the case. Medication may be prescribed for mild cases but for severe solar dermatitis, surgery may be needed. Damaged ear flaps may require surgery.

Keeping your cat indoors during the strongest hours of sunlight is the best way to avoid the damaging effects of ultraviolet rays. Cats who love to lounge in the sun for long periods are especially at risk.

Your veterinarian may recommend the use of a sunblock to cover areas such as the ears. Don't apply one without consulting your veterinarian first because you need to make certain it'll be safe if ingested.

CYSTS, TUMORS, AND GROWTHS

Any lump found on your cat should be immediately checked by the veterinarian. Don't assume that a bump under the skin is benign (noncancerous) just because it doesn't seem to be bothering your cat.

Tumors can occur anywhere on the cat's body, from the head to between the toes. Cancerous tumors are discussed under "Cancer" in this chapter.

RESPIRATORY SYSTEM DISORDERS

Upper respiratory infections can range from being similar to what would be a mild cold in humans to a life-threatening condition. Many of the initial symptoms are so similar (such as sneezing, nasal discharge, runny eyes) that you might postpone taking the cat to the veterinarian, thinking it's just a case of the sniffles. Don't play "wait and see" with any suspected upper respiratory infection.

Asthma

A cat with chronic asthma may have a dry, hacking cough and wheeze a lot. He often sounds as if he's gagging. This is sometimes misinterpreted by owners who assume the cat is just coughing up a hair ball. As he struggles to breathe, you may notice he sits with his head extended, trying to take in enough air. In acute cases, the cat may go into respiratory distress as he fights for oxygen.

Asthma can be aggravated by exposure to dust, pollen, grass, litter dust, cigarette smoke, flea sprays, hair sprays, perfume, cleaning sprays and deodorizers, and air/carpet fresheners.

Immediate veterinary treatment is needed. Oxygen therapy may have to be administered along with a bronchodilator. Acute asthma is a very scary thing for a cat (just as it is for humans), so his stress level will be elevated. Try to use minimal restraint as you transport him to the veterinary hospital. Stress can be a deadly accomplice to an asthma attack.

For chronic asthma, medication will be prescribed. Avoidance of the irritant (if known) is crucial. Many times the specific irritant that triggers attacks is difficult to pinpoint. You can reduce the chances of an attack by using dust-free litter, avoiding household sprays and carpet cleaners, hair sprays, air fresheners, and other common allergens. Cigarette smoke is also something to be avoided, so if you smoke in your home, it is aggravating your cat's condition.

With chronic asthma, be prepared for a life-long maintenance commitment.

Upper Respiratory Infection

Cats generally become infected through direct contact with another cat. Signs may include: conjunctivitis, sneezing, discharge from nose and eyes, and you may notice open-mouth breathing. The discharge may change from clear to yellowish green as infection worsens.

Chronic upper respiratory infections can be especially hazardous for short-nosed breeds such as Persians and Himalayans.

Upper respiratory infection is really a broad term. There are two main viral groups that produce most of the upper respiratory infections in cats—the *calicivirus* group and the *herpes* virus group. In addition to the viral component, secondary bacterial infections can also occur.

Treatment involves medications to relieve symptoms and administration of antibiotics. It's important to make sure the cat continues to eat and drink, since very often his decreased sense of smell can cause appetite decline. If the cat is dehydrated due to the fact that he's not eating or drinking, fluid therapy will be administered either intravenously or subcutaneously.

Pneumonia

Bacterial pneumonia is a lung inflammation and infection that can be a secondary condition to a respiratory illness when the weakened immune system can't fight off the bacteria. Aspiration pneumonia can be a result of aspirating mucous, fluids, food, or medication. Aspiration can occur during force-feeding, vomiting, seizures, or while the cat is under anesthesia. This is where you must be very careful when you medicate your cat with a liquid or are instructed to force-feed. Cats are very susceptible to aspiration pneumonia. Be sure you get detailed instructions from your veterinarian to avoid aspiration pneumonia.

Symptoms of pneumonia can include: noisy, wet-sounding breathing, fever, coughing, lethargy, and respiratory distress of varying degrees. Diagnosis for pneumonia is made through examination, radiographs, and lab tests. Treatment is based on the primary cause. Antibiotics will be prescribed.

Bacterial pneumonia is more common in dogs than cats.

Pulmonary Edema

Pulmonary edema refers to fluid in the actual tissues of the lungs. This is a secondary condition that can result from asthma, pneumonia, cardiomyopathy, obstruction, exposure to toxins, injury to the chest, or poisoning. It can also occur as a result of an electric shock or a severe allergic reaction. Signs can include: breathing difficulty, wheezing, coughing, rales (crackly lung sounds), and open-mouth breathing.

Veterinary treatment is immediately needed. Once the diagnosis is made, oxygen therapy is used. Diuretics are also administered to pull the excess fluid out of the lungs. Further treatment depends on the primary cause.

Pleural Effusion

This is fluid accumulation in the chest surrounding the lungs, making breathing difficult due to the inability of the lungs to expand properly.

The fluid accumulation can be due to disease such as the wet form of *feline infectious peritonitis* (FIP), which causes a buildup of thick, sticky pus in the chest. Other causes of fluid can include heart failure, liver disease, tumors, or heartworms.

Signs include: breathing difficulty and open-mouth breathing, coughing, loss of appetite, and no energy. The cat may be unable to lie down and remain seated with his head far forward in an attempt to gasp air. As breathing becomes more difficult, the cat's lips and gums may turn gray or blue, indicating oxygen deprivation.

Causes can include heartworms, chest trauma, heart failure, infection, overhydration, and liver disease.

Emergency veterinary attention is needed. The fluid will be drained from the chest cavity by way of aspiration. Further treatment depends on the primary cause, but the prognosis is often not very optimistic.

Pneumothorax

Air in the chest cavity can be the result of a blow to the chest. This can happen when a cat falls from a tree or window, or sustains an open chest injury (as a result of a blow from an object or from being hit by a car). It can also occur in some chronic lung diseases. Air leaks from the lungs into the chest. This creates less room for the lungs to sufficiently expand, causing respiratory distress.

Signs of pneumothorax begin as shallow, rapid breathing. As the condition worsens the cat begins abdominal breathing and mucous membranes turn blue. Emergency procedures by your veterinarian are needed to remove the accumulated air in the chest and then treat any injury.

One way to prevent pneumothorax is to keep your cat indoors to eliminate chances of falls from trees or being hit by automobiles.

URINARY SYSTEM DISORDERS

Lower Urinary Tract Diseases

Lower urinary tract refers to the bladder and urethra. The bladder is the sac that holds the urine. The urethra is the tube extending from the bladder in which the urine travels to exit the body. LUTD (lower urinary tract disease) is actually a broad term, covering various urinary diseases.

Feline Lower Urinary Tract Disease

FLUTD is a general description that refers to problems connected with the lower urinary tract, including cystitis and obstructions (stones or plugs).

SIGNS OF URINARY PROBLEMS

- increased or decreased urination
- voiding outside of litter box
- frequent trips to the litter box
- crying or straining upon urination
- voiding only small amounts of urine
- inability to urinate
- blood in urine
- change in urine color
- change in urine odor
- incontinence
- frequent licking of penis or vulva
- painful abdomen
- distended abdomen
- loss of appetite
- weight loss
- depression
- restlessness
- irritability
- ammonia odor to the breath
- vomiting
- excessive meowing or crying

FLUTD can occur at any age. Both male and female cats are affected, though the long narrow urethra in the male cat increases the chances of urinary obstruction.

Many of my clients have reported that the only way they knew that their cats were experiencing urinary problems was because they were urinating in the bathtubs or in sinks. Blood-tinged urine was visible against the light-colored tubs. Those owners were very lucky that their cats gave them such definite signs. You may not be so lucky and that's why it's important to be very familiar with your cat's normal litter box habits.

One cause of obstructions with FLUTD is the development of *uroliths* (crystals that harden to stones) in the urinary tract. For many years, the majority of crystals that developed were *struvite* (comprised of magnesium ammonium phosphate). The urine pH is claimed to influence the formation of these crystals. Pet food companies responded by creating diets that maintain a more acidic urine pH, thereby limiting the amount of magnesium which helped in controlling the formation of struvite crystals. Unfortunately, though, the acidic urine that helps prevent struvite crystals may contribute to other problems. For instance, a diet that promotes an acidic urine wouldn't be indicated for a cat with *calcium oxalate* crystals that are now being diagnosed with increasing frequency. Therefore, it's important that each case be individually diagnosed by your veterinarian. Don't assume that one of your cats has the same urinary problem as the other just because of similar symptoms.

Male cats are more predisposed to developing a urethral plug. This soft, sandy material, composed of crystal fragments and mucous, accumulates in the urethra. If not treated, this material will actually "plug" the opening of the penis. The cat then becomes *blocked* as urine continues to build up in the bladder. THIS IS AN EMERGENCY, AND DEATH WILL RESULT IF NOT IMMEDIATELY TREATED. On appearance, your cat may repeatedly lick his penis. You may also be able to feel his distended abdomen. Lethargy and dehydration will soon result. Don't delay in getting veterinary help. This blockage can cause death within a few hours. Don't assume the cat is constipated and waste valuable time attempting to administer a laxative.

Treatment involves first relieving the bladder. The veterinarian may insert a needle through the skin and into the bladder to withdraw the urine into a syringe. Sometimes a plug can manually be removed under mild anesthesia. In most cases, a catheter is then inserted temporarily to keep the urethra open and free of obstruction. Recurrent cases sometimes require a surgery called *perineal urethrostomy*. The narrow part of the urethra (at the penis) is removed and a wider opening is created. This surgery isn't always successful and is considered a last resort. The use of prescription diets has greatly reduced the need for this surgery.

Long-term treatment for FLUTD involves dietary management with a specific prescription food, based on the individual condition. Make sure the cat's water intake is adequate and don't let him become obese. Exercise is also important. Stress may additionally play a role in recurrences, so keep an eye on changes in the environment that could cause your cat to worry.

Providing clean, easily accessible litter boxes is essential to helping prevent FLUTD. If the box is too dirty or too difficult to get to the cat may void too infrequently. This can predispose him to FLUTD.

Preventing FLUTD

- Feed your cat a high-quality, premium diet. If your veterinarian prescribes a specific diet for your cat, stay on it and don't supplement with table scraps.

- Provide an adequate number of easily accessible litter boxes.

- Keep the litter boxes clean.

- Supply fresh, clean water. Wash the bowl every day before refilling. If your cat eats dry food exclusively, monitor his water intake to make sure he's getting enough.

- Encourage exercise through interactive play.

- Limit the cat's exposure to stress.

- Monitor litter box habits on a daily basis, so you'll be familiar with each cat's routine.

- Take the cat to the veterinarian at the first sign of potential urinary problems.

Incontinence

Various diseases can cause incontinence (involuntary voiding of urine). Injuries to the spinal cord can also result in the inability to control the bladder muscle.

Treatment is based on the underlying cause. Drug therapy is sometimes helpful in regaining bladder control.

Kidney Disease

The *upper* urinary tract refers to the kidneys and the *ureters*, which are the two tubes that lead from the kidneys to the bladder. One of the jobs of the kidneys is to filter the blood, removing wastes. Without this function, wastes would build up in the body to a toxic level.

Since the kidneys are the filtration system for the blood, infections, diseases, and poisons can adversely affect and damage the kidneys themselves.

With reduced kidney function, no matter what the cause, fluid therapy is administered to replace lost electrolytes, correct dehydration, and serve the function of dialysis. Dietary changes are also recommended. The prescription diet will be lower in protein and phosphorus, which reduces the workload on the kidneys.

SIGNS OF POTENTIAL KIDNEY PROBLEMS

- increase or decrease in normal water consumption
- increase or decrease in normal urine output
- blood in urine
- halitosis
- vomiting
- diarrhea
- sensitivity or pain in back, near kidney (cat may have a hunched posture)

- weight loss and anorexia
- dull haircoat
- excessive shedding
- fever
- lethargy
- joint pain
- tongue discoloration
- mouth ulcers

Kidney Failure

The filtering components of the kidneys are called *nephrons*. There are thousands and thousands of these. When a large amount of nephrons become damaged or destroyed, it results in renal (kidney) failure.

Kidney failure can be acute, resulting from such things as poisoning, trauma, or blockage in the lower urinary tract.

Kidney failure can also be chronic and occurs due to disease (such as *feline infectious peritonitis* or *feline leukemia*), infection, hypertension, age, prolonged exposure to toxins, cancer, or long-term use of certain medications.

A cat is in *chronic* renal failure when about 70 percent of the kidney has been destroyed. Usually, the first visible sign that the cat is in kidney failure is increased urination. There will also be an increase in water consumption. Accidents outside of the litter box may occur due to the increased volume of urine produced. Chronic renal failure can cause anemia.

Many cats in chronic renal failure also become hypertensive. Routine blood pressure readings should be done.

As the kidneys continue to deteriorate, waste products that are no longer able to be filtered out remain in the bloodstream and in the body's tissues. This is called *uremia*. If left untreated, the cat will go into a coma and die of uremic poisoning.

In *chronic* cases, fluid therapy is used to restore electrolyte (mineral) balance. A therapeutic diet will be prescribed to slow the progression of the deterioration. This prescription diet will reduce the workload on the kidneys. A cat in kidney failure always needs fresh, clean water available. A cat who fails to eat or drink enough water will have to be hospitalized and rehydrated by intravenous fluid therapy. In some cases, ongoing subcutaneous fluid therapy is needed at home and your veterinarian will instruct you on how to do this.

Symptoms may include: vomiting, increased thirst, depression, constipation, diarrhea, anorexia, weight loss, blood in urine, and increased urination.

Treatment for *acute* kidney failure involves trying to reverse damage before it permanently destroys the kidney tissues.

DIGESTIVE SYSTEM DISORDERS

Vomiting

Vomiting is almost always included in a list of symptoms for just about every disease or disorder.

Due to their self-grooming behavior, cats often vomit as a result of swallowing hair. There are commercial hair-ball-prevention products that should be given to the cat who routinely vomits hair or who grooms very often. Long-haired cats should regularly be given the hair-ball prevention.

SIGNS OF DIGESTIVE PROBLEMS

- diarrhea
- constipation
- changes in appearance of stool
- blood in stool
- weight gain or loss
- change in appetite
- change in water consumption
- vomiting
- restlessness
- abdominal swelling
- painful abdomen
- swallowing difficulty
- flatulence
- change in hair coat appearance
- halitosis
- appearances of worms in vomitus or feces
- excessive meowing or crying

Another common cause of vomiting is due to eating too fast or too much. In multicat households, *competitive* eating may develop where one cat tries to eat not only his own food but that of his companion cats' as well. This can be addressed by either feeding the cats in separate locations, training them to eat out of their own bowls (by now you know that cats can be trained), or by leaving food-dispensing puzzle toys out for cats to enjoy throughout the day. Provided none of the cats are overweight you can also leave some dry food out for free-choice feeding.

Cats who nibble on grass or chew on houseplants will usually vomit shortly thereafter. Nibbling on grass is safe, but chewing on houseplants is very dangerous since many are poisonous to cats. For more on this, refer to the section on poisoning in this appendix or "Emergencies and First Aid" in Chapter 18.

Motion sickness can cause vomiting. Often, withholding food before traveling will prevent stomach upset. It's also important to get the cat used to travel by making short trips around the block at first to build up the cat's tolerance for travel. If the cat still has motion sickness, ask your veterinarian about the use of medications.

If your cat has an occasional episode of vomiting but he otherwise seems healthy and normal, with no other behavior changes, it may just be a mild stomach upset. If he vomits more than one time during that day or evening, withhold food and water for twelve hours in order to give his stomach a rest. Contact your veterinarian for specific instructions on whether this is indicated in your cat's case.

What and *how* a cat vomits can provide possible clues as to the cause. For instance:

Vomiting a foreign object. This is serious because you don't know what damage has already occurred and if any part of the object is still somewhere in the digestive tract. Because of the backward-facing barbs on a cat's tongue, foreign objects that he may lick or chew are often doomed to be ingested. String, ribbon, rubber bands, and yarn are especially difficult for a cat to avoid swallowing. Anytime a foreign object is vomited, consult your veterinarian because a radiograph may need to be taken in order to be sure no damage or blockage has occurred.

Vomiting worms. Roundworms (they resemble spaghetti) may be vomited if the infestation is serious. Virtually all kittens have roundworms, and so you may see one in the vomitus. Your veterinarian will need to deworm your cat.

Vomiting feces. This could indicate an obstruction or injury. Immediate medical attention is required.

Projective vomiting. Possible causes include obstruction or tumor. Get immediate veterinary attention.

Vomiting several times per week. If no hair balls are present and the vomiting isn't related to meals, kidney or liver disease could be the cause. Vomiting also occurs with inflammatory bowel disease, pancreatitis, and chronic gastritis.

Your veterinarian needs to do a complete exam, including blood tests and radiographs.

Obviously, if the cat shows any signs of illness, vomits up anything suspicious, or there's blood or feces in the vomitus, immediate medical attention is required.

Gastritis

This inflammation of the stomach lining can be caused by any number of irritants. *Acute* gastritis may be the result of ingesting a poison, spoiled food, plants, or a medication that irritates the stomach lining. Vomiting is the most common sign of gastritis. The cat may also have diarrhea.

Treatment involves identifying the irritant. If the cat has ingested a poison, contact your veterinarian or emergency animal hospital immediately (refer to the section on poisoning in this appendix).

Chronic gastritis can be the result of long-term drug therapy, chronic hair balls, or ingestion of foreign objects. Chronic gastritis can also be secondary to another underlying disorder such as pancreatitis, renal failure, heartworm, liver disease, or diabetes.

Treatment of *chronic* gastritis involves identifying the underlying cause. Your veterinarian will perform numerous diagnostic tests. Dietary changes may need to be made based on the primary disorder. *Chronic* gastritis usually requires the use of a low-fiber, easily digestible food. Treatment may involve antibiotics and gastric protectants.

Diarrhea

Diarrhea is another one of those symptoms that can be connected to various underlying diseases and disorders. The odor, color, and consistency of the diarrhea may produce some clues as to the possible underlying cause.

Dietary changes can give a cat a case of diarrhea, which is why all adjustments should be done gradually to avoid intestinal upset. Overfeeding is another common reason cats develop diarrhea.

A change in water can cause diarrhea. Carrying an extra supply when traveling is always a good idea.

Outdoor cats run the risk of developing diarrhea by ingesting prey, eating garbage or rotting foods, as well as poisons.

Most kittens, once they're weaned, become lactose intolerant. *Lactase*, which is the enzyme needed to digest the milk sugar lactose is no longer present once kittens begin eating solid food. This is why adult cats often develop a case of diarrhea after being fed a bowl of milk.

Food allergies can make specific ingredients difficult for your cat to digest. Feeding table scraps is especially dangerous and can result in a case of diarrhea.

Diet isn't the only thing that can cause diarrhea. Stress can play a role as well. When a cat goes to the veterinarian, is boarded in a kennel, or experiences any major upheaval in his life, he may experience a mild or even severe case of diarrhea.

Diarrhea that lasts longer than a day can result in dehydration. Left unchecked, this can cause shock.

A cat with diarrhea should be checked by the veterinarian if:

• It lasts longer than a day.

• It's accompanied by vomiting, fever, or lethargy.

• The diarrhea contains blood or mucous.

• There is a putrid odor.

• There is an unusual color to the stool (normal color is brown).

• You suspect that the cat may have ingested a toxic substance.

Stool Appearance

Brown	normal
Tarry black	digested blood, possible bleeding in the upper portion of the digestive tract
Fresh, red blood	bleeding in the lower portion of the digestive tract
Green or yellow	undigested, having gone through the digestive tract too fast
Very light	possible liver disease
Gray, foul-smelling	digestive problem, parasites, or internal infection
Very watery	irritation in the digestive tract, lack of absorption
Oily-looking stool	malabsorption
Soft, nonformed stool of normal color	possible overfeeding, change in diet, food of lower quality, or parasites

Treatment of diarrhea: a mild case of diarrhea that has no other accompanying signs may be treated at home upon the advice of your veterinarian.

Constipation

This results when stools are retained in the colon, causing them to become hard, dry, and difficult to pass. Constipation can have many causes, such as hair balls, obstruction, low water intake, dietary factors, or certain diseases. Cats afraid to go to the litter box for fear of ambush by a companion cat can become constipated.

Cats on the average have at least one stool per day. The cats who have bowel movements only every couple of days are the ones inclined to become constipated.

Symptoms of constipation can include: straining to defecate with little or no feces eliminated, hard stools, small stools, small amount of stool with presence of mucous, blood present in stool, decreased appetite, depression, and presence of blood in stool after straining to defecate.

Owners can often miss the fact that their cat is constipated in a kind of "out of sight, out of mind" way. With diarrhea, the cat often misses the litter box, so you're left with the evidence on the middle of the carpet. Even if the cat does make it to the box, with diarrhea it's very apparent that the stool is abnormal. With constipation, though, an owner may easily lose track of the last time the cat had a bowel movement. It may not be until you see the cat straining or you notice the rock-hard fecal balls left in the litter that you're aware of the problem.

Chronic constipation is commonly the result of hair balls. Long-haired breeds are more prone to this—as are the short-haired cats who live with them, due to allogrooming. You may notice that the cat not only vomits hair balls but you may see hair in the stool. The use of a hair-ball-prevention product is recommended in that case. There are also hair-ball-prevention-formula foods available. Ask your veterinarian for a recommendation if you feel your cat should be switched over to that diet.

A diet with an inadequate amount of fiber can cause constipation. Cats who don't drink enough water will often have difficulty passing stools as well.

Megacolon is a condition where the colon becomes enlarged and is unable to contract sufficiently to evacuate the stool (see section on megacolon).

Stress is another psychological factor that can cause a cat to become constipated. A change in the cat's routine, a move to a new home, a new baby, being left in the care of others, intercat conflict, etc., can all upset a cat's normal routine. Often when there's a move to a new environment it's not uncommon for the cat to not have a bowel movement for a couple of days. During any family upheavals or potentially stressful times, be extra aware of your cat's litter box habits and notify your veterinarian if the cat goes longer than two days without a bowel movement.

Serious constipation can cause *fecal impaction*. Treatment for this requires veterinary attention. The veterinarian will give a laxative orally as well as administer an enema. Commercially available enemas should never be used. They're extremely harmful to cats. Never attempt to give an enema to the cat yourself. This is best left up to the veterinarian. Severe cases may require hospitalization and the administration of several enemas.

Treatment for constipation depends on the underlying cause and the severity of the condition. Mild cases can be treated with veterinary laxatives and the addition of higher fiber foods. Bran added to canned foods is a good bulk-producing agent to help keep the stool soft and more easily passable. There must be sufficient water present for the bran to work so it should only be added to canned food. Ask your veterinarian before adding bran to the diet so he/she can advise you on whether it's appropriate in your cat's case and if so, how much and how frequently to add. A little canned pumpkin is an excellent source of fiber as well. In addition, make sure clean, fresh water is always available. Cats with *chronic* constipation often need to be on high-fiber diets indefinitely.

Severe fecal impaction may require surgery so the veterinarian can manually remove the impacted feces.

Keep your cat active and at a good weight to help prevent constipation as well. Incorporate regularly scheduled interactive playtime with your cat. Maintain him on a good quality diet without the addition of tablescraps. Monitor his water intake to ensure he is staying adequately hydrated.

Inflammatory Bowel Disease
This is actually the broad name that refers to several gastrointestinal disorders.

Food allergies are usually a contributing factor toward IBD. Allergens such as preservatives, additives, specific proteins, and wheat are commonly associated with IBD. Definite diagnosis requires endoscopy or biopsy. Endoscopy is performed with a thin fiber-optic tube called an endoscope that can be placed in the digestive tract. Other diagnostics include barium studies, ultrasound, blood tests, X-rays, and fecal analysis (to rule out parasites).

Symptoms can include: diarrhea, abdominal pain, gas, weight loss, blood in stool, vomiting, and audible abdominal sounds.

Treatment for IBD may include the use of corticosteroids and immunosuppressive drugs to recue inflammation. There is no cure for IBD, so diligent, ongoing dietary management is crucial in treating IBD.

Megacolon

Megacolon occurs when a section of the large intestine (colon) enlarges and balloons out, causing feces to become lodged there instead of traveling down to the rectum. The longer the waste remains trapped, the more water is resorbed, resulting in rock-hard feces. The cat then becomes constipated.

Megacolon is believed to be caused by prolonged or chronic constipation. This is something owners of cats who suffer from repeated bouts of hair-ball-cased constipation need to be aware of. Other causes include dehydration, tumors, or complications from pelvic fractures (the injury is often the result of being hit by a car). It can also be congenital, as is often seen in Manx cats. Another possible cause to be aware of is when a cat attempts to retain feces in order to postpone using a dirty or undesirable litter box.

Symptoms include: hardness to the colon upon manual palpation, fecal impaction, inability to pass gas due to complete fecal blockage in colon, poor haircoat, weight loss, and dehydration.

Diagnosis consists of a history of the cat's health and bowel habits, physical examination (the veterinarian can usually feel the rock-hard feces when palpating the abdomen), rectal exam, and blood tests (to rule out underlying conditions). Additional diagnostics may be needed as well such as ultrasound, barium studies, and X-ray.

I'm always lecturing my clients about being diligent in their litter box maintenance because in addition to keeping a clean box, this allows an owner to know what is or isn't happening when it comes to kitty's elimination habits.

Treatment involves determination of the underlying cause (not always possible), attempted removal of fecal impaction by way of warm water enemas (so the veterinarian can manually remove the impaction), and correcting dehydration. Surgery is needed in some cases. Long-term care involves treating for constipation by feeding a specific prescription food and administering a feline laxative or stool softener. Your veterinarian will instruct you on exactly what kind to use. In some cases, surgery is performed to remove the ballooned section of colon.

Flatulence

The passing of gas can be related to eating a diet high in fiber. It can also be a problem for cats who are fed diets containing beans or highly fermentable vegetables such as cabbage, cauliflower, and broccoli. Additionally, milk can cause gas (as well as diarrhea). Cats who gulp their food and swallow a lot of air can end up being a bit gassy.

Flatulence accompanied by an abnormal stool can be a symptom of a more serious underlying medical condition.

Don't give your cat any commercial anti-gas medication intended for humans. Consult your veterinarian to determine the primary cause. He/she may then make dietary changes. Medication can be given after meals to ease the problem. For cats who gulp their meals, leaving food available free-choice may alleviate the need to eat so much so fast. I usually recommend that my clients incorporate the use of food-dispensing puzzle toys instead of switching to free-choice. This way, the cat is required to eat slowly and gets the added bonus of having fun while eating. All of my clients' cats who had problems with gulping food too quickly have been successfully treated using the puzzle feeders.

Impacted Anal Glands

There are two sacs located on either side of the anus at about five o'clock and seven o'clock. The purpose of these sacs is to mark the cat's stool with a very malodorous secretion to help identify that particular cat and his territory.

The contents of the anal glands are normally emptied upon defecation. The secretions can vary from being thin and liquid to thick and creamy. Color can range from brown to yellow. The odor, of course, is always unmistakable.

Cats usually don't have difficulty with impaction of the anal glands but if it does happen, they can be manually expressed by your veterinarian. If it becomes an ongoing problem, your veterinarian can show you how to express them yourself (it's not difficult, just not one of the more pleasant aspects of being a pet owner).

The most common sign of anal gland problems is "scooting." You'll notice your cat dragging his rump along the carpet in an effort to express the contents of the glands.

If you notice a particular odor coming from the cat's rear end, it may indicate an anal gland problem. Sometimes, you may notice the odor on the cat's *breath* due to his licking the anal glands. This is a sign that they may need manual emptying.

Anal glands can also become infected or abscessed. Signs include: swelling on either side of the anus, frequent scooting, and pain. Blood or pus may be visible in the secretions. Seek veterinary attention immediately for treatment. For infection, the glands will be expressed and an antibiotic will be injected into them. Oral antibiotics will be prescribed as well. You may be instructed to use moist warm compresses at home. An abscess will be lanced and drained. The wound must heal from the inside out so it will have to remain open to allow drainage. This is done usually by flushing diluted *Betadine* two or three times a day. An oral antibiotic is administered as well.

Hepactic Lipidosis (HL)

Also called fatty liver disease, this disorder occurs when fat accumulates in the liver cells. Hepatic lipidosis is usually due to an underlying primary cause, such as kidney disease, starvation, obesity, cancer, liver disease, pancreatitis, or diabetes. Hepatic lipidosis may result from any disease process that stops a cat from eating—the reason being that as the body begins to break down fat, fat and by-products begin to accumulate in the liver. Since cats lack certain enzymes that are important for complete fat metabolism, the fat stays in the liver. *Idiopathic* hepatic lipidosis refers to cases where no underlying cause can be identified.

When fat accumulates in the liver it becomes enlarged and turns yellow. As liver failure progresses, jaundice becomes visible.

Symptoms include: anorexia, diarrhea, constipation, muscle wasting, weight loss, vomiting, depression, drooling, and jaundice.

Treatment involves fluid therapy and nutritional support. In cases of anorexia, force-feeding or the administration of a stomach tube are needed. After the cat begins eating on his own, a prescription diet will be required long-term. Regular follow-up visits will be needed.

Overweight cats who are put on drastic weight reduction diets by well-meaning owners are at great risk of hepatic lipidosis. It's crucial that when planning a diet for a cat, the weight loss is done very gradually. If your cat is overweight, consult your veterinarian before starting any nutritional change so you can be given safe guidelines on how much to feed and at what rate your cat can safely lose weight.

Pancreatitis

The pancreas has two main jobs: it produces insulin for metabolization of blood sugar and it produces pancreatic enzymes used for digestion. *Diabetes mellitus* (sugar diabetes) is a common disorder in cats that results from an insufficiency in insulin production.

Pancreatitis (inflammation of the pancreas) can occur after eating meals too high in fat. Other possible causes may include too much fat in the blood, trauma to the pancreas, and toxins.

When the pancreas becomes inflamed, its digestive enzymes can flow into the abdomen. The kidney and liver usually are affected by pancreatitis as well.

Symptoms can include: abdominal pain, loss of appetite, weight loss, fever, vomiting, diarrhea, dehydration, and depression.

Diagnosis involves blood tests to determine pancreatic enzyme levels along with performing diagnostic imaging procedures such as ultrasound, biopsy, and radiograph.

Treatment varies, based on case severity.

Obesity
Refer to Chapter 10.

MUSCULOSKELETAL SYSTEM DISORDERS

Arthritis

There are different kinds of arthritis. *Osteoarthritis*, the most common form, is also known as *degenerative joint disease* because the cartilage layer on the surface of the joint deteriorates. It mostly occurs as a result of aging but can also develop as a result of injury to the joint surface.

Lameness is the most common symptom and is made worse by cold, damp weather or occurs after strenuous activity. The cat may also appear stiff upon getting up after sleeping.

Polyarthritis is an inflammatory disease that may be connected to one or more viral infections.

Hip dysplasia is not common in cats. It refers to a shallow ball and socket hip joint, which results in degenerative problems.

Treatment depends on the type and severity of arthritis and the underlying causes. Surgery may be required. Keeping your cat warm will also lessen pain, since arthritis is aggravated by cold and damp conditions.

Unfortunately, aspirin and Tylenol—commonly used for arthritis in humans—are toxic to cats. If your cat is uncomfortable, consult your veterinarian regarding possible pain medication. There is a feline arthritis formula food available that is also kidney-friendly for older cats. Ask your veterinarian if the food would be appropriate for your cat.

Glucosamine is a product that seems to be effective in helping restore some joint function by increasing synovial fluid and repairing some of the damage done by osteoarthritis. Synovial fluid acts as a lubricant to the cartilage and when there isn't enough lubrication, cartilage hardens and the joints stiffen. Glucosamine comes in tablet, capsule, and liquid form.

Preventing your older cat from becoming obese will lessen the pain associated with arthritis by reducing weight load on joints.

SIGNS OF MUSCULOSKELETAL SYSTEM PROBLEMS

- lameness
- reluctance to move
- pain
- limited range of motion
- constipation
- weight loss
- sensitivity to being touched
- flaky skin
- greasy hair coat
- fishy odor to the coat
- fever
- loss of appetite
- loose teeth
- curvature of the back
- stiffness upon rising

Parathyroid Diseases

The four parathyroid glands, located in the neck (at the thyroid), secrete *parathyroid hormone*. This hormone helps maintain proper blood calcium and phosphorus levels. Calcium is one of the most important minerals in the body. If the amount of calcium in the blood falls or the amount of phosphorus gets too high, the parathyroid glands release parathyroid hormone (PTH) to raise the calcium level. They do this by pulling it from the bones. The consequences of this can lead to a thinning of the bones. The more brittle they become, the more at risk of fractures the cat becomes.

Successful treatment depends on early diagnosis. Treatment includes calcium supplementation and dietary changes.

Nutritional Secondary Hyperparathyroidism

This is caused by a diet too high in meat and low in calcium and vitamin D. This is where homemade diets can be potentially dangerous. Good-quality commercial cat food is nutritionally balanced to provide the right amount of meat and minerals. Demineralization of the bone can result from feeding an all-vegetable diet as well.

This disease is seen more in kittens who are on all-meat diets, which doesn't provide the extra calcium requirements needed to promote bone growth and development.

Symptoms in kittens appear as a reluctance to move, lameness, and bowed legs. Limping may also be seen due to possible fractures. In adult cats, the thinning of the bones causes brittleness and high risk of fractures. The teeth can also become loose. Left unchecked, curvature of the back develops and can cause the pelvis to collapse.

Treatment involves correcting the diet to address the kitten or adult cat's nutritional needs and administering calcium supplementation. A cat with fractures should be confined to a cage to allow healing and to prevent additional fractures.

If diagnosed early, prognosis is good. If the disease has progressed to where the bones have become deformed, recovery is very doubtful.

Renal Secondary Hyperparathyroidism

Due to kidney disease, which creates a high level of phosphorus, the parathyroid glands secrete an excessive amount of parathyroid hormone to raise the calcium level. As with *nutritional secondary hyperparathyroidism*, calcium is pulled from the bones causing thinning and demineralization. The prognosis is usually guarded.

Steatitis

Also known as *yellow fat disease*, it's caused by a vitamin E deficiency and is now rare in cats. Excessive amounts of unsaturated fatty acids fed to the cats is what causes the destruction of vitamin E. The result is a painful inflammation in the body fat. The fat turns yellow and becomes very hard.

Red meat tuna has high levels of unsaturated fatty acids and a cat eating sufficient quantities will develop this extremely painful disease. An ongoing diet consisting of fish in general may commonly lead to steatitis if not properly supplemented with vitamin E. Canned tuna intended for humans is the most dangerous of all because it isn't supplemented with vitamin E. Other causes include cancer, pancreatitis, infection, and fish-based diets.

Initial symptoms include a greasy coat and flaky skin. The hair coat may develop a fish odor as well. As the disease progresses, the cat becomes reluctant to move or be handled. Even petting becomes too painful. The cat runs a fever and has a poor appetite.

Diagnosis is based on the dietary history and is confirmed by taking a biopsy of the fat.

Treatment involves the dietary correction of switching to a well-balanced food and supplementing with vitamin E. In some cases, tube feeding is necessary. Surgical removal of fatty lumps may also be needed.

Prevent this disease in the first place by never feeding any tuna to your cat, even if it's in commercial cat food. Especially avoid canned tuna intended for humans. Tuna, having such a strong taste and odor, can cause a cat to become addicted to its flavor. Once you start feeding it to your cat, you may find him rejecting his other more balanced food.

If you want to feed fish-flavored cat food to your cat, limit it to occasionally.

Vitamin Overdosing

Excessive amounts of fat soluble vitamins (A, D, E, K) can adversely affect the cat's normal growth, development, and health. Good-quality commercial foods are formulated to be nutritionally complete and well balanced to meet a cat's needs. Supplementing with additional vitamins and minerals can cause bone problems, deformities, lameness, and pain.

Vitamin A is stored in the liver, so excess amounts won't wash out of the body in the urine. Overdosing this vitamin either through supplements or diets containing liver, milk products, and carrots can result in severe neck and back pain and joint swelling. As the disorder progresses, the cat develops very limited range of motion in the neck. Other symptoms include constipation, weight loss, and sensitivity to being touched.

If diagnosed early, dietary correction (and discontinuation of any supplementation) may reverse symptoms. If allowed to progress, the symptoms are irreversible.

ENDOCRINE SYSTEM DISORDERS

Hypothyroidism

The thyroid gland, located in the neck, is responsible for maintaining the body's metabolism. The thyroid produces two major hormones, triiodothyronine (T3) and thyroxine (T4). When the gland fails to manufacture sufficient amounts of these hormones, hypothyroidism (underactive thyroid) results. Though extremely rare in cats, it can, however, be the result of surgical removal or destruction of the thyroid gland in treating for hyperthyroidism.

SIGNS OF ENDOCRINE PROBLEMS

- change in appetite
- change in weight
- lethargy
- low body temperature
- restlessness
- increased or decreased water consumption
- increased or decreased urination
- behavior change
- change in bowels

Hyperthyroidism

Excessive amounts of the thyroid hormones triiodothyronine and thyroxine result in *hyperthyroidism* (overactive thyroid). It's a disease more commonly seen in aging cats (the average is about eight years of age). Hyperthyroidism can lead to a form of heart disease known as *cardiomyopathy*.

Symptoms of this disease include: restlessness, increased appetite, weight loss (despite an increased appetite), rapid heart rate, dull hair coat, vomiting, increased water consumption, and increased urination. A behavior change you may notice is increased activity and, in some cases, aggression. Also, as the excessive hormone level increases the workload of the heart, the cat may develop *hypertrophic cardiomyopathy*—a thickening of the heart muscle. Left untreated, hyperthyroidism can also cause hypertension, which can lead to kidney damage.

Treatment for hyperthyroidism may include antithyroid drug therapy, surgical remove of the gland, or the administration of radioactive iodine. Choice of treatment is based on your cat's specific condition, whether heart disease is present, and if there's a veterinary specialist in your area who performs radiation therapy. The thought of radioactive iodine may sound scary but is, in many cases, the best treatment because it doesn't require anesthesia and usually only one dose is needed to bring the thyroid back to producing normal levels of hormones. This method has a very high cure rate. The downside of treating with radioactive iodine is that the cat will have to be quarantined for about a week or two, so the radioactive iodine has time to leave the body before owners can safely handle the cat. Upon discharge, you'll be given specific instructions on handling your cat and his litter for a while. Surgery is an option if radiation therapy isn't available where you live. Surgery may not be an option if your cat already has heart damage or is in a weakened state.

The drug *methimazole* is sometimes used to control hyperthyroidism. The cat must be given a pill for the rest of his life. This drug can be compounded into a transdermal form and applied to the inside ear tip. Some cats may suffer side effects from the drug including vomiting, loss of appetite, or lethargy. Cats on antithyroid medication need to be monitored regularly. As time goes on, more of the drug is usually needed.

Cost may be a concern when deciding which method is best for your cat. Keep in mind that drug therapy may initially seem the most economical, but long-term the ongoing cost adds up. Radioactive iodine is often the best option.

Diabetes Mellitus

Diabetes mellitus occurs when there is an inadequate amount of insulin produced by the pancreas. Insulin, which is secreted into the circulatory system, enables the body's cells to metabolize sugar into energy. Without insulin, the sugar levels in the blood become elevated. The excess sugar is eliminated by way of the kidneys since it can only be excreted in urine. This means there will be increased urination and thirst. Testing the cat's urine will reveal the presence of sugar. Because the cells in the body aren't able to utilize the glucose (sugar) in the blood, the cat becomes lethargic. He also will begin losing weight despite having a large appetite.

Diabetes can be found in cats of any age but is seen more frequently after the age of six. Obesity puts a cat at great risk as well. Cats on long-term corticosteroid or progestin therapy should be routinely tested for diabetes.

When the body can't metabolize sugar, it begins using its own tissues for energy. This results in the presence of *ketones* (acid) in the blood. If the disease has progressed this far, an acetone odor may be detected on the cat's breath. As the condition worsens, breathing becomes more difficult and eventually the cat goes into a diabetic coma.

Diagnosing diabetes is done by testing for the presence of sugar and ketones in blood and urine.

Treatment depends on the severity of the condition. In cases of dehydration and electrolyte imbalance, fluid therapy will be administered. Insulin injections will be started and monitored, and the cat will remain hospitalized until the correct dosage has been established.

Before the cat is discharged, you'll be given instructions on how to administer insulin injections under the skin. The cat will need to be monitored carefully because dosage adjustments may have to be made. You'll have to return to the veterinarian on a regular basis for a while. Dietary instructions will also be explained to you.

In some cases insulin injections aren't used, and instead, diabetes is controlled through dietary management and oral drugs. Not every cat is a candidate for this, though.

If your cat is obese, you'll be instructed to put him on a calorie-restricted diet to better control his diabetes. The diet change needs to be very gradual, so follow your veterinarian's instructions carefully. High fiber diets help control glucose levels in the blood in addition to aiding in weight reduction. The timing of feedings will need to coincide with insulin injections. The cat's day-to-day meals need to be consistent because insulin requirements vary, depending on the diet.

Home care of a diabetic cat can be done relatively easily as long as you follow instructions and are committed. You'll also need to bring the cat back to the veterinarian regularly to test blood glucose levels.

SIGNS OF HEART TROUBLE

- weakness
- coughing
- lethargy
- abnormal pulse
- irregular heart rhythm
- pale or bluish mucous membranes
- breathing difficulty
- cold limbs
- swollen abdominal cavity
- vomiting
- fainting
- heart murmurs
- crying
- lameness or paralysis
- head tilt
- loss of appetite

CIRCULATORY SYSTEM DISORDERS

Cardiomyopathy

Cardiomyopathies are diseases that affect the heart muscle, making it unable to function efficiently.

Dilated cardiomyopathy occurs when the heart muscle is stretched, and becomes thin, weak, and unable to effectively contract. The chambers of the heart enlarge and fill with too much blood. Dilated cardiomyopathy is seen more commonly in cats middle-aged and older.

A deficiency of the amino acid *taurine* is linked to being one of the major causes of dilated cardiomyopathy. Since that connection was made in the 1980s, cat food manufacturers have supplemented their products with taurine. As a result, dilated cardiomyopathy is now rarely seen. This is one very important reason to feed your cat a good quality cat food and never dog food. Dog food isn't supplemented with taurine.

Signs of dilated cardiomyopathy can come on relatively quickly (over a matter of days) and can include breathing difficulty, loss of appetite, noticeable weight loss, weakness, erratic pulse, and lethargy. As breathing becomes more difficult, the cat may sit with his neck extended in an attempt to get enough air.

With *hypertrophic* cardiomyopathy, the walls of the left ventricle thicken, decreasing the size of the ventricular chamber. The amount of blood pumped in and out of the heart decreases.

Hypertrophic cardiomyopathy isn't related to taurine deficiency. One of the causes is high blood pressure as a result of hyperthyroidism or renal failure. Symptoms can include loss of appetite, decreased activity, and respiratory distress. Sudden death may occur.

Diagnosing cardiomyopathy (and more specifically, which type) requires electrocardiogram, ultrasound, radiographs, and blood chemistries.

Treatment for cardiomyopathy starts with easing the workload on the heart. Depending on the specific condition, therapy may include the use of diuretics (to correct fluid retention), digitalis drugs, and other medications that improve the heart function. Most of the medicines are the same ones used for human heart disease. These drugs can be very toxic, so close veterinary monitoring is required.

A sodium-restricted diet almost always is prescribed. Treatment for *dilated* cardiomyopathy may also include taurine supplements.

Arrhythmia

Arrhythmias are changes in the normal heartbeat rhythm. There can be many causes of arrhythmias, including electrolyte imbalance, stress, heart disease, certain drugs, fever, hypothermia, and exposure to toxins. Arrhythmias may result in sudden death.

Cats with severe ongoing diarrhea or vomiting, diabetes, or kidney disease may develop *hypokalemia* (low serum potassium), which can result in an arrhythmia. Hyperthyroid cats may develop a fast heart rate (known as *tachycardia*), as can cats with cardiomyopathy or under stress. A slower than normal heart rate is called *bradycardia*, which can occur due to many conditions—among them, hypothermia.

Treatment is based on the underlying primary condition.

Heart Murmur

Heart murmurs occur when the normal flow of blood is disturbed as it travels through the heart. With a stethoscope, instead of hearing the normal "lub dub," you hear abnormal sounds.

Murmurs are graded on a scale of 1 to 6 (6 being the most serious). They can be caused by many things, including congenital birth defects or heart disease. Many cats who are otherwise healthy can have a murmur. Less serious murmurs that don't appear to be connected to any underlying condition are graded and monitored during each veterinary exam.

Heartworm

Refer to the section on "Internal Parasites" in this chapter.

Anemia

Anemia refers to an inadequate number of red blood cells, which are the oxygen carriers for the body's tissues.

Anemia can be caused by blood loss due to hemorrhaging and also parasite infestation or poisoning. A severe coccidian or hookworm infestation can result in a large amount of blood loss. Bloodsucking external parasites such as fleas can inflict an alarming amount of damage to a cat's blood supply. Flea-infested kittens are especially vulnerable to becoming anemic, as are weaker, older cats.

Diseases that interfere with bone marrow production or cause destruction of cells can result in anemia such as *feline leukemia* and *feline infectious anemia*. Abnormal reactions to certain toxins and drugs can also lead to anemia.

Signs of anemia include pale mucous membranes, weakness, lethargy, loss of appetite, and decreased tolerance to cold.

Treatment is based on the primary cause. With severe anemia, blood transfusions are performed.

Arterial Thromboembolism

A blood clot in the artery, arterial thromboembolism causes the flow of blood to become obstructed to that artery. Causes can include trauma (such as an injury to the heart), cardiomyopathy, or heart disease.

Symptoms depend on the area of the body affected. The cat may appear lame or even experience paralysis in the legs. The legs may also be cold to the touch.

This is an extremely painful condition and affected cats may vocalize incessantly. Treatment is often unsuccessful.

SIGNS OF NERVOUS SYSTEM DISORDERS

- restlessness
- weakness
- loss of balance
- abnormal eye movements
- fixed pupils
- irregular breathing
- semiconsciousness or unconsciousness
- slow heart rate
- seizures
- skin twitching
- tail lashing or biting
- sudden aggression
- vomiting
- head tilt
- paralysis of any body part (including tail)
- incontinence

NERVOUS SYSTEM DISORDERS

Head Injuries

This commonly occurs as a result of the cat being struck by an automobile. Other causes include falling from a tree or a window, or being hit with an object.

The brain is protected by a surrounding layer of fluid and then encased in the skull. Even with all the cushioning and protection, a major blow to the head will fracture the skull and possibly cause injury to the brain. A brain injury can also occur without a fracture to the skull.

After a head injury, brain swelling can occur, which creates pressure on the brain. This is an emergency because if not treated it will lead to brain damage and death.

Any time your cat sustains a blow to the head, however minor, he should be examined by the veterinarian. If you aren't sure if he suffered a blow to the head but he seems weak, his gait is strange, he's dazed, or his eye movements appear abnormal or fixed, seek immediate medical care.

Years ago when I worked as a veterinary technician, I was always amazed at how many people would call on the phone to say that their cat had just been hit by a car, and that the cat seemed dazed but was otherwise okay. The owners would be calling to see if a veterinary exam was *really* necessary. I couldn't imagine not having my little *eight-pound* cat examined for possible internal injuries or concussion after being struck by a *thirty-five-hundred-pound* vehicle.

Increased pressure on the brain occurs in the first twenty-four hours after the injury. Depending upon the severity of the injury, the swelling may be *mild, moderate,* or *severe.* Even mild pressure is a serious condition and needs immediate veterinary attention. Any delay can result in irreversible brain damage or death.

Epilepsy

This is a recurrent seizure disorder that can be brought on by many causes such as trauma, tumor, exposure to toxins, kidney failure, or hypoglycemia.

A seizure results from an abnormal pattern of brain activity. Seizures are more common in dogs than in cats.

Epilepsy becomes a catchall term in veterinary medicine for seizures due to an undiagnosed cause. For example, seizures caused by renal failure shouldn't be classified as epilepsy because correction of the underlying cause would control the seizures. In this case, the drugs *phenobarbital* or *valium,* normally given to treat epilepsy, would be of no use long-term.

The area of the brain affected will determine the type and severity of a seizure.

A seizure can be as insignificant as staring off into space for a few seconds or as major as a grand mal.

Prior to a seizure, the cat may appear restless. Once a grand mal seizure begins, the cat falls onto his side and becomes very stiff while exhibiting jerking movements of the limbs. He may chew or experience facial twitching. Urination, defecation, or vomiting are also very likely during a seizure. Cover your cat with a towel and keep him safe from thrashing against dangerous objects. Keep the room quiet and dark so you don't stimulate another seizure. Any seizure that lasts more than a few minutes requires immediate veterinary care to prevent brain damage. When the seizure passes, the cat may appear disoriented.

Veterinary care involves diagnosing and treating the primary cause. The seizures themselves can be controlled through medication.

Feline Hyperesthesia Syndrome

Also known as rolling skin disease, this is a disorder that mostly affects young cats under five years of age, but can still be seen in older cats as well. The cause of feline hyperesthesia syndrome is unknown but some experts describe it as a neurotransmitter malfunction in the brain during periods of anxiety.

This syndrome causes cats to be super sensitive to being touched, usually along the spine and down the tail.

The majority of cats with feline hyperesthesia syndrome groom excessively, sometimes to the point of mutilation. Skin twitching and tail lashing is also exhibited, followed by sudden bursts of activity such as darting around wildly. This behavior can range from mild skin twitching to actual seizures. Some cats become aggressive during these episodes and attack companion pets or even their owners. Other signs may include dilated pupils, increased vocalization, biting at the tail, and sensitivity to being touched on the back or base of the tail. Cats who are highly aroused or living in chronic anxiety seem to be more at risk.

Underlying conditions such as spinal problems, epilepsy, arthritis, abscesses, cancer, wounds, and skin conditions must be ruled out before a cat is diagnosed with feline hyperesthesia syndrome.

This disorder is usually controlled by antianxiety or antidepressant medication. It's also important to reduce causes of anxiety. Improve environmental enrichment and provide your cat with opportunities for stimulation, energy release, and fun.

Peripheral Vestibular Dysfunction

The vestibular system is responsible for detecting certain types of head movement and reacting to maintain balance.

The *labyrinth* is a bony part of the ear that's crucial for equilibrium. Should it become inflamed or broken, peripheral vestibular dysfunction will occur. Infections of the middle or inner ear can also cause this condition.

Symptoms include: loss of balance, circling, head-tilt, vomiting, and abnormally rapid eye movements (nystagmus).

Treatment is based on the underlying cause.

Early medical attention is required to prevent progression of the disease, which could lead to permanent damage.

Spinal-Cord Injuries

These are caused most commonly by falls and being hit by an automobile.

A cat who is unable to stand or walk may have sustained spinal-cord injury and should be transported very carefully to the veterinarian. Transfer him to a flat board or onto a blanket (carry it as a stretcher) to prevent doing further damage.

A cat's tail is very vulnerable to being run over, which can cause spinal cord separation as the cat tries to escape. This leads to tail paralysis, nerve damage, and loss of bladder and rectal function. Even if a cat seems fine except that his tail hangs limp, immediate veterinary attention is required to assess damage to the bladder (which may be permanent or temporary).

Treatment of spinal cord injuries depends on whether it has been severed. For bruising, medications are administered to reduce swelling. If the spinal cord has been severed, the cat will be paralyzed.

Spina Bifida

Common in the Manx cat, this birth defect is a malformation of the bones in the lower back. These cats run the risk of not having properly formed sacral and coccygeal (tail) vertebrae. Severely affected cats may have a weakness in hind leg movement or difficulty urinating and defecating. These cats should be monitored for constipation.

REPRODUCTIVE AND NEONATAL DISORDERS

Vaginitis

Vaginitis is a vaginal inflammation and infection. There is often a discharge with vaginitis. If left untreated, the infection may spread up into the bladder. The sign you'll most commonly see will be the cat continually licking at her vulva.

Treatment usually involves the use of topical medication.

SIGNS OF REPRODUCTIVE SYSTEM PROBLEMS

- abnormal heat cycles
- vaginal discharge (other than normal heat)
- discharge from penis
- undescended testicles
- swollen or irritated testicles or penis
- swollen or inflamed vulva
- foul odor
- tenderness or pain
- unretracted penis
- frequent licking of penis or vulva
- swollen, tender, or red breasts
- lumps
- fever
- vomiting
- reluctance to nurse
- restlessness
- lethargy
- loss of appetite
- increased water intake
- increased urination

Mammary Tumors

These are relatively common in cats. Mammary tumors are mostly found in females but males can develop them as well.

Mammary tumors that are *malignant* (cancerous) are mostly found in older cats. Treatment involves mastectomy. The cat must be rechecked on a regular basis, because recurrence is quite common.

The risk of mammary tumors can be virtually eliminated by spaying prior to the first heat cycle.

Cystic Endometrial Hyperplasia

The tissues of the uterine wall (endometrium) thicken and develop cysts. This occurs in cats that cycle repeatedly without mating. The follicles of the ovaries produce an abnormally high level of estrogen, which leads to the formation of these cysts. The cat may show no signs of illness.

The best preventive treatment for cystic endometrial hyperplasia is spaying.

Metritis

This is an infection that causes the uterine lining to become inflamed. It's usually caused by unsanitary conditions when the cat is giving birth or by trauma to the birth canal during parturition. It can also happen after a miscarriage, or artificial insemination if done under non-sterile conditions.

Symptoms can include: swollen abdomen, bad-smelling discharge from the vulva, appearance of pus in the discharge, bloody discharge, fever, poor appetite, neglecting kittens, poor milk production, and depression.

This is a serious infection. The cat will need to be hospitalized and might also need fluid therapy. Treatment involves the use of antibiotics. Kittens may need to be hand-raised to prevent transmission through infected milk and to protect them from exposure to antibiotics.

Pyometra

This life-threatening infection causes the uterus to fill up with pus. There are two forms of this infection: open and closed.

With *open* pyometra, the large amount of pus becomes visible as a discharge. With *closed* pyometra, the pus accumulates in the uterus without discharging, creating a very toxic situation for the cat.

Symptoms of pyometra can include: a firm, distended abdomen, loss of appetite, discharge (with *open* pyometra only), increased water intake and increased urination, and vomiting (*closed* pyometra).

This is a life-threatening condition. Veterinary attention is needed immediately. The treatment for pyometra is surgery (hysterectomy).

False Pregnancy

More commonly seen in dogs, false pregnancies can occur in cats whose eggs weren't fertilized during ovulation.

The usual sign is that the cat will begin displaying nesting behavior. Some cats may even have some degree of mammary development.

There is no veterinary treatment required for this specific condition, but have the cat examined to rule out the possibility that there may have been an aborted pregnancy.

A cat who repeatedly exhibits false pregnancy behavior should be spayed.

Mastitis

Mastitis is an infection of the mammary glands (it can affect one or more of the glands) caused by bacteria. A wound or scratch to the breast can introduce bacteria into the gland. The kittens' nails can even cause a scratch as they nurse. The milk from the infected glands is toxic and can infect the nursing kittens.

Signs of mastitis include breasts that are swollen, hot, tender, or red. The cat may have a fever and lose her appetite. The milk may or may not appear normal. The nursing kittens should be removed immediately and hand-raised with kitten milk-replacement formula.

Treatment involves the administration of antibiotics. A warm, moist compress should be applied to the breast several times a day.

In cases that aren't severe, your veterinarian may recommend that the kittens continue to nurse. If the infection is systemic, the cat will need to be hospitalized and the kittens should be hand-raised.

Eclampsia (Milk Fever)

Due to the calcium demand during nursing, a cat with a low serum calcium level can develop eclampsia. This is more apt to happen when the mother cat has a large litter.

Eclampsia results in muscle spasms. Initially, the signs are rapid breathing, restlessness, pale mucous membranes, uncoordinated gait, and dangerously high fever. The muscles in the face tighten, exposing the teeth. Eventually the cat goes into full body muscle spasms, and finally, paralysis.

Eclampsia is an emergency. The cat needs to be taken to the hospital immediately for calcium replacement therapy (given by IV). Feed the kittens using a milk-replacement formula.

Once the cat has recovered from the emergency, she'll be given vitamin/mineral supplements but the kittens shouldn't be allowed to continue nursing.

Kitten Mortality Complex

A broad term that refers to the various neonatal infections and diseases as well as other influences (such as low birth weight) that can cause death in kittens.

The first two weeks of life are the riskiest for newborns. Of the fatalities that occur, they mostly happen within this time frame. Kittens are at risk of diseases transmitted from the queen in utero. Congenital defects also can affect the mortality rate. Another factor is that kittens are unable to regulate their body temperature, so if the area in which they're kept isn't warm enough it can lead to hypothermia. Low blood sugar and dehydration are additional dangers at this young age. Poor sanitary conditions will also put kittens at risk of disease. Then there are the possibilities of injuries sustained during birth, lack of milk production from the mother cat, as well as the chance that she may not provide adequate care and attention. Not every would-be mom reads the manual on what her kittens will need. Some cats can even reject their own kittens.

Inadequate milk production is a common cause of kitten mortality. This can be due to the size of the litter or as a result of the mother being fed a poor quality diet.

Fading Kitten Syndrome

This can happen in utero, at birth, or during nursing.

Fading kitten syndrome usually is the result of a birth defect and the cause may be that the mother didn't receive adequate nutrition while pregnant. It can also be caused by a traumatic birth or infection.

Contact your veterinarian immediately if any of your recently born kittens are failing to thrive. Treatment depends on age of the kitten and the cause and severity of the symptoms.

Hernia

A hernia is a hole in the abdominal wall. This can be felt as a little protrusion on the cat's underside. The bulge may be soft and you may be able to temporarily push it back. If the protrusion can't be pushed back or feels hard, swollen, or is painful for the cat it needs immediate attention because blood supply to the tissue may be cut off. Umbilical hernias are the most commonly seen.

Umbilical hernias, if they don't recede on their own within the first six months, can be surgically repaired. This is commonly done during the spay or neuter surgery. If you're planning on leaving your cat intact, the umbilical hernia surgery will have to be done by the time the cat is six months old.

If you feel any type of lump on your kitten's belly, have it examined by the veterinarian.

Birth-Related Infections

Umbilical Infection

The kitten's navel may look inflamed with pus drainage. Clipping the umbilical cord too close to the abdomen can lead to this kind of infection. Unsanitary conditions can put a kitten at risk of umbilical infection as well.

If the cord was severed too close to the abdomen, cleanse the area and apply an antibiotic ointment such as Neosporin. Don't allow the mother to lick the kitten in that area because she could make the condition worse. If you're in doubt about how to properly care for the area, consult your veterinarian. If an infection has already taken hold, contact your veterinarian because more specific treatment is needed.

Toxic Milk Syndrome

Breast infections such as *mastitis* cause the milk of the mother to become toxic to her kittens. Commercial milk replacement that has not been properly prepared or has turned bad may also be toxic. Signs of toxic milk syndrome can include excessive kitten vocalization, diarrhea, or a bloated stomach. *Septicemia* can result from toxic milk syndrome.

Treatment involves removing the kittens from the mother. If the mother has an infection, immediate veterinary attention is required and the kittens shouldn't nurse from her again until after you get approval from the veterinarian. Diarrhea and dehydration must be treated, and the kittens will have to be hand-fed. Antibiotics may be administered by injection.

Septicemia

This infection can enter the bloodstream by way of an infected umbilical cord. Bacteria-infected milk can also lead to this condition. This is seen in kittens under two weeks of age.

Symptoms include: vocalization, distended and bloated stomachs, and difficulty in defecation. It may appear as if the kitten is constipated, but if you look at his bloated abdomen you'll see it has developed a dark red or blue color. As the septicemia gets worse, the kitten will cease nursing, develop a low body temperature, lose weight, and become dehydrated.

Treatment involves determining the underlying primary cause. If it's due to infected milk, the kittens must be removed from the mother and both she and her kittens will need care. Kittens must be treated for diarrhea and dehydration.

Insufficient Milk Supply

If kittens appear hungry, cry excessively, or aren't tended to by the mother (which can occur with first-time mothers), there may be an insufficient supply of milk. Contact your veterinarian for a milk-replacement formula.

Paraphimosis (penis that is unable to be retracted)

Normally, when the penis is retracted, it slides back into the sheath. Long hair that sticks to the penis after mating may prevent it from sliding back. The most common cause is when hair collects around the penis and over time forms a ring.

Trimming the long hair around the penis before mating your male cat is recommended to prevent this condition.

Paraphimosis is an emergency because the penis can quickly become swollen and painful.

To treat, gently slide the *prepuce* (skin) back away from the penis and remove any trapped hairs. Gently hold the penis head and check for hairs caught on the spines. Next, lubricate the penis with a little *K-Y* jelly. Very gently slide the prepuce back over the penis. If the penis still doesn't retract, take the cat to the veterinarian. If the cat is difficult to handle or gets too anxious, don't attempt to remove the hairs from the penis by yourself—just get the cat to the veterinarian right away.

Hair caught on the spines of the penis can cause irritation and even infection. If the penis looks irritated, or has a discharge or odor, veterinary treatment is required.

Even if the penis can be retracted back into the sheath, if any of the above signs are present or if the cat frequently licks at his penis, veterinary attention is needed.

Cryptorchid Testicles (undescended)

A male cat should have both testicles descended into the scrotum at birth. If one or both fail to descend, they're referred to as *cryptorchid.*

A cat with either one or both cryptorchid testicles should be neutered and not used for breeding. If left undescended, the testicle can develop a tumor.

Male Infertility

Attempting to breed the male cat too often (more than twice a week) can result in a low sperm count. On the other hand, mating too infrequently can lead to a low sperm count as well.

A cat with both testicles undescended may be sterile. If one testicle has descended he might be fertile but shouldn't be bred.

Age also affects fertility, as does obesity, poor nutrition, and other diseases.

In terms of genetics, male tortoiseshell and male calico cats are almost always sterile.

Diagnosis involves determining the underlying cause by way of clinical tests, history taking, and physical examination. Treatment will be based on case specifics.

Female Infertility

Infertility in females can be caused by cysts on the ovaries or abnormal heat cycles (especially as the cat gets older). Abnormal heat cycles can be the result of insufficient daylight (an initiating factor in estrous cycling). Treatment for cysts involves surgical removal. Treatment for abnormal heat cycles is based on the specific cause. If it's due to lack of daylight, increasing the cat's exposure to at least twelve hours of light per day is usually recommended.

INFECTIOUS DISEASES

Viral Diseases

Feline Viral Rhinotracheitis (FVR)

Feline viral rhinotracheitis is produced by a *herpes* virus. It's the most serious of the respiratory diseases for cats and is fatal for kittens. FVR is spread by direct contact with saliva, nasal/eye discharge, or by contact with an infected litter box or water bowl. Feline viral rhinotracheitis is more common in kennels, catteries, and multicat households when there is poor hygiene, inadequate ventilation, stress, poor nutrition, and overcrowding.

Symptoms start with a fever, then progress to sneezing, coughing, and eye and nasal discharge. The eyes become inflamed, which can lead to ulcerations, eventually forcing the eyelids shut. The nose can become totally blocked due to the thick discharge, causing open-mouth breathing. Symptoms can also include drooling and sometimes stomatitis (mouth ulcers), which makes eating extremely painful, so the cat loses weight. Even if the mouth doesn't become ulcerated, the compromised sense of smell due to congested nasal passages can cause a loss of appetite. Warming the food slightly will help release the aroma, making it more appealing.

Treatment includes antibiotics, topical eye ointments, IV fluids, and nutritional support. The nose and the eyes have to be kept clear of discharge. Use a cotton ball moistened with water to clean the eyes and nose. A little drop of baby oil can be used over chapped areas of the nose.

Severe infections can leave a cat susceptible to recurring colds.

A yearly vaccination will help prevent your cat from developing this disease.

Feline Leukemia Virus (FeLV)

This is a highly contagious viral disease that grows in bone marrow and spreads via secretions. FeLV-positive cats have suppressed immune systems that leave them highly susceptible to other diseases and FeLV-potentiated cancers.

Transmission occurs most often through exchange of infected saliva. Possible transmission may occur as a result of sharing food and water bowls or allogrooming. Sexual contact and bite wounds are definite forms of transmission. Kittens can acquire the disease in the mother's uterus or by nursing on the infected milk.

Some cats can be carriers without showing active symptoms themselves. Some cats exposed to FeLV may develop an immunity. This is called *primary viremia*, where the virus is in the blood and saliva but the cat's antibodies are able to stop progression.

Secondary viremia refers to the virus that continues to be present in the cat's blood and saliva. Having taken a firm hold of the cat's immune system, the virus causes the body to become susceptible to any number of diseases. This is where FeLV-potentiated diseases become fatal to a cat.

Signs of FeLV are rather nonspecific. Initial symptoms of illness may include: fever, loss of weight, depression, change in bowels, and vomiting. The cat may also become anemic, showing pale mucous membranes. Specific signs then change when the other diseases develop as a result of immunosuppression.

Your cat can be tested for FeLV. There are two types of FeLV tests available: ELISA (enzyme-linked immunosorbent assay) can be done in the veterinary clinic and tests for both primary and secondary viremia. IFA (indirect immunofluorescent antibody assay) is sent out to a diagnostic lab. IFA tests are done to detect secondary viremia.

Treatment involves providing relief for the cat and prolonging life if possible. Antibiotics, vitamin supplements, IV therapy, and anticancer drugs are available, but both the owner and the veterinarian must work together on the ethical questions of the cat's quality of life. Anticancer drugs are very powerful and you have to consider how much the cat should have to endure. In addition, there is the risk of treating a cat who may continue to shed this virus, putting other cats at risk.

Prevention involves testing any cats before introduction into your household.

If you had a FeLV-positive cat in the household, disinfect the home, replace all litter boxes and food/water bowls. All remaining cats should be tested.

If an FeLV-positive cat was recently removed from your single-cat household, disinfect the home, throw out the litter box and food/water bowls, and wait at least one month before bringing in another cat.

There are vaccinations available against FeLV. Discuss your cat's risk factors with your veterinarian.

If your vaccinated cat has been bitten by a cat whom you suspect could be FeLV-positive (i.e., any unknown cat), have him tested because no vaccine is 100 percent foolproof.

Feline Immunodeficiency Virus (FIV)

FIV was first identified in California in the 1980s. It's related to the human HIV virus, but FIV doesn't produce HIV in humans and HIV will not produce FIV in cats.

FIV is shed in saliva and is spread mainly through bite wounds, which puts outdoor cats, especially roaming males, at greatest risk. Casual contact is not a main form of transmission.

The immune suppressed conditions caused by FIV can be hard to distinguish from FeLV, such as anemia, infections, and low white-blood-cell count. Signs of FIV can include various symptoms, depending upon the route of infection. Gingivitis, periodontitis, and stomatitis (mouth ulcers) are relatively common, which lead to the inability to eat and eventual emaciation. Skin infections, anemia, urinary infections, eye and ear infections, diarrhea, and respiratory infections are also possible. Delayed healing may be an important clue.

There are several stages of FIV; as with HIV, it begins with the acute stage following exposure where the cat develops a fever and enlarged lymph nodes. The cat may then go through a lengthy stage of being an asymptomatic carrier. Following that, there is the final AIDS-like stage. The cat's immune system, which is no longer functioning, leaves the cat open for infections that become severe.

Diagnosis is based on testing that can be performed in the veterinarian's office. Confirmation can also be done by doing additional tests that are sent out to a diagnostic lab. Treatment includes supportive therapy based on specific infections involved.

A positive diagnosis of FIV shouldn't mean an immediate death sentence for your cat. FIV-positive cats (if they're healthy) can live for months and even years. A positive diagnosis does mean, though, that the cat must strictly be an indoor cat and no other new cats can be introduced into the home.

The only way of preventing FIV is to limit your cat's exposure to the virus by keeping him indoors. The most effective method is nonexposure.

If you do allow your FIV-negative cat outdoors, have him neutered to reduce his inclination to roam and fight. Keep him up-to-date on all of his other vaccinations and have him checked at the first sign of anything awry.

A vaccine against FIV was approved for use several years ago but it's not recommended. Vaccinated cats will have positive antibody test results and the vaccine hasn't proven to be 100 percent effective.

Feline Panleukopenia

Also known as *feline infectious enterititis* and *feline distemper*, this is a highly contagious and serious disease. It can attack a cat at any age and is one of the primary causes of death in kittens. Kittens can develop the virus in utero or from infected mother's milk.

The disease is spread by direct contact with infected cats or their secretion. Infected cats shed the virus in their feces. Fleas that bite an infected cat can spread the virus to other cats.

The feline panleukopenia virus can survive temperature extremes and can remain in the environment for more than a year. Thorough cleansing and disinfecting with a diluted bleach solution must be done by anyone who handles or treats an infected cat to prevent passing infections on to other cats.

Signs of illness vary but can include fever and vomiting. The cat often develops a hunch pose, due to abdominal pain. He may sit with his head hanging over the water bowl. If he is actually able to eat or drink, he often vomits afterward. A yellowish diarrhea develops, sometimes streaked with blood. The cat's coat usually develops a dull appearance. When you handle or pick up the cat, he may cry out due to abdominal pain.

Panleukopenia attacks the cat's white blood cells. As the number of healthy white cells diminish, the body is susceptible to secondary infections.

The earlier you get to the veterinary hospital when symptoms first appear, the greater the chance of a cat surviving this disease. Treatment includes: antibiotics, IV fluid therapy, and nutritional support. Cats who survive this disease develop an immunity against future infections.

The best prevention is to vaccinate your cat. The vaccine is very effective.

In an environment where panleukopenia has been present, thorough cleansing and disinfecting must be done with a solution of bleach and water. Throw out anything in the cat's environment that can't be disinfected.

Feline Infectious Peritonitis (FIP)

Caused by a strain belonging to the *coronavirus* group, FIP is spread by direct contact with secretions. Transmission can occur through direct contact with an infected cat or by coming in contact with surfaces or objects such as litter boxes, food bowls, bedding, or toys that have been exposed to an infected cat's secretions. The cats most often infected are under three years old. A few cats who are exposed to the virus may develop only mild respiratory infections but can then become carriers while remaining asymptomatic. For the majority of cats, though, FIP is fatal.

The most at risk for FIP are catteries, households with a dense cat population, undernourished cats, kittens, or cats already suffering from another illness.

There are two forms of this disease: *effusive* (wet) and *noneffusive* (dry). Both are fatal. In the wet form, fluid accumulates in the chest or abdomen. You may notice breathing difficulty as the lungs become unable to expand. Fluid that accumulates in the abdomen causes it to become enlarged and painful to the touch. Other symptoms include: fever, loss of appetite, diarrhea, anemia, and vomiting. Jaundice may also develop. Cats with the *effusive* form of FIP don't usually survive more than a couple of months.

The *noneffusive* form of FIP doesn't involve fluid production, but rather attacks the organs, such as the brain, liver, kidneys, pancreas, and eyes. Symptoms can include: liver failure, kidney failure, neurologic disease, retinal disease, blindness, and pancreatic disease. Cats with *non-effusive* FIP may survive several months. Outward symptoms may initially be vague such as loss of appetite, weight loss, pale appearance of the nose, jaundice of the inside of the eyelids, rough or dull haircoat, and recurring fever.

Diagnosis is made through a series of tests to first determine if there is enough of an FIP profile present. Your veterinarian will check antibody levels, kidney and liver functions, blood count, and fluid analysis (if present).

Treatment is unfortunately limited to supportive therapy to provide relief: antibiotics and anti-inflammatories. There is no cure. The prognosis for cats infected with this disease is, sadly, very poor.

If your cat is in a high-risk category, make sure his health is maintained through proper nutrition, veterinary checkups, and appropriate vaccinations. Address all health concerns immediately, however minor they may appear (that means fleas, other parasites, or the slightest sniffle or sneeze). Keep the area where the cat lives disinfected regularly. Use a solution of a half-cup bleach in a gallon of water to disinfect the environment. In a densely populated cat environment, this is crucial.

Feline Calicivirus (FCV)
FCV is spread by direct contact with nasal or eye discharge and saliva. It can also be spread by coming into contact with the litter box or food and water bowl of an infected cat.

Initial symptoms include: eye and nasal discharge, fever, and sneezing. As the disease progresses, drooling is seen due to ulceration of the mouth and tongue. The cat stops eating, loses weight, and has more and more breathing difficulty.

Treatment involves the use of antibiotics and anti-inflammatory medications. You can help keep the nose and eyes clear of discharge by using a cotton ball moistened with water or saline solution. A drop of baby oil can be used on chapped portions of the nose. There are various strains of this virus and some are more dangerous than others.

There is a vaccine available.

Rabies
This fatal disease enters the body usually by way of a bite from an infected animal. The virus, which is in the animal's saliva, enters the open wound and travels through

the central nervous system to the brain. The incubation period can range from a couple of weeks to several months, depending upon how close the initial bite wound was to the brain and how long it takes for the virus to infiltrate the nervous system—its transport route to the brain.

Rabies takes two forms, *furious* and *paralytic*. Infected animals may exhibit signs of both. The *paralytic* form is presented in the time close to death but an animal may not reach that form if death occurs during a seizure during the *furious* stage.

If rabid, the cat may appear nervous, restless, or irritable. He may become sensitive to light and loud noises. He'll seek hiding places and become withdrawn. These symptoms may last a few days before the cat goes into the *furious* stage.

The *furious* phase can last anywhere from a day to a week. The cat becomes aggressive, biting at the air or imaginary things. He may suddenly attack and bite any approaching human or animal. Restrained cats will attempt to gnaw through crates or cages. In a short time, the cat develops tremors and muscle twitching, leading into convulsions.

When the *paralytic* stage takes over, it affects the head and neck first as the muscles become paralyzed. The image most people associate with rabies is the animal who seems afraid to drink water. It's actually paralysis that causes an inability to swallow. The cat drools and often paws at his mouth. The paralysis prevents him from fully closing his lower jaw so his tongue can be seen hanging out. This partial paralysis soon gives way to complete paralysis. The cat collapses and death follows soon after.

The only true diagnosis is through microscopic examination of brain tissue, which is done by way of necropsy. Treatment is not available.

If your *unvaccinated* cat has been bitten by a rabid animal, it will most likely be recommended that he be put down or placed in quarantine. If your cat has been vaccinated and is bitten by a rabid animal, he will be given an additional booster vaccination and placed under observation.

Prevention comes down to making sure you have your cat vaccinated against rabies. Although rabies in cats is rare, you need to vaccinate against this disease. Kittens can be vaccinated starting at three months of age. A booster is given one year from that date. Then, depending upon the type of vaccine and your state's law, boosters are administered yearly or every three years.

When it comes to animal bites, all wounds should be immediately cleaned with water and disinfectant. If you have any questions or concerns about a bite that your cat received, consult your veterinarian.

Bacterial Diseases

Feline Infectious Anemia

Caused by an organism called *hemobartonella felis*, which attaches to the red blood cell surface of cats, feline infectious anemia results in anemia.

It's presumed that blood-sucking parasites and insects such as ticks and fleas may pass the contaminated blood to a healthy cat after biting an infected one. Kittens can be infected in utero if the mother is infected.

Signs can include pale gums and mucous membranes, and vomiting. If the disease progresses slowly, significant weight loss may be noticeable. An acute case may not show weight loss but rather weakness, fever, loss of appetite, and the skin will appear jaundiced due to the breakdown of red blood cells. An anemic cat may start eating litter or dirt in an attempt to get iron.

Diagnosis is made through microscopic examination of blood smears. More than one sample may need to be taken because there's a period when the parasite isn't visible in the blood. A more accurate test can then be done using a PCR (polymerase chain reaction) blood test.

Antibiotic treatment, in addition to other medication, is usually administered for several weeks. Extreme cases may require blood transfusions. Provided that the anemia isn't too far advanced, treatment is often successful, however, the parasite may never be completely eliminated from the body and the disease may recur following stress.

Flea and parasite control should also be part of the comprehensive program to reduce the cat's exposure to feline infectious anemia. Cats allowed outside, male cats who roam, and cats under the age of six seem to be at higher risk.

Bordetella Bronchiseptica (FeBb)

Once known primarily as causing *kennel cough* in dogs. FeBb is now recognized as a possible respiratory pathogen that can cause similar signs in cats. Upper respiratory infections resulting from FeBb can lead to pneumonia.

Symptoms can include: fever, loss of appetite, listlessness, runny eyes, coughing, nasal discharge, sneezing, and increased lung sounds. Although coughing is a common sign in dogs, it may or may not appear in cats.

It's believed the transmission primarily occurs through oronasal exposure to secretions and excretions of infected cats—sneezing, hissing, biting, licking, spitting, etc.

Bordetella alone can't be diagnosed based on physical examination or clinical signs due to the similarity of symptoms associated with other respiratory pathogens. Culture swabs must be taken and sent to the laboratory.

Cats who have clinically recovered from FeBb can continue to shed the organism for about nineteen weeks. Shelters, boarding facilities, and multicat households are most at risk, especially if there is a history of respiratory disease.

Affected cats are treated with antibiotics.

A vaccine for FeBb is available but is considered a noncore vaccinate. Talk to your veterinarian about your cat's risk factors.

Salmonellosis

A bacterial infection caused by a type of salmonella (there are many). Cats often seem to be asymptomatic carriers and appear relatively resistant to salmonella. The cats most susceptible are the ones under stress, living in unsanitary or overcrowded conditions, malnourished, or already weakened by illness. Bacteria is shed in the feces of carrier animals.

Cats can acquire salmonella by ingesting raw food, rodent or bird feces, and canned food that has been contaminated.

Symptoms of salmonellosis include fever, loss of appetite, abdominal pain, dehydration, diarrhea, lethargy, and vomiting. There are some cases, though, where no sign of diarrhea is exhibited.

Diagnosis is made by examination, fecal cultures, urinalysis, and blood tests. This infection is difficult to diagnose. Treatment involves fluid therapy to correct dehydration. Antibiotics may also be used.

To help prevent salmonellosis, never feed your cat raw or undercooked meat. If your cat is an outdoor hunter, he's at a greater risk of contracting this bacterial infection. If you choose not to confine him indoors, make sure his immune system stays in peak condition through premium nutrition, booster vaccinations (there is no salmonella vaccine), regular veterinary checkups, and a sanitary environment. Finally, don't let your cat ingest captured prey.

Cat Scratch Disease

I'm including cat scratch disease in this chapter because so many people don't understand exactly what it is. They only know that it's connected somehow to cats.

This disease is one that affects humans. Cats can be asymptomatic carriers. Cat scratch disease is usually self-limiting and consists of a red sore at the location of the bite or scratch. An enlargement of the lymph nodes closest to the wound may develop, usually lasting several weeks or even months. In most cases, the lymph nodes then return to normal size. In a few cases, cat scratch disease results in a more severe condition, including fever, fatigue, headache, and loss of appetite. For immunosuppressed humans, the disease can become life-threatening.

Always clean and disinfect any scratch or bite you receive from a cat, however minor. This disease is more apt to occur when scratched by a stray cat rather than a known pet. Consult your doctor if you have any questions about a cat-related wound.

Instruct children on the proper and gentle handling of cats, so hopefully they will avoid getting scratched in the first place.

Feline Chylamydiosis

Also known as *feline pneumonitis*, it's a respiratory infection that can range from mild to very severe and is spread through direct contact.

Symptoms include: conjunctivitis, which causes redness and discharge from the eyes; sneezing, loss of appetite, coughing, and breathing difficulty are also signs.

Young cats seem most at risk, especially those living in a multicat environment where there has been a history of disease.

Treatment includes the use of oral and ophthalmic antibiotics. Cats usually recover from this disease, although recurrence is common.

There is a vaccine available that may or may not be included in routine vaccinations. The vaccine doesn't prevent the disease but may lessen the severity.

Fungal Diseases
Histoplasmosis

This disease is caused by a soil fungus. Transmission occurs through inhalation. Histoplasmosis is rarely found in cats, however, young cats are more susceptible.

Symptoms can include: respiratory difficulty, fever, weakness, loss of appetite, and diarrhea.

Diagnosis is made by taking a culture and treatment involves the use of long-term antifungal medication. The prognosis, though, is usually not very good.

Aspergillosis

Signs of infection by this fungus, which is found in soil and decaying debris, usually include respiratory and digestive disorders.

Cats already infected with panleukopenia seem to be the most susceptible to aspergillosis.

Antifungal drugs are part of the therapy used to treat this disease. Prognosis is guarded.

Cryptococcosis

A common fungal infection in cats, cryptococcosis is found in bird droppings and is usually acquired by way of inhalation.

The infection usually results in respiratory illness with symptoms such as sneezing, thick nasal discharge, coughing, breathing difficulty, and weight loss. Hard growths may develop across the nose.

Diagnosis is made by sending samples to the lab for culturing. There is also a blood test available for diagnosing cryptococcosis.

Antifungal drugs are used to treat this disease. In some cases, surgery may also be necessary.

Ringworm

Refer to section on skin disorders.

DISORDERS OF THE MOUTH

Retained Deciduous Teeth

Kittens have twenty-six deciduous (baby) teeth, which eventually get replaced by adult teeth. The transition begins at about three months of age and is usually completed by the time the kitten reaches seven months.

Occasionally, one or more of the baby teeth don't come out and as the adult teeth emerge they get pushed out of proper alignment. When you look in the kitten's mouth you'll notice two sets of teeth. If left alone, this leads to a badly aligned bite and rapid progression of dental disease.

Treatment consists of pulling the retained baby teeth.

Halitosis

This isn't the primary problem but rather a symptom of another condition, and finding the cause is crucial. You can't just treat this as a simple case of bad breath.

Gingivitis, periodontal disease, certain infectious disease, or even urinary problems can cause halitosis. A strange mouth odor can also be a sign of poisoning. Diabetes may also produce a characteristic odor due to acetone. Anytime you notice a strange or foul odor to your cat's breath, have him checked by the veterinarian so the primary cause can be accurately diagnosed.

SIGNS OF MOUTH OR THROAT PROBLEMS

- inflammation of lips or gums
- change in appearance of tongue
- receding gums
- yellow or brown deposits on teeth
- halitosis
- loss of appetite
- excessive drooling
- pawing at mouth or face
- swelling on the face or neck
- ungroomed hair coat
- difficulty in swallowing

Following a regular program of cleaning your cat's teeth will help prevent gingivitis, which can cause bad breath. Refer to Chapter 12 to learn how to care for your cat's teeth.

Gingivitis and Periodontitis

Gingivitis, a common problem for all pets, refers to the inflammation of the gums. Gingivitis begins when the bacterial film known as *plaque* coats the tooth. The invisible plaque is caused by the growing bacteria in food that gets trapped between the teeth. *Calculus*, or *tartar*, forms as the soft plaque appears yellow or brown on the teeth.

Signs of gingivitis: a thin red line on the gums. It'll almost look as if someone outlined your cat's gums with a red pen. As the disease progresses, you may notice bad breath. As the infection worsens, the inflamed gums form pus pockets and your cat may begin drooling.

Periodontitis refers to the inflammation of the periodontal membrane around the tooth. At this stage teeth may be loose, roots abscessed, and gums receded. The infection may have spread to the bone. Eating and chewing become painful for the cat.

Left untreated, the infection in the bones can become life-threatening if it spreads to the cat's organs.

Scaling and polishing of your cat's teeth should be done by your veterinarian as often as needed. At that time, loose teeth will need to be extracted. The whole procedure is done under anesthesia, so your cat doesn't feel any pain.

For instructions on caring for your cat's teeth, including brushing, dental rinses, and tartar-reducing foods, refer to Chapter 12.

Excessive Drooling

Salivary glands secrete saliva, a fluid that aids in digestion of food. Drooling is more commonly associated with dogs, but a cat might drool when given oral medicine. You also may notice drooling during displays of affection if he seems to get too carried away with his joy. Cats often drool when sprayed with flea-control products if they lick their fur afterward.

Excessive drooling can be a sign of many health problems as well. Dental disease can cause drooling, as can foreign bodies caught in the mouth or throat. Drooling can be a sign of poisoning. Heat stroke is another possible cause. Runny noses, watery eyes, or sneezing that accompanies drooling can indicate a respiratory infection.

Stomatitis (sore or ulcerated mouth)

Periodontal disease can cause inflammation and ulcers of the mouth. The cat will have a strong mouth odor, puffy red gums, and a dark brownish saliva. This condition is also known as *trench mouth*.

Stomatitis can also be connected to certain respiratory diseases, as well as FeLV, FIV, and renal diseases, among others.

Symptoms include: pawing at the mouth, inflamed mouth, drooling, inability to eat, and head shaking.

Treatment involves diagnosing the primary cause, cleaning the mouth, treating the ulcers, pulling loose teeth, and placing the cat on appropriate antibiotics. An at-home oral hygiene program will be prescribed and the cat must stay on a very soft diet while the mouth heals.

EYE DISORDERS

Conjunctivitis

This is an inflammation of the lining of the eyelid and sometimes the bulbar conjunctiva as well. One or both eyes can be affected. There is usually a discharge that may be clear and watery or thick and puslike. The eyes will be red or inflamed. Sometimes edema will be present. The cat may blink often and paw at his eyes. They may even appear to be swollen shut and crusts may form on the eyelids.

Conjunctivitis can be caused by an irritant such as dust, dirt, or some type of allergen. A clear watery discharge may indicate a viral upper respiratory disease or allergies. If the discharge is thick and changes color, it could suggest a secondary bacterial infection.

There are several causes of conjunctivitis. Specific treatment will depend on the underlying cause. Eye drops or ointments will be prescribed and if there are crusts on the eyes, warm soaks will be administered.

SIGNS OF EYE PROBLEMS

- bleeding from or around the eye
- squinting
- rapid blinking
- unusual movement of the eye
- eye discharge
- pawing or scratching at eye
- appearance of third eyelid
- swelling in or around the eye
- pain

- fixed pupils
- one pupil of different size
- opaque film covering the eye
- bloodshot eyes
- irritated, red, or inflamed conjunctiva
- crusting over eye
- sunken or protruding eyeball
- eyelid drooping
- tearing

If your cat is squinting or appears to have conjunctivitis, don't administer any previously prescribed medicine until you've seen the veterinarian. If a corneal ulcer is present, using the wrong ointment can cause more serious injury.

Some cats sabotage recovery by continually scratching or rubbing at the eyes. If this is the case, your veterinarian will recommend the use of a special collar that prevents him from gaining access to the eyes.

Appearance of the Third Eyelid

Injury or illness can cause the third eyelid to become visible. If only one eye is involved, it's most likely an infection or injury to the eye itself. If the membrane is visible over both eyes, illness may be the cause.

Have your cat seen by the veterinarian for a complete exam to determine the cause of the third eyelid appearance and begin appropriate treatment.

Haws Syndrome

This is a relatively common condition in cats that results in a protrusion of the third eyelid. Its cause is unknown and may be associated with self-limiting diarrhea. The condition is temporary, lasting anywhere from one to two months. Treatment may include topical medication. If diarrhea is present, that must be treated as well.

Horner's Syndrome

A constant partial appearance of the third eyelid, Horner's syndrome is due to the loss of nerve stimulation of the muscle that keeps it retracted. In addition to third eyelid protrusion, symptoms may include: small pupil, retracted eye, and lid droop.

Horner's syndrome is a sign of a neurologic problem. Causes can include injury to the neck or upper spinal column, along with middle ear infection. Treatment is based on primary cause.

Blocked Tear Ducts

Normally, excess tears drain into the tear duct, which leads into the nose. If the normal tear drainage system becomes blocked, the tears spill out over the eyelid and run down the face, causing the hair to become stained. A cat with a chronic clear discharge not accompanied by redness to the eye may have blocked tear ducts.

There are several causes for the tear ducts to become blocked: it can be the result of the sharp turns that the drainage system has to take in short-nosed, flat-faced breeds such as Persians; it can also be caused by injury, thick secretions, infections (especially chronic ones), tumors, and even dirt or litter can cause the blockage.

To check for adequate drainage, the veterinarian will use *fluorescein*, an ophthalmic dye in the eye. Under a special light, the dye should be apparent at the nostril opening if the drainage system is functioning. Sometimes only one side is blocked.

Treatment depends on the underlying cause. Infections are treated with antibiotic therapy. Reduction of inflammation by using ophthalmic steroid drops may open the ducts. Flushing the ducts with saline is often done to loosen whatever is causing the plug. This procedure is often performed under an anesthetic.

Corneal Ulcers

Usually caused by an injury, corneal ulcers can also be the result of secondary infection. Eye injury due to a cat fight is a common cause of corneal ulcers. Inadequate tear production that results in dry eyes can also cause ulcers.

The ulcer may be large enough to be visible to you or it may be too small to see with the naked eye. Early treatment is crucial to preventing a more serious condition. To find small ulcers, the veterinarian will stain the eye with fluorescein, an ophthalmic dye. The eye is then rinsed and under a special light, any ulcers will retain traces of the dye.

If your cat is squinting, don't assume it's conjunctivitis and place previously prescribed medicine in the eye. Certain medications can cause very serious injury to the eye when ulcers are present.

Keratitis

An inflammation of the cornea that can affect one or both eyes. Symptoms include: appearance of the third eyelid, squinting, discharge, and sensitivity to light. The cat may also paw at his eye. This inflammation is painful to the cat. If left untreated, the cat may suffer permanent loss of vision.

Keratitis can be the result of a traumatic injury or *entropian* lesion (where the eyelid rolls inward and the lashes irritate the cornea). Many infectious agents can also be the cause.

A veterinarian should be seen immediately. Antibiotics are usually prescribed. To reduce pain, a topical ointment will also be administered.

Glaucoma

This is increased fluid pressure inside the eyeball itself. Glaucoma in cats is usually secondary, caused by things such as injury, infection, cataracts, or tumors. The fluid builds up because something scars over or blocks drainage.

As fluid pressure increases, the eye gets larger, harder, and begins to bulge. It is a painful process. Glaucoma can affect one or both eyes. Other symptoms may include: dilated pupils, squinting, and increased appearance of vascular structures in the sclera.

Left untreated, retinal damage occurs and the cat could lose vision.

Eye pressure can be measured by the veterinarian, using an instrument that is placed over the eye's surface.

Hospitalization and possible surgery are required to relieve pressure for acute cases of glaucoma. In severe cases, removal of the eye is necessary. Chronic glaucoma may be treated with topical and oral medication.

Cataracts

With a cataract, there's an opacity of the lens that gives it a milky appearance. Normally, a healthy lens is clear. Cataracts can develop as a result of injury or infection, which is how it's most commonly seen in cats. Not just a condition of old age, cataracts can develop in cats at any time. Diabetic cats may develop them as they age.

Symptoms: changes in appearance of the eyes, squinting, inflammation, reluctance to go up or down stairs, and may seem unsure when walking.

Depending upon the cause of the cataract, surgery can be performed if needed, but it may not restore total vision.

Nuclear Sclerosis

A common eye disorder that occurs with aging. As the cat gets older the lens continues to grow, pushing toward the center of the eye, creating a buildup of cells. This results in a grayish or bluish haze. This condition, normal to the aging process, doesn't seem to obstruct vision. No treatment is usually needed. This condition is not the same as cataracts.

Uveitis

This is an inflammation of the inner eye that's commonly seen in connection with various infectious diseases in cats, such as *feline leukemia* or *feline infectious peritonitis*. It can also be the result of physical trauma. With uveitis, the eye becomes increasingly soft.

Symptoms include: red, watery eyes, squinting, constricted pupils, and sensitivity to light. This condition is very painful.

Veterinary care includes diagnosis and treatment of the primary illness or cause, along with medication to reduce inflammation and relieve discomfort.

Left untreated, uveitis can lead to blindness.

Blindness

Numerous disorders can cause blindness as can injury. If you suspect that your cat is going blind or is blind, contact your veterinarian to determine the cause.

If your cat is blind or has diminished vision, he must never be allowed outdoors. Kept indoors, a blind cat can do well as long as his environment remains consistent. Refrain from rearranging furniture and keep his food, water, bed, and litter box in the places he's familiar with.

DISORDERS OF THE NOSE

Infections

A nasal infection can be the result of respiratory disease, injury, or the presence of a foreign object. Symptoms usually include: nasal discharge, sneezing, breathing difficulty, noisy or wet sounding breathing, and loss of appetite. You may notice open-mouth breathing as the cat's nose becomes more congested.

SIGNS OF NASAL PROBLEMS

- sneezing
- discharge
- crusting
- bleeding
- pawing at face
- breathing difficulty

- open-mouth breathing
- swelling
- lumps or tumors
- severe dental/oral infections
- decreased appetite
- change in nasal appearance

A nasal discharge that is yellow or puslike indicates a bacterial infection.

After diagnosing the specific condition, appropriate antibiotics will be given. A decongestant may also be prescribed. Helping your cat to breathe comfortably is of the utmost importance, so gently wipe any discharge or crusts from the nose with a moistened cotton ball. You can also use a drop of baby oil on the nose to keep it from becoming chapped. Your veterinarian may recommend the use of a vaporizer.

IMPORTANT NOTE: Cats who can't smell usually become anorexic.

Sinusitis

Symptoms of sinusitis can include: sneezing, and a white or yellow nasal discharge, which may or may not contain blood. Sinus infections can be a secondary result of an allergy, respiratory infection, injury, or fungal infection. A tooth abscess can also lead to sinusitis.

The underlying cause must be treated. Antibiotics will be prescribed and in extreme cases, surgery may need to be performed to allow drainage.

DISORDERS OF THE EAR

Otitis

Cats can develop inflammation of the outer ear (*otitis externa*) from bacteria, wax accumulation, ear mites, or infected wounds.

Symptoms include: inflammation, scratching or pawing at ears, odor, appearance of exudates, head shaking, or ear flaps held at an unusual angle.

Treatment involves cleansing the ear (see Chapter 12 for instructions on how to keep the ears clean) and the application of a topical antibiotic medication.

SIGNS OF EAR PROBLEMS

- scratching or pawing at ears
- head tilt
- discharge
- swelling of pinnae (ear flaps)
- bleeding
- odor
- appearance of gritty black material in ears

- excessive wax
- inflammation in or around ears
- crusting
- hair loss around ears
- lumps on or inside the ear
- abnormal ear movements

Middle ear (*otitis media*) inflammation can be caused by parasites, bacteria, fungi, or foreign bodies.

Symptoms include head tilt and lack of balance.

Treatment may include the use of antibiotics or antifungal medication. In some cases, surgery may be required.

Inner ear infections (*otitis interna*) are extremely serious and can result in irreversible damage and even death. Symptoms can include: hearing loss, vomiting, loss of coordination and balance, circling, and abnormal eye movements. Treatment may include the use of antibiotics or antifungal medication.

Deafness

Deafness can be caused by a variety of things, including: injury, infection, aging, obstructions, tumors, poisons, and certain drugs. It can also be congenital. White cats with blue eyes are often deaf. In odd-eyed white cats, the deafness occurs on the side with the blue eye.

If your aging cat is going deaf or has already become totally deaf, avoid startling him. You can announce your arrival or intentions to handle him through the vibrations of your footsteps. When approaching a deaf cat who is sleeping, make your footsteps heavier (don't stomp, though) so he'll feel the vibrations. If the cat is awake and his attention is focused elsewhere, slowly come into his visual field. Don't just come up behind a deaf cat and pick him up.

If you suspect deafness, have your cat examined by the veterinarian to check for infections, injuries, or obstructions.

Ear Mites

The most common cause of ear problems in cats, these microscopic parasites feed off skin tissue. They live and breed in the ear canal, causing itching and irritation, but they can also travel to other parts of the body.

Ear mites are extremely contagious to other pets, so if one pet has an infestation, there's a good chance that his companions will have them as well. Even though ear mites are primarily found in the ears, they can actually show up anywhere on the body so it's easily spread from pet to pet.

Left untreated, ear mite infestation can cause serious trouble as the ear canal becomes irritated and raw.

The most common sign of ear mite infestation is constant scratching and repeated head shaking. The cat may also hold his ears at an unusual angle. When you examine the ears you'll find dry, dark, crumbly brown debris, resembling coffee grinds. During violent head shaking or scratching you may notice some of the debris expelled out onto the haircoat.

Ear mites are actually white in color. The brown debris in the ear is the digested material and wax.

A confirmed diagnosis of ear mite infestation is made by taking a sample of the debris in the ears for examination under the microscope. There, you're able to see the tiny mites moving all around. One look at the numerous mites under the microscope and it's easy to understand how itchy and irritating they must be for the cat.

Veterinary treatment involves careful and gentle cleaning of the ears. It has to be done gently because the ears will be very irritated and raw. After cleaning, you'll notice how red and inflamed the ear canals are. Cleaning is important for the miticide to be effective so the mites won't be able to hide in the accumulated debris.

Follow the instructions concerning length of time for treatment because ear mites have a three-week life cycle. If treatment is stopped too early, infestation will reappear.

There are several ear mite treatment products available. Specific dosage instructions may vary, depending on the product.

During ear mite treatment, keep the nails trimmed on your cat's hind feet to reduce scratching-related damage to the ears and surrounding area.

Treating the environment isn't usually indicated since ear mites don't survive for long off the animal.

Hematoma

When a cat violently shakes his head, a blood vessel can rupture, causing a bulging pocket of accumulated blood and fluid in the ear flap between the cartilage and skin.

Such severe head shaking and scratching can be the result of ear mite infestation, allergies, or ear infections. A hematoma causes so much swelling that it becomes painful for the cat. Surgery is often required to prevent a recurrence, otherwise the pocket that was formed from the blood clot will fill up with fluid again.

Other causes of a hematoma can include cat fights and trauma to the head.

To help prevent hematomas, check your cat's ears regularly for signs of mites, redness, or irritation. If you notice anything or if your cat shakes his head often, paws at his ears, or holds his ears at an unusual angle, have him examined by the veterinarian.

Sunburned Ears

To prevent this condition, limit the cat's access to the outdoors, especially on sunny days. When the cat does go outdoors, apply a sunblock to the ears. Check with your veterinarian regarding which one is safe for cats. Check the ears regularly and seek immediate attention for any signs of sunburn or ulcers. This can develop into skin cancer.

Frostbite

The tips of the ears are especially susceptible to frostbite. This subject is covered in Chapter 18, "Emergencies and First Aid."

CANCER

Cancer can develop anywhere in the body: the skin, the mouth, lymph nodes, blood cells, or any internal organ.

Since many cancers aren't outwardly detectable, anytime your cat displays symptoms of not feeling well, consult your veterinarian.

Neoplasia is a word you'll commonly hear in connection to tumors. It refers to a tumor that continues to grow (a neoplasm).

One of the most common cancers in cats is *lymphoma*, a cancer associated with feline leukemia virus.

Another cancer, *fibrosarcoma*, is the one often known as injection site sarcoma and is associated with some vaccinations.

Tumors are divided into two categories: *benign* and *malignant*. A benign tumor is noncancerous, generally grows slower, doesn't spread to other areas of the body, and is very often able to be surgically removed if necessary. A tumor that's diagnosed as malignant is cancerous, grows rapidly, has an irregular shape, and spreads to other parts of the body. Surgery may or may not be successful in removing a malignant tumor.

Treatment for malignant tumors depends on the specific case. One rule does apply to all cancers, though: early detection provides a greater chance of a successful cure.

Different types of treatment include:

Surgery (sometimes used with other therapies)
Chemotherapy (anticancer drugs)
Radiation therapy (sometimes used with chemotherapy or surgery)
Cryosurgery (freezing the tissue)
Hyperthermia therapy (heating the tissue to a very high temperature; sometimes used with other therapies)
Immunotherapy (natural and chemical immune boosting agents; sometimes used with other therapies)

SIGNS OF CANCER

- lumps or bumps
- swelling
- growths on the skin
- weight loss
- loss of appetite
- nonhealing wounds
- weakness
- depression
- lethargy
- anemia
- coughing
- breathing difficulty
- chronic diarrhea

Each treatment has advantages and disadvantages. Tumors that have spread or are in difficult-to-reach locations may need a therapy such as radiation. It's not unusual to employ a combination of treatments to control and hopefully eliminate the cancer. Cancer is, unfortunately, relatively common in cats.

Resource Guide

Other books by Pam Johnson-Bennett
      Starting from Scratch (Penguin Books, 2007)
      Psycho Kitty (Ten Speed Press, 2008)
      Cat vs. Cat (Penguin Books, 2004)
      Hiss and Tell (Penguin Books, 2001)

Visit Pam's Web site for information on behavior consultations, quick behavior tips, video tips, and to find out about her other best-selling books:
    www.catbehaviorassociates.com

Follow Pam on Twitter:
    www.twitter.com/thinklikeacat

Where to Find Certified, Professional Behavior Help
International Association of Animal Behavior Consultants
    www.iaabc.org
American Veterinary Society of Animal Behaviorists
    www.avsabonline.org
Animal Behavior Society
    www.animalbehaviorsociety.org

Air Travel with Animals
FAA
    www.faa.gov/passengers/fly_pets/
Animal and Plant Health Inspection Service
    www.aphis.usda.gov
      Site contains information regarding requirements associated with air travel with your pet.

Health and Welfare Information

American Humane Association

www.americanhumane.org

> Contains information on training, welfare, animal protection, child protection, therapy animals, and PAWS (Pets and Women's Shelters program).

ABRIonline

www.abrionline.org

> A site for both animal behavior professionals and owners that contains the latest behavior information. ABRI is part of the American Humane Association.

American Heartworm Society

www.heartwormsociety.org

> Contains current information and treatment guides for feline and canine heartworm disease.

Winn Feline Foundation

www.winnfelinehealth.org

> Information on feline health-related studies.

PetMD

www.petmd.com

> Lots of information on pet health and care.

Association of American Feed Control Officials

www.aafco.org

Pet Food Recall Products List

U.S. Food and Drug Administration

www.fda.gov

Veterinary Organizations

The Academy of Veterinary Homeopathy

www.theavh.org

American Association of Feline Practitioners

www.aafponline.org

American Holistic Veterinary Medical Association

www.ahvma.org

American College of Veterinary Surgeons

www.acvs.org

American Veterinary Medical Association

www.avma.org

International Veterinary Acupuncture Society
   www.ivas.org
American Veterinary Chiropractic Association
   www.animalchiropractic.org

Hotlines
ASPCA National Animal Poison Control Center
   www.aspca.org/pet-care/poison-control/
Dr. Louis J. Camuti Memorial Feline Telephone Consultation Service
Cornell Feline Health Center
Cornell University
   www.vet.cornell.edu/FHC/
Tufts University Pet Loss Support Hotline
   www.tufts.edu/vet/petloss/
Cornell University College of Veterinary Medicine Pet Loss Support Hotline
   www.vet.cornell.edu/org/petloss/
University of Illinois College of Veterinary Medicine C.A.R.E. Pet Loss
Hotline
   http://vetmed.illinois.edu/CARE/
U.C. Davis Center for Companion Animal Health Pet Loss Support
   www.vetmed.ucdavis.edu/ccab/petloss.html
Washington State University's College of Veterinary Medicine Pet Loss Hotline
   www.vetmed.wsu.edu/plhl/
   Note: Many veterinary universities offer pet loss support hotlines. Check
   with the university nearest you.

Pet-Sitter Organizations
National Association of Professional Pet Sitters
   www.petsitters.org
Pet Sitters International
   www.petsit.com

Disaster Preparation
The American Veterinary Medical Association
   www.avma.org/disaster
The Cat Fanciers' Association, Inc.
   www.cfa.org

The American Red Cross
  www.redcross.org

Breed Information
The Cat Fanciers' Association, Inc.
  www.cfainc.org
The International Cat Association
  www.tica.org

Index

psychoactive drugs, 145, 176–77
psychogenic alopecia, 119–20, 342
psychotropic medications, 127
pulmonary edema, 319, 345
pulse, 69, 307
pumpkin, 294, 356
punishment, 84–85, 116, 171–75, 180
puppies, 228
purebred cats, 6–7, 10, 212, 276
purring, 28
puzzle feeders: and anxiety relief, 120; and behavioral issues, 130; and depressed cats, 127; and diets, 213, 214; and digestive systems disorders, 352, 358; and geriatric cats, 297; and nighttime activity, 108–9, 129; and sleeping arrangements, 88; and traveling with cats, 265; and weight management, 109
pyometra, 373

rabies, 382–83
radiation therapy, 364
"raised underfoot" cats, 12
rashes, 246
raw foods, 194, 206–7, 208, 385
rectal thermometers, 68, 316
Red Cross, 327
refrigerators, 39
registered cats, 12
rehabilitation, 15
Reis, Pedro M., 24
relationships, 216–36; addition of second cats, 217–22; babies, 232–34; dogs, 224–29; and multicat households, 222–23; partners, 229–32; and redirection tactics, 223–24; responsibility for cats, 235–36; small children, 234–35, 236; social nature of cats, 216–17; strangers, 122, 229
remains, 300

renal failure, 197, 199, 288, 292, 293, 316, 350–51
renal secondary hyperthyroidism, 362
renovations, 167–68
reproductive system disorders, 371–77
rescue groups, 8–9, 11, 15
respiratory disorders, 343–46
respiratory rate, 22, 69, 307, 310–11
retina, 22
ribbons, 36, 54, 111, 352
ringworm, 339
rodent poisons, 320
rodent ulcer, 342–43
rolling skin disease, 370
rooms for cats. See sanctuary rooms
rope, 184
roundworms, 330, 352
routines: and attention-seeking behavior, 128; and behavioral issues, 115; and changes to the household, 230; and depression, 127; and geriatric cats, 292–97; and grooming, 241–42; and new babies, 234; prebedtime routines, 129; and travel, 257
rubber bands, 36, 43, 111, 352
rubbing, 31
runts, 17

saliva, 30
salmonella, 206, 385
salt, 45
sanctuary rooms, 48–50, 218, 226, 271–72
"Save Our Pet" signs, 57, 327
scaling teeth, 388
ScareCrow Sprinkler, 140, 169
scent analysis, 24–25
scents. See also marking; odor control: and allogrooming, 31; babies, 233–34; boarding cats, 269–70; introducing new cats, 219; scented litters, 151; scent glands, 33, 181
Science, 24
"scooting," 358

scratching and scratching posts, 180–89; and behavioral issues, 114; building, 184–85; and ear mites, 396; and false nails, 188–89; furniture, 4, 114, 183, 186–87, 188; and geriatric cats, 287–88, 292–93; location of, 184–85; and removal of old nails, 25; replacing, 189; scratching posts, 4; and training cats, 80–81, 82, 185–86, 186–87; and traveling with cats, 265; typical design, 182–83
screaming, 111
scruffing technique, 262
sebaceous glands, 33, 341
secondary viremia, 379
second-degree burns, 318
sedation, 65, 263
sedentary cats, 217
seizures, 369–70
sensitivities, 138
septicemia, 376
sexual contact, 30, 275, 378
sexual maturity, 283
shampoos, 247, 248–50
shedding, 122, 238
shelters, 1, 5, 9–11, 56, 259–60, 273
shock, 313–14, 324
short-haired cats, 8, 22, 238, 239–40, 242–43
show cats, 12
shrieks, 29
Siamese cats, 117, 118, 121, 212
side stepping, 31
SIDS (sudden infant death syndrome), 3, 232
sight, 283, 290. See also eyes
sinusitis, 394
sisal, 184–85
size of cats, 6–7, 18–19, 47, 204–5, 281, 283. See also obese and overweight cats
skin, 18, 214, 246, 322, 334–38, 337. See also hair and coat
skunks, 251